SCHOOLCRAFT COLLEGE LIBRARY

W9-AEU-827

WITHDRAWN

HC
106.6
.E85
1972

Estall, Robert
Modern geography of
the United States

DATE DUE

#47-0108 Peel Off Pressure Sensitive

A Modern Geography of the United States

A Modern Geography of the United States

Aspects of Life and Economy

Robert Estall

CHICAGO
Quadrangle Books
1972

HC
106.6
.E85
1972

A MODERN GEOGRAPHY OF THE UNITED STATES.
Copyright © 1972 by Robert Estall. All rights
reserved, including the right to reproduce this
book or portions thereof in any form. For
information, address: Quadrangle Books,
Inc., 12 East Delaware Place, Chicago 60611.
Manufactured in the United States of
America. Published simultaneously in Canada
by Burns and MacEachern Ltd., Toronto.

First published in England in 1972 by
Penguin Books Ltd., Harmondsworth,
Middlesex.

FIRST AMERICAN EDITION

Library of Congress
Catalog Card Number: 77-183732
International Standard
Book Number: 0-8129-0242-4

To R. Ogilvie Buchanan
Teacher, Colleague and Friend

Contents

List of Figures

Preface

The United States of America is a country of enormous size, blessed with immense natural wealth. The potential of this area has been exploited with a technical skill, a spirit of competition and a desire for achievement that have driven material standards to the highest levels. The per capita Gross National Product in the USA is almost one third as great again as that in the second-ranking country (Sweden) and more than twice as high as in the UK. Levels of production and consumption which have no parallel are sustained. In the achievement and maintenance of this situation there is much to be admired and much to be deplored, but such a society is bound to present a fertile ground for social scientists of all kinds. For geographers in particular, however, the USA, with its great internal diversity of physical and human landscapes and spatial variations of experience, provides a laboratory without peer for the examination of the patterns, trends and problems of an advanced, mature economy. The study of such an economy has value for anyone who seeks to understand the world in which we live in the second half of the twentieth century, for the socio-economic problems and achievements of the present time in the United States are, on past experience, inevitably to be those of other nations in future years.

This study adopts a systematic approach to the examination of the modern geography of the USA, but on each topic regional patterns and variations are probed at some depth. This approach was adopted for its value in providing a relatively full view of the geographical patterns and problems of modern America, for an overall grasp of these matters cannot easily be obtained from the series of regional analyses which are presented in most existing studies. In form, the study divides into three unequal parts. Chapters 1 to 4 provide background essays on population, land use and patterns of economic activity. Chapters 5 to 12 examine the major productive systems – agriculture, mining and manufacturing – in some detail, and Chapters 13 and 14 review the urban geography and Federal government activities. In each part, the issues specific to the system under discussion are examined, but one or two themes recur throughout, notably the increasing role of government and the problems of resource use and of the underprivileged.

The selection of themes is a personal one, and several important aspects of modern geographical study have been omitted to permit treatment at satisfactory length of the chosen topics. Particularly regretted is the absence of specific chapters on the geography of transport, water and poverty. Each is a matter of great current interest and significance, but their treatment has here been confined to passing mentions in chapters devoted primarily to other subjects. It need hardly be added that each theme examined here is itself worthy of a book – and, indeed, many detailed, specialized works have been produced. The studies offered here, therefore, do not pretend to give an exhaustive appraisal of all the issues involved in each case. For those who wish to pursue some matters to greater depth, a brief guide to further reading is provided at the end.

A word on the statistics. The student of the United States is in most instances faced with a superabundance of statistical material, flowing from numerous sources, some quite unexpected. The difficulties are to know where to look and how to render manageable the vast mass of data. This is a problem at once easier and more satisfying than that faced by students of areas where data are lacking, but it is a problem none the less. Moreover, on some matters new data are continuously forthcoming so that the selection of a terminal year is difficult. No sooner is one set of data absorbed and interpreted than a new set is published. Such new figures, fortunately, do not often change the patterns in any fundamental way, but there is clearly the issue of where to draw the line. In general, the most recent data available at the time of writing have been used. This is sometimes, as with population estimates, data for 1969; in other cases, much earlier. For example, the full results of the 1967 Census of Manufactures are not available in mid 1970, and on occasion material from the 1963 Census must still be relied upon. Again, for agriculture, the

1964 Census remains the most recent source for many kinds of data. On some occasions, too, when time series are used, the terminal date may be several years past, but must be adhered to so that the data are comparable. For such reasons, then, the terminal dates used here vary from one theme to another.

In preparing a study of this kind, one inevitably depends heavily on help and advice from many people. I wish particularly to thank Professor R. Ogilvie Buchanan, who spent many hours formulating numerous detailed suggestions for removing many thousands of words from a heavily overweight manuscript. Nesta Herbert typed all of the early drafts, and much of the final copy, with great efficiency. At the later stages valuable assistance was also cheerfully given by Meda Briggs, Janet Fox, Megan Rikof and Gail Cockwill, and I am very grateful to them all. I would like also to acknowledge my debt to Jean-Marie Stanton of the cartography department at the London School of Economics for expert assistance in drafting maps and diagrams, and to my wife, Mary, for much aid and support throughout. Finally I record my thanks to the American Council of Learned Societies, who generously sponsored, at the London School of Economics, the Readership in the Economic Geography of North America which I hold. Their support has enabled me to become involved in the deepest possible way in the examination of the economic geography of what I find to be the most fascinating country in the world.

1 : Fundamentals of Population Geography

This study of the modern geography of the United States begins as naturally with population as did older texts with physical environment. It is not that the physical environment is considered to lack significance in the modern world. Its role in shaping the form and manner of economic life is obvious and it would be absurd to consider this great area as if it were a uniform plain, with an equitable distribution of resources. Mountain ranges, climatic régimes, soil properties, mineral occurrences and so on are vital facts of life which must be taken as given, although their precise significance changes over time. Here, however, we will assume these facts as known and the treatment will emphasize the activities of man, the spatial arrangement of his economic and social life and the human problems issuing from such activities and arrangements. Population studies therefore intimately concern geography, and few significant geographical problems are not in some way also demographic problems. Population geography is a fundamental basis from which an analysis of modern life and economy may logically proceed. This is particularly true of the United States, where patterns of population growth and change, of migration and counter-migration, provide a fascinating kaleidoscope reflecting the very essence of man's search for different and, it is hoped, better things.

It follows that any assessment of the situation is like a photograph, capturing the scene at a given moment – a scene which is changing from that very moment. The evaluation of population characteristics does not thereby become a hopeless task, devoid of reality. Much of the effervescence is of no immediate significance except to those directly concerned, though possibly offering portents of things to come. Although volatile, patterns of population geography are not revolutionized every day or every year, but are sufficiently stable to permit a rational appraisal of the status quo, an assessment of current characteristics and trends and of possibilities and implications.

The appraisal will be organized under several headings. National size and rate of growth is the subject of this chapter. Regional variations in size and growth rates, the varying experiences of rural and urban areas and some aspects of the racial characteristics of the population are discussed in Chapter 2. These are only selected highlights from the possible topics for discussion under this heading. Others will be considered later (e.g. the structure of employment) but some must remain unexplored. Naturally, great variations of experience result from local or regional socio-economic conditions, and it is difficult to divorce the account of the processes from the discussion of possible influence or causes. These opening chapters, however, are concerned primarily with evaluating the facts, rather than probing for underlying explanation. The causes are numerous and complex, acting in different ways in different areas to produce widely divergent experiences. This will be demonstrated in the succeeding chapters, which will provide clues and at least partial answers to how and why such marked differences in population experience and characteristics exist within the boundaries of one nation.

Population Size: The Current Situation

As 1970 is a Population Census year, many valuable facts and figures will flow from the Census Bureau in the next few years. Unfortunately, no data from this source are yet available, and we must rely on estimates for earlier years, and even return to the inter-censal decade 1950–60 for essential detail in some parts of the work. The lack of current Census data is not, however, a major impediment to a broad, general study. When the official figure of total population appears it will probably give a 1970 population of about 205 million. A difference of a million or two either way will matter little. The Census itself is subject to a margin of error which can be surprisingly large, as the experience of the 1960 Census shows.

The total resident population for the 1960 Census count was given as 179·3 million. This was later found severely defective because of misreporting and under-enumeration, the error being estimated at about 5·7 million missing people, or 3·2 per cent of the Census total. The fact that the lost population was largely in significant groups like the Negro (undercounted by more than 2 million), and the poor generally, is doubly unfortunate. Federal assistance funds are often allocated on numbers involved. Be that as it may, the important point is that, even after a full census, there is some vagueness about how many Americans there actually are, and therefore about their detailed characteristics. A national event of 1967 is worth recalling. At about 11 a.m. on 20 November that year the National Census Clock in Washington DC, ticking off one new citizen every 14·5 seconds, struck for 200 million Americans. The milestone was duly acknowledged by President Johnson and other notables, but the facts of this apparently precise, computer-controlled event lend themselves to a useful lesson. For better or worse Americans are neither as programmable as computers nor as regular as clockwork in their child-bearing habits, while computers are only as accurate as the material they are fed. In this case, the defective 1960 Census had provided the raw data for the calculations. Thus, even as President Johnson spoke under the Census Clock, the population was far ahead of the milestone he was commemorating. We must, therefore, beware of the pedantic accuracy which impels people to use figures to the final digit and the nth decimal place. All statistics, including those of population, are only approximations, which must not be invested with an accuracy they do not possess.*

The impressive inaccuracy of the Census Clock and the precise moment when the population of the USA passed the 200 million mark are of little significance. The indisputable facts are that the nation currently has a population considerably above this number and that the USA is only the fourth nation on earth to exceed it.† Reactions to the event were somewhat mixed: pride and anticipation in some quarters, apprehension in others. Traditionally, an expanding population in America has brought economic and social benefits.

* It is already being claimed that the 1970 Census has miscounted, with the possibility of an error equivalent to that for 1960. At this time, therefore, the total population *could* be about 210 million.

† China, India and the USSR are the others.

An increasing labour force, larger and more varied markets and an ever-widening range of opportunities have brought a steadily rising standard of living.

Less attention has been paid in the past to the problems accompanying rapid growth and change in patterns of living and geographical distribution – problems of water supply, waste disposal, pollution of environment, urban sprawl and blight and traffic congestion, for example. Now, however, concern about these and associated issues is growing and, in commenting on the passing of the 200 million mark and on concurrent projections for the year 2000 (some of which approached 400 millions), an apprehensive school of thought considered further growth of population a threat rather than a blessing. The US Department of the Interior, for example (concerned among other things with 'conservation'), was quite blunt in its reaction. Stewart S. Udall, then Secretary of the Interior, in a Foreword to his department's publication, *The Population Challenge* (1967), stated flatly, 'The greatest threat to quality living in this country is over-population,' and referred to the shrinking amount of space per head and the gathering conflict on space allocation, resource utilization and the preservation of the quality of the environment. The headings to the various sections of this report (e.g. 'A Rationed Tomorrow', 'So Much and No More', 'Planning for the Pinch') show serious concern over further rapid population growth. This approach rejects the optimism of other sections of American opinion as based on narrow preoccupations. 'Commodity dealers tend to see only the business impact of a larger market. Chambers of Commerce and local officials still trumpet "growth".' Such people should show concern for broader issues, for the problem of 'stretching natural resources' and for preserving the 'quality of life'

Those who are less worried by such issues are not, however, confined to commodity dealers and Chambers of Commerce. Many people believe that further population growth is acceptable both on economic and social grounds, and that the country still has room to spare. In some respects the 'population pressure' case has been overstated and the argument can be reversed by placing emphasis on the exceptionally favoured situation of the USA, as in the concern

4

expressed about space standards. Crude density calculations, despite their inadequacies, prove useful in this context. In the mid 1960s, with a crude density of about 55 per square mile, the US was more fortunate than all but three of the world's twenty most highly populated countries (which have four fifths of total world population). Of the three, Mexico has a density similar to that of the USA; Brazil and the USSR crude ratios of only 24 and 26 per square mile respectively. But even in relation to these, the Americans' superior endowment of 'usable' or 'productive' land offsets, or more than offsets, an apparent space disadvantage. Compared with the seventeen other highly populated countries, the US measures up extraordinarily well, even by crude density standards. Fifteen have crude densities of over 100, nine over 200 and five over 400 per square mile. Clearly the United States currently enjoys space standards (and especially productive space standards) far superior to most of the rest of humanity. Even with double its present population, the USA would still rank among the best-endowed nations of the world in this respect.

The Department of Commerce, Bureau of the Census, briefly takes up the issues of overpopulation, overcrowding and prospects for living standards in a report entitled *200 Million Americans* (1967). 'Are there too many of us? . . . Will we be swamped by a wave of people?' The feeling here is that this kind of thinking is highly coloured by the daily experiences of those living in large metropolitan areas. The report points to the many thousands of uncrowded acres (ten States in fact have under 20 persons per square mile) and to the rapid rise in the output of goods and services and in the general standards of living that have accompanied recent population growth and, looking ahead, the American reader is here warned to 'beware of predictions of dire times ahead because of overpopulation', especially since population projections are themselves so unreliable.

There is nevertheless a problem. One may legitimately reject the thesis of 'dire times ahead' while recognizing the obvious difficulties, both economic and social, of population growth and geographical distribution. The problem is, in essence, not of overall numbers *v.* resources, but of *where*, how *adequately* and how *efficiently* the

5

increasing numbers may be catered for. Massive new demands for homes, schools, jobs and facilities for health and leisure activities and so on must be met, while at the same time solving large problems of underprivileged sectors of society and underprivileged areas of the country. The adequacy of plans for dealing with these matters is of concern to all Americans, and the issues involved are at once of local, of regional and of national significance. Because of their dimensions, such problems must be squarely and cooperatively faced at all three geographical levels; a requirement not as simple as it sounds. Such issues will emerge again in subsequent chapters. At present, we shall briefly consider rates of population growth, in their historical context.

Population Growth: Past Experience

Table 1 presents statistics of population for fifty-year periods from 1800 to 1950. Obviously this summary conceals many fluctuations, but it is the broad pattern of growth that is significant here.

Table 1: Population Growth, 1800–1950 and Projection, 2000

	Population (nearest million)	Increase (per cent)	Increase (million)
1800	5	—	—
1850	23	338	18
1900	76	228	53
1950	151	98	75
[2000	280	85	129]

Source: Census of Population. Projection selected from *Current Population Reports*, 1970 (Series P-25)

The table shows that, while the *rate* of growth has fallen steadily over the century and a half represented, the *actual increment* in population becomes larger and larger. The possibilities of such significant differences between absolute and relative growth rates must always be remembered, and one must guard against conclusions drawn from a study of relative growth rates alone. Certain erroneous impressions about regional change in the USA have gained wide currency through disregarding this simple rule. Looking ahead very briefly at this point, the rate of growth will doubtless fall again over the period 1950–2000, but there is no doubt, either, that the actual increment will dwarf that of previous periods, as the projection in Table 1 indicates.

In examining population growth it is necessary to comment on the movements of the three relevant variables, birth rates, death rates and net migration. Throughout the nineteenth century both birth rates and death rates were falling, and they have continued to fall in the present century (Table 2), although with major fluctuations in birth rate caused by volatile economic conditions and the effects of war. Thus in 1933 the birth rate was as low as 18·4 per thousand. Thereafter it increased, especially in the later 1940s. At the peak in 1947, birth rate reached 26·5 per thousand, as returning service men completed, or started, their families. Subsequently the general trend has been down, reaching an all-time low of 17·5 per thousand in 1968. Death rates have also continued to fall this century and, contrasting with the birth rate, pretty steadily (Table 2). This trend reflects the tremendous strides in death control, which have significantly prolonged the life expectancy of the average American. In 1920 the average male American baby could anticipate a life span of some 54 years, and by the late 1960s, 67 years. American females, like females everywhere, did rather better at both times, but have made a larger jump, from 55 to 74 years. Such developments have affected the population structure. For example, in 1940 there were only 9 million Americans (under 7 per cent of total population) aged 65 years or more. By 1968 there were 19 million of these 'senior citizens', i.e. nearly 10 per cent of the population. More importantly, however, medical, nutritional and other advances at the origin of this process have improved the general health of the population at all ages, and thus benefited all aspects of human life and economy in the country. Obviously, the pace of advance in death control achieved in the first half of the twentieth century could not (without some new, major breakthrough) be indefinitely maintained, and only a marginal lowering of the death rate has been achieved since about 1950. The

7

most optimistic current forecast does not visualize an average rate below 9 per thousand until the 1980s.

Table 2: Components of Population Growth, 1900–1968

	Birth rate (per 1,000)	Death rate (per 1,000)	Natural increase (per 1,000)	Immigration rate (per 1,000)
1900	32·3	17·2	15·1	5·9
1910	30·1	14·7	15·4	11·3
1920	27·7	13·0	14·7	4·0
1930	21·3	11·3	10·0	2·0
1940	19·4	10·8	8·6	0·5
1950	23·9	9·6	14·3	1·6
1960	23·8	9·5	14·3	1·5
1965	19·6	9·4	10·2	1·5
1968	17·5	9·6	7·9	2·3

Source: Long-term Economic Growth 1860–1965, and Statistical Abstracts of the United States

With these movements in birth and death rates, the rate of natural increase has fluctuated from year to year and decade to decade. The lowest point was 7·7 per thousand in depressed 1933, the highest 16·4 per thousand in the boom year 1947. This represents a very considerable disparity but, over all, the falling death rate has offset the full effect of the long-term declining birth rate and thus, until recently, kept the rate of natural increase relatively high. The 1950 and 1960 rates of 14·3 would be sufficient to double the population in forty years. The sharp fall in birth rate in the 1960s, however, brought a steep decline in natural increase (Table 2). Whether this will be permanent is the crucial question, the answer to which demographers, planners and many others would dearly love to know.

The third factor in population growth, net migration, has also proved highly volatile, with numbers affected by economic and social circumstances both in the USA and in the countries of origin. Decade by decade, however, the number arriving in the United States rose steadily during the nineteenth century, except for the 'difficult decades' of 1860–70 and 1890–1900. In the peak nineteenth-century decade, 1880–90, no fewer than $5\frac{1}{4}$ million immigrants

8

arrived; but even this was dwarfed by the $8\frac{3}{4}$ million in the first ten years of the twentieth century. Clearly, up till then, immigration had been a very important source of population growth. From 1820 to 1910 28 million migrants settled in the USA, chiefly from Europe. This was over one third of total population growth in that time, and markedly affected the structure and character of the American people and economy.

High rates of immigration continued, in fact, until the outbreak of war in Europe in 1914, whereupon the number dropped sharply, never to return to the former levels. As a rate per thousand of the population, the immigration figure slumped from 12·3 in 1914 to 3·2 in 1915. It has remained below the 1915 level ever since, apart from a few exceptional years in the early 1920s. Table 2 illustrates the broad pattern. The main reason for this sustained fall in immigration was a growing concern about the numbers and kinds of migrants. A quota system was introduced in 1924 which, reinforced in 1929, operated with only slight modification (and occasional suspension*) until 1968. The 1929 system was designed to preserve the ethnic balance which existed in the country at the 1920 Census, offering the largest quotas of entry permits to those countries whose nationals provided the largest groups in the existing population. British, Irish and German emigrants could therefore, if they wished, make up some 70 per cent of total admissions since, in 1920, people of these origins accounted for some 70 per cent of the population. Since nationals of these favoured countries did not, in fact, take up all the places allocated, total immigration fell considerably short of the permitted levels. The shortfall could not be made up from elsewhere, and the desperate attempts of would-be eastern and southern European migrants to enter and to stay in the country provided a true-life basis to many a Hollywood film of the period. The system was modified in 1965, by allocating unused portions of national quotas to a pool from which immigrants from other nations could be admitted. In 1967 a new law abolished the quota system, substituting a preference system which operated from July 1968, and which will be mentioned again below.

* E.g. after the Second World War, the barriers were temporarily raised to allow about 1 million aliens to enter as displaced persons or war brides.

Thus immigration has not in recent decades retained its earlier significance as a contributor to population growth. From 1930 to 1965, for example, $5\frac{1}{2}$ million were admitted, amounting to less than 8 per cent of the total population growth over that period; a sharp contrast indeed with the pre-1914 situation. This does not mean that the flow of foreigners into the country at present, and in the recent past, is without significance. The lower immigrant rates recorded in Table 2 are measured against a considerably rising base population. In absolute numbers, immigration has not fallen below a quarter of a million a year since 1950, and has often been above 300,000. This is a large number, and an inflow of this order will have affected the character of the national population, and have had an especial impact in the ports and larger metropolitan areas where many of them congregate.

Population Prognosis

The concern felt by some about population growth in the United States has been noted. A brief glimpse into what the future may hold now seems appropriate, leaving the implications to be gathered later in the treatment of various other aspects of US life and economy. That a large increase in population is in prospect cannot be doubted. With the current size of the population even a low birth rate means a substantial number of new citizens. The all-time low of 17·5 live births per thousand of the population in 1968, for example, still represented a quite impressive increment of some $3\frac{1}{2}$ million babies. Thus, in default of any fundamental change in child-bearing habits, the population will grow in substantial steps through the foreseeable future. All projections are liable to error, but perhaps in matters of population people become even more unpredictable than in other fields – which is saying a great deal. Early post-war projections, for example, suggested a US maximum population of 158 million by 1980. Plans built on that assumption had quickly to be revised. None the less, the need for future bench marks remains essential and, undeterred by past errors, the Bureau of the Census produces regular estimates and projections of the total population and its component parts. Reference to these is made below.*

Birth rates provide the major uncertainty in making projections. The possible future variation in death rates and net immigration are, apparently, small compared with the possible range of fertility, and may be treated first. The reasonable current assumption about the death rate is that it may decline from the 9·6 per thousand of 1968 to, at best, 8·4 by 1990. The calculation is significant as affecting the numbers of 'senior citizens' who will need to be catered for in future years, the size of the 'non-productive' sections of the population, and so on. In the present context of guessing at the total *size* of population, however, the range of possible variation is small, and thus of minor significance. Despite the 'spectacular accomplishments in surgical technique . . . relating particularly to the use of artificial and transplanted organs . . . (the) kind of "breakthrough" required for a significant increase in life expectation is not yet in sight'.†

Since the volume of immigration is largely determined by Federal laws, this element in population growth is controllable. Under the 1968 law the quota system was replaced, for countries outside the Western Hemisphere, by a system of preferences. This gives most visas to relatives of existing US residents and then to people with desirable skills and talents on a 'first come, first served' basis, with a limit of 170,000 for such immigrants. Western Hemisphere native immigrants were limited to 120,000, and early applicants again get priority, irrespective of nationality. In addition there is an exempt category of special immigrants. The new system will certainly alter the character of migration, and work to the 'disadvantage' of the hitherto privileged areas of north-west Europe. Early results indicate a large increase of Italian, Portuguese, Greek, Chinese and Filipino immigrants. On the matter of future population size, however, although the number admitted can be varied (e.g. 362,000 in 1967; 454,000 in 1968) the range of possible variation is small relative to

---

* The chief source used is the Bureau of the Census publication *Population Estimates*, Series P–25, No. 381, Dec. 1967, amended by reference to preliminary 1970 data.

† ibid., p. 37.

other elements, and the official projections, allowing for a net annual gain by migration of 400,000 persons, should not be far out on this score.

Thus the accuracy of the projections to 2000 rests principally upon assumptions about possible variations in the birth rate, and four different Bureau projections (1967) reflect, chiefly, varying estimates of fertility. A 'high-fertility' projection, assuming birth rates similar to those of the 1940s, gave a 1980 population of 250 million, rising to 360 million by 2000. A 'low-fertility' projection, assuming birth rates similar to those of the middle 1960s, gave a 1980 population of about 228 million, and a 2000 figure approximately 283 millions. Already, by 1970, it seemed that the latter projection was the more likely and that the 'crisis' level of nearly 400 million people by AD 2000 recently feared by the 'apprehensive' school was unlikely to be reached. Adding another 80 million or so to the population by the end of the century is, however, itself considerable, and will certainly provide numerous problems.

In sum, population growth in the United States will continue to be large in absolute numbers, and American attitudes to the prospect are decidedly ambivalent. On the one side, many still see population growth as providing continuing economic stimulation and the prospect of better standards over all. Uncle Sam has room and to spare. Thus expressions of indignation and accusations of error in enumeration have already come from States, cities and townships whose populations are recorded as having declined over the inter-censal decade 1960–70. On the other side are fears that further large increments to population will present almost insuperable problems and be inevitably marked by a deterioration in the quality of life of the average American and by problems of resource adequacy, pollution and environmental damage. In a world context, it may appear to be nonsense to talk of 'overpopulation' in America in the foreseeable future. However, if the country is to cater adequately for further large increases in numbers, and at rising levels of real income per capita, it must change its attitude to the use of land and other resources. In the past, shocking waste has characterized the development of the American landscape and economy – a point which will be developed further. In this context P. R. Erlich (founder of a US organization called 'Zero Population Growth' in 1969) asserts that population growth is much more serious in America than elsewhere because of the very heavy demands of Americans on natural resources. He suggests that each American baby requires fifty times the resources of a baby born in India. If the attitudes of Americans to the use of their still abundant resources can be changed by such propaganda, something positive will have been achieved towards the better ordering of future patterns of development.* In the world of today, however, what is immediately significant to our analysis is the manner in which the population has arranged, and is arranging, itself over the land. This provides one theme of the following chapter.

* In this context, the work of the Commission on Population Growth and the American Future established by President Nixon early in 1970 may help further to influence opinion.

2: Regional Aspects of Population Growth and Change

Since the first Census of 1790 the United States has added not only over 200 million to its population, but also over 2 million square miles of territory to the 0·9 million square miles of its original area. Effectively, possession of this vast new territory was secured during the first half of the nineteenth century but the whole period up to about 1900 can be regarded as a 'frontier' period. Till then the Americans were broadly testing out the population-supporting potential of different regions of the area now known as 'conterminous USA', the area referred to throughout.* The urge to 'go West' was felt by millions of pioneering spirits and the tide of settlement surged unevenly across the Mid West and the Central and Southern Plains to the Pacific borderlands. This movement is reflected in the location of the 'centre of population', a neat device for summing up the total effect of regional population change (Figure 1). This centre is the point on which the USA would balance if it were a rigid, weightless plane and each person thereon had equal weight, and exerted an influence on the central point proportional to his distance from that point. In 1790 the centre was 23 miles to the east of Baltimore, but by 1900 it had moved 530 miles due west to the vicinity of Columbus, Indiana, reflecting the general trend of population movement and settlement to that time.

The year 1900 provides, of course, no neat dividing-line for an analysis of population geography, and twentieth-century developments, especially in the early decades, broadly continued the lines established in the nineteenth century. The pace was, however, slower. In the first 40 years of this century, for example, the centre of population moved west on average only 21 miles per decade; for the 110 preceding years the average had been about 50 miles per decade. This

* 'Conterminous' USA excludes Alaska and Hawaii.

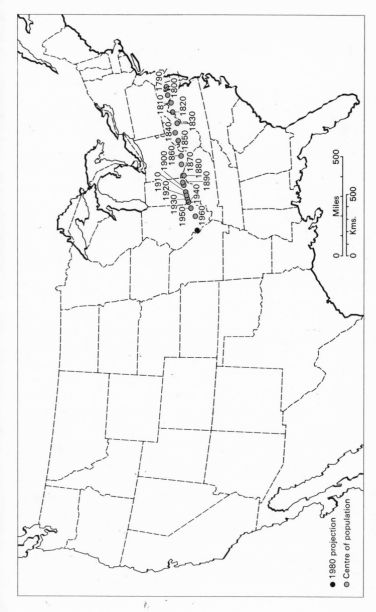

Figure 1. Centre of Population 1790–1980

1980 projection
Centre of population

Miles
0   500
Kms.
0   500

greater geographical stability of the population in the first 40 years of the twentieth century probably owes much to the periodic difficulties and economic uncertainties of the times. Figure 1 indicates, too, that the centre moved slightly south of west from 1900 to 1940, marking the onset of a more complex pattern of population distribution, a pattern we shall examine in greater detail for the period from 1940 to the present. This analysis will refer to Regions, Divisions and States, and a key to these geographical areas is provided in Figure 2.

On a preliminary view of the four major regions, the West has undoubtedly continued to outshine all other regions in its attractions. Table 3 presents Census figures for 1940 and 1960 and estimates

Table 3: Population of Conterminous USA by Region, 1940–69

Region	1940	(million) 1960	1969	Increase 1940–69 million	%
North-East	36	45	49	13	36
North Central	40	52	56	16	40
South	42	55	63	21	50
West	14	27	33	19	136
Total	132	179	202	70	53

Source: Census of Population and Current Population Reports

for 1969 for the four regions of conterminous USA. While the total population increased by over 50 per cent between 1940 and 1969, that of the West rose by 136 per cent, dwarfing the growth rates of other regions. The increase in the West was on a comparatively small 1940 base of 14 million, and therefore looks most impressive expressed in relative terms. Nevertheless the West, which had only 11 per cent of the American population in 1940, had 27 per cent of the total national population increase between that date and 1969. This performance has often, rightly, been singled out for special emphasis, but it must not be permitted completely to obscure the significance of growth elsewhere. A rather larger absolute increase came in the South, but here *rates* of growth are much affected by the large base population of 1940. Such points are further illustrated in Figures 3 and 4, which

16

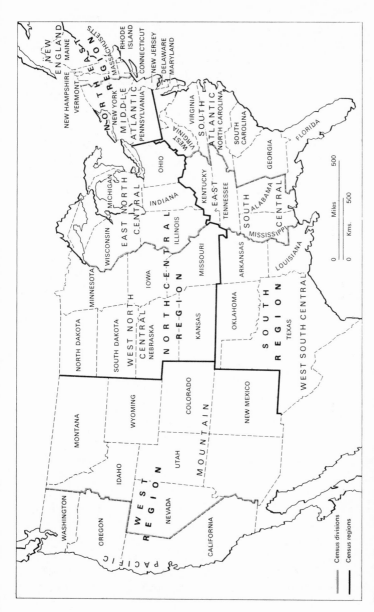

Figure 2. Key to Regions, Divisions and States

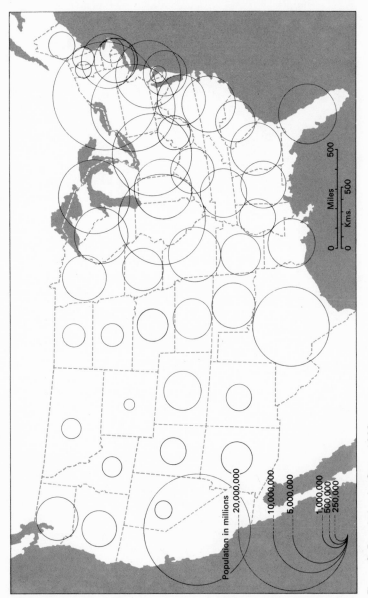

Figure 3. Population by State, 1968

Population in millions

20,000,000

10,000,000

5,000,000

1,000,000
500,000
250,000

0   500
Kms.
0   500
Miles

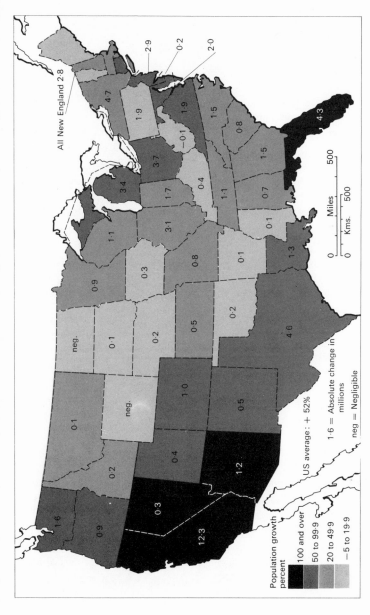

Figure 4. Population Change 1940–68

depict for each State the present size of population and the absolute and relative growth since 1940.

A word on the estimates used may be in order at this point. Clearly, it is an advantage to use the latest available statistics rather than terminate the analysis with 1960 Census data. Not only is this more satisfying in itself, but also in this highly volatile subject significant changes can occur over a very few years. The only proviso is that the figures should be reliable. Bureau of the Census estimates for intercensal years are based on the average of the results of two different estimating procedures.* Undoubtedly there are errors (especially problematic is the problem of estimating changes resulting from net migration) but even full Census counts are, as we have seen, not free from sizeable error, and these estimates normally prove consistent with the results of censuses taken by State governments at various times. The average error of the Bureau's estimates for the States is, according to recent tests, about 1·5 per cent and, even allowing for the variations around this figure, such accuracy is not only quite acceptable but even impressive. Since our analysis is not concerned with changes from year to year, and we normally use figures rounded at least to the nearest 100,000, the use of recent estimated figures is justifiable.

Let us now return to Figures 3 and 4 and attempt to get an objective view of regional population change, despite the quite extraordinary *rates* of growth in some areas that leap to the eye and attract most attention. In the north-eastern USA population was already dense (by American standards) in 1940. Yet some States in this north-eastern area have experienced a considerable upsurge of population since then. New York, for example, has added nearly five millions. Only California has added more. New York, however, has a low *rate* of population change over the period shown in Figure 4. Further, over three million people were added to the populations of each of Ohio, Michigan and Illinois. Such increases may not look impressive beside that of the 'Pacific Paradise', but none the less they rank among the largest in the nation. Moreover, California stands alone as a major western centre of population (see Figure 3), whereas

* See note on methodology in Bureau of the Census, *Population Estimates*, No. 436, Jan. 1970, p. 25.

in the North-East there is a whole series of contiguous, highly populated States which, year by year, add considerably to their total. Such large absolute increases in the 'older' areas of the country are less dramatic than those occurring elsewhere, but they raise issues no less significant than those of the favoured south-western areas.

Broadly, therefore, although the general movement has remained toward the West, the population of the United States is still heavily concentrated in the eastern half of the country and especially in the north-eastern 'quadrant', which comprises the Middle Atlantic, East North Central and New England divisions. This is demonstrated by the 1960 position of the centre of population in central southern Illinois, about 90 miles from its 1940 position. The move to the West has speeded up again since 1940, averaging 45 miles per decade, but the direction of movement remains somewhat south of west, reflecting the counter-pull of developments in south-eastern areas. The centre is, moreover, still within the north-eastern quadrant, only some 750 miles from the Atlantic, but nearly 1,800 miles from the Pacific coast. Despite the much publicized attractions of the West, the older north-eastern centres retain their hold upon a massive population.

Figure 4 illustrates that in each of the major Census regions there has been a wide diversity of experience. A few instances may be selected from each region. The South, for example, experienced the largest absolute increase of population between 1940 and 1968, but West Virginia actually lost population, and numbers in Arkansas and Mississippi remained virtually unchanged. Florida, however, made remarkable gains. Between 1940 and 1968 it increased its population by over four million and (benefiting from its small population base), ranks with Nevada and Arizona as one of only three States with growth rates of over 200 per cent in the period. Of these three, Florida can claim by far the largest absolute increase.

The central areas of the country have, over all, not done very well. Every State of the West North Central division has increased its population at below the national average rate, and sometimes hardly at all. With the base population already relatively small, the total addition to population for the whole division has been negligible, only 2·6 million over the twenty-eight-year period. A similar experience characterizes other central areas. In fact, of all States lying between Longitude 90° and 105° West, only Texas has experienced notable growth.

The Mountain States, as a group, still rank low on population size, although southern parts have experienced higher than average growth rates since 1940. Particularly impressive have been the expansion rates, 308 per cent and 234 per cent respectively, of Nevada and Arizona. This has been featured in the popular press, but Figure 4 shows that the absolute additions have normally been small compared with those elsewhere.

Along the Pacific coast, the outstanding absolute and relative expansion of California has already been noted. In 1964 California replaced New York as the most populous State in the nation. In Washington and Oregon, however, a rapid spurt in population between 1940 and 1950 has not been maintained, and both remain somewhat sparsely populated.

Finally, the States of the north-east quadrant also experienced varying fortunes. The large absolute gains of some of these States (New York, Ohio, Michigan and Illinois) were mentioned above. A notable further element, however, is the high growth *rate* of all the north-eastern seaboard States from Connecticut to Virginia (except New York), broadly representing the rapid growth of megalopolis. By contrast, the New England States, except Connecticut, have an unimpressive record, as does Pennsylvania, the western parts of which share with West Virginia and East Kentucky the grave problems of that afflicted area, Appalachia.

There is also a great diversity of experience within each State. For example, within West Virginia, where population has declined absolutely, some counties along the western margin of the State have continuously increased in population since 1940. In Florida, by contrast, where growth has been extraordinarily rapid, counties in the extreme North-West have lost population continuously. This situation is summarized in the fact that, in a nation which gained in population by 47 million between 1940 and 1960, about half of all the 3,100 counties experienced continuous population loss. The counties concerned were chiefly rural and covered much of the deep South, Appalachia and the Ozarks and the Great Plains. In the 1960s, the number of counties losing population diminished. In the South, particularly, most of the previously declining counties began again to grow. In the West North Central and Mountain divisions, however, as well as in Appalachia, numerous counties are still losing population.

What emerges is a picture of an exceedingly mobile population. In large numbers people respond, as they did in the past, to the varying assessments of the opportunities for satisfactory living and working conditions in different parts of the country. But the consequent patterns of regional growth or decline have become much more complex in modern times. The conditions of economic life and the location of attractive economic opportunities have been changing as the economy has matured and society, in general, has become more affluent. The simple, stirring cry to the young man to 'go West' is still raised, but carries less resoundingly through the land. Numerous forces now interplay in determining the choice of area in which to 'live, work and play' (a standard advertising phrase). Consequently the geographical pattern of population change increases in intricacy as counter-migration is superimposed on migration and as the components of natural population increase vary in response to regional or local conditions. These elements are considered in the following section.

Components of Regional Change

Birth rates and death rates naturally vary widely across the country. In 1968 (the special case of the capital* excepted) the birth rate ranged from approximately 15 per thousand in Kansas to 23 per thousand in Utah (US average 17·4). The death rate also varied greatly, from 7 per thousand in Utah and New Mexico to over 11 in Florida (US average 9·6). Figure 5 depicts the consequent variations in the rate of natural increase by State in 1968. The situation is complex, but one or two broad features are worthy of comment.

The rate of natural increase is consistently high through the South

* Washington D C in 1968 had a birth rate of 33·8, a death rate of 13·2 and a natural increase of 20·6 (rates per thousand). Each of these is by far the highest in the nation.

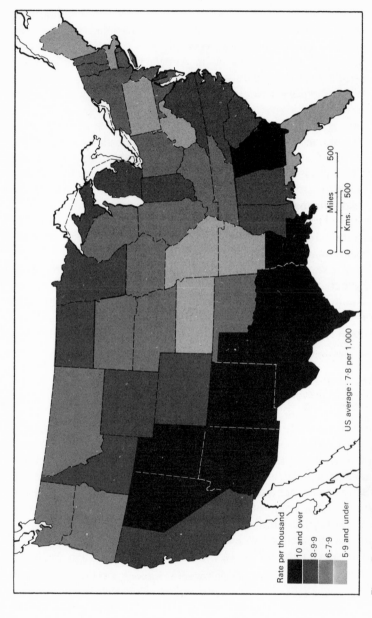

Figure 5. Natural Increase by State 1968

Rate per thousand

■ 10 and over
■ 8·9-9
■ 6·7-9
□ 5·9 and under

US average: 7·8 per 1,000

Miles
0   500   500

Kms.
0   500

and South-West. In fact, with the single exception of Florida, every peripheral State from Virginia south and west to California falls in the high or moderately high classes of natural increase adopted in Figure 5, normally because of both high birth rates and low death rates.* Florida's exceptional situation reflects the lower birth and higher death rates associated with an unusually high proportion of retired and elderly people.

Throughout the Mountain division, except for Montana, rates of natural increase are above the national average, in the south of the division well above. The moderately low natural increase in the Pacific North-West reflects an average death rate and a rather low birth rate. The central areas of the country, too, have many States with below-average natural growth rates; some indeed, in the very lowest rank. A group of largely agricultural States in mid Continent fall into this class, as do also the troubled Appalachian States of West Virginia and Pennsylvania and parts of New England. In each, declining economic opportunities lead to out-migration of persons in the chief child-bearing age groups.

Net migration can greatly alter population growth in different regions and, according to its type and direction, ultimately produce different rates of natural increase in various parts. Figure 6 distinguishes States according to net migration rates between 1960 and 1968. The figures include foreign migrants. They represent *net* movements and behind them lies an enormous volume of infinitely complex interchanges which we must ignore. The figure shows, however, that net migration losses characterize most interior States. These losses have been particularly severe in relation to population size, or natural increase rates, in West Virginia, the Dakotas and Wyoming. In each of these States total population fell over the eight-year period. In Iowa too, natural increase has barely offset migration losses. For the East North Central States, however, the net migration losses are small compared with the absolute size of the natural increment. Over the whole division natural increase amounted to 3·6 million, and net migration loss to barely a quarter of a million.

* Of the eleven 'peripheral' States concerned, only Virginia had a lower than national average birth rate and only Mississippi a higher than national average death rate.

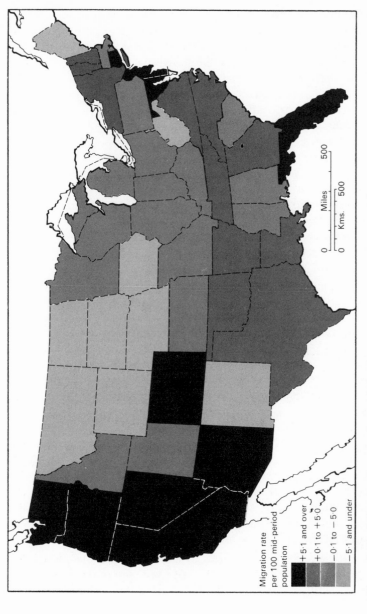

Migration rate
per 100 mid-period
population

+5.1 and over
+0.1 to +5.0
−0.1 to −5.0
−5.1 and under

Miles
0   500
Kms.
0   500

Figure 6. Net Migration Rates by State, 1960–68

By contrast, peripheral areas have been the chief gainers from migration. Particularly impressive, absolutely and relatively, have been the gains in California ($+1.7$ million in the period) and Florida ($+0.8$ million). The north-eastern seaboard States have also done particularly well, with high migration gains extending from Connecticut to Maryland, giving a net gain of almost a million persons between 1960 and 1968. Many of these, especially in New York and New Jersey, are, of course, foreign immigrants, without whom the record here would be much less impressive.

Migratory movements can, of course, be particularly volatile, likely to change sharply in strength or direction. Washington State, where post-war migration has been heavily influenced by the fortunes of a single employer – Boeing in Seattle – illustrates the point. Through the 1950s Washington had small net migration gains, but from 1960 to 1965 it had a net loss as Boeing laid off large numbers of workers. Subsequently the company expanded its aircraft production, producing a net migration gain for the State – in fact the highest rate in the nation between 1965 and 1968. Recently, however, the Boeing payroll has fallen sharply once more and the pattern of migration is changing yet again. Over all, however, it appears from available evidence that the volume of inter-State movement has declined somewhat in the late 1960s. The average net migration gain of California, for example, 280,000 per year between 1960 and 1965, was only about 80,000 between 1965 and 1968. Florida continues to attract large numbers, but Arizona and Nevada seem to be losing appeal. Meanwhile the rate of net out-migration for large north-eastern States (notably Massachusetts and Pennsylvania) appears to have slowed, and the East North Central division has turned a long-standing migration loss into a small gain. Intercensal estimates for migration are subject to a considerable margin of error, but the patterns described are unlikely to be much changed by the 1970 Census data.

The complexity of the total migration movement is at least partially illustrated by Figure 7, which maps the annual average flow of migrants among the four major regions between 1955 and 1965. (This map excludes foreign migrants and the North-East region thereby shows a net deficit. On the statistics used for Figure 6, which

27

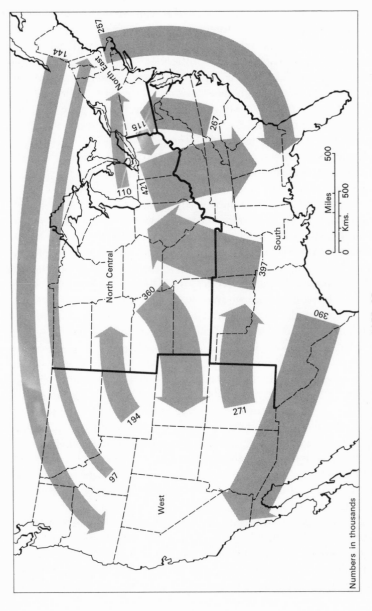

Figure 7. Inter-Regional Migration, Annual Average, 1955–65

Numbers in thousands

included migration from overseas, the North-East region made an average annual net migration gain of 100,000 from 1960 to 1965.) Over the decade, the West was the biggest gainer from this movement, but the large out-migration shows that not everyone is satisfied with what he finds. From 1960 to 1965, for example, about one million people moved into the West on average each year, but 600,000 per year moved out. Within the West, California remains the chief goal of the migrant, but reactions to this State, though always positive, are becoming more mixed. The American columnist Russell Baker has noted, 'visitors usually decide immediately that there is no place on earth, or run screaming to pick up return reservations to get them out . . .'

Another important element in the flow is the large interchange between the South on the one hand and the North Central and North-East regions on the other. Numerically these movements practically cancelled themselves out in the ten-year period shown, but the characteristics and the purposes of the people concerned could hardly be more different. The flow to the North included many Negroes and poor whites, often from rural areas, who hoped to find employment and opportunity to live a better life in the big northern cities like Chicago, New York and Detroit. This inflow of hundreds of thousands of normally poor and ill-educated people added greatly to the problem of the cities to which they moved, and especially to the difficulties of their central areas. This theme, with others only lightly touched upon here, will be taken up again. By contrast, the flow to the South was chiefly to Florida, and contained many relatively affluent and recently retired people, supplemented by younger persons whose skills permitted the realization of their desire to live in this highly advertised area by working in the space industry there.

Figure 7, based as it is on only the four major Census regions, inhibits the direct identification of other major migration patterns (such as the large flow from the Prairie States of unemployed farm workers to the urban-industrial zones both east and west) and conceals completely other large but more localized movements from, for example, city to city and from city to suburb. None the less the map indicates that the kinds of opportunity and the 'good life' sought are

29

not identical for all Americans, and produce many contrasting movements.

The Urban-Rural Dichotomy

Highly significant among these trends in population geography is the movement from farm to city (the terms are used in a broad sense): a movement which is changing the character and pattern of American life. We mentioned above the remarkable fact that in recent decades, although population has increased by many millions, hundreds of counties have had a continuous population decline. The affected counties, chiefly agrarian, mirror the changing role and structure of the farm and rural areas generally, changes that have often induced large-scale depopulation. The counterpart of this process has been the steady growth of cities and, especially, of the large metropolitan areas. The traditional dominance of rural over urban population, which penetrated well into the twentieth century, has thus been overthrown. Reasons for, and consequences of, this continuing development will be reviewed later. Here in examining salient characteristics of population geography, we only present the essential facts.

There are problems of definition here, but we shall not become deeply involved at this stage. Basically the difficulty is to make an acceptable division of the population into 'urban' and 'rural', since frequently the dividing-line is by no means clear. The practice in the USA, as elsewhere, is to define the 'urban' population, the 'rural' population comprising the balance. Clearly, in this procedure judgements which may be controversial must be made. Moreover, judgements may, with time, lose whatever validity they originally possessed, and new definitions to cover new developments must be made. This affects the accuracy of historical comparisons. In the United States an important change in definition came in 1950, which therefore becomes a dividing-line in the study.

However unsatisfactory the definitions, the statistics reflect correctly a substantial change in the character of the American population. Throughout the nineteenth century the rural population dominated the urban, but decreasingly so as the urban-industrial sector grew vigorously in the second half of the century. Even so, by 1900 six out of ten Americans were still classified as rural (Figure 8), and from then until 1950 the rural population continued to grow steadily in absolute size. None the less, with urbanization proceeding much more rapidly, the rural *proportion* of the population declined equally steadily. In fact, over this time the old definition of 'urban' became increasingly unrealistic as large numbers of truly urbanized Americans came to live in areas falling outside its scope (e.g. in unincorporated settlements or urban fringe areas). The new 1950 definition attempted to correct the grosser inaccuracies in this situation, with the consequences shown in Figure 8. From 1950 to 1960, on this evidence, the entire growth of the American population was accounted for by urban areas, and the rural proportion fell to 30 per cent.

Within both categories of population other important changes have taken place, especially perhaps in the structure of employment of people living respectively in rural and urban areas. The term 'rural' conjures up visions of fields and crops, animals and farmsteads, but the rural population of modern America is not chiefly involved in occupations relevant to this image. Of the 54 million people classified as 'rural' in the 1960 Population Census, under a quarter were sub-classified as 'farm population'. Department of Agriculture figures show how great the change has been in recent years. In about 1910 the total *farm* population reached its peak of 34 million, and it remained high until 1940 (31 million). Subsequently the number dropped sharply to 15·6 million in 1960 and about 10 million in 1969. Clearly, whereas up to about 1940 most persons classified as living in rural areas still made a living from farming, or in serving farmers and farm workers, they no longer do so.

While the truly 'rural' ways of earning a living in rural areas have declined, however, the opportunities for employment in large urban communities have multiplied. Industrial activities are more numerous, more varied and more sophisticated; and an enormous range of highly remunerative careers has developed in the 'services' category of employment. Such tremendous changes have affected settlement patterns and brought associated problems of various kinds which

31

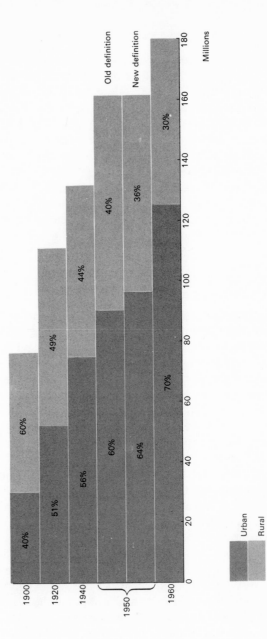

Figure 8. Urban and Rural Population, 1900—1960

are not easily summarized. In essence, opportunities for making a satisfactory living in truly rural areas have greatly diminished, but in urban areas greatly increased. This is naturally reflected in the level of incomes in the two types of environment. According to the 1960 Census, 34 per cent of rural families were living on incomes below $3,000 (then approximately the poverty line for a family of four), compared with 16 per cent of urban families. At the opposite extreme 40 per cent of urban families flourished on incomes above $7,000, compared with only 22 per cent of rural families; and we may safely assume that many of these latter families belonged to the adventitious 'rural' population, i.e. urban in all but name. Such distinctions lie at the roots of the migratory movements, which have developed at great speed in recent years with consequent problems for every area concerned.

So far has urbanization gone and so deeply has the countryside been penetrated by its influence that some consider that the division of population into urban-rural categories has lost its value. In fact, however, it remains significant and important, especially towards the extremes of the urban-rural spectrum, which avoid the special problems of the rur-urban zone. Even a cursory examination of the American scene reveals the contrast between the experiences and impact of population changes in distinctively rural areas on the one hand and distinctively urban areas on the other. While the Jeffersonian concept, in which farm families provided the indispensable backbone of a democratic society, has long gone, a sizeable population still lives in a demonstrably rural society, pursuing a truly rural economy and facing specifically rural difficulties. American democracy, though now expressing an advanced urban-industrial civilization, cannot afford to discount the problems of its rural population.

Some Significant Racial Characteristics

The racial character of a population remains important in studying current population geography. Americans are of very mixed origin and, in particular, large numbers of the whites (almost 20 per cent

33

of the total population in 1960) are either foreign born or children of foreign-born parents. This gives a special character both to the US population and to the environments, urban and rural, where individual nationality groups have concentrated. Although this is interesting and important, we must forgo its detailed consideration in this study. The major ethnic groups tend to maintain their distinctiveness for several generations after their entry into America, but the main problems of white newcomers are normally less enduring than those of other racial types, both because of their backgrounds and because they are less visible as members of racial minorities. Thus, for the continuing problems of settlement and absorption the non-whites emerge as most significant in the racial structure. Even when they have been Americans for generations, they remain highly visible and, for this and other reasons, suffer consistently from under-privilege, both social and economic. In the late 1960s the non-whites were about 12 per cent of the total population – a sizeable minority of over 25 million persons which, with a high birth rate, is growing considerably faster than the population as a whole.

A practical Census division of the non-white population separates it into 'Negroes' and 'other races'. Of these the former are by far the more numerous and significant, and will receive most attention here. The 'other races' number less than 2·5 million and comprise chiefly American Indians, Japanese, Chinese and Filipinos.* The last three are concentrated mainly in Hawaii and California (which together have half the total non-white population, excluding Negroes), with the States of Washington and New York following, but far behind. The American Indian is more widespread, but the central and western States are well represented, as would be expected. Over all, however, the 'other races' do not greatly affect the population picture. In only two of the nine Census divisions (Mountain and Pacific) do they amount to more than 1 per cent of the total population. Thus, while they are of considerable local significance, and while the particular difficulties of these minorities (especially the Indians) are now stirring American consciences, they do not impel such urgent attention as the Negro, whose problems have notable

* Persons of Mexican birth or ancestry (about 6 million in number) are normally classified as 'white'.

economic and social expression over wider and wider areas of the USA.

In 1969 22·4 million American Negroes provided over 11 per cent of the total population whereas, in 1940, 12·9 million had provided only 9·8 per cent. Clearly the Negro population has grown more rapidly than the white in recent decades. This reverses the historical situation in which a growing Negro population had provided a steadily decreasing proportion of the total. In 1800, for example, almost 20 per cent of the American population was Negro, but in 1850 only 15 per cent, in 1900 12 per cent and in 1940 9·8 per cent. The consistently higher Negro fertility rates had, historically, been offset or more than offset by higher death rates and by the effects on population totals of a vigorous white immigration. Both conditions have changed. Since the First World War there has been rigorous control over immigration and, since about 1940, a decline in the Negro death rate far sharper than that of the whites, so that the two groups had approximately equal death rates by 1967. So, with fertility rates remaining considerably above the white level, the Negro population has been growing the faster – indeed, in the late 1960s almost twice as fast as the white population. This situation may be expected to continue.

Not only is the Negro population growing rapidly in size, but its geographical distribution is changing dramatically. Throughout the nineteenth century Negroes were concentrated overwhelmingly in the South, with the balance chiefly in the North-East. Up to about 1860, in a rapid geographical movement, the Negro followed the extension of the cotton-growing area of the South towards, and then beyond, the Mississippi. From then to about 1910, little change took place in relative geographical distribution. As Hart expresses it, 'In terms of interregional migration this half century was essentially a slack tide between the great westward surge which had preceded it and the great northward diaspora which was to follow.'* It was not that no movement took place over this period, but what there was was insignificant compared with what went before and what followed.

From about 1910, the geographical distribution again changed

* J. Fraser Hart, 'The Changing Distribution of the American Negro', *Annals of the Association of American Geographers*, Sept. 1960, p. 242.

significantly, as continuing difficulties in southern agriculture and the demands of northern industries for labour during the First World War attracted more and more Negroes to industrial areas in the North-East and North Central regions. The flow slackened during the depression years, but from 1910 to 1940 just over $1\frac{1}{2}$ million Negroes (net) migrated from the South. This is an impressive total, but it was surpassed in the single decade 1940–50, when wartime labour demands in non-southern regions were again important. The flow has remained strong ever since, under the continuing pressures of agricultural change in the South, and the Negroes' hopes of better employment opportunities elsewhere. Between 1940 and 1970 about 4 million Negroes (net) left the southern region. This movement, coupled with the high natural increase rates of the now considerable Negro populations in non-southern cities, has transformed and is transforming the geography of the race. The 'colour problem', once essentially a southern matter, has swiftly become a national problem.

This is reflected in Figure 9, which requires little commentary. As recently as 1940 over three quarters of the Negro population remained in the South. By 1975, if present trends continue, more will live outside the South than within it. Although the Negro population is increasing in the southern region, the increase is less rapid than elsewhere. Indeed, substantial areas in the South (including the whole of Mississippi and Arkansas) have had continuous decline of the Negro population since 1940. Meanwhile very rapid increases occurred in the three non-southern regions. By 1940 the North Central region, industrializing energetically since 1900, was replacing the North-East in having the largest non-southern Negro population. It has continued to outgrow the North-East, but obviously both regions have greatly increased their Negro populations. Growth since 1940 in the West has also been vigorous. While the total Negro population here remains relatively small, the *rate* of increase is impressive and, moreover, the movement west has been largely concentrated into California, which between 1940 and 1960 increased its Negro population by nearly 1 million, or over 700 per cent. Such growth puts special strains on local areas favoured by the Negro, and requires rapid adjustment in all spheres of life and work; adjustments not always easily made.

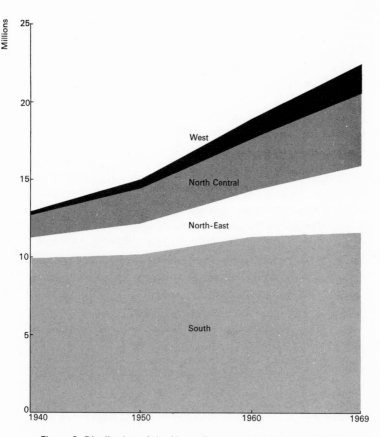

Figure 9. Distribution of the Negro Population by Region, 1940–69

Two further geographical aspects of these great Negro migrations are noteworthy, the one a matter of considerable interest, the other of explosive significance. The first is the quite consistent connection between certain districts of origin and particular destinations. Significant Negro migrations from the South began in the South Atlantic division, and the participants chiefly moved up the coastal areas towards the north-east coastal cities. As migration got under way, increasing numbers moved from the central and the western portions of the southern region. Those from the central South mainly moved directly northwards to the industrial areas of the Mid West, those from the western parts of the South established a strong orientation towards the West. In this manner the Negro has penetrated every region of the United States, and the movement, if continued, must ultimately produce a broad equalization of the Negro population in all regions.

The second, more urgent, aspect is that the Negro migrant, to whichever region he has gone, has moved almost exclusively to a city, and especially to a few of the very largest cities. R. I. Morrill's estimates of the major destinations of the 3 million Negroes who left the South between 1940 and 1960 indicate that about 85 per cent of the migrants were destined for one or other of only ten cities.* New York, Philadelphia, Washington DC and Baltimore were the major destinations along the north-east coast, Chicago, Detroit, Cleveland and St Louis in the North Central region and Los Angeles and San Francisco in the West. By 1967, according to Bureau of the Census estimates, Negroes comprised over 30 per cent of the population in seven of these ten cities, whereas as recently as 1950 only Washington DC had such a proportion. Despite a recent decline in the Negro migration rate, their high rates of natural increase mean that many large cities will have a majority Negro population well before the end of this century. Washington DC and Newark are already in this position. (N.B. 'city' here refers to the central city core of the metropolitan area.)

Such developments have fundamentally changed the pattern of life of many Negroes. Historically, the Negro was a rural person first

* R. I. Morrill, 'The Negro Ghetto: Problems and Alternatives', *Geographical Review*, July 1965, p. 340.

and foremost, and the 'urban' proportion has until recently been considerably lower than for whites. The situation has been rapidly changed by the migration movements outlined and also by the changing character of farming and other developments in the South, which have brought a sharp increase, even here, in the numbers of 'urban' Negroes. By 1960 the American Negro had become, on average, more highly urbanized than the white, with 73 per cent of all Negroes living in urban areas compared with about 70 per cent of all whites. The trend has continued. Naturally, there are considerable regional variations. At the 1960 Census, 42 per cent of Negroes in the South were still 'rural'. The North-East, however, had only just over 4 per cent entered as 'rural', and other regions have similarly small rural Negro populations. The general situation is clear, and the 'Negro problem' of today is, essentially, an urban problem or, more precisely, a problem of the metropolitan areas.

One further and quite vital geographical distinction remains. The Negro has, for historical, economic and social reasons, settled almost exclusively in the central areas of the great metropolitan communities to which he has migrated, while the white population has become increasingly suburban. The central cities of the major agglomerations have thus seen a rapidly increasing population of Negroes and a steadily decreasing white population. In 1969 about four out of every five Negro citizens of US metropolitan areas lived in the central cities of those areas, whereas only two out of five white citizens did so. The implications are very grave, and will be further discussed in the chapter on urban geography.

The conditions of life of the average American Negro are reflected in various indices of economic and social conditions, in which, invariably, he measures up poorly compared with his white compatriot. For example, the unemployment rate for Negroes is, over all, some twice as high as for whites, and has been for many years. In many large industrial cities, unemployment rates of 10–15 per cent were not uncommon among Negroes in the later 1960s, compared with city-wide averages of 2·5–4·5 per cent. Overwhelmingly, too, Negroes work as labourers, machine-minders, cleaners and messengers, with correspondingly low incomes. In 1968, for example, the median family income for non-whites was $5,600; for whites $8,900.

39

Some advance has been made recently. In 1960 the non-white median family income was only 55 per cent of the white, but the discrepancy remains very great. Moreover, Negro families averaged 4·4 persons compared with 3·6 for whites and are about three times as likely to be headed by a woman – indicating a substantial incidence of broken homes and unsatisfactory home life. Of outstanding significance, however, both as a consequence of past conditions and as a cause of their perpetuation, is the situation in education. Over 18 per cent of adult Negroes have had less than four years in school, compared with only 5 per cent of whites. Only half of the 400,000 or so Negroes attaining the age of 18 each year have completed their full twelve years in school, and even these are on average more than three years behind a similar white youth in educational attainment. Thus estimates suggest that up to 90 per cent of Negroes entering the labour market are educationally unfit to compete in a modern, highly technical, society. Clearly, advance in education is a key to any solution of the Negro problem.

Other socio-economic characteristics of the Negro could be mentioned but the essential point has been made. Whether urban or rural, the Negro is massively underprivileged. He, however, is not the only member of the underprivileged class in the USA; there is no simple correlation of low economic status and deprivation with race. The Negroes are a large and perhaps uniquely afflicted people, but other distressed minorities (the Indian, for example), and very many 'poor whites' bear an equivalent, or sometimes an even more degrading, burden. The poor whites in fact greatly outnumber the poor Negroes, and districts (e.g. of Appalachia or the Ozarks) with dominantly white populations, besides those predominantly coloured, have areas of social and economic distress. In 1968, 25·4 million Americans were living below the poverty line, and two thirds of this number were white. Of course, the incidence of poverty is greater for non-whites, one in three of them falling into the poverty class in 1968, compared with one in ten whites. None the less, poverty is certainly not exclusively a Negro problem.

Conclusion

In these opening chapters various problems of population and population geography have been introduced, but several important areas of population study have been neglected. Age structure and sex structure are examples. Both are changing and altering the structure of American society and economy. The numbers in various age groups, for example, directly affect the demand for goods and services of varying types, and various 'critical' ages have considerable economic and social importance (e.g. the age of 6, when children enter school, 18 when young people move on to college, the armed forces or the labour force, 62 when people can retire, and so on). Regional variations in age structure, which can be considerable, are therefore important. The same applies to sex structure; and the number of women of child-bearing age is critical for population forecasting. Nowadays too, women outnumber men in the total population, a new phenomenon of American society. Up to the Second World War the males had dominated (numerically!) – the 'frontier syndrome' – but the 1950 Census recorded, for the first time in history, a female superiority, which is progressively advancing in the age of the 'new frontier'. None of these topics can be pursued here; this introductory treatment has merely highlighted certain major aspects of American population geography to provide a basis for further analyses.

3: Land Resources and Problems of Land Use

Turning from population geography to land resources and their utilization is turning from one truly seminal topic to another. An examination of the land, its resources and the way they are used could itself provide a method for analysing practically all the significant aspects of life and economy touched upon in this book. All man's activities use land in some way or another, and create problems of competition, of conservation and optimal use and of spatial relationships. Each claim for land could provide a key to a full analysis of the activity concerned and set that analysis in the context of possible conflicts of economic and social interests and values. An examination of mineral extraction, for example, could lead to a comprehensive study of mineral endowments and patterns of economic exploitation. Subsequently it could study the implications for other possible uses of the land in question (e.g. for agriculture, urban or recreational development), reaching value judgements on its impact on environment. In other cases this would permit a very detailed analysis of the allocation of land to various *types* of agricultural activity, different *kinds* of industry, differing *styles* of urban development and so on.

Such an approach is mentioned here, however, chiefly to emphasize the key significance of land. Attempting a full geographical analysis through land use has real attractions to a modern geographer, but also has problems, some apparently insuperable at present. A special difficulty is the paucity of data on various important aspects of land use in the United States, especially on land use in urban–industrial systems. This situation, when first faced, invariably surprises the student of North America, which prides itself (often justifiably) on the extent and comprehensiveness of its statistical resources, yet has no system of regular collection, analysis and publication of land-use

42

data. Clawson and Stewart, among others, have drawn attention to growing population, rising real incomes and other influences which are intensifying the competition for land in the USA; and to the numerous and complex changes in land use. Therefore, they conclude, 'accurate, meaningful, *current* data on land use are essential'. But, 'by and large land use data for the US are a hodge-podge. It is very difficult to obtain national total acreages for many land uses on a consistent and meaningful definition. . . . Moreover, the situation is much worse if one attempts the same data compilation . . . on a regional, state or smaller geographical basis. Errors which average out, or are concealed, in national totals may become glaring for smaller areas.'* So to attempt an entire systematic review on the general theme of land resources and utilization would be, at the least, frustrating. None the less land remains, with population, the key resource of the nation and in this chapter we discuss, in a broad way, the land endowment of the USA and the division of this dowry amongst the various claimants; while some problems associated with land use and the 'philosophy' of land use in this country will also be touched upon. This chapter, then, like the previous ones, provides a foundation for later studies.

Land Areas and Attitudes

Land does not seem particularly scarce in the United States. Conterminous USA embraces almost 3 million square miles, or 1,900 million acres. Thus in the late 1960s the US crude population density remained under 60 per square mile, extraordinarily low compared with advanced industrial countries of Western Europe or with Japan. Some of the total area is, of course, classed as 'unproductive'. The precise definition of 'unproductive' or 'waste' land varies greatly from area to area and country to country, depending upon economic, social and technological conditions. This makes international comparisons difficult, but not necessarily invalid when used in a very general way. The amount of true 'wasteland' in the United States

* M. Clawson and C. L. Stewart, *Land Use Information*, Resources for the Future, 1965, Foreword.

comes to only some 10 per cent of the total area, a relatively small proportion compared, say, with Canada (58 per cent 'waste'), Russia (43 per cent 'waste'), and a world average of about 45 per cent. Americans have up to 9 acres per head of land capable of some productive use compared with the U K, for example, with under one acre for each person. Even the land currently in farm use (which, at about 1,100 million acres is below its historical peak, and well below the area technically capable of food production) gives over five acres for each American. This situation, again, contrasts very sharply indeed with that of other advanced industrial countries.

The inclusion of Alaska and Hawaii raises the total area of the US from 1,900 million to 2,270 million acres. Hawaii, in fact, adds only 4·1 million acres, but Alaska is the largest State of all (365 million acres, compared with the next largest, Texas, 168 million and California, 100 million). Adding Alaska thus greatly alters any calculations and conclusions involving land-area relationships. Moreover, Alaska has such enormous areas of 'unproductive' land and its ownership pattern is so unusual that its inclusion with conterminous USA greatly affects the 'average' picture. These non-conterminous States are consequently excluded from the discussion, except where otherwise stated.

Clearly the problem of US land resources and their management differs greatly from that of other comparable societies. Nevertheless there *are* land-use problems – problems of conservation and reclamation in areas destructively deforested, over-grazed or over-cropped (fortunately a problem of past rather than current creation); of controlling spoliation by mineral working; of optimum land use in areas of greatest population pressure, as around Megalopolis; of efficiency in land use and of amenity preservation. There are responsibilities and duties too (belatedly recognized) in the use of land, which the present generation holds in trust for the future.

That land resources are abundant is clear, but there is need for a more responsible attitude to their use. The population is large, is growing rapidly and, most important, is concentrating geographically in certain areas where competing pressures on land are creating serious problems. Especially in such areas, major developments in land use should have only one eye on immediate profitability, and the

other fixed on more fundamental or permanent issues of conservation of resources and quality of environment. In fact, however, vital
decisions in this context are often taken by private interests, not
informed by any clear national or local policy and not concerned
with wider public issues or costs. Many activities involving the use
of land are highly expensive and (more important) almost completely
irreversible. Further, the pace of modern constructional development is so swift that irremediable damage can be done, resources
permanently sterilized or amenity destroyed, before adverse consequences are noticed and opposition can become effective. A careful,
informed forward planning of land use appears, therefore, to be
essential, but there is little evidence that this need is so far widely
appreciated.

A major difficulty is that of widely prevalent mental attitudes.
There has been a traditional faith in the superabundance of land
resources, a notion of the inexhaustible endowment of Mother
America, fostered by government land-disposal policies both before
and after the Homestead Act of 1862. This inherited faith naturally
affects the way of looking at things, so that relatively few Americans
are really concerned about the way in which the land and its resources
are used or abused. This notion of abundance has been reinforced by
uncritical attitudes to private entrepreneurial activity in pursuit of
profits, and by highly critical attitudes to government 'interference'
with the activities of individuals. It is not being suggested that the
pursuit of profits is not beneficial; but that the unqualified pursuit of
self-interest can have detrimental effects elsewhere – in this case in
the abuse of land and resources and a carelessness about future needs.

The traditional attitude to land, therefore, has been to exploit it at
the earliest opportunity without regard for the consequences. This
attitude contributed notably to the rapid development of the American economy in the nineteenth century, and perhaps such a phase
was unavoidable or even essential. Unhappily, it was agonizingly
prolonged, inflicting irreparable and increasing damage upon the
land and its resources, ruining the lives of hundreds of thousands of
less fortunate Americans, and still affecting attitudes of mind. The
situation was eloquently summed up early this century by Gifford
Pinchot, an outstanding American conservationist: 'The American

Colossus was fiercely intent on appropriating and exploiting the riches of the richest of all continents – grasping with both hands, reaping where he had not sown, wasting what he thought would last forever. . . . The man who could get his hands on the biggest slice of natural resources was the best citizen. Wealth and virtue were supposed to trot in double harness.'*

In the nineteenth century, therefore, Acts of Congress showed no thought for waste, or for the changing needs of a maturing economy, but sought consistently to transfer the nation's land into private ownership, to create a nation of small farmers – the democratic ideal visualized by Jefferson at the outset of the Union in totally different times. The disposal policy assumed that most land was suitable for cropping, and that that was all that was worth considering. This naïve assumption about land potentials in agriculture, and thoughtless attitude to the non-agricultural potentials of land, is termed a 'nonpolicy' by Thomas le Duc, a modern critic, who says 'the heart of this nonpolicy [was] the failure of Congress to formulate and support a program for the protection of the public interest in timber, coal and metals found on the public property. These resources were neither managed affirmatively nor opened to private development on a basis that would guard the people's equity. Congress chose, instead, to tolerate depredation and depletion of such resources as did not pass [into private ownership] by sale or donation under laws contemplating the transfer of lands suited primarily for agriculture.'†

Contemporary observers, such as Agassiz, Guyot and Marsh, sought to draw attention to the realities of the situation, but to little purpose until the end of the century, when the 1891 Forest Reserve Act indicates the beginnings of a conservationist movement. The fact, and consequences, of the rapid depletion of timber resources were at last becoming obvious and the President was authorized to set aside areas of Federal land as forest reserves, not to be homesteaded or otherwise privately 'developed'.

The conservationist movement made some progress during

* Gifford Pinchot, *Breaking New Ground*, quoted in *Surface Mining and Our Environment*, Department of the Interior, 1967.

† H. W. Ottoson (Ed.), Land Use Policy and Problems in the United States, 1963. p. 22.

Theodore Roosevelt's presidency (1901–8), but thereafter quickly lost popular appeal and became a national movement again only in the 1930s, as part of the New Deal programmes. The National Resources Board, established in 1934, produced a Report whose tone was contrary to the traditional American attitude. It maintained both that national resources were a heritage of the whole nation, to be conserved and utilized for the benefit of all rather than misused for the benefit of the few; and that this was a proper sphere for government activity. 'Ignorance, inattention or greed has devastated our heritage almost beyond belief. . . . Public policy should aim at effecting such ownership and use of land as will best subserve general welfare rather than merely private advantage.'*

In general, however, the chief concern of this period was with land use in agriculture. Over wide areas the land was suffering gravely from wind and water erosion deriving from agricultural and timber-felling practices, while farmers were also seriously affected by the economic depression. Programmes for soil conservation and for re-settling farmers and redeveloping farms in marginal areas were initiated, and some are still operative.† While a notable advance in land-use practices was thus achieved, it remained limited in scope. There was little effective concern for other major uses of land or for the developing range of possible conflict in land-use matters. Further, the general attitude was little changed by the 1934 Report, and the urgency of that submission, which had struck a chord in tune with the urgency of the period, was subsequently lost.

Interest in conservation and orderly resource-use programmes has revived since about 1960, stimulated by the thought of the 'New Frontier'. Important publications have presented the work of private researchers, notably under the banner of the 'Resources for the Future' organization, while appropriate themes enter numerous official reports and publications and presidential statements. Major legislation on environmental matters (water and air pollution, recreational space, etc) was passed in the 1960s and the increasing

* *Report to the President*, National Resources Board, December 1934, Foreword and p. 8.

† See *The Land Utilization Program 1934 to 1964*, Department of Agriculture, Economic Research Service, Agricultural Economic Report No. 85, 1965.

47

involvement here is bound to spill over into related issues of land use. A major landmark may have been reached with the National Environmental Policy Act of 1969. Here the rights and duties of individuals in environmental matters were stressed, but the Federal government declared it as its own responsibility, in cooperation with State and local governments, 'to create and maintain conditions under which man and nature can exist in productive harmony'. A Council on Environmental Quality was set up to report to, and advise, the President on relevant matters, and all Federal agencies are now required to examine the environmental impact of their policies and proposals. This Act was followed in 1970 by the creation of an independent Environmental Protection Agency, with wide powers. Land-use matters have not yet received specific attention, but are clearly going to be involved.

It is too early to judge the effectiveness of such measures. Specific programmes have been marred by a lack of funds, and the perennial problem of the division of power between State and Federal authorities. None the less, the careless attitudes of former years appear to be changing and few would now support the common nineteenth-century approach. Yet whole-hearted support for effective land-use planning programmes is lacking, a feeling of those limitless horizons lingers and suspicion of governmental activities and controls remains widespread. Considerable pressure, for example, still exists to release to private interests the land still in Federal ownership, and many still honestly believe that the best interests of *all* Americans can be served only by the unrestricted activities of private enterprise. In fact, with American population and society growing rapidly in size and complexity and with increasing conflicts over the optimum use of land, the market mechanism cannot satisfactorily resolve the problem. Waste and distress can be avoided only by thoughtful forward planning of land use. 'We have no land to waste, and we should provide for the adequate protection and use of every acre.' This statement was not made recently when, for example, the population moved over the 200 million mark, but in the 1934 Report of the National Resources Board (p. 105). The population was then 127 million, of simpler tastes and lower expectations, and generally thought to be heading for stabilization at well below the 200 million reached only some 30 years later. One wonders what would be the reactions of the compilers of that report to the situation of today.

Land Acquisition and Survey

Attitudes to land and its resources and practices in its disposal and use have been coloured by Federal government policies. These policies and practices can best be appreciated with a broad knowledge of the manner and speed of acquisition of this enormous territory. Further, the patterns of development themselves have been markedly affected by the survey procedures adopted so that land allocation and settlement could take place in an orderly way. Acquisition and survey, therefore, now receive a brief treatment.

The early colonists acquired land in various ways, but the areas of land designated in grants, charters or patents were ill defined (a natural consequence of the lack of knowledge of the country, especially of the interior) and often in conflict, as were the colonies themselves. In essence, however, the colonies held land, directly or indirectly, from the Crown, and they sold or rented it. The most confused situation was in the westward limits of the 'grants' and the claims of the various settlements overlapped seriously. Thus, at the formation of the new nation, practically the whole area east of the Mississippi, except Florida and the Gulf coastlands, was claimed and disputed by various member States. To avoid persistent conflict these land claims were ceded to the Federal government at various times between 1784 and 1802. So the central government gained possession of all the territory outside the areas of the original colonies, except the land already privately owned. This ceded land became known as the Federal Domain.

Quite as important as the cession of these claims by the new States was the precedent established. The Federal government could acquire and own land, and dispose of it in ways agreed by Congress. This proved very significant as the young country proceeded, through the first half of the nineteenth century, to acquire vast additional territories and extend its bounds to cover what is now 'conterminous

USA'. In 1790 the gross area of the USA was under 0·9 million square miles. By 1853 it was above 3 million square miles. Rarely has so enormous an empire been so quickly established. Figure 10 shows the timing and extent of these acquisitions. With few exceptions, the areas of all these territories became part of the Federal Domain. The chief exception was Texas, which, at first an independent republic, joined the Union in 1845 but kept its rights to public land in its own area and thus contributed nothing to the Domain. Subsequently, however, the State disposed of its land in a manner similar to that adopted by the Federal government. The remaining exceptions to the Federal ownership of acquired lands were of land already privately owned – a relatively small amount. While new land areas were being added to the Federal Domain, existing possessions were being disposed of in various ways touched upon below. In consequence, the total area of Domain in conterminous USA did not rise commensurately with the total area of the nation. In 1802 some 200 million acres were public land, in 1850 1,200 million. Subsequently, with acquisitions almost completed and disposals proceeding vigorously, the area fell to about 600 million acres by 1912.

There is much debate about the wisdom or necessity of the land-disposal policies, which are discussed in the following section, but the original decision to dispose of the public land was accompanied by a practical decision of great wisdom. This was that the size and location of every grant of land should be precisely recorded by applying a uniform system of land survey. Such a universal system was essential for the orderly use of, or disposal of, land. In essence the system adopted by Congress closely resembled that developed in New England in colonial times, and reflected the experiences of the earlier colonists – especially in New England and the South. In New England township boundaries were surveyed by the colonial authority, and the settlers were then required to make a survey and record of the area within the township. Some results were crude, but this imposition of a common system was clearly advantageous. Land holdings were demarcated and could be upheld in law, while the settled land consisted of a mosaic of adjacent holdings. In the South, by contrast, settlers had been permitted to choose their area of settlement without prior demarcation. Surveys should have been

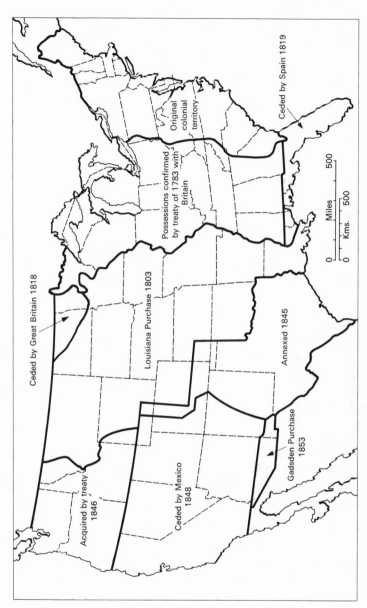

Figure 10. Territorial Expansion of the USA

carried out subsequently and deposited with the authorities, but in fact were not always done. The lack of a uniform system meant that those that were done were not always comparable; many were executed on the basis of an ephemeral landmark; tracts of land between patches of early settlements were left unclaimed and unsurveyed, and so on. Difficulties inevitably followed from such a situation, and acrimonious disputes were numerous. Congress therefore understood the need for a well-defined and orderly system, universally applied, to provide the basis for settlement and ownership.

The system selected involved the drawing up of rectangular areas of standard size, based on prominent, permanent local features, which became the starting-points for the survey. The method requires little explanation here. Briefly the principal meridian runs north–south through the initial point and a base line runs east–west through the same point. A series of further lines, six miles apart, parallel to the base and the meridian, divides the land into six-mile square 'townships'. These townships are further divided into thirty-six sections (one mile square, or 640 acres), and these subdivided into quarter sections, 160 acres each. If necessary, further subdivisions can be made.

On this system the location of each township can be described precisely with reference to the initial point; smaller areas can be described according to their position in each section, quarter section etc. Every tract of land can thus be accurately identified. In practice various problems and imperfections naturally arose. For example, it is impossible to have square townships with true north–south boundaries – i.e. following lines of longitude – and adjustments became necessary here and there. Further, the system was not everywhere suitable to the local physical environment, while there were also erratic or deliberately dishonest surveys. None the less it was a highly valuable innovation and 'as a way of meeting contemporary problems it represented a victory of order over anarchy'.* Some parts of the western USA remain to be surveyed, but most of the land area has been surveyed and occupied on this basis, leaving marked visual impressions on the landscape and having consequences, too, on the organization and geographical patterns of life in rural areas.

* Thomas le Duc in H. W. Ottoson (Ed.), op. cit., p. 6.

The Public Domain: Its Disposal and Use

The way the enormous Federal-owned territories should be used was a major political and social issue throughout the nineteenth century in America. Yet the prevailing attitude and practice remained one that had been established by Congress in the late eighteenth century. Thomas le Duc says: 'We can see now that the most fateful and basic decision was one taken at the outset and allowed to stand until the end of the nineteenth century; that the lands should be disposed of rather than retained in public ownership. The corollary of this principle was that nothing should be done to protect or develop the land . . . so long as it remained in social ownership. . . . Starting from the premise that farming was the use to which the lands in the interior would be put . . . it was taken for granted that investment and development, as well as farm operation, should be left to the private sector of the economy. . . . Akin to this complex of ideas was the physiocratic view that the yeoman farmer, the owner-operator, was not merely the salt of the earth but the flesh of the body politic.'* Following naturally and directly from this 'most fateful and basic decision' the official attitude towards land was oriented merely towards its disposal, not to its conservation and proper management; an attitude which, as noted above, contributed cumulatively to waste and destruction.

Le Duc's view is that of a modern, conservation-minded critic of nineteenth-century policy. Most people then (and many even now) agreed that the public domain should be disposed of. The questions and arguments were about how, and how quickly; whether it should be given to farmers to achieve the settlement and development of the nation, or sold to raise revenue for the republic; about the quantity to be handed out – large areas for later subdivision or small family holdings, and so on. The amounts of land involved were astonishing. Over two thirds of the area of conterminous USA has, at one time or another, belonged to the Federal government. Most of this (i.e. over half the land area of the nation) was disposed of during the nineteenth century. The impact of this great land-disposal programme

* ibid., pp. 4 and 5.

on the political, social and economic life of the nation cannot be overstressed.

To modern historians the immediate objectives of the policy are not entirely clear. Most commonly it has been maintained that the new nation, heavily in debt, decided on its land-disposal policy in order to raise revenue by the sale of land. Other historians reject this. Rather, they maintain, the object was to promote migration and economic development, especially in the context of the yeoman-farmer mythology then universally accepted. The revenue motive was there, but secondary. This latter view appears the more likely, since the government seemed to go to considerable lengths to avoid raising as much revenue as it could have from the sale of land. For example, such large areas were offered for sale at any one time (normally by auction) that the realized price was bound to be low. Moreover, squatters had often pre-empted the better lands before they were put on sale, and methods of resolving this problem often meant little or no money flowing into the Treasury. Yet further, large quantities were given away, thus effectively undermining the sales policy. Le Duc maintains that almost half the disposals up to 1828 were free donations. Free grants of land were made for public purposes, such as for schools and other public institutions (the land being granted in the first instance to the State authorities). Other gifts were for road- and canal-building enterprises, and from about 1850, enormous grants were made to the railway-builders.

These large grants of public land laid the foundation for the Homestead Act of 1862. Under this Act anyone who would settle upon and improve the western land was offered a quarter section of the Federal Domain, free. Additional unoccupied land could be pre-empted and, when developed, purchased for a mere $1·25 per acre. This system did not entirely replace the previous methods of operation, being grafted on to them rather incongruously. Land sales and other forms of land grant continued, making the situation complex, even chaotic. Ignoring all these complexities, we may note that the area obtainable by settlers under the Homestead laws was raised from 160 to 320 acres by 1909, and to 640 acres in 1916 – a belated acknowledgement that settlement had extended into more arid lands where the original 160 acres was of little economic value.

These various programmes and processes did not work entirely smoothly nor without considerable abuse. The rules were not always followed, and the government and the courts did not rigorously insist that they should be. There was much undesirable and illegal speculation in land, and considerable fraud and trespass infringements, all of which brought the Homestead Act, and the disposal policy generally, into disrepute. But some such programme was doubtless necessary, and today most students of the situation might agree broadly with Marion Clawson's judgement: 'One need not endorse every step taken to assert that the end product was magnificent. . . . Perhaps the process could have been more orderly, with the wisdom that comes of hindsight; but the qualities that made the pioneer willing to push out onto the frontier were impatient of restraint, and it may be doubted if a slower and better controlled land disposal system would have been acceptable to the nation at the time.'*

In the late nineteenth century, with mounting evidence of the undesirable consequences of the policy of pure disposal, contemporary conservationists became more influential. Opinion favouring retention of large areas in Federal ownership slowly grew. Withdrawing the Yellowstone National Park from settlement in 1872 was a notable, if isolated, landmark in this development. For this reason, and because much of the remaining Federal area was difficult western arid or semi-arid country, disposals declined in the present century. In 1912 the area of Domain was 600 million acres; it is now approximately 400 million† (conterminous USA only). The major period of land disposal in fact ended during the inter-war years, though disposal on a small scale still continues, partially offset by the government's acquisition of land for various reasons (e.g. for tax delinquencies) and purposes (e.g. for conservation, roads, reservoirs and parks). Apart from the Federal holdings, State governments still own about 100 million acres of land – the residue of grants made to them from the Federal land – plus later acquisitions, while local governments own a further 18 million acres or so.

* *Man and Land in the United States*, 1964, p. 81.

† The total for 1968 is officially 407 million acres. Of this, 352 million acres are the remnants of the original public domain, and 54 million have been acquired by 'other methods'. See *Statistical Abstracts of the U.S.*, 1969, Table 275.

The situation in respect of the Federal Domain in conterminous USA may now be summarized statistically. According to recent calculations by Clawson, of the total land area of 1,904 million acres, about 1,442 million have been part of the Domain at one time or another. Of this total about 1,031 million acres have been disposed of, leaving something over 400 million in the government's hands. Clawson's calculations of the various methods by which the disposals were made are given in Table 4. The disposals, then, have

Table 4: Methods of Public Land Disposal

	million acres
Homesteads	285
Grants to States	225
Cash sales and miscellaneous methods	300
Military bounties and private claims	95
Railroad grants	91
Timber culture and other related activities	35
	1,031

Source: M. Clawson, *Man and Land in the United States*, 1964, p. 75

attained awesome proportions. The total area of England and Wales is some 37 million acres, i.e. hardly more than the smallest class of disposal shown in the Table. None the less, about 21 per cent of the total area of conterminous USA remains as Federal Domain, with a further 5 per cent or more owned by State and local governments. Thus a large proportion of the nation's land area is still owned by government at various levels and, despite some continued pressure for disposals, the consensus is that most of it should remain in governmental hands.

The current geographical distribution of public land is important. Inevitably, given the lateness in deciding to retain land, much of it is what was left early this century after the settlers had chosen the land they wanted. Thus by far the largest areas are in the West. Figure 11 shows the broad distribution of the holdings under the three major

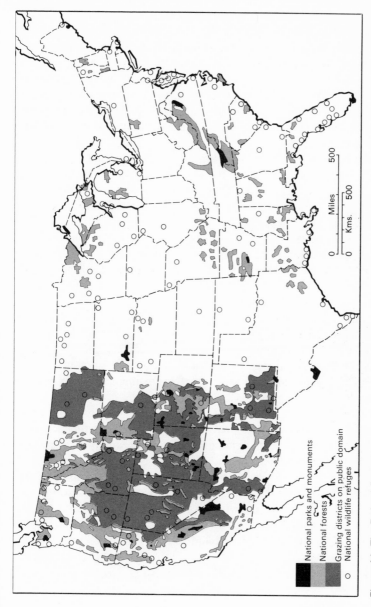

National parks and monuments
National forests
Grazing districts on public domain
National wildlife refuges

Figure 11. The Federal Domain

classifications of National Forests, National Parks and Grazing Districts. This terminology reflects the major, but not the only, uses of these areas. Federal lands are mostly west of longitude 105°, and the map shows that they often account for much of the total area of individual western States. In the Mountain and Pacific divisions nearly half the total area is public land, and the two divisions contain 88 per cent of all Federal land in conterminous USA.* Clearly, this pattern reflects the fact that these were the only large areas of land left unclaimed after the idea of a permanent Federal reservation had taken hold. The increasingly significant recreational functions of these lands, however, make the smaller areas in the eastern half of the country very important. These areas, classified mainly as National Forests or National Parks on the map, have mostly been purchased or in other ways acquired by the Federal government since 1900.

The use of the great public lands is obviously of significance. It is inconceivable that this land should be held in idleness, and controlled attempts are made to exploit the resources of the domain, although controversy exists over its 'optimum' use. Important are timber growing, grazing, watershed management, wildlife and natural vegetation reserves, and recreation. Such uses are not always mutually exclusive. Grazing areas, for example, may also provide public open space, some timber and watershed management services. National Forests are similarly used in multiple ways but, in the main carefully managed, they are providing an increasingly important part of the national timber harvest.

The demand on public lands is growing, most notably for recreation. The National Parks provide a major service in this field, and recreation is their prime function. Visitors are rapidly increasing on all Federal lands. From 1950 to 1969 visits to National Park properties rose from 33 million to 164 million and pressure on the National Forests has grown commensurately, with some unpleasant consequences. Hopeful visitors who have travelled long distances have in recent years been turned away from overcrowded parks or forests. Other uses of the public land include the extraction of minerals under

* In Alaska over 98 per cent of the land area is owned by the Federal government. This unparalleled situation makes it desirable to deal here only with conterminous USA.

lease and the use of land by the military. The former activity uses small areas intensively and makes an important contribution, both to the economies of the Mountain States (where copper, uranium and various other materials are won) and to the nation as a whole. The latter involves large areas and is normally, of course, a highly restrictive form of land use. Recreation, timber and watershed uses, however, appear to be the major trio in national significance, and the value of these uses to the nation will certainly rise further in the coming years.

Controls on the Use of Land

The attitudes of Americans towards official control over the use of land have normally ranged between the downright hostile and the decidedly ambivalent. There is, therefore, no system of land-use planning such as has been in force in the United Kingdom since the Second World War. None the less government at various levels has several means of keeping some control of land use. None is as rigorous or as comprehensive as planning controls in the U K, but the methods can be effective when it is decided that they should be. Again we must distinguish between public and private ownership, the extent and degree of official control being obviously greater over the public lands.

Public ownership of itself does not prevent conflict amongst various possible users. Conflicts can arise between grazing or forestry uses, for example, or between either of these and recreation, or between recreation and wildlife preservation. Moreover, such conflicts cannot be resolved once for all, for the various pressures build up unevenly and earlier policies and decisions periodically need review to meet changing circumstances. Thus bodies concerned with the management of public land often face difficult decisions as to its best use. With public land, too, the market mechanism is not considered an appropriate means of achieving a rational allocation among competing uses. The general public, however, influences policies and decisions in various ways. Numerous organizations, for example, focus the views of individuals and apply pressure at appropriate

59

points to further their own interests. Again, the public evince their desires by such things as their attendance at national parks, and the land managers are influenced by the numbers and types of applications for licences or leases to utilize Federal lands, and so on. But final decisions are taken by, or for, a government department which, reflecting the policies and regulations of President and Congress, directly controls the use of public land.

The administration of the public domain has grown up rather haphazardly, numerous bodies having powers of one kind or another. The Department of the Interior controls the largest area, and within this department responsibility is shared amongst the Bureau of Land Management, the Bureau of Outdoor Recreation, the National Parks Service, the Fish and Wildlife Service and the Bureau of Indian Affairs. The Department of Agriculture controls most of the rest of the area, through the Forest Service, but the Department of Defense is also important. The division of responsibility between these bodies is not always clear-cut, problems of duplication are bound to arise, and relations between them are not always amicable. Our present point, however, is simply that the enormous areas managed in this way have their manner of utilization supervised by an official body.

While the public lands are very significant, most of the land in conterminous USA (above 70 per cent) is privately owned. Since early times government has retained some rights even over private land, and could pass laws with some relationship to, or effects on, its use. The rights of the individual owning the land to determine its disposition were, however, also recognized. Some conflict is inherent in such a situation but throughout the nineteenth century the rights of the individual were strongly insisted on, and it became common belief that the owner should have unrestricted control over the use (or, one assumes, abuse) of his own land. Evidence that such a system can have disastrous results has already been presented. In sum, huge tracts of land have been ruined by ill-advised or careless agricultural and mineral extraction activities, while the wholesale 'mining' of forest lands has had appalling consequences for land, wildlife and water control. Urban development often sprawls for miles in thin and unpleasant ribbons, and, in attractive rural country, gigantic road-side hoardings add further blemishes to those of badly sited commercial undertakings and huge, unscreened used-car graveyards.

Recently toleration of this situation has been weakening, and the rights of the general public have received increasing stress, and were confirmed in the 1969 National Environmental Policy Act. It is clear that, in the past, the high degree of freedom allowed in these matters was not matched by responsible behaviour among the developers of private land. Thus, since the range of conflict between alternative possible uses of one piece of land, or between the uses of adjacent pieces of land, is now so wide, the permissible degree of freedom has declined somewhat. Several powers can be used to control privately owned land. None is really new, and they derive their authenticity from long-established precedents, but their degree of application has increased in recent years. Few private land-owners will be completely unaware of the powers exercisable (but still frequently not exercised) by public authorities over their use of their land.

Very important among these powers is that of eminent domain. This is the power to take, compulsorily, the private land needed for public purposes, e.g. for road-making or for slum clearance. Not everyone is happy about the use of these powers, or about the rights of the individual to appeal or to be properly compensated. But the power is generally accepted as essential to permit the proper and efficient implementation of public schemes involving the use of land.

Another power, 'zoning' and 'subdivision' controls, comes under the general 'police power' of governments – i.e. the right to make rules for the public good, in this case in respect of land and its use. Zoning has become the chief way for local authorities to control the future development of land in their areas. Effectively, a zoning ordinance sets down the use(s) to which a given area of land must *not* be put. Zoning has been widely used to preserve the value of land and quality of environment in 'desirable' residential neighbourhoods by prohibiting industrial and commercial developments. It is also used by some authorities to set out the broad aims of their programme of development for their areas. Subdivision regulations are similarly used, giving an authority power to control the way in which a given area is divided into separate lots for development, setting a *minimum* area on which a given building can be constructed. By using these zoning and subdivision powers some local authorities have achieved very effective control of the type and character of development in their area, if sometimes for dubious motives.

Another method of influencing private land use is found in the government's right to tax, and local governments in the USA raise most of their funds by taxing private land and land users. Applying varying rates, changing the rates, assessing the land for special levies or exempting certain land from taxation, can all influence land use, in both kind and intensity. The counterpart of taxing is the spending of moneys raised. Government spending, unlike land taxation, is not confined to local governments. The Federal authorities are massive spenders, and support various programmes and schemes which directly affect the use of land. Government programmes, for example, are directly reflected in the type and distribution of land uses in agriculture; government funds support urban developments, such as slum clearance and massive road-building programmes.

Such powers offer a considerable degree of public control over the private use of land. Not everyone is yet convinced that their use is either necessary or desirable. Much depends on the scale of the view. At local level numerous authorities see no real reason, apart from maintaining property values in high-income areas, why the powers should be diligently used or comprehensive land-use plans drawn up; but at higher level the problems of uncontrolled development are often more manifest. Thus, some State governments intend to pass laws which will empower them to provide plans for areas where local authorities have failed to do so, while Federal legislation on land-use matters *per se* seems imminent. Such moves will be bitterly opposed, but it becomes increasingly accepted that, in this field as well as in others of traditional respectability, some individual freedom must be sacrificed for the good of the whole.

Current Land-use Patterns

In this final topic of the present chapter we must first remember the lack of a reliable statistical base and of agreed methods of classifying the statistics that *do* exist to make them comparable over time and space. Even in agricultural and forest uses, where information has long been collected, there are no widely accepted methods of classification, and figures vary from time to time and place to place according to the judgement and current practices of the compiling agency. Admittedly problems exist as to where, in a classification of types of agrarian or forest uses, a given piece of land is properly to be placed, but uniformity, at least in official practice, might legitimately be expected. The most disturbing statistical gaps, however, are in land uses outside agriculture and forest. Such uses are often relatively small consumers of surface space; but they include some, quite vital to the nation's life and economy, whose land requirements are becoming matters of increasing concern. Here the statistics are scanty, and those that do exist reflect the methods of collection and interpretation of individuals or interested bodies, and are thus rarely comparable with data collected by others. The figures in Table 5, therefore, need to be viewed with caution.

The Table is drawn from two major 'Resources for the Future' publications. The estimates for the years 1900 to 1940 are from *Land for the Future* by M. Clawson, R. B. Held and C. H. Stoddard; those for 1960 to 2000 from *Resources in America's Future* by H. H. Landsberg, L. L. Fischman and L. L. Fisher. The limitations of each part of the data and the basis of each projection should be appreciated, and the reader seeking a closer acquaintance with this problem should refer to the detailed footnotes and textual comment in the sources. It will be seen that the projections for the year 2000 over-allocate the total land area by about 50 million acres. This helps, perhaps, to emphasize the haziness of projections of these kinds.

The 1960 pattern of land use reflects the end product, to date, of processes of trial and error, rather than the results of careful appraisal of land types and possible uses. Thus, although many adjustments towards an 'optimum' use will have been made, the best lands for any particular purposes may not be currently used for that purpose. The pattern, that is to say, is not an accurate guide to potential. Furthermore, the position is changing, and as important as the present situation is the trend in different uses. Table 5 thus sets the 1960 estimates against those for past years and projections for the future.

(million acres)

	1900 Area	1900 %	1920 Area	1920 %	1940 Area	1940 %	1960 Area	1960 %	1980 Area	1980 %	2000 Area	2000 %
(a) Agriculture and Forest Uses												
Cropland, including temporary pasture	396	20·8	480	25·2	467	24·5	447	23·5	443	23·3	476	25·0
Grazing land*	808	42·4	730	38·3	740	38·9	700	36·8	700	36·8	700	36·8
Farmland, non-producing	53	2·8	58	3·0	44	2·3	45	2·4	45	2·4	45	2·4
Commercial forest land	525	27·6	500	26·3	488	25·6	484	25·4	484	25·4	484	25·4
(b) Special Uses												
Recreation (excluding reservoir areas and city parks)	5	0·3	12	0·6	41	2·2	44	2·3	76	4·0	134	7·0
Cities of 2,500 population or more (including city parks)	6	0·3	10	0·5	13	0·7	21	1·1	32	1·7	45	2·4
Transportation	17	0·9	23	1·2	24	1·3	26	1·4	28	1·5	30	1·6
Wildlife refuge	neg.	—	1	neg.	12	0·6	15	0·8	18	0·9	20	1·1
Reservoirs	neg.	—	2	neg.	7	0·4	12	0·6	15	0·8	20	1·1
Total Specified	1,810	—	1,816	—	1,836	—	1,794	—	1,841	—	1,954	—
Residual†	94	4·9	88	4·6	68	3·6	110	5·8	63	3·3	−50	−2·6
Total	1,904	100·0	1,904	100·0	1,904	100·0	1,904	100·0	1,904	100·0	1,904	100·0

* Includes open permanent pasture in farms and grassland range not in farms (e.g. on Federal land)

† Includes certain small uses (e.g. for mineral production) and miscellaneous and unaccounted for land. The projection for the year 2000 over-allocates the land by 50 million acres

Clearly, however, if the estimates for recent years are suspect, those for earlier years and forecasts for the future will be more so, and the Table is at best an approximate guide. Again, these are national figures, and land-use patterns and trends will differ from place to place. Understandably, regional and local data are even more subject to variability and error than the national. However, estimates for 1964 have been compiled by the Department of Agriculture (*Major Uses of Land and Water in the United States*, Report No. 149, 1968), and these are used to illustrate the patterns in the various agricultural regions in Figure 12. The data are not closely comparable with that used in Table 5, but these various sources provide an acceptable basis for a broad review.

The 1960 estimates indicate that nearly 1,200 million acres, about 63 per cent of the total area of conterminous U S A, are in some form of agricultural use (although not necessarily in farms). Another 25 per cent is classified as commercial forest land. All other uses, therefore, account only for about 12 per cent of the total area. Size of area alone, however, does not necessarily reflect the relative importance of different uses. Nor do other possible measures, such as the value of the land, the numbers of people involved per acre or the value of product per acre. These may overweight smaller uses, such as urban transport development. In fact, many different uses of varying intensity are all essential to a functioning modern economy and society, and it is idle to speculate on which is the more 'significant'. Nevertheless a shallow view of the smallness of acreages involved in uses outside agriculture and forestry can produce indifference to the land requirements of these uses, failure to appreciate the reality and importance of the conflicts between different uses in different areas, and a toleration of a profligate consumption of land by the 'small' users, to the detriment, perhaps, of highly productive

---

Table 5: Use of Land in Conterminous USA: Estimates for Selected Years 1900–60, and Projections for 1980 and 2000

Sources: M. Clawson, Held and Stoddard, *Land for the Future* (for 1900 to 1940)
H. H. Landsberg, Fischman and Fisher, *Resources in America's Future* (for 1960 to 2000)

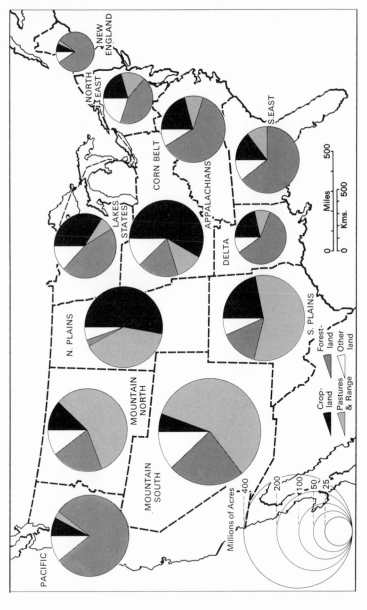

Figure 12. Major Regional Uses of Land, 1964

segments of the 'major' users. A balanced and realistic attitude to each class of use, in proper perspective, is therefore necessary.

Of the land labelled broadly as agricultural, the larger proportion, some 700 million acres, is classed as *grazing land*. Like other classes it embraces land of widely differing types and levels of productivity. Some can be grazed relatively intensively (as, for example, the permanent pastures on farms), some only very extensively (such as the poor Federal grazing lands in the West). Some is pure range, some provides a woodland grazing, and so on. Much of it is of low potential on current standards, a residual, left in these low-yielding grazing uses after land suitable for other purposes had been taken up. Thus it lies chiefly west of the Mississippi ('pasture and range' in Figure 12), much of it part of the Federal Domain. Table 5 shows that land so used has decreased substantially in the present century, chiefly in the early decades. This reflects its nature as 'residual': mixed farming and other uses having expanded at the expense of grazing. Moreover, grazing is sometimes combined with other uses, such as recreation. If it becomes subsidiary to them, the land-use category may be altered. The projection suggests, however, that future change is likely to be negligible.

The *cropland and pasture* acreage now amounts to nearly one quarter of the total area. Cropland includes not only the area harvested but also cropland which was fallow, idle or in cover crops, or on which the crop failed in the year in question. The pasture land included here means land considered to have potential as cropland but used only for pasture in the relevant year. In 1960 such pastoral uses totalled about one seventh of the total 'crop and pasture' area – rather less than formerly. The Table indicates that total crop and pasture acreage rose early this century, possibly to a peak at about 1930 (some 486 million acres). There followed a small decline, reflecting not a falling farm output but a massive rise in productivity. The serious problem of farm surpluses indicates that even the current acreage is too large in current conditions of demand.

The future is of course uncertain, especially as to what extent a continuing productivity rise will meet the demands of a growing domestic population and overseas requirements. For the near future problems of surplus will almost certainly remain the more significant and thus contribute to a continuing, if small, decline in crop acreages. Over the longer term estimates differ markedly. Clawson, Held and Stoddard, for example, assume that 'The most likely outlook appears to be for an ample, even over-generous, supply of cropland for the period up to 2000. Surpluses of cropland are much more probable than deficiencies in this country during the next forty years.' They therefore see total cropland areas continuing their mild decline for the rest of the century. Landsberg, Fischman and Fisher, however, whose projections are given in the Table, foresee a slowly rising pressure on cropland capacity after 1980. It is currently estimated that the total area of cropland available in the USA is approximately 470 million acres. This represents land capabilities as assessed at this time. On the projections given, therefore, there will still be an excess of available cropland in 1980, but a small deficit by the year 2000. The Soil Conservation Service has made a comforting estimate, however, that 200 million or more acres currently in woodland or grass could, with some improvement, be used for cultivation. Given the continuing great advance of farm technology little, if any, of this reserve should be needed this century.

While total crop and pasture land uses have changed relatively little over recent decades, regional patterns have altered considerably. Some areas have experienced marked decreases in cropland uses, especially since the late 1940s, as poorer areas have been abandoned, retired under conservation programmes or converted to other uses. The losses have been greatest in the Northern and Southern Plains regions but most eastern regions have been affected. The gains have come notably in the Corn Belt, but the Mountain and Pacific regions have also increased their cropland areas. Such changes indicate a continuing adjustment to potential, concentrating cropping functions on the most productive lands. Over all, as Figure 12 indicates, the traditional crop-producing regions of the north central States still have the largest areas in this use. Cropland is dominant in the Corn Belt and the Northern Plains regions, and ranks high in the Lake States region. Elsewhere this land use never exceeds 25 per cent of the total area, and, despite recent growth, is relatively minor in the Mountain and Pacific regions. Of course, area of land *per se* is only one variable in crop production. Others include productivity, application of capital and market organization. With all such elements included, some cropland in the 'minor' areas (e.g. the Pacific region) becomes of outstanding value and makes a formidable contribution to total agricultural production.

In the past, attitudes towards *forest land* seem to have been even more regrettable than towards other resources. While contributing notably to life and livelihood, trees were often, and perhaps understandably, regarded as an obstacle to development. Thus, as exploitation became more commercialized during the nineteenth century, forest resources were pillaged without thought for, or awareness of, the consequences. For good reason, then, the first steps in conservation were taken in respect of forest resources. Attitudes and practices have changed, but the old feelings persist in some areas. Nevertheless, commercial forest remains a major land use, covering some 25 per cent of conterminous USA.

Here again special problems of calculation and definition arise – from the millions of small forest holdings, and from the numerous areas in multiple use, for example. But, while details for regions and smaller areas are suspect, the national totals (Table 5) are probably not far out. These figures suggest that the commercial forest area has decreased in the present century, again most notably before 1920. With the slowly falling total, however, has come a dramatic development in management. In 1900 virtually none of the estimated 525 million acres of commercial forest land was under 'continuous management', i.e. involving tree-farming rather than 'cut and quit'. By mid century three quarters of the slightly reduced acreage was under continuous management, a welcome reversal of nineteenth-century practices. The treatment of commercial forest may continue to improve, but despite firm predictions that the demand for forest products (lumber, plywood and pulp) will continue to outstrip supply, the area of commercial forest can hardly rise significantly and, under pressure from other uses, especially recreation and water supply, may even diminish. The projections in Table 5 leave this area in doubt, being satisfied not to 'balance the land budget' precisely for the year 2000, and carrying forward the current acreage. In any case, the USA will almost certainly need massive imports of forest products.

Figure 12 shows that forested land occupies an important position, absolutely or relatively, in all regions except the Plains and the Corn Belt. The country is thus quite neatly divided into eastern and western forest zones, separated by an area where forests are less significant. The West is the major area for commercial softwoods, the East for hardwoods, though not exclusively. More importantly, the West has a larger proportion of virgin forest, much in public ownership; in the East most is second or third growth and the areas are predominantly privately owned. Generally, areas in public ownership have been better managed and contain a larger proportion of the volume of standing timber than they do of forest area. A most welcome feature of the geographical pattern is the wide distribution of forest areas, especially in the more populated parts of the country. Through their aesthetic contribution and the possibilities they provide for multiple use (dovetailing with wildlife preservation, recreation and watershed services, for example), forest uses have great significance, quite apart from their purely productive functions.

With the agricultural and forest uses, all but 12 per cent of the total land area is accounted for. The remaining area, identified as 'Special Use', is none the less of great importance, both in itself and in its effects on people and land use generally. This is also an expanding sector in its land requirements, as Table 5 shows. While estimates disagree widely on the particular uses to which this residual land is put, all agree with the data presented here that the largest distinguishable category is *recreation*, which is becoming an increasingly intensive form of use. Much of the land concerned is in the National Park system and, consequently, is mostly in the western States. With the growth of the National Parks, the areas used primarily for recreation have expanded rapidly and will certainly continue to grow faster than most other uses. Since the highly populated eastern half of the country is less well served than the West, considerable areas may well be brought into this use near the large urban concentrations, probably in numerous smallish parcels rather than in great expanses such as in the West. This is a major land use that also permits various subsidiary activities to continue. Such multiple use will doubtless be increasingly important in the more expensive areas that will be embraced by the Americans' quest for outdoor leisure facilities. The separately classified uses of wildlife refuges and reservoirs (Table 5) could also come under this general umbrella of multiple land use in which some recreational functions are, or could be, served.

Among other types of 'special use' areas is the land devoted to *transport*, the total of which has naturally risen in this century, especially through nation-wide road building. The area of land so covered will never be very large, and the projections to AD 2000 imply a growth rate considerably less than for other special uses. While transport takes relatively small areas of land in total, however, it has a vital impact on other forms of land use, as well as on economic conditions. Here, indeed, we have a form of land utilization with implications far beyond anything implied in the relatively small areas involved.

The same could be said of the last identified use in Table 5, i.e. land in *city uses*. Expansion here has been rapid this century (more than threefold between 1900 and 1960), but the estimates in the Table certainly understate the true 'urbanized area' of the United States. More will be said of this in Chapter 13. Under any definition, however, urban uses will cover only a tiny fraction of the land area of the nation, but these acres have great influence on all areas around them – and, indeed, on land use generally. Rapid expansion of urbanized areas will continue as the population rises and most seek an urban, or suburban, home. Precise estimates are not possible, as so much will depend on the wishes and the judgement of individuals and the evolving attitudes of the community as a whole. That a repetition of the kind of urban expansion experienced in the past two or three decades would bring intolerable burdens and lead to intolerable waste is surely a commonplace. But such considerations are best postponed until a later chapter.

4: Patterns of Employment and Economic Activity

Many aspects of the developments traced above – the changing urban–rural balance of the population and the changing requirements in the use of land, for example – are direct consequences of developments in the patterns of economic activity. Such changes have been considerable in recent decades and, although the pace of change will slow, the situation can hardly ever be stable. The form and direction of the trends, both national and regional, are of considerable importance, and not only to Americans. The patterns of economic life in the USA will almost certainly provide the models towards which other nations will steadily evolve.

Various measures can be used to chart developments in the structure of economic activity, none of them entirely satisfactory. For our present purpose the most useful appear to be data on employment, which have several advantages. There is the fact that quite long runs of national and regional statistics are available. In addition a unit of labour is, superficially at least, a pretty constant concept, whereas indices utilizing monetary values present greater problems of historical comparability because of inflation, and are less reliably documented. Moreover, employment data are relevant to all forms of economic activity and are highly significant social phenomena. Unused or underemployed capital may escape general notice; unused or underemployed labour is more obvious, and receives constant political attention.

Like all indices, of course, employment data must be used with care, and conclusions based upon their use must be suitably qualified. In inter-industry comparisons, for example, relatively high levels of employment in a given activity may not be reflected by an equally high relative level of output. On the other hand an industry may, by very high labour productivity, reach much higher status in economic life than its employment figures suggest. Again, over time, changes in employment can be an inadequate indicator of the growth or decline of a given activity, because of changes in technique and productivity. It is possible also to criticize the concept of labour as being a constant unit over time and place. Labour varies, among other things, in age, sex, skills, education, attitudes and productivity. The mixture of these, although often interdependent, variables may well change in time and be different from place to place at any one time. Over time and space, too, employment figures are affected by differing social customs, practices and rules. Legal regulation of hours of work and of the employment of youths and women are cases in point. All such considerations affect the value of the data and, despite attempts to adjust the statistics, can affect the validity of findings based upon them. Such a catalogue of difficulties could, however, be compiled for all statistical indices. Here statistics of employment are used, with awareness of their shortcomings, as data which are available and highly significant in the patterns and conduct of economic life, and which illustrate the changing character of national and regional economies. Other indices, such as sector contribution to national income, total output, or value added in manufacturing, will be introduced at relevant points in subsequent chapters.

From 1947 to 1969 the total civilian labour force, employed and unemployed, rose from 59 million to 81 million persons. The rate of increase was very similar to that of total population, and the overall labour-force participation rate (i.e. the proportion of the total population aged sixteen years or more employed or seeking work) scarcely changed over the period. None the less, the composition of the labour force altered significantly. Since the Second World War young Americans (especially males) have increasingly tended to stay on at school and college so that, for many, the age of entry into the labour force is being postponed. In the higher age groups increasing affluence has enabled more Americans to retire earlier than was once customary. The large gap thus created has been filled chiefly by women. In fact, two thirds of the addition to the labour force since 1947 has been provided by women, who now represent over 37 per cent of the total. In sum, the labour-force participation rate of males

73

Table 6: Employed Persons, 14 Years Old and Above, by Major Occupational Group, 1947–66, and Projection 1975

| | White collar | | Blue collar | | Service | | Farm | | Total employment |
	million	% of total	million	% of total	million	% of total	million	% of total	million
1947	20·2	34·9	23·6	40·7	6·0	10·4	8·1	14·0	57·8
1957	26·5	40·6	24·9	38·3	7·6	11·7	6·1	9·3	65·0
1966	33·3	45·0	27·2	36·7	9·7	13·1	3·9	5·2	74·1
Projection 1975	42·6	48·1	29·9	33·7	12·7	14·4	3·4	3·8	88·7
% change 1947–66	+65		+15		+62		−52		+28

Sources: Manpower Report of the President, 1967; Occupational Employment Patterns, 1960 and 1975, Bulletin 1599, US Department of Labor, 1968

under the age of 20 and more than 55 years old has fallen pretty sharply, whereas that for females in practically all age groups has risen.

This significant change in the composition of the working population has been accompanied by changes in its character. These are reflected in the differential growth of major occupational groups. Official statistics designate four major occupational categories (Table 6). The Table covers the years from 1947 to 1966, the longest span of years, to date, for which comparable data are available. (After 1966 the age for inclusion in labour-force statistics was raised from 14 to 16 years, and existing data cannot be adjusted further back than 1954.) Over this period clear trends occur. Employment has risen in all except *farm occupations*, comment on which is reserved for Chapter 5. *White-collar* employment has grown very rapidly. Within the group, most expansion has been in the 'professional, technical and kindred worker' category (+145 per cent). A smaller, but still very impressive, growth rate occurred among 'clerical and kindred workers' (+64 per cent) and 'sales workers' (+40 per cent) while the 'managers, officials and proprietors' category expanded at the national average growth rate of 28 per cent. Employment in *service* occupations has also risen sharply, especially in service jobs excluding work in private households (e.g. food and hotel services, police, health and personal services). In *blue-collar* occupations, by contrast, growth rates have been small. But while the new jobs created in this group as a whole have been comparatively few, it is significant that the growth becomes smaller as the level of skills required diminishes. Thus, for labourers, job opportunities rose by a mere 165,000 (5 per cent) over a period when all employment rose by more than 16 millions (28 per cent). Meanwhile jobs in the 'operative and kindred workers' category rose by 13 per cent and in the 'craftsmen and foremen' category by 23 per cent.

The broad trends are therefore fairly clear; new job creation has been most prolific in occupations requiring better education and higher skills, while the occupational pattern as a whole has moved in favour of a structure in which women play a larger part. Almost one third of all female employment in 1966 was in the clerical category, and a further quarter in the service occupations. In both types of job numbers have grown sharply, and women are much more important today than formerly. Less predictable, perhaps, has been the female permeation of the professional and technical occupations, where the rate of job creation for females has roughly equalled that for males. Over all, the number of women in white-collar occupations grew by over 7 million between 1947 and 1966, the number in blue-collar jobs only by 770,000. Women have, therefore, advanced steadily into the chief growing classes of employment where rather higher standards of education and training are often required.

The significance of the changing situation is reflected in various socio-economic indicators. Unemployment may be used for illustration. Generally speaking this has been mild in occupations requiring higher levels of education and training, but much more serious in the semi-skilled and unskilled sectors. In 1966, for example (a very good year for the American economy), the average unemployment rate was 3·9 per cent. In white-collar occupations it varied from 1 per cent for managers and proprietors to 2·8 per cent for clerical workers. In the blue-collar class the rate was 2·8 per cent for craftsmen and foremen, 4·3 per cent for operatives and 7·3 per cent for labourers. A similar pattern is found in every post-war year to 1970, except that in over half of these years the unemployment rate for labourers has been above 10 per cent. The significance of this goes deep. It is well known that the non-white population contains a larger than normal proportion of the poorly educated and meagrely skilled. Thus the relatively sluggish rates of new job creation in the less skilled and unskilled occupations hits the non-white population harder than the white, and the condition of non-whites worsened as the trends outlined above gathered speed from the middle 1950s. Unemployment rates in the non-white labour force have always been considerably higher than those for the white. But, since about 1954, the non-white rate has normally been close to double that for whites, reflecting the pressures exerted on this semi- and unskilled sector of the labour force by modern patterns of economic growth.

Much of the difficulty at this low end of the labour force, both for whites and for non-whites, is associated with educational standards. During the rapid and sustained economic expansion in the 1960s serious personnel shortages existed in certain occupations where trained and flexible ability was required. Meanwhile, high unemployment continued for other classes of labour. The gap between the two conditions of urgent demand for workers and the inability of large numbers to find employment is made unbridgeable by the low educational attainment of many of the unemployed. The median number of school years completed by the employed civilian labour force aged 18 years and over rose from 10·6 in 1948 to 12·3 in 1966, indicating the general rise of standards. But in 1966 the median for clerical grades was 12·5 years and for the professional and technical occupations 16·3 years. These are the occupations which have had a rapidly growing demand for labour. By contrast, the median number of school years completed by blue-collar operatives was only 10·7 and by labourers a mere 9·5 years. Persons in these two classes of occupation, however, accounted for over 30 per cent of all the unemployed in 1966 and for a large proportion of the long-term unemployed. It follows that many are out of work because they lack the skills or educational background being asked for in those jobs which are available. The trends shown in Table 6 for the first two post-war decades will continue. Projections to 1975 indicate that employment will rise to some 15 millions above the 1966 total, but only about 2·7 million of these new jobs will be in blue-collar occupations. Moreover, within that class, no measurable expansion at all is to be expected in the demand for labourers. At least the policy implications in this case seem clear.

The Structure of Employment

Such changes in the composition and character of the labour force reflect changes both in the structure of the US economy and in the operating procedures within each sector of the economy. The latter will be discussed in appropriate chapters below and attention here will be confined to structure and associated issues. Economic evolution must involve adjustments to the relative roles of different sectors. Measuring such change by jobs, we find that some sectors have grown continuously, but at varying rates, while others have attained a peak of employment from which they have since declined. Whatever the individual experiences, the inevitable consequence has

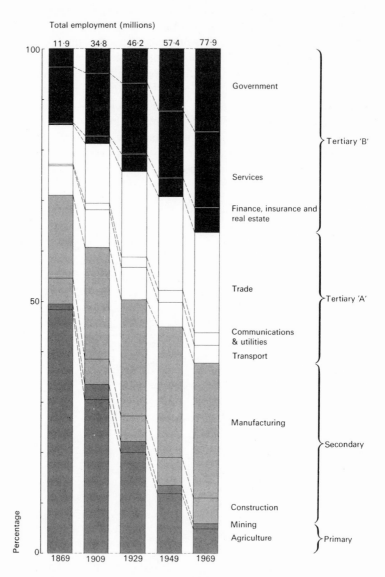

Figure 13. Structure of Employment, 1869–1969

been an alteration in the overall structure of employment. Figure 13 illustrates the changing patterns over the century 1869–1969. While the estimates for any given year may be imprecise, the broad pattern of change is undoubtedly shown accurately.

Perhaps the most remarkable situation is that in the *primary sector*. Unfortunately, agricultural employment is combined with that in forestry and fishing in the sources utilized here, but the latter are relatively small employers. Thus, what is demonstrated in Figure 13 is the change in agriculture from a dominant to a relatively minor position, and since about 1909 the employment decline has been absolute as well as relative.* Mining, for its part, has never been a very large employer of labour. At its peak, early this century, it had about 3 per cent of the total labour force, but since about 1919, it, too, has experienced both relative and absolute decline. These primary (or 'extractive') industries certainly remain of crucial importance to the operation of the American economy, yet they currently provide less than 6 per cent of all jobs. This apparent paradox will be discussed in subsequent chapters.

The *secondary industries* (here including both construction and manufacturing) have experienced secular growth in total employment, so that the highest recorded levels of employment are being attained now. (The secular trend, of course, smooths out sharp cyclical fluctuations.) Of the two categories, manufacturing is by far the more important. Having overtaken agriculture during the First World War, manufacturing has since provided the largest single category of employment among the ten classes of activity identified in Figure 13. The fortunes of this sector are particularly changeable, reflecting the general level of business conditions and confidence and the state of international affairs. It appears, however, that the very rapid rates of growth in manufacturing employment which characterized the first two decades of this century and the years spanning

* The point made above about the limitations of employment data may be recalled here. Total *output* in agriculture has risen tremendously, and is far greater today than, say, fifty years ago, when over twice as many people were engaged. Figure 13 shows only the changing structure of employment, giving a guide to the changing patterns of employment opportunity, which are significant in themselves. No other conclusions should be drawn as to the status of any sector on the basis of these data alone.

the Second World War will not be repeated. At its highest point in relative terms, manufacturing accounted for nearly 28 per cent of all employment (this was in the boom year of 1953). Subsequently the ratio has been about 26 per cent, indicating that higher growth rates have occurred in other classes of activity.

Such classes are found in the *tertiary group* of industries, which embraces the six remaining classes of activity represented in Figure 13. Over all, these have advanced continuously. In 1869 they accounted for 28 per cent of all jobs. By 1929 they provided half of all employment in the USA and, with continued expansion, by the late 1960s about 62 per cent. The tertiary group is very cosmopolitan, however, and it would be advantageous if it could be satisfactorily subdivided, particularly as it is now of such huge proportions. This is not the place to develop a theme on classification, and we must accept the six groups as internally indivisible. It appears both valid and useful, however, to distinguish here between the transport, communications, utilities and trade categories on the one hand (which we shall term the 'tertiary A', or 3A sector) and the finance, insurance, real estate, service and government categories on the other ('tertiary B', or 3B sector). The former have more or less direct connections (though not exclusively so) with the operations of the primary and secondary groups of industries, providing their utility service needs in production and their transport and marketing requirements. Tertiary A employment thus depends largely on the production and movement of, and trade in, goods. Intra-regional levels of primary and secondary production have significance, therefore, for the size of the 3A sector interest in the region concerned. The tertiary B categories naturally have some links with the 'goods-producing' sectors (and this is a main weakness of this attempted division of the tertiary group), but often less directly. The 3B sector has usually a more intimate contact with individual members of the public, with the business, educational and other aspects of their lives and with the general protection and ordering of society. The level of employment here depends largely on the wealth generated in other sectors of the economy, and grows as the level of affluence rises. This concept also applies at the regional level. Of course wealth can be transferred across regional boundaries in support of large tertiary populations (as when one city provides national services). But the indigenous wealth-producing capacity of a region is normally vital to the size and stability of its 3B sector, usually having, for example, played an important role in the early stages of its growth.

Growth in tertiary A employment was more significant before 1929, when the foundations of American economic power were being laid. Up to that time this sector grew on the whole more rapidly than the tertiary B, and by 1929 accounted for 25 per cent of all employment. Each of the branches of 3A activity grew absolutely and relatively until about 1919. In that year employment in transport reached a peak, alone accounting for 8 per cent of all employment. Thereafter the secular trend has been slowly downwards, although with considerable fluctuation. Employment in communications and in the utility services (gas, electricity, water, sanitation) has never been very high, but has grown consistently up to now. Since about 1929 this sector of activity has maintained a fairly constant 2 per cent of all jobs. Wholesale and retail trade has always been the largest branch of tertiary A activity and numbers employed have grown continuously to the present. The pace of growth slackened, however, after about 1939, since when the sector has accounted for 18–19 per cent of all employment.

Tertiary B activities have been expanding throughout the twentieth century, but most remarkably in more recent decades, as seems appropriate in a society of increasing productivity and affluence and high, and constantly rising, expectations. In 1929 they still employed rather fewer than the 3A group, but by 1969 accounted for 37 per cent of all employment. Each class of service in this group is currently at its peak of both absolute and relative stature.* The period since 1949 has brought remarkable advance throughout this sector (Figure 13). Fourteen million jobs were added between 1949 and 1969 – no less than 74 per cent of the entire increase in the employed labour force over those years.

Of the three classes of tertiary B activity, employment in govern-

---

* For government employment, the wartime years of 1943–5, when Federal government employment alone reached 14 million, are considered abnormal and are excluded from this statement.

ment and government enterprises perhaps merits special mention for both its outstanding size and its rate of growth. In the nineteenth century the lack of popular demand in the USA for the kinds of services that governments provide meant that less than 4 per cent of the labour force was normally engaged. The decade including the First World War brought a leap forward (the numbers employed more than doubled between 1909 and 1919) and another such advance was made over the depressed decade 1929–39. The modern demand for governmental services of various kinds, however, was by no means satiated, and employment has continued to expand impressively. Since the mid 1950s, however, growth of employment in the Federal government and its enterprises has slowed down, and most expansion has been concentrated in State and local government. Government employment here covers civilians only, including, for example, people engaged in legislation, administration, police work, and civilians employed in government enterprises and establishments, such as arsenals, defence establishments and navy yards.

There must, of course, be a limit to the possible extension of the relative position of the tertiary sector, even in the USA. The precise position of the limit will, however, essentially depend upon the level of technology and productivity in primary and secondary sectors. No national economy could survive merely by having its working population providing each other with services. The 'goods-producing' sectors thus hold the key. This is true for a national economy, but it is also at least partially true for a regional economy. Special conditions may, of course, allow a very high level of tertiary activity in a local area within which little 'support' exists from the primary and secondary industries. That such a situation could satisfactorily exist for the whole of a major region is scarcely possible without a massive inflow of supporting resources from other regions, and this would appear in turn to require intervention by the Federal government.

Regional Patterns of Development: The General Experience

Having identified the national pattern and trends we proceed to evaluate the varied experience in the major geographical regions.

Since the changes in employment structure outlined here have been accompanied by a steady advance of economic well-being in the country as a whole, we may fairly assume that the structural trends have been materially beneficial; that the presence of the growing sectors reflects a favourable economic climate and rising incomes and that this in turn promotes further development. Certain implications for geographical regions appear to follow. Those regions that have participated more fully in this type of economic progression will be those with higher material standards of life. Those where such trends have been less marked will show less prosperous conditions. This is not to say that the optimum pattern of economic life in each region is identical with that for every other. This would be manifestly absurd. Much regional and national advantage is gained from regional specialization in those activities in which comparative cost advantages are greatest (or disadvantages least). But, while it remains true that regional economies will, in optimum conditions, show bias in favour of certain activities, it remains true also that a region isolated from developments and trends elsewhere will probably be relatively backward. Its economy will increasingly reflect the requirements of a previous stage of economic development, and become steadily less prosperous. Regional experiences must, therefore, be looked at against broad national trends, and significant divergencies may be expected to be accompanied by abnormal conditions in other respects.

The factors governing the process and the pace of regional economic development are complex, and their operation remains only partially understood. Two major theoretical frameworks have been suggested as embodying the essence of the regional development processes. Firstly, there is the 'stages' theory, which suggests that regional development can be explained as resulting from an internal evolutionary process which can be outlined as a series of steps following each other in logical sequence. Thus improvements in transport are followed by increasing specialization and trade, a growth in goods-processing activities, more ancillary development and so forth. Various important elements such as capital and entrepreneurial ability can be introduced at appropriate points in the model. The second major framework has been the 'export base' theory, which suggests that most regions develop because of the advantages they possess for export production, which attracts capital and thus stimulates the cycle of development. The two models are not really incompatible but, either singly or moulded together in some way, they leave great gaps in our understanding both of the processes and the mechanisms. Leaving possible models aside, however, we can identify the essential ingredients of regional economic growth.

Certainly resource endowment has played a part, and continues to do so, although the nature of the resource base that most effectively encourages economic growth has changed over time. Conditions of access to regional, national and international markets, and the changing structure of market demand itself, have also been important. So have the availability and relative cost of the factors of production, and the speed of adoption of technological innovations. The establishment of a large and sound employment base, with its associated infrastructural development, itself has a multiplier effect; the accumulation of advantages thus provided encourages the growth of more enterprises, of steadily broadening range. As economies develop and mature, the prospect for further regional growth depends on the industrial mixture: whether employment is concentrated in growing or declining industries, or the kind of balance between these types. The competitive pressure from other regions also continues to have effect, an effect which can in certain conditions have great influence on a mature economy. Technological advance becomes more crucial in maintaining standards. In addition there are intangible elements, such as confidence, prejudice and ignorance, and immeasurable factors like human unpredictability. All these, and more, have contributed to the regional economic development process, affecting both the type and the pace of growth in different areas and leading to major regional contrasts. Government activity at all levels (Federal, State and local), and in various ways, has also been important, and has expanded considerably in recent decades, introducing increasing complexity into the problem of establishing the true causes of regional economic growth. Be that as it may, the wide differences in the economic structures of regions as they have evolved so far are reflected in equally wide inequalities of income, which become a matter for investigation in outline here.

The range of differing economic development experiences that may be perceived clearly depends in part upon the number of regions which are identified. A detailed treatment would recognize, on the one hand, areas of difficulty (such as southern Appalachia, the northern Lakes Region and the Ozarks) and, on the other, areas of great or rapidly growing prosperity (such as southern California or Connecticut). Between such extremes would lie a broad and important range of experience. In this outline, however, sketched on the basis of the nine geographical divisions, the variety is not quite so startling. The greatest variations are at least partially lost by local contrasts within the divisions themselves. Thus, all of the divisions have recorded an overall expansion of employment since 1940, but within their boundaries experience may be as disparate as that of West Virginia (where employment has declined during these years of unprecedented economic expansion in the nation) and Florida (which has one of the fastest growth rates in the country). Both belong to the South Atlantic division. Some mention of similar local experiences will come in later chapters. Here, with the nine divisions as our study areas, the differentiation is found in the varying pace of growth and in the changing structures of employment. This regional investigation will be chiefly confined to the period 1940–67. An earlier base year could be used, but only by considerably lengthening the treatment. In essence, it is correct to assume that the period from 1940 has everywhere brought a continuation of trends established before that date, but in general at a quickening pace. The year 1967 was the latest for which comparable regional data were available. Figure 14 shows the size and structure of employment in each division in 1940 and 1967, while Figure 15 illustrates the differences between the divisions in per capita income for the same years and 1900. These provide the basis for the following discussion.

Regional Patterns in 1940

By 1940 the processes that were greatly diminishing the relative role of extractive industry were well advanced, and the primary sector accounted for only about one fifth of US employment. All regions

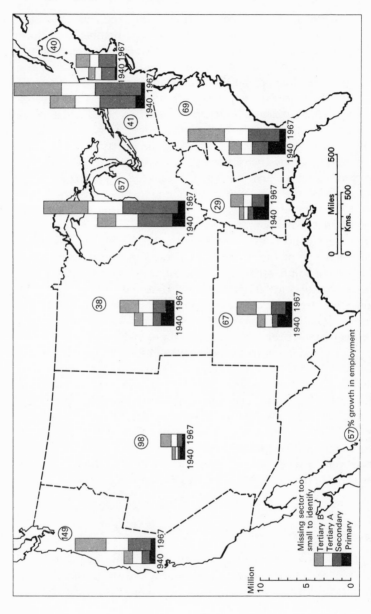

Figure 14. Employment by Division and Major Sector, 1940 and 1967

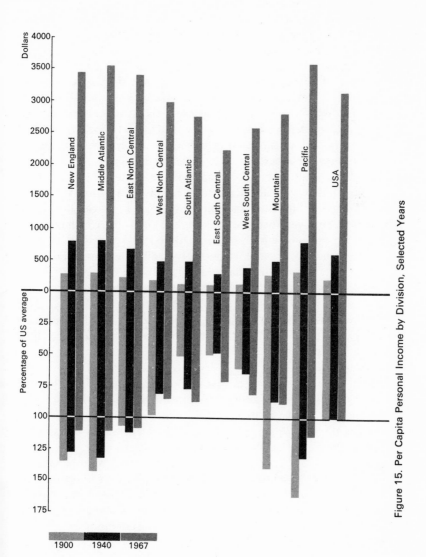

Figure 15. Per Capita Personal Income by Division, Selected Years

had participated in this trend, but to varying degrees, and there remained sharp contrasts, as Figure 14 shows. Five divisions retained over 30 per cent of their total employment in the primary sector, while the remaining four had 16 per cent or less. Throughout the South the extractive industries continued in the forefront of economic life, and only in the South Atlantic division was there a manufacturing sector of notable size. In the East and West South Central divisions at this time, 51 per cent and 41 per cent respectively of all employment was in the extractive activities. Since the incomes of the majority of those engaged were relatively low (especially in agriculture, the largest employer), such high degrees of dependence had direct implications for the economic status of the South, as Figure 15 demonstrates. Each southern division had in 1940 a per capita income far below the national average. In the South Atlantic division, however, there had been a quite vigorous growth of manufacturing since the turn of the century, and the steady improvement of the structure of employment in that division was marked also by a steady advance in relative income. In the two South Central divisions, by contrast, there had been little improvement in economic structure prior to 1940, and the difficult economic conditions and the rundown of employment in the primary sector had brought very grave problems. In per capita income these areas had advanced little in the first forty years of the century.

Similar difficulties, though less urgent because of the smaller populations and the comparative lack of social problems of the kind inherent in the South, faced the two other divisions with high levels of dependence on the primary activities in 1940. In the West North Central division 36 per cent of all employment was in the primary sector. Per capita income was, chiefly as a consequence, only 81 per cent of the US average; and this compares unfavourably with the situation in 1900, when West North Central incomes approximated to the US norm. The deteriorating trend reflects the changing place of agriculture in the economy. A similar trend is also evident in the Mountain division. In 1900, due to the special conditions of the time in the demand and supply of primary goods (especially minerals) the relatively small working population in this division enjoyed a per capita personal income 40 per cent above the national level. By 1940 the relative level had slipped to only 87 per cent of the national average, as shown in Figure 15. In that year the primary sector was still providing 37 per cent of all jobs in the Mountain division.

By contrast, in each of the three divisions which, broadly, comprise the Manufacturing Belt (i.e. New England, Middle Atlantic, East North Central)* a very high proportion of total employment was in the secondary occupations. Indeed, in 1940 these three divisions accounted for two thirds of all employment in manufacturing in the nation, and this was supported by some 53 per cent of national employment in the tertiary sectors. As a consequence, the primary sector – although sometimes sizeable, as in the East North Central division – was of much less relative importance. Moreover, the conditions of supply and demand for primary produce were relatively favourable here, and more conducive to high productivity, so that the primary sector, too, was generally in better shape than in the regions already discussed. The structure of economy in the Manufacturing Belt at this time, therefore, was quite outstanding, favouring high incomes and relative prosperity. In each of the three divisions per capita personal income in 1940 was above the national average, becoming highest in the two North-Eastern divisions, where the secondary and tertiary sectors were most strongly developed. The trend is important, however. The economic advance of the East North Central division in the period up to 1940 raised its relative income position while helping to diminish the relatively extreme status of the older-established North-Eastern economy. An equalizing trend among these divisions is evident from the data in Figure 15. It is also apparent in the changing positions of other divisions, and more comment on these phenomena will be made below.

Relatively prosperous conditions also prevailed generally in the Pacific division in 1940. Both the primary and the secondary sectors were relatively less important in the provision of jobs here than in the country as a whole, the tertiary occupations being already represented to an unusually high degree. Together the two tertiary categories accounted for 58 per cent of all employment in this division in 1940, compared with 47 per cent nationally. A very large trade sector and high levels of employment in service activities (including enter-

* The concept of the Manufacturing Belt is discussed in Chapter 11.

tainment) and government placed the division in this advanced position. In the primary activities the high technical standards and concentration on high value products (especially in agriculture) were also advantageous to the region's income standards. None the less, the changing balance of economic advantage, away from the primary and towards the secondary industries, together with improvements in transport connections with other regions, had caused a decline in the formerly extreme position of this division in the per capita income league (Figure 15). Note also that the numbers of the employed population in the Pacific division in 1940 were not very large. With under 8 per cent of the nation's labour force, the division ranked only sixth in size among the nine divisions.

Regional Developments Since 1940

The changes in the size and structure of employment in the nine divisions between 1940 and 1967 are indicated in Figure 14. Some general points may usefully be made before the individual regions are examined. Firstly, in the country as a whole employment rose by 59 per cent. In the East North Central division there was a roughly identical growth rate but four other divisions were above and four below the average rate. To some extent the process represents an evening-out of employment opportunities over the country, and this accords with the tendency for regional discrepancies in per capita income to become less. Regions of the North-East, already with high levels of employment in 1940, although still growing substantially in absolute terms, have tended to lose ground relatively. The major beneficiary has been the Western region, where the growth of total employment has been very vigorous, but the South Atlantic and West South Central divisions of the Southern region have also done comparatively well. The levelling process has not, however, affected all parts of the nation. The East South Central and West North Central divisions, with low to moderate employment in 1940, have experienced very little growth since then and have thus declined still further in relative stature.

A second general point relates to structure. The outstanding fact is that nationally, by 1967, under 6 per cent of the total employed population were engaged in primary activities, and the highest regional proportions ranged only from 10 to 13 per cent. Against this background, manufacturing and tertiary A employment both rose slightly in relative stature, while the tertiary B sector experienced a major expansion. Such trends, bringing increasing numbers into higher income employment, offer clear benefits. At the regional level, however, the change in structure must be viewed alongside the actual experience of employment growth in different sectors: beneficial effects do not necessarily follow automatically from a structural change. The *proportion* engaged in manufacturing, for example, can be impressively raised simply by a sharp decrease in agricultural employment. No significant gain of employment in manufacturing is essential for such a statistical adjustment.

A third general comment recalls the increase of government employment and of government involvement in economic affairs. This has roots in the 1930s, but grew greatly during and after the Second World War. Government programmes tend to vary, whether deliberately or not, in their geographical impact. This is significant in regional growth, enabling established roads to economic development to be by-passed and time phases of development to be foreshortened. With such generalizations in mind, the highlights of the developments charted in Figures 14 and 15 may now be reviewed. Detailed treatment of individual sectors follows in subsequent chapters.

The eye-catching performance for the twenty-seven years is that of the Western region, where both divisions have growth rates far above the national average and have thus advanced in stature. Despite its great area and rapid *rates* of growth, however, the *Mountain division* remains the smallest in the country for employed population. Detailed statistics show some very striking growth performances, but the high rates of expansion really reflect the very low levels of employment in the base year. Thus, this division has the highest growth rate in manufacturing in the nation over the period; but absolutely the increase was the smallest of all the divisions, and even by 1967 employment was barely measurable on the scale adopted for Figure 14. More notable in this division is the extraordinarily high proportion of the employed population in the tertiary activities (73 per cent in 1967). This is chiefly in the tertiary B category, within which government employment here accounts for half of all jobs. Civilian employment in government establishments, especially defence establishments, is very high. Over all, however, the structure of employment in this division is not too favourable. The primary sector is relatively large, the secondary sector small, a situation that is reflected in the worsening per capita income status of the division in recent decades. There are local exceptions, of course, as in Phoenix, Arizona, where rapid growth in manufacturing has helped lift per capita incomes to about the national level, but the growth rate record for the division as a whole is deceptive.

The *Pacific division* scores, as usual, several distinguished 'firsts'. The highest overall rate of employment growth is here coupled with the lowest rate of decline in the primary sector and the highest rates of expansion in both A and B tertiary categories. In manufacturing the division has the second highest growth rate but its expansion dwarfs in absolute size the increase in the Mountain division. In every major sector of economic life, therefore, the Pacific division has advanced significantly in national status. Tertiary occupations now account for two thirds of all jobs (as usual, government employment has made the most substantial advance), but here the tertiary growth is well supported by primary and secondary sectors of vast capacity and outstanding productivity.

Such growth-rate performances, however, must be kept in focus. In fact since 1940 the East North Central division has experienced an absolute growth in employment greater than that in the Pacific, but because of the much larger base level of employment, the growth *rate* has been only average. Together the three divisions of the *Manufacturing Belt* (each with average or below average growth *rates*) added over 11 million new jobs, 40 per cent of all new jobs created in the USA over the twenty-seven-year period. Yet their proportion of total US employment fell. This fact helps to re-emphasize an important point touched upon earlier. Journalistic interpretation of comparative regional growth rates have sometimes given an impression (fostered by advertisers with sectional interests) of a great migration of work and workers from the older regions of the North-East to the newer and, supposedly, more favoured areas. This is far from the truth, which is that these decades have brought a great expansion of employment opportunities in both 'new' and 'old' regions. There has been no massive job migration in the sense which implies an uprooting, a moving and the extraction of jobs from the originating area. The term 'migration' can here be used acceptably only in the sense of a change in the geographical distribution of the totality of jobs.

During the war strategic considerations, coupled with a serious shortage of manpower and deficiencies in energy supply in the old Manufacturing Belt, encouraged a wider geographical spread of manufacturing activities, and consequently of other forms of employment. In some cases the effects did not long outlast the war, but in others the vigorous twist then given to the economic development spiral has had permanent results. Since the war the great and continued expansion in demand, the processes of cumulative advantage, the development of economic activities requiring new types of location, the changing distribution of population and the continuing high levels of government expenditure have confirmed these changes from established pre-war patterns. Thus the proportion of all manufacturing jobs in the Manufacturing Belt fell from 66 per cent in 1940 to 55 per cent in 1967, and there were corresponding relative movements in the tertiary sectors. These older areas, however, have not been in decline in absolute terms. Rather they have, over all, moved from strength to further strength, adjusting their economies in ways now familiar to us.

Within the Manufacturing Belt itself, however, the important changes already under way before 1940 have continued. Increasingly, the 'balance of power' between the eastern (the Middle Atlantic and New England divisions) and the western (East North Central) sections of the belt has shifted in favour of the latter. This is exemplified in the differences in overall employment growth rates (Figure 14) and these differences are repeated in each of the four sectors of activity defined here. Primary employment has declined more slowly, and each of the other three sectors has expanded more rapidly, in the East North Central division. By 1967 this area had displaced the neighbouring Middle Atlantic as the leading national employer of labour in the secondary and 3A sectors. In 3B employment the Middle Atlantic, with its enormous financial, business and other service interests, still held pride of place, but the East North Central division follows close behind and is, characteristically, expanding the faster. The East North Central division is a leader, too, in the primary activities, with sizeable, and highly productive, interests in agriculture and mining. This, then, is currently the outstanding centre of economic activity in the nation, the power-house of the national economy.

Not unnaturally the economic ebullience of the East North Central division produces 'fall-out' effects on neighbouring areas, and not least significant are those along the eastern margins of the *West North Central* division. But, over all, the performance of this latter division is among the poorest in the nation. Employment in primary occupations has declined at slower than average rates, and in 1967 nearly 13 per cent of all jobs remained in this sector – the highest proportion in any division. Employment in other sectors has expanded, but neither absolutely nor relatively has this development been notable. At present, therefore, this area represents something of a backwater. The slow advance of the economy has not sufficed to retain the region's population growth, and over large areas (as indicated earlier) absolute declines in population have been recorded. In some respects the situation resembles that of parts of the South.

The economic structure of the *South* as a whole has undoubtedly improved since 1940, but this largely arises from the very sharp decrease in the numbers employed in the primary industries. This sector employed 5·3 million in the South in 1940, 39 per cent of all jobs; in 1967 it gave employment to rather under 2 million, only 9 per cent of all employment. This very large absolute loss of jobs has not (in the region as a whole) been sufficiently offset by gains in secondary employment, which remains under-represented. Much has therefore depended on a massive expansion of tertiary activities, which provided $7\frac{3}{4}$ million new jobs over the period. In the main, however, this tertiary growth has not been achieved by 'natural' outgrowth from high capacity and production in primary or secondary activities. It has largely been 'imposed' upon a relatively immature economy, and is sustained by the transfer of resources from other regions. The 'natural' progression from primary or secondary development to an increasingly sophisticated superstructure of tertiary employment is not, of course, the invariable route of regional economic development. In some instances (Florida, for example) a substantial service sector may be created early in the development process and subsequently serve to stimulate growth of secondary and primary activities. But this is an 'induced' rather than a 'natural' process, because the development of the service sector in the first place depended upon the attraction of resources from elsewhere, resources which must in the end be rooted in the goods-producing sectors of other regions. The point is that over much of the South very high proportions of employment (higher, often, than in the nation as a whole) are in the tertiary sector, especially in tertiary B occupations. These, we have seen, depend for their existence upon high levels of affluence – which are manifestly not common in the South. Employment in government activities has grown very rapidly here, and one third of the entire national expansion of government payrolls in the 1940–67 period was concentrated in the South. This has naturally benefited other forms of employment. The wage and salary payments to the large tertiary sector cannot be fully met from the region's own resources, however, and to this extent at least the economic situation is not yet satisfactory.

These generalizations do not of course apply equally to all parts of the South. At the divisional level they apply most fully to the East South Central area. Here primary employment fell by over a million jobs between 1940 and 1967. Secondary employment rose, but sufficiently to replace only about 70 per cent of the lost primary jobs. The large deficiency was extremely significant in this area, with its high natural increase in population. In the event the deficiency was made good and a small further growth of employment achieved (Figure 14) by increased tertiary activity. This was especially sharp in the 3B sector, which provided only 16 per cent of all jobs in 1940 but 32 per cent in 1967. Government and government enterprises figured very strongly in this growth, with their employment rising by over 170 per cent. The observations made in the previous paragraph thus apply closely to this division as a whole.

The neighbouring southern divisions have, over all, fared rather better. Before the war the South Atlantic division showed the largest totals of employment outside the Manufacturing Belt, and since 1940 continuing vigorous growth has raised further its proportion of all US employment. A similar rate of growth, but from a much smaller base (Figure 14), has occurred in the West South Central area. In both, the wartime and post-war development processes commented upon above help to explain the trends, but the oil and gas resources of the West South Central division merit special identification. In both divisions, the advances in secondary employment have more than offset the large declines in primary job opportunities, and the considerable tertiary expansion has significantly raised employment totals. Over all, therefore, these divisions have fared much better than the East South Central, but numerous problems, and problem areas, remain. In Appalachia, in the South Atlantic coastal plains and in the Ozarks, for example, are areas in which experience more closely resembles that of the East South Central division than the better overall situation which characterizes their respective divisions.

Some General Conclusions

In the discussion of total employment changes among regions mention was made of a certain 'levelling out' which appears to be affecting most parts. Employment is growing more rapidly in regions where lower relative levels of activity prevailed at the earlier date. This adjustment affects the several categories of employment and is causing the regional structures of activity to become more and more alike, especially if the analysis, as here, is confined to broad classes of economic activity and to large regions. This is illustrated in Figure 16, which demonstrates the changing regional positions by superimposing the 1940 and 1967 divisional *shares* of national employment in the four sectors of activity. In the secondary sector the proportion of all employment contributed by each division of the great Manufacturing Belt has declined, whereas in all divisions outside the Belt it has increased. A similar situation is found in both tertiary categories, with the single exception of the West North

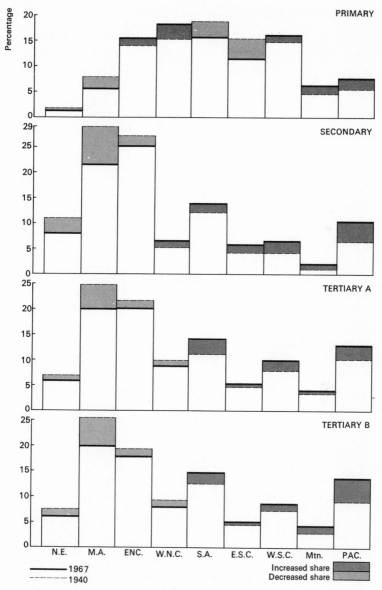

Figure 16. Regional Share of Employment by Sector, 1940 and 1967

Central division which has lost ground. A more complex trend appears in the primary sector. Within each region this sector has declined relatively, and to that extent regional trends have been similar, but within this condition, the varying rates of decline are enhancing the differences between regions rather than diminishing them.

In sum, the secondary and tertiary occupations have become more dispersed throughout the nation, as part of a process of levelling out of employment generally, whereas primary occupations are concentrating in greater degree in regions west of the Mississippi, and in the Middle West. Despite these trends regional inequalities in size and variations in structure remain very considerable, and there is nothing to suggest that the equalization and conformation processes will, or can, be carried through to completion.

Partly consequent on these general trends, the disparity between regions in per capita incomes has also diminished (Figure 15), but remains notable. The existence and apparent persistence of strikingly different levels of per capita income between regions in a single national economy has naturally stimulated a search for likely explanations of the phenomena and of the processes at work. A very brief résumé of suggested theories may be useful at this point. Traditional 'free-market' theory has maintained that, if the factors of production were mobile, in conditions of free competition, great regional inequalities could not continue long. Factors would move from centres of low reward to those of higher reward. This would decrease the returns to factors in the latter centres, and perhaps also raise the returns in the former, because of an increasing scarcity of factors there. Thus a trend towards equalization of income is established. This theory has proved inadequate, basically because the factors of production, for many reasons, are not sufficiently mobile. No marked convergence of regional per capita income thus appears to occur in conditions approximating to free competition, unless possibly in the very long term. Indeed, in medium- and short-term experience the converse has sometimes occurred, and some regions have found their situation deteriorating. Given freely competitive conditions, that is to say, the forces at work appear to reinforce existing inequalities rather than smooth them out.

This latter idea was developed by Gunnar Myrdal in the 1950s, when he introduced the concept of 'cumulative causation'.* According to this theory, the regional development processes, once under way, attain a momentum in which investment and other changes, brought about to support existing activities, in fact create conditions for yet further growth. Such expanding and prosperous conditions attract much of the nation's developmental effort to the region concerned, and so the differentials between the advancing regions and others are reinforced, and not diminished, by the operation of free market forces. The flow of capital, labour and goods towards the expanding and more prosperous region has what Myrdal terms 'backwash effects' on other regions. These tend to lose capital and skilled labour, which perhaps they can ill afford, and their own existing industries may be hard hit by effective competition from the technologically superior enterprises in the 'growth' region. Such processes can be cumulatively injurious to the poorer region, lowering its relative income standards. On the other hand, the theory identifies certain 'spread effects' which may benefit other regions. The advance of the growth region may, for example, require supplies from other regions, which in turn may stimulate capital investment and initiate processes of growth elsewhere, which may (unless completely offset by the deleterious backwash effects) lead on to the cumulative developmental sequence. This brief summary of the Myrdal theory may be assessed against the actual developments in the US regional economy outlined here. The basic model applies, however, to a free-market economy and in addition to the forces identified as affecting regional incomes, the possible consequences of governmental intervention must be assessed. Government activity may serve to counteract the 'backwash' and support the 'spread' effects. How far does this theoretical structure fit regional development experience in the United States?

Comment has already been made on the situation in 1940, when the relative differences between the wealthiest and the poorest regions were quite startling. Figure 15 illustrates the developments from 1900

* G. M. Myrdal, *Economic Theory and Underdeveloped Regions*, 1957. An almost identical model of the processes was developed independently at about the same time by A. O. Hirschman in *The Strategy of Economic Development*, 1958, Chapter 10.

to 1940. The relative standing of the wealthiest regions was somewhat reduced, but remained very superior; some poorer areas became relatively even worse off; others made notable advances. There is no room for detailed discussion, but, in general terms, a slow and uncertain equalization process was under way, and this process appears at least superficially to fit the Myrdal theory fairly well.

Between 1940 and 1967, however, the degree of inequality between regions became markedly less. The wealthiest divisions became relatively less outstanding, while the poorer all improved their relative position. Trends in economic development in recent decades have apparently diminished the extremes of experience. The improved relative position of the backward regions, however, to an extent which varies from area to area, owes much to the transfer of resources from other regions. In part this is the normal operation of the spread effect, as private investors seek to capitalize on opportunities they perceive developing in the backward areas. More important, however, has been the transfer of resources by Federal government programmes, introducing a new element into the regional economic development process. (We may note, in passing, that to some extent the 'voluntary' shift of resources has been aided by State and local governments, many having become active in the industrial promotion business.) Direct Federal participation in regional economic activities dates effectively from the establishment of the Tennessee Valley Authority in 1933. The legal basis of that intervention was disputed, however, and acceptance by the Federal legislature of some responsibility for regional economic growth is probably better dated from 1961, when the Area Redevelopment Act was passed. But other programmes involving huge Federal expenditures necessarily had an uneven geographical impact, and the regional effect of Federal operations of all kinds has been considerable since 1940. Federal programmes for agriculture; the strategic location of industry in wartime; expenditure on defence installations and other government facilities; investment in aerospace programmes; Federally supported road construction; assistance to distressed areas and subventions to State governments under various other programmes, as in education, health and welfare and urban affairs: all have succeeded, whether by intention or by accident, in achieving a considerable redistribution of the nation's resources, which, while not confined to the backward regions, has selectively assisted them towards economic advance. This advance is reflected in per capita incomes, which have in every case risen more rapidly in 'backward' than in 'wealthy' regions since 1940, a process which has automatically reduced the relative disparity between regions.

We must, however, again be wary of oversimplified conclusions from growth *rate* data. Absolutely, each of the four divisions with per capita incomes above the national average gained, between 1940 and 1967, increases higher than the national average per capita increase of $2,540 (Figure 15). By contrast the five divisions that fall below the national average in per capita income all experienced increases below that level. In other words, the *absolute* discrepancy between the wealthy and the not-so-wealthy continued to widen over the period, despite the faster rates of growth in the latter. Of course, if the superior growth rates in the poorer areas are maintained, the absolute gaps will begin to narrow and, eventually, be eliminated. The big question is whether such growth rates can be maintained, and in which regions they are the more likely to be maintained. Despite the direct, and subsequent multiplier, effects of large Federal expenditures, this of itself, at recent levels, will not ensure income equalization. In the long run the relative economic stature of regions must depend chiefly upon their own productive resources, and the way they use them, and not least on the competitiveness of their own primary or secondary sectors. For most regions it is the indigenous wealth-producing capacity that is vital to the eventual size and importance of their economy.

Finally, economic growth is not essential all the time, everywhere, nor is the achievement of high growth rates for every region a legitimate policy objective. This cannot be so in an efficient and advancing economy. In a dynamic situation some regions inevitably grow faster than others in any given period, and a given region grows faster at one period than at another. It is also inevitable that changing circumstances will set in train processes which, over a long term, run against the economic development interests of certain areas which have figured more prominently in the past. This will give rise to the phenomenon of the distressed area in a generally growing regional economy,

101

a situation that became of great political concern in the 1960s. Not all are agreed on the proper policy to be adopted, and no doubt a proper policy would be one which varied according to the situation. A moderate 'pump priming' operation, for example, might restart the processes of cumulative causation. On the other hand it might be that no realistic input of financial and other supports would achieve that objective. Areas with few saleable resources will remain areas of relative underprivilege and in some circumstances local, regional and national interests may be best served by permitting a certain run-down of economic activity. The problems of such areas of difficulty, and the expanding role of government in connection with them, will be touched upon again after the detailed treatment of the several major sectors of the economy which follows.

5: Characteristics of the
Modern Farm Economy

In treating population and land use brief reference was made to great changes in US agriculture over recent decades. These developments have revolutionized the farm and farm economy, altered fundamentally the socio-political context of US agriculture and had far-reaching consequences outside the agricultural sector. Many elements involved can be easily quantified, but not all of them. Much damage has been done, for example, to the traditional image of the yeoman farmer and to the mystique of rural values and rural ways of life. Such images have had important political and practical consequences as, for example, in nineteenth-century land disposal policies, and have led to a suspicion of (if not hostility to) urbanism, somewhat anachronistic in a highly urbanized and very rapidly urbanizing nation. These attitudes are changing and more realistic views of both urban and rural societies are gaining currency. But old beliefs die hard, and traces of the 'Jeffersonian dream' persist, affecting the form and the pace of development in different areas of the country.

While the decline of the 'agrarian ideal' can be assigned no numerical value, the facts of the changing situation are impressively demonstrated in the statistics. The farm population stood at 31 million in 1940, very similar to the level for several preceding decades. By 1970 it had declined to about 10 million. Similar trends are naturally evident in farm employment. This reached a peak of 13·6 million in 1910, declined modestly to 11 million in 1940 and 10 million in 1950, but has plummeted to about 4 million at the present time. Thus, from providing 30 per cent of all US employment before the First World War, the industry now provides under 5 per cent. Such figures suggest the size of the change in American agriculture, but the end is still not in sight. Most farm economists consider the industry still heavily overmanned. The inevitable further decline in number of farm workers, plus continuing employment growth elsewhere in the economy, will lower the proportion of farm employment to 3 per cent or less in the next decade or so. Yet this greatly reduced labour force is able to provide the food needs, and many relevant raw material requirements, of a population more than double that of sixty years ago, and indeed is able to create massive surpluses despite strict production controls.

This issue, which concerns productivity, is discussed below. At present we can emphasize the paradox that this industry, so fundamental to life and economy and of such large productive capacity, should command an almost insignificant place, not only in the number of jobs it provides, but also in its share of national income. Even in 1910, the total net income of farm proprietors and workers was only 14 per cent of total national disposable personal income (i.e. personal income less tax), but by 1967 it was a mere 2·7 per cent. Even allowing for the great fall in numbers concerned, the income of the farm sector as a whole appears extraordinarily low. Moreover, the distribution of this income among the farm population is grossly uneven, so there is a high incidence of poverty among farm families. The low incomes in agriculture also affect regional patterns of income. Agriculture, being virtually ubiquitous, takes its influence and its problems to every part of the nation. Its relative position regionally and locally varies greatly, however, and in areas where it occupies a larger than normal place in the economy, income potentials are often low, producing various difficulties.

Patterns of Farm Land Use

The broad situation of agricultural land use in conterminous USA has already been outlined. Not all land used in some way for agricultural purposes, however, is actually in farms. At the 1964 Census of Agriculture, the area of land in farms constituted about 58 per cent of total land area, whereas 70 per cent was considered as having agriculture as its major use. Most land used primarily for agriculture, but not in farms, is Federally owned land in the West, leased for grazing. Here we shall look briefly at the pattern of use of land on the farms themselves, which is shown for 1950 and 1964 in Figure 17.

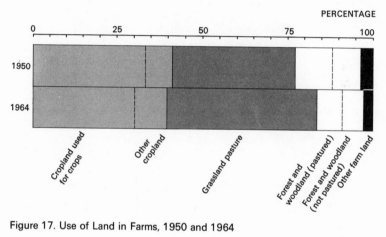

Figure 17. Use of Land in Farms, 1950 and 1964

In 1964 about 40 per cent of the land in farms was classified as 'cropland', but not all of this was actually used in crop production. A fair proportion was under soil improvement cover, used for temporary pasture, or simply left idle. The amount of cropland treated in this way has tended to rise in the post-war years, i.e. the amount of cropland actually used for crops has been falling. About 44 per cent of farm land was in permanent pasture and a further 13 per cent in forest and woodland, of which over half was also used for pasture. The small residual area was used for homesteads, farm buildings, farm roads and so on. Total land in farms fell a little

105

between 1950 and 1964, from 1,159 million acres to 1,106 million. Except for the permanent pasture, the area under each major use has also fallen. In the pasture category, the expansion of area has sharply raised its status in farm land use (Figure 17), reflecting changes in farm organization and technique.

There are, of course, marked regional variations in the incidence of farm land. Compared with the national average of 58 per cent of total area in farms, the proportion ranges from little over 30 per cent in the North-East, where they have many other fish to fry, to 80 per cent in the Corn Belt and 96 per cent in the Northern Plains States of North and South Dakota, Nebraska and Kansas. The use of the land in farms also varies regionally. Cropland accounts for 72 per cent of the total in the Corn Belt, but only 16 per cent in the Mountain States. The intensity of cropland use also varies. Nationally, in 1964, 75 per cent of cropland was actually cropped. In Appalachia (where land is being withdrawn from agriculture, and conservation measures applied) only 50 per cent was cropped, whereas in the Mountain division (with cropland relatively short and heavy investment in water-supply schemes) the proportion rose to 80 per cent. Again, permanent pasture is very important in the Mountain division (over three quarters of farm area), but very minor in the Corn Belt (one tenth of the total). Finally, forest and woodland areas also vary widely around the national 13 per cent of farm land. In the Northern Plains, for example, farm land in this use is under 1 per cent, but in the South-East it reaches almost 50 per cent. Such variations are discussed in the following chapter, where differing regional patterns of agriculture are considered.

Patterns of Agricultural Production

The kinds of product making up the total output of farm commodities respond over time (and as permitted by developing technology) to changes in the pattern of consumer demand. In response, therefore, to developments in the American economy and in the structure of consumer preferences, we find gradual changes in the 'mixture' of agricultural commodities and, following this, changes in the regional patterns of farming. 'Global' changes in demand and supply obviously affect the total pattern of national farm output. Sometimes more significant, however, is the changing *regional* demand–supply relationship, which is affected not only by changes in taste and the structure of demand, but also by changing economic and technological circumstances which may, for example, affect market accessibility and the competitive position of different regions in relevant products. We shall, however, examine changes in the national pattern here, and discuss the regional effects separately in the following chapter.

Changes in the structure of farm product demand have markedly altered the global pattern of US agriculture this century. The effects would probably have been yet greater had not Federal farm policies often delayed adjustment to new conditions, and to some extent ossified established patterns. The changing demand mixture is not always reflected in an actual decline in the output of given commodities. Population has grown and the total demand for most farm products has thus risen also. But within the rising total of farm output, the product mixture has altered in response to changing market conditions.

Production of natural fibres offers a good illustration. The position of cotton and wool in the national pattern of farm production has declined steadily over recent decades. Since the Second World War, for example, the total USA consumption of cotton has changed little, despite the rise of over 60 million in population. Consumption of wool has fallen sharply. Per capita cotton consumption in 1945 amounted to 32 pounds per head, in 1969 to only 19 pounds. In 1945, too, each American consumed 4·6 pounds of wool, in 1969 a mere 1·5 pounds. This reflects the competition of man-made fibres. Until very recently, total cotton production showed no major change and the crop was therefore losing ground only relatively. Actual wool production, however, has declined sharply – an additional element here being strong competition by imports.

Amongst the various food products also, long-term change has been considerable. Trends in American food consumption have

107

been, first, to decrease the intake, by both weight and calories, per capita and, secondly, to shift the balance from crop products to animal products. These developments reflect not only the dietary preferences of Americans, but also their affluence and the productivity of their farming. The processing of grains and roots by animals to prepare them for human consumption means a considerable loss of food value. This luxury underdeveloped nations cannot afford, but Americans can, with margins to spare. Important changes have also occurred *within* the crop and livestock categories, but some of these serve merely to support the broad trend as outlined above as, for example, the increased cultivation of certain crops as animal feed.

Figure 18 illustrates the changing pattern of farm output over a period of forty years. Being based on the farmer's cash receipts from his actual marketings, it accurately reflects his final production preferences. Such a pattern of final output, however, does not necessarily reflect the *internal* patterns of farm operation. For example, much effort may go into producing feed for internal farm use, and a sizeable production of hay, feed grain and fodder crops will appear in the figures not as 'field crops' but as livestock or livestock product sales. Overall, livestock and products sales have come increasingly to dominate the farmer's cash receipts. An outstanding rise has been in the value of cattle and calves sold, increasing their contribution to total cash receipts from about 13 per cent to nearly 27 per cent from 1929 to 1969. This results from a massive expansion in the American appetite for beef. As recently as 1950 under 19 million head of beef cattle were slaughtered, in 1969 almost 36 million. Because of the increased 'productivity' of each animal, the total weight of beef produced has much more than doubled in the period.

Room for this expansion has been made by adjusting almost all the other farm products (Figure 18). The sales value of most other livestock products has risen (the principal exceptions being sheep and wool), but much less than for cattle and calves, and the structure of farm marketings has changed accordingly. The relative position of poultry and egg production, for example, has declined somewhat in the overall pattern, yet production has greatly increased. Egg

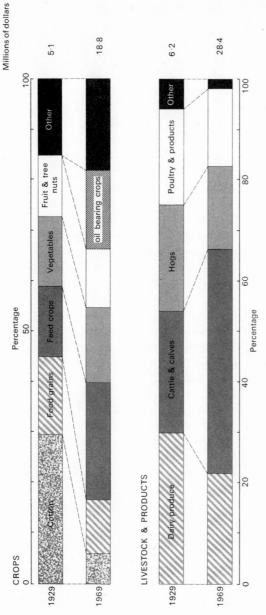

Figure 18. Farmers' Cash Receipts from Marketings, 1929 and 1969

production has risen steadily, while broiler production has proved a major growth point in American agriculture. Even so, the farm sales value of poultry and products has not risen nearly as much as that for cattle and calves.

The fall in the relative position of dairy products is more complex. Milk production has increased, following the rise in population, but not commensurately. Dietary preferences have moved away from animal fats since the war, because of alleged risk to health, and the contribution of dairy sales to total farm cash income declined sharply from 18 per cent in 1940 to 13 per cent in 1950, at which it has since remained. Different dairy products have had different experiences, conforming to changes in consumer preference. Factory butter production has fallen, whereas cheese production has risen; the output of evaporated whole milk has declined, whereas that of non-fat dry milk solids has risen. Over all, however, consumption of milk and milk products per head has fallen and, between 1950 and 1969, when total population rose by 33 per cent, the quantity of milk produced on farms increased hardly at all.

In crops, a notable feature is the decline of cotton, mentioned above, from its 1929 position as the major source of income. In other field crops the major change has been from producing crops as direct human food to producing animal feeds. Food grain production (chiefly wheat, rye and rice) has lost ground, while the output of feed crops (chiefly corn, sorghums, oats, barley and hay) has expanded to contribute nowadays about one tenth of the farmers' market receipts. Among the food grains, too, increasing quantities of wheat (nearly 200 million bushels in 1969) are in fact being used for cattle feed. Within the feed-crop group the production of oats (formerly the major feed for farm-work horses and mules) has markedly declined while that of sorghums has risen sharply. Another notable development is the rise to prominence of oil-bearing crops (soybeans, peanuts and flaxseed are included in this category in the figure. Cotton seed is included in the totals for cotton.) These were not identifiable in the graph for 1929 as they contributed under 1 per cent of total cash receipts. By 1969 they provided above 6 per cent. This development reflects partly the increasing American dietary preference for vegetable oils and fats, but oil seeds also make nutritious animal feeds, and provide another link between an expanding field crop and the ubiquitous and growing livestock interest. The rise of soybean farming has been outstanding. Before the Second World War soybeans were a minor interest. Now they provide the chief source of protein for livestock feeding. In the early 1940s, for example, production was only 170 million bushels. Today it is above 1,000 million bushels, and soybeans are the second crop by value in eleven States, and first in one (Arkansas).

The Productivity Revolution

Developments in the broad patterns of farm population, employment, land use and output are clearly significant, but the outstanding change in agriculture, the key to the changes already outlined and the very essence of the modern agricultural dilemma, has been the phenomenal rise in productivity. Table 7 shows spectacular advance

Table 7: Farm Productivity Indexes; 1940–69
(1957–9 = 100)

	1940	1957–9	1969
Farm output per man-hour	36	100	189
Crop production per acre	76	100	129
Production per animal unit	75	100	119†
Cropland used*	103	100	94

  * Harvested areas plus crop failure and summer fallow
  † 1967

Source: Statistical Abstract, 1970

in output per unit of labour, land and livestock since 1940. The degree of advance understandably varies with the type of farming done, but throughout the whole range of farm operations gains have been most impressive. Nor is the progress of this second agrarian revolution slackening. The data indeed suggests a quickening pace in the sixties. While in research the speed of advance has slowed recently, large gaps still exist between average farm yields and experimental results. Performance under normal commercial production conditions will never, of course, match the best experimental standards, but the existing gaps hold promise of further general advance. Other sectors of the US economy have been unable to match the productivity gains in agriculture. With 1957–9 as 100, output per man-hour on farms rose to 174 by 1968 while, in the non-farm sector, the index rose merely to 133. (N.B. This index differs slightly in its compilation from that used in Table 7.)

The factors contributing to this remarkable record are clear. Research laboratories and experimental stations have developed new strains of plants, new breeds of livestock, new kinds of fertilizer, new pesticides and chemical treatments for plant and animal diseases and new guides to agricultural practice. Throughout the farming industry these advances have been assisted in their practical and economic application by new machinery, equipment and techniques including, for example, the use of electronic devices and aircraft, and the more scientific use of water. None of these advances could, by itself, have anything like the same impact, and it is the complementary and supplementary nature of the developments which has resulted in the outstanding impact on the total performance of the farm sector.

Not all of this has been universally welcomed, of course, and some troubles have followed. This is not new in a period of rapid change and innovation. Anxieties about the prolific use of chemicals and chemical derivatives on farms increased following the publication in 1962 of Rachel Carson's *Silent Spring*, with its disturbing pictures of possible secular consequences. Since early 1969, after considering the findings of research into the effects of concentrations of DDT in animal life, several States have banned its use, while several other chemical products now widely used are under suspicion. In economic and social affairs, too, the productivity revolution has had unwelcome effects, exacerbating various undesirable elements in the nation's 'farm problem', which is touched upon below. Be this as it may, there are numerous telling illustrations of the achievements of US farms, one or two of which are now outlined.

Over the decade 1959–69, feed-grain acreage fell by 26 per cent, yet output rose 12 per cent. The yield per harvested acre, in other words, rose by more than 50 per cent in a ten-year period. Of these grains we may look more closely at corn. From early this century to the Second World War, yields averaged some 26 bushels per acre. Advance since then brought the average in the late fifties to an impressive 49 bushels and, by 1969, to a spectacular 84. The new corn hybrids use plant food more efficiently, grow more swiftly, resist disease more effectively, stand more strongly, accept mechanical methods more readily and yield more abundantly. Not only, then, has yield per acre risen so impressively, but man-hours of work required for a given output have fallen dramatically. Before the Second World War 108 man-hours were required per 100 bushels produced; by the later 1960s only 9.

Among major non-food crops, cotton has made similarly striking improvements. Because of advances in breeding and fertilizing and other developments (including changes in major areas of production) yield rose from 226 pounds per acre just before the Second World War to more than 500 pounds in the 1960s. Further, with mechanization (to which this crop had been thought to present insuperable problems) the average man-hours required per bale fell from 209 immediately before the war to a mere 36 in the later 1960s.

All of these are *average* figures, too. The best performances far exceed them, indicating, no doubt, the shape of things to come. Yields of corn of over 100 bushels per acre are now not uncommon and about 150 bushels is considered possible in normal commercial operations with full use of research information. For cotton, outputs of 1,000 pounds per acre have been recorded in ordinary farm conditions, while nearly 2,000 pounds has been reached at a Texas experimental centre. On the other hand, however, poor conditions and results also remain widespread. Many farmers still obtain yields which would have been considered poor two decades ago. This indicates a disturbing range of performance in the farm sector, which has wider implications.

Advance in water supply and use has played a considerable part in the achievements outlined. Not only has this extended the area capable of sustained cultivation (as in cotton production in western Texas, Arizona and California) but also raised yields in existing farm areas. In 1939, total irrigated areas measured some 18 million acres,

113

by 1964 37 million. Irrigation schemes have not only provided regular and reliable water to areas with insufficient rain, but have supported agricultural improvements in areas of generally adequate, but unreliable, rainfall. Even where rain is generally ample and dependable, irrigation has enabled water to be applied at critical times, well repaying the effort and capital involved. In such areas the practice is still not widespread, but is growing. At present, however, most irrigated farm land is still in the subhumid, semi-arid and arid land west of 90° longitude (Figure 19). Many of the schemes provide multi-purpose services – water supply, flood control, hydro-power and, sometimes, navigational and recreational services.

Enough has been said to characterize the revolution that is taking place in US agriculture. The extent of the change in methods can be summarized by comparing the major farm inputs in pre-war and post-war years (Table 8). Total farm input has risen fairly steadily over the 34 years (and output even more, from an index of 51 in 1934

Table 8: Index Numbers of Farm Inputs by Categories, 1934 and 1969 (1957–9 = 100)

	Total input	Farm labour	Farm real estate	Mech- anical power and machinery	Ferti- lizer and lime	Feed, seed and livestock purchases	Miscel- laneous
1934	86	190	86	32	14	24	69
1969*	112	66	107	115	217	147	134

* Preliminary figures

Source: Agricultural Statistics, 1967 and Statistical Abstract, 1970

to 121 in 1969), but the composition of that input has changed dramatically. Outstanding is the fall in labour input occurring in conjunction with sharp rises in that of mechanical power and machinery, fertilizers, feed, seed and livestock. A different example illustrates strikingly how the declining input of labour has been offset. In 1900 every US farm worker could provide 7 persons with their farm-product needs. By 1940, following a very slow rise in productivity, he could provide for 11. By 1969, however, his output

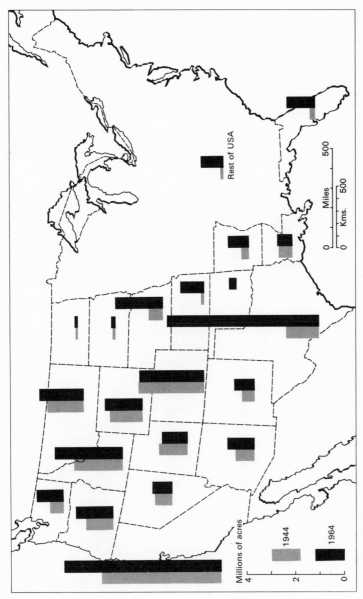

Rest of USA

Millions of acres

4

2

0

1944

1964

Miles
0   500

Kms.
0   500

Figure 19. Irrigated Land in Farms, 1944 and 1964

supplied the needs of 45 persons, a prodigious achievement, and one that holds out some hope for the hungry world. Such advance exacts a price, however, and we proceed to examine some consequences of this modern agrarian revolution.

Numbers and Scale

The technical advance is reflected in the number of farms, which has declined, and in the average size of farm, which has risen. According to the Census, a peak of 6·8 million farms was recorded in 1935. By 1969 there were under 3 million, the rate of decline being especially fast since 1950. Over this period the total area in farms changed little, however, and average farm size rose from 155 acres in 1935 to 378 acres in 1969. The average figure, while useful, conceals the extreme positions, and it may be added that farms of over 1,000 acres, which number less than 5 per cent of all farms, account for more than half of all land in farms.

Yet the increasing acreage of the average farm, however impressive, is only one indicator of the rise in the scale of profitable farm operation. There has also been a rising commitment, per farm, of technical, capital and managerial resources, reflecting an increasing *commercial*, as well as physical, scale. The dominance of the big business unit is evident in Table 9 which ranks farms by number and share of the value of farm products sold. (N.B. The definition of a 'commercial farm', relating to sales value, age of operator and number of days worked, is both complex and controversial, but need not delay us here. Suffice it to say that the 1964 Census classified 70 per cent of the then 3·2 million farms as 'commercial'; the remainder being 'part-time', 'part-retirement' or in other ways abnormal.) Units with sales below $5,000 accounted for 36 per cent of the number of commercial farms in 1964, but only 6 per cent of total sales. The claims to 'commercial' status of many of these units are dubious, but this does not affect the present argument. As the sales class of farms rises to above $10,000, the units concerned account for fewer, proportionately, of all farms, but for more and more of the sales. The increasing market dominance of the largest farms is

Table 9: Distribution of Commercial Farms by Number and by Value of Farm Products Sold per Farm, 1959 and 1964

	$50–2,499		$2,500–4,999		$5,000–9,999		$10,000–19,999		$20,000–39,999		$40,000 and above	
	1959	1964	1959	1964	1959	1964	1959	1964	1959	1964	1959	1964
Per cent of farms	14	16	26	20	27	23	20	22	9	12	4	7
Per cent of sales	2	1	8	5	16	11	23	19	19	21	33	44

Source: Statistical Abstracts, 1966, 1970

demonstrated by comparing the figures for 1964 with those for 1959. The only farms to raise their proportions of total sales were those with sales of $20,000 or more, and the largest gain was made by those in the $40,000 plus class. Preliminary data for 1969 indicate that this latter class now accounts for over half of all sales.

Clearly, such farming requires heavy capital investment in farm equipment, machinery, fertilizer, seed and stock and even, in expanding 'agribusiness', in processing and packing facilities and market outlets. Investment per worker in agriculture (some $30,000 in 1966) has risen above that in manufacturing ($25,000). This can place the small farmer in a very difficult position. Without adopting new and more productive methods he cannot compete effectively, but the new techniques and equipment often cannot be applied properly, or earn adequate return, in a small farm business. Again, being a small farmer, he often experiences difficulty in acquiring the capital needed to make himself more competitive. Some have survived in this situation by joining cooperatives, sharing the costs and benefits of capital investments, marketing organizations and purchased specialist services. Others, unable to earn an adequate income from their farm, have sold out and moved to town. Many continue to run their farms part-time, supplementing their incomes with earnings from elsewhere. Yet others have soldiered on, living near or below the poverty line, sometimes unable even to feed themselves and their families adequately and contributing to an aspect of American society that has only recently become widely recognized as pervasive and serious, the problem of rural poverty. Meanwhile the better placed, or the higher skilled, or the simply lucky, have extended their farm areas, raised the loans they need and, supported by Federal programmes for agriculture, participated with varying success in the new capital-intensive agriculture. In sum, a major consequence of recent developments has been a rise in the scale of effective farm operations from every point of view, and this has altered the very fabric of rural life in the USA.

The Income Paradox

Productivity in agriculture has risen at an unparalleled rate in recent years; man-hour productivity advance on the farm has far out-paced that in other economic sectors; and the agricultural labour force has duly reflected these great developments in a massive con-traction. Now, if society and economy worked smoothly, and if there were justice in the ordering of economic affairs, the rewards to those still engaged in agricultural enterprises would have improved correspondingly. The fact is, however, that personal incomes in agriculture, traditionally well below those of the non-farm popula-tion, have not advanced commensurately. In 1969 the per capita disposable personal income of the farm population was only 77 per cent of that of the non-farm. Even this was far better than in most preceding years. As recently as 1959 the ratio was only 50 per cent, but the gap, though closing, remains sizeable. The discrepancy persists at all levels of farm occupation. In 1969 the median earnings of all civilian male full-time workers in the USA were $7,660. Those of farmers and farm managers were, by contrast, only $3,350, and of farm labourers and foremen a mere $2,870.

These low incomes are not notably, if at all, offset by those per-quisites of cheap food, cheap housing and other low costs assumed by urban workers to accrue to the farm population. Home-produced foods are limited these days in range and value, and food has to be bought at local stores or supermarkets at the same price as obtains for the urban population (sometimes higher). Housing is often cheaper, but also often low in quality and amenities, while costs of transport, medical care, clothing and various services are normally higher for the rural than for the urban population. But even with a generous allowance for these doubtful perquisites, the incomes gap cannot be narrowed greatly and, in its income status, the farm population as a whole appears very obviously to be under-privileged. It has been argued that the average figures for the farm population are to a degree falsified by the inclusion of large numbers of very small operations, which should not be thought of as farms at all, much less as 'commercial' undertakings. While it can be argued, however, that such 'farms' heavily weight the average, they are at least partially offset by the other extreme. Some tens of thousands make a good, or even enviable, living from their farms. Neither group is 'typical' of the farm community as a whole, and the essential fact remains: that despite his extremely high productivity, the 'average' commercial farmer commands a standard of life considerably below that of his urban counterpart. While we cannot resolve this paradox, which is not confined to the USA, we can note one or two contributory elements.

Firstly we note that the growing wealth of Americans has not resulted in increased per capita purchases from the farm. Rising population has, of course, raised total demand, but not sufficiently to absorb fully the expanding output of farm products. The farm sector has thus shared progressively less in total consumer spending. Moreover, the demand for many farm products in America is highly inelastic, so that if prices were lowered, farmers would achieve a smaller total return rather than greater sales. On the other hand, even if it were possible to raise the prices of given farm commodities in attempting to achieve a better return, the availability of substitutes would probably cause total sales to fall, while output would rise so greatly that the increased prices could not be sustained.

The prices of farm products have therefore risen less than other prices. In consequence the farmers' relative position has deteriorated, since he consumes non-farm products. Indices have for long been compiled to show the degree of change from a 1910–14 base, and to construct the 'parity ratio'. In 1969 the index of prices received by farmers for all farm products was 275 (1910–14 = 100); while the index of prices paid for commodities bought (including interest, taxes and wages) was 373. The ratio $275/373(\times 100)$, the parity ratio, thus stood at 74, having fallen from a peak of 115 in 1947, indicating a worsening post-war situation for farmers as a whole.

Another element in the situation is that increasing proportions of the consumers' dollars that *are* being spent on foods are meeting marketing costs and not rewarding the farmer. Between 1947 and 1968, for example, for every one dollar by which the farm value of foods purchased rose, the marketing bill rose by about 4 dollars. Much could be said on this score, but whatever justification there is for the increasing role of intermediaries, the impression remains that something has got a little out of focus in the business of growing and marketing food.

Farm income is also affected by Federal policy, of which more is said below. Here we note that one objective of official farm support has been to stabilize farm income and remove some of the risks and uncertainties in farming. Over all, it has had some success. Numerous independent studies agree, for example, that without government support net farm income would, by 1965, have been 25–50 per cent *below* the 1955 level and that, if major government support ended now, net farm income would fall substantially, at least in the short term, with possibly disastrous results.

Federal activity has, then, helped keep farm income higher than it would otherwise have been. But the manner of operation of the policy has spread the Federal input very unevenly over the farm population. President Eisenhower, in the *Economic Report of the President* in 1959 (p. 57), said 'Actually the majority of farm people derive little or no benefit from our agricultural price support legislation. . . . Only some 1·5 million of our commercial farmers are the recipients of price support outlays in any material amounts, and, within this group, those with the higher incomes are the main beneficiaries. More than 2·5 million farmers whose annual sales are less than $2,500 . . . receive only very small supplements, or none at all, to their incomes from Government expenditures for price support.' This situation remains broadly unchanged. Recent complaints from Congressmen indicate that some big operators net over a half a million dollars per year from 'cultivating Washington'. Indeed, in 1968 two Californian farm syndicates netted $3 million and $2·8 million respectively, while many poor farmers received nothing. Federal policy on farm income thus seems to reinforce success rather than raise incomes generally. This may, of course, be a laudable objective, although never officially held as such, but the fact remains that, while the large operators have increased in prosperity (aided by substantial direct and indirect government support), many of the modest operators find it more and more difficult to maintain their standards, and very large numbers of small farmers and farm workers have been unable to earn a livelihood from their farms.

It is not suggested here that this process is necessarily morally wrong. The point is that a sizeable problem of rural poverty is being maintained and the flow of population from rural to urban areas constantly stimulated. In 1968 it was estimated that 23 per cent of the farm population was living in poverty, compared with 12 per cent of non-farm population. Rural poverty is not restricted to poor farmers, of course. There are numerous non-farm rural poor, many with backgrounds as miners, forestry workers or service workers for example, but for most the roots of their present poverty go back to the virtual collapse of farming as a means of earning a reasonable livelihood for the 'small man'. The nature and extent of rural poverty has only recently been generally appreciated, and is still being investigated. An estimate for 1967 put the actual number concerned at some 14 millions. The definition of 'poverty' may well be generous by world standards, but the condition is real enough for many millions. Thus, Americans have been disturbed to discover an extraordinarily high incidence of the common diseases of malnutrition (comfortably thought of as eliminated in the United States) in many rural areas. The report of a 1967 survey in rural areas of the South had this to say: 'We saw children . . . for whom hunger is a daily fact of life. . . . We do not wish to quibble over words, but "malnutrition" is not quite what we found; the boys and girls we saw . . . are suffering from hunger and disease and directly or indirectly they are dying from them – which is exactly what "starvation" means.'* Federal farm policy has not alleviated this situation, chiefly because this was not its major objective.

Poor incomes and poor prospects have, of course, driven many away from rural areas. About 22 million people migrated from rural to urban areas between 1940 and 1960, many of them ill-prepared for urban life, with little in the way of resources or saleable skills. During the 1960s the rate slackened off to about 0·75 million per year but, clearly, movement on this scale has serious consequences for all concerned. The rural areas lose active and enterprising people; supporting employment declines; populations become imbalanced with rising proportions of the old and indigent; tax revenues decline;

* Quoted in the Report of the President's National Advisory Commission on Rural Poverty, *The People Left Behind*, 1967, p. 5.

services of all kinds (medical, educational, shopping, transport) decrease in standard. Given such conditions the rural community has often disappeared as an effective unit for the organization of life, and people living in such areas may lead their lives in virtual isolation from the affluent market economy of which they nominally form a part.

We may set beside the comment on the poverty and hunger of certain rural farm and non-farm families another highly significant consequence of the productivity revolution, i.e. the huge surpluses of farm products. Such surpluses grew in size and value until the early 1960s, despite Federal schemes of production control and surplus disposal. Various measures often resulted, not in eliminating the surpluses, but in transferring their ownership to the Commodity Credit Corporation. The extent of the problem is thus indicated by the total value of the commodities owned by the CCC, nearly $2,000 million in 1950 and $6,400 million in 1959. Subsequently, massive inroads were made into the stocks, whose value was only $1,200 million (not *quite* the post-war lowest) in 1969. Even so, it remains considerable, and is on the rise again; while its magnitude illustrates the degree of Federal involvement in agriculture, which we will now examine.

Federal Involvement and the Farm Problem

Government involvement in the farm sector of the US economy is immense and has grown rapidly since the war. For example, in 1950 direct government payments to farmers totalled $283 million, just 2 per cent of the US farm operators' total net income from farming. By 1969 direct payments were $3,800 million, more than one fifth of total net income from farming. This is only part of the full cost of the farm programme, which runs at between $7,000 and $8,000 million annually. Federal policies are consequently a matter of considerable controversy, on the one hand regarded as essential to the reasonable ordering of a major sector of the economy and on the other as bordering on an 'un-American' activity. Federal involvement with agriculture, however, has a considerable pedigree, as

123

governments since the foundation of the republic have adopted measures aimed at helping the farmer. The nineteenth-century land disposal policies, the creation of the Department of Agriculture in 1862, the establishment of the land-grant colleges and other policies were designed to aid and support this sector of the economy, even in the heyday of *laissez-faire*.

In the present century, and particularly after the First World War, it became increasingly clear that agriculture presented a special social, political and economic problem in which the government had to play a direct and increasing role. The 'farm problem' involves the three related issues of unstable incomes, the considerable poverty of many of the farm population and the farm product surpluses. Without support schemes, farm incomes can fluctuate violently because of the nature of agriculture itself, the hazards of production, the unpredictability of the harvest, the delayed returns to investment (e.g. in livestock), the low degree of control exercisable by numerous farmers on market conditions, and so on. In recent years the problem has been accentuated by the tremendous advances in productivity and changes in market demand. With the prices of farm products rising much less than the prices of farm purchases, the individual farmer would in any case be striving to increase his output to maintain his real income. This in itself leads to surplus production (and, incidentally, further worsening farm prices, so that the individual's logical response to his problem of income maintenance worsens the situation for all farmers) but, added to the productivity revolution, has produced the enormous surpluses mentioned above. It is argued that, without Federal schemes for controlling this situation, the glut would have proved disastrous, farm prices would have collapsed and a slump on the old 1930 model might have ensued.

To face such problems, for which there appeared to be no effective and politically acceptable private solution, the Federal government erected a large, unwieldy system of price supports and production controls dating from the early 1930s. These programmes were overtaken by the agrarian revolution of the 1950s and 1960s – and, far from resolving the problem, they have in some respects (e.g. the surpluses) worsened it. But the system, having once been established, could not easily be dismantled, and it became difficult even to change direction without risk. Let us, then, examine in outline the types of Federal farm activity and briefly indicate their historical origins.

Pressures for greater government involvement built up in the 1920s as post-war prosperity seemed to be passing the farmer by. Tariff protection, aid to cooperative movements and other such measures had little effect, but more direct participation came in 1929 when a Federal Farm Board was set up. There was no immediate crisis behind this move, but rather the generally poor condition in farming which, it was hoped, could be improved by controlling marketing and stabilizing prices. The Great Depression, however, arrived almost immediately, the Farm Board became overloaded with surpluses and was abolished in 1933.

In that year, however, as part of Roosevelt's New Deal, the first Agricultural Adjustment Act was passed. The aim was to establish price support and production control programmes for certain major crops and livestock products. Later that year the Commodity Credit Corporation (CCC), a government agency, was created to buy, store and sell farm commodities, and to make cash advances to farmers for their products before the harvest. Although the Act of 1933 was declared unconstitutional by the Supreme Court, the CCC has remained a major part of the organization for farm support.

Another Agricultural Adjustment Act was passed in 1938, which provided for mandatory price support for stipulated crops (initially corn, wheat and cotton), for marketing quotas for these and other commodities (controlled through acreage allotments), and legalized price supports for other farm commodities where necessary. This scheme, amended by later Acts, remains the basis of Federal policy. Under it, the CCC has used its powers to support numerous farm products, most notably and consistently corn, wheat, rice, cotton and tobacco. The effects of such government activities in the 1930s are difficult to judge. The parity ratio had fallen to 58 in 1932; it rose to 93 by 1937, and remained comparatively high thereafter (81 in 1940). The farmer's situation had improved relatively, but this improvement cannot be ascribed solely to government action, for agriculture shared in the general economic recovery.

During the 1940s the Federal mechanisms were adapted to achieving a massive increase in output to overcome the wartime and early post-war world food shortages. For nearly ten years high support prices and other measures encouraged the farmer to invest heavily and undertake much development to achieve the highest possible output. Parity ratios were above 100 through most of the 1940s, reaching a peak of 115 in 1947. In the early 1950s, however, with overseas demand reduced by the recovery and advance of agriculture in war-afflicted areas, the redirection of the farm economy to meet a new situation was extremely difficult, and massive surpluses accumulated. Modifications to the 1938 Act (e.g. in 1954) permitted greater flexibility in the use of price supports, allowing prices to fall to lower parity ratios. Surpluses still grew. Acreage reductions were applied but resulted in more assiduous cultivation of the reduced acreages, so that output actually rose, while the remaining areas were often put into other crops, increasing their output and thus raising fears of other surpluses.

The fight against the surpluses included various direct efforts to reduce the farmed area. The Agriculture Act of 1956 established the famous 'soil-bank' scheme, creating two types of land reserve, the 'acreage reserve' and the 'conservation reserve'. The acreage reserve scheme enabled farmers to be paid for taking land out of crops in surplus supply and placing it in the bank. This was intended, hopefully, to reduce the surpluses of particularly troublesome crops and at the same time help the conservation movement. The scheme lasted only until 1958 and had little effect. At its peak in 1957 about 21 million acres were in this account at the 'bank', but farmers understandably desposited their poorest land, and continued to cultivate their remaining acres more intensively so that output rose once more. The experiment ended with surplus stocks at record levels. The conservation reserve programme, however, continues, although no new land could be included after 1960. Under this scheme farm land was leased to the government and held by it as part of the reserve, the farmer applying approved conservationist measures, aided by Federal funds. A major aim here, however, has been conservation, and production control was never significant. The area involved reached a maximum of some 29 million acres in 1960 but with land being released from contract annually, the total fell to 3 million acres by 1969.

Other attempts made since 1960 to persuade farmers to retire land include, for example, the Emergency Feed Grains Programme of 1961, aimed at retiring land out of corn, grain sorghum, barley and oats, and offering considerable financial incentive. Retirements under this programme ranged between 25 and 39 million acres from 1961 to 1969. Again, a Cropland Adjustment Programme, inaugurated in 1966, has many similarities with the soil-bank scheme of ten years earlier, but provides only for longer terms of retirement (5–10 years) and offers less inducement. Only 4 million acres were retired under this programme in 1969. None the less, under the various schemes the total 'diverted' area rose from 14 million acres in 1956 to a peak of 65 million in 1962, thereafter declining for some years, but recovering to 58 million acres in 1969.

To summarize, the policy for agriculture consists of price supports, related to 'parity' as explained above. Enforcement has normally been by the CCC, which has either purchased the crop or advanced a loan upon it (based on the support level), by which the crop became government property if the farmer could not raise a better price elsewhere. To participate, the farmer must apply the requested acreage control, or keep to quotas, which are set annually for relevant crops by the CCC. Various additional programmes have attempted to retire land out of crop production, either temporarily or permanently.

The CCC also attempts to stimulate demand. Efforts have been made to dispose of food surpluses by domestic programmes of aid to needy sectors of the American population. The school lunch programme, the food-stamp scheme (by which the poor may purchase food to several times the value of the food stamps they have bought) and direct distribution of free food to the poorest families are examples. But the total of such welfare disposals has had almost no effect on the surpluses.

Far more important in reducing the surpluses after 1960 was the large increase in overseas demand, especially in areas such as India and Pakistan, where poor harvests had brought serious consequences. Massive subsidized exports of foods raised the volume of agricultural exports to the highest recorded levels. By 1966 the volume of all agricultural exports was 57 per cent above the 1957–9

127

level, the export of grains and feeds 130 per cent above. This disposal was supplemented by more vigorous internal action, with low support prices (the parity ratio has not risen above 80 since 1959, and has often been down in the 70s) and sharply cut acreages. Thus the value of the surplus owned by the CCC fell rapidly from the 1959 peak. As individual instances, stocks of wheat fell from 1,133 million bushels in 1960 to 216 million in 1966, corn from 1,500 million bushels to 156 million.

The alleviation may prove only temporary, for the position is complex and subject to rapid alteration. An example from wheat may illustrate the problem. The large disposals since 1960 greatly eroded the stocks and sharply reduced the annual carry-over. At one time it seemed as if these overseas shipments would remain important both for the US farmer and for the consumers in South-East Asia. Support prices rose and payments for wheat land placed in reserve were dropped. Good harvests in overseas areas, however, and the apparent achievement, at long last, of improved productivity in these areas, sharply reduced wheat exports in 1967. Thus 5 per cent acreage cuts were imposed for 1968, on which the farmer, aided by exceptionally favourable weather, raised the yield per acre by 10 per cent, thus increasing total output. Since the world wheat carry-over at the end of 1968 was very large, the position again looked serious from the point of view of surplus creation. The American wheat farmers' acreages for 1969 were cut back again by 15 per cent, and the conservation reserve programme was again urged upon the farmer.

It seems, then, that the situation is still not under effective control but, whatever the faults of the policy, numerous independent studies agree that it has brought an unusual stability to total farm income since the war; has cushioned the impact of large shifts in demand and supply relationships, giving more time for adjustment, and has provided (by sustaining a farm economy of high production capacity and by holding considerable stocks) some insurance for national and international emergencies.* It is also, however, widely felt that farm policy is in a rut, really represents the patching up of schemes

* See L. G. Tweeten in F. V. Waugh *et al.*, *Agricultural Policy, A Review of Programmes and Needs*, 1967.

designed for meeting the problems of different times, and is of dubious cost effectiveness. Different policies have aimed at opposing objectives, and control emphasis has always been on land areas, ignoring all other inputs and their effects. The cost of the programme has risen rapidly, but the number of persons served has decreased equally rapidly, and more and more of the aid goes to that section of the farm community which needs it least. These are powerful arguments.* E. Higbee, in his comment, points to a major deficiency: 'Less thought has been given to the problem of surplus men than to that of surplus crops.'† The 'farm problem' in fact is a complex inter-relationship of various difficult issues. The farm programme has not achieved the hoped for success, partly because of the complexity and diversity of needs in different sectors of the farm economy and different regions of the country, and partly because of the great technological advance.

The high cost of the support programme and other defects have brought increasing pressure for change. Re-apportionment of seats in Congress, taking into account recent population movements, is bringing to the legislature more politicians with urban interests in their hearts, and massive urban problems on their hands. Such men cast envious eyes on the vast sums allocated annually to agriculture. The problem, however, is to find an acceptable and workable alternative. In 1970 a new Agriculture Act had to be passed and, despite all criticism and pressures, it turned out to be much the same as its predecessors. A limit has been set to the amount payable to a single farm, but it is so high ($55,000 per crop per farm) as to mean little in practice, and merely establishes the principle of a ceiling, which could be useful in the future. No provision is made for the low-income rural population and, for a few more years, things will run largely as in the recent past.

Federal programmes for agriculture are not confined to those described above. Amongst others the Cooperative Extension Service, founded in 1914, assists in the diffusion of knowledge of new techniques and new ways of rural living. County agricultural

* They are expounded further in M. Clawson, *Policy Directions for U.S. Agriculture*, 1969.
† *Farms and Farmers in an Urban Age*, 1963, p. 4.

agents, supported by Federal, State and county funds, and familiar alike with farm problems and with the latest work at agricultural experimental stations and land-grant colleges, are found in every significant agricultural county. The Soil Conservation Service too, established in 1936, draws support from the Federal government, and has impressive achievements to show.

Moreover, official intervention in the farmers' affairs is not restricted to the Federal level. State governments (and, indeed, local county officials as well as Federal agencies) concern themselves with the interests of their agricultural sectors. The larger and more important that sector, the more care is taken to support it, for political and economic reasons. 'Buy at home' laws often stipulate that, wherever possible, food purchases for public institutions should originate in the State. Anti-margarine laws have bolstered consumption of locally produced butter in major dairy States. Milk sanitation laws often aim at ensuring quality and hygiene and also at giving some control over out-of-State supplies, to which more rigorous standards may be applied, or transport limits set, etc. State systems for controlling the supply of major farm products also exist beside the Federal system, and rigorous limitations have sometimes been enforced, for example, to prevent the over-supply of certain fruits. In sum, even in the most avowedly 'free-enterprise' areas, such as California, the unique problems of farming have stimulated forms of State protection, support and jurisdiction reminiscent of a semi-socialist society.

6: Some Spatial Variations in Agriculture

The examination of general issues at a national level, however essential to understanding modern American agriculture, nevertheless leaves large gaps, for it conceals significant regional variations. A detailed examination of all the variables in regional or local context is beyond the scope of this study, but it will be useful to give some illustrations of their differential geographical impact before attempting a general regional appraisal of present patterns of agricultural production. The areas used here will be the nine standard geographical divisions. Significant differences will occur more locally, of course, while the divisional boundaries themselves have little validity in the delimitation of true agricultural regions. However, they are used here to demonstrate the range of geographical experience. This is justified by the limited aim, the comparability thus achieved with other sections of the book, the availability of statistics at this level and, not least, by the need for brevity.

Regional Changes in Employment and Farm Land

Figures 20 and 21 show divisional changes in farm employment and land in farms for 1945 to 1967 and 1945 to 1964 respectively. During this period the definition of a farm changed, but notably in relation to small farms which, although numerous, cover very small proportions of farm land, production and sales. For our purposes, therefore, this complexity may be ignored. As a direct result of the technological advance, total farm employment fell by just over half in the period. Divisional experiences vary greatly, however, reflecting continual post-war regional adjustments. The North Central

131

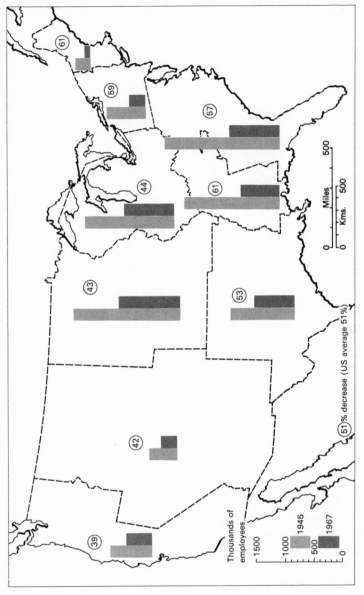

Figure 20. Employment in Agriculture, 1945 and 1967

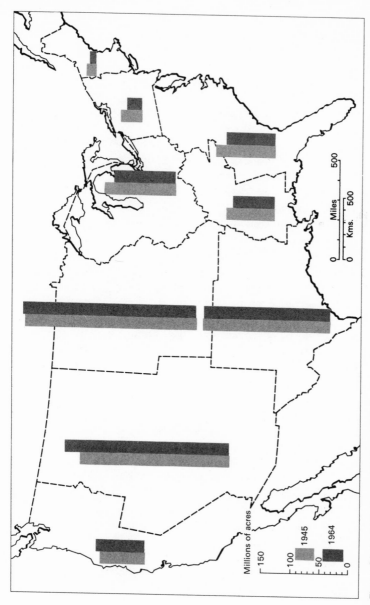

Millions of acres

150 —
100 —
50 —
0 —

1945
1964

Miles 500
Kms. 500

Figure 21. Land in Farms, 1945 and 1964

divisions (East and West) and the Western divisions (Mountain and Pacific) experienced rates of employment decline considerably below average. Much greater loss of farm jobs occurred in the three Southern divisions and in the North-East (New England and Middle Atlantic) divisions. The total area of land in farms moved broadly with these employment trends. The total national area altered little but considerable inter-regional movement occurred, as Figure 21 illustrates.

Sharp losses of farm land occurred in the Middle Atlantic and New England divisions, continuing long-established regional trends. By 1964 the proportion of the national farm area in the North-East was under 3 per cent. This loss, together with the rapid decline in farm employment, reflects the evolving character of this major area. Farm land decline is a complex process with many possible interacting causes but, in this region as a whole, two elements have played a major role. Farmers in the north-eastern USA have long suffered severe competition from other better-endowed parts of the country – competition which has sharpened with each advance of productivity in 'newer' areas, and with advances in transport, processing and storage techniques. In addition, the tendency of the new industrial, commercial and residential facilities to sprawl at low densities has notably affected farm uses. Considerable areas have been used directly in construction; but there has also been a far-reaching impact on farm land in the vicinity of major developments. Much has become unusable or unprofitable under the strains of urban fringe farming, and large areas lie practically idle, awaiting the high prices obtainable for further urban-industrial development land. Such effects on farm land use have been supplemented by employment considerations. The sprawling suburbs offer wider employment opportunities and higher incomes to suitable farm workers. This works both ways: proximity to other employment helps some families to remain in farming who might otherwise have been forced off the land. On the whole, however, in this area of the country the chief effect for decades has been to attract farmers and farm workers from the land. Here, then, the push of advancing farm and transport technology has been re-inforced by the pull of urban opportunities to produce rates of

134

decline in farm land and farm employment which are among the highest in the nation.

Other notable overall losses in farm area, accompanying high rates of employment decline, are in the South Atlantic and East South Central divisions of the Southern region. Here many old, worn-out farms have been converted (or allowed to revert) to other uses, especially forest. In these divisions the depletion of area and employment can be compared with that in the North-East. But here the causes lie more especially in the changing character of southern agriculture, and less directly in massive urban-industrial growth. Moreover, within the North-East the decline in farm area has been pretty general, whereas within these two Southern divisions the situation varies considerably. In Florida, for example, the total farm area has notably increased, aided by irrigation and by large-scale drainage schemes. Often also resulting from drainage programmes, farm area has risen in parts of other southern States, as along the Mississippi Valley. However, these two divisions have, overall, suffered substantial farm land loss. In the adjacent West South Central area there has again been marked local variation, but the losses of farm land in some sections have been balanced by the taking-in of new areas elsewhere. Consequently, little overall change has occurred. The rate of decline in farm employment has also been lower than elsewhere in the South, and both conditions reflect the slightly superior relative conditions and prospects of farming here.

In the North Central region each of the four most westerly states (the Dakotas, Nebraska and Kansas) has raised its farm area since the war. Elsewhere local gains and losses have given a net decline in farm land, which increases in size towards the east. The East North Central division as a whole thus sustained a sharp loss, whereas in the West North Central losses in Minnesota, Iowa and Missouri were almost precisely balanced by the increases mentioned above. Farm employment losses have been comparatively moderate in the region as a whole, but again have been heavier to the east. Simple explanations must be tentative, but non-farm employment opportunities and non-farm land use potentials are clearly considerably greater in the eastern half of the region.

The Dakotas, Nebraska and Kansas mark the transition between kinds of experience in farm area and employment. Further west the area of land in farms has consistently increased and losses of employment have, by contrast with experience in the East and South, been moderate and much more a reflection of improving technology than of the push of competition or the pull of urban opportunity. Millions of new acres have been taken into farms in the Mountain division since the war, so that this division now accounts for almost a quarter of all farm land. The lack of other intensive pressures on land use is worth noting. This recent expansion of area continues the trend of past decades, reflecting particularly the advance of irrigation. Numerous, but relatively small, areas of irrigated land provide an essential basis for huge farm operations which control or lease large tracts of grazing land (often Federal Domain). Of the eight Mountain States, only New Mexico has failed to increase its area of farm land since 1945.

Increases in total farm land have also been widespread in the Pacific division, but much smaller in size than in the Mountain areas. However, on average, acres are much more intensively cultivated in the Pacific coast States. This is partly why the decline of farm employment here has been slower than in any other division. In sum, with a smaller total farm acreage the Pacific division far outstrips the neighbouring Mountain division in output and in productivity.

With farm employment as a guide a worthwhile distinction can be made between the Eastern and Southern regions on the one hand, and the Central and Western regions on the other. The latter have experienced relatively low rates of employment loss and now possess over half the nation's farm employment, compared with about 43 per cent in 1945. The decline of the East and South is also reflected in farm land areas, but less consistently. A more precise comparison here would be of areas east and west of the Mississippi. In 1945 the former still had 30 per cent of total farm land, but by 1964 under 25 per cent

Regional Changes in Output and 'Productivity'

Further illustrations of the changing regional balance in agriculture arise from a comparison of the value of farm products sold in 1945 and 1964 (Figure 22). Each division's proportion of total national sales may also be compared with its proportion of total employment to give a crude index of 'labour productivity'. For example, in 1964 the East South Central division provided 6·7 per cent of total US farm sales, but 12·8 per cent of farm employment. The ratio 6·7/12·8 equals only 52, giving this division the lowest comparative productivity ratio in the nation. Table 10 shows the ratios for 1945 and 1964 for each division. Over all the gap in 'productivity' between regions has narrowed since the war, but the rank order remains much the same.

Table 10: Index of Comparative Labour Productivity* on Farms by Division, 1945 and 1964

Division	Ratio		Division	Ratio	
	1945	1964		1945	1964
Pacific	182	161	East North Central	124	102
Mountain	147	150	Middle Atlantic	95	100
West North Central	145	126	West South Central	80	91
New England	113	105	South Atlantic	57	68
			East South Central	43	52

* Ratio per cent of farm sales to per cent of farm employment

The evidence of farm sales again reflects the relative decline of the North-Eastern divisions. By 1964 only 7 per cent of total US farm sales originated here and the region accounts for roughly the same proportion of output as of employment. The evidence for the South, however, shows a different aspect of agricultural change. Each Southern division *raised* its proportion of total national output between 1945 and 1964. True, the rise is small (especially for the ESC division where the rounded proportion remains 6·7 per cent) but the South accounted for 28·6 per cent of farm output by value in 1945, and for 30·2 per cent in 1964. Here, then, is an excellent

137

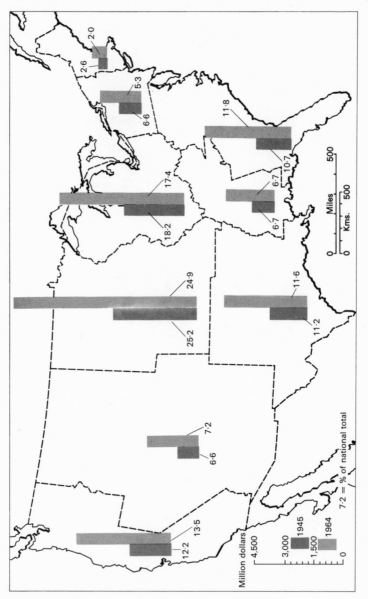

Figure 22. Value of Farm Products Sold, 1945 and 1964

illustration of the fact that in an 'underdeveloped' area a rapid decline in farm employment and the transfer of land out of agriculture can contribute to the improvement of the farm economy, as well as result from that improvement. Thus the relative standing of southern agriculture has been raised. In the past, the farm sector here was characterized by its poor yields and very low productivity. The changing patterns of agriculture have gone some way to redressing the balance, as the statistics show. Clearly, however, much room remains for further improvement. In 1964 the South still provided 43 per cent of total farm employment, but only 30 per cent of total output. The index of comparative labour productivity stands only in the range of 52 to 91 in the Southern divisions. This contrasts with the range of 43 to 80 in 1945; but, although advance has certainly been made, the South still has a long row to hoe.

In total output from farms, the North Central region remains outstanding. Here is the true heart of American agriculture, a kind of agrarian power-house without parallel on earth. Figure 22 shows that the East and the West North Central divisions together accounted for over 42 per cent of the total value of farm sales in the USA in 1964, accomplishing this with just under 37 per cent of the farm labour force. The North Central region as a whole has, since the war, maintained its relative position, having provided some 43 per cent of these sales in 1945. This is no ordinary achievement for a well-established region, which may normally expect to lose ground in relation to vigorous growth elsewhere. Here, however, is a most extensive and highly productive area, in which the new agrarian revolution has most fruitfully produced good solid food rather than the peripheral delicacies. Comparisons of this kind are perhaps invidious but the advances made here in producing grains and livestock offer more hope to the hungry of all nationalities than the achievements elsewhere in growing a heartier lettuce, a machine-harvested tomato or a flawless (and sometimes tasteless) apple. Within the North Central region an increasing economic emphasis on farm activities is discernible as one moves from east to west. Clearly, both the East and the West North Central divisions are raising their farm output but the western area has been growing rather faster, for reasons intimated above.

However impressive the scale of agrarian activity in the North Central region, in pure growth its performance is less spectacular than that in the Western region. Over one fifth of total US farm sales originated in the West in 1964 with only 13 per cent of the farm labour force involved. The index of comparative 'productivity' (Table 10) puts both the Mountain and the Pacific divisions far ahead of their nearest rivals, and on this, as on other criteria already reviewed, these divisions are outstanding in the recent advance of their agriculture.

Regional Developments in Scale

Another index of the changing national farm economy discussed above was the rising scale of farm operations, both in area of units and in commercial scale of operations. Every region has participated in this trend, but with marked variations. Figure 23 illustrates the average acreage of farms in each division in 1945 and 1964. Calculations of differing *rates* of growth in area are of little value here because of the varying impact of the changed definitions of a farm. Farm acreages east of the Mississippi, however, remain below the national average, those west of it above average. This is a consequence of environmental conditions, historical stages of development and types of farming, and needs no elaboration.

More significant is the commercial scale of operations, an element measured earlier by the sales classes of commercial farms. Figure 24 indicates proportions of all commercial farms in each division falling into each of three sales classes. Remarkable regional differences are evident. This is not the best index for regional comparison, for clearly the optimum commercial scale of operations varies with the type or types of agricultural commodity produced, conditions of market access and so on. However, the positions at the extremes (referred to here as Class 1 and Class 3 farms respectively) deserve comment, and of special significance is the number of farms in Class 3, the lowest category. This class, with sales below $5,000, contains the problem farms. (The middle category also contains at its lowest end many problem farms which just enter the $5,000 sales range; but this re-

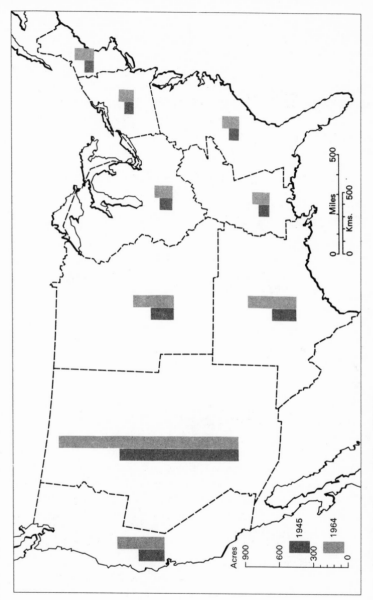

Figure 23. Size of Farms, 1945 and 1964

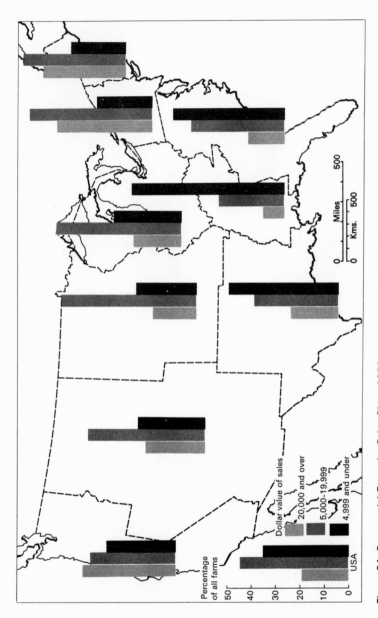

Figure 24. Commercial Farms by Sales Class, 1964

finement cannot be pursued here.) Areas where Class 3 farms are numerous must in consequence be in some respects areas of difficulty. Frequently, as we have seen, the incomes derived from farm sales are supplemented by off-farm earnings by one or more members of the family. In some parts of the country, however, opportunities for off-farm activity are very limited, and the existence of many farms in this low commercial class implies severe rural poverty. The net income derived from sales even of $5,000, at the top of this class, is around $2,000 or less, well below the current 'poverty line' and, even allowing for some home-produced foods, implying a very low standard of life.

The USA as a whole in 1964 had 36 per cent of all its commercial farms in Class 3, but this proportion is much inflated by conditions in the South, where all divisions have proportions well above the national average (Figure 24). In the East South Central division about 180,000 farms, two out of every three, fell into this class: an astonishing situation, reflected in the general poverty of the division. The South Atlantic and West South Central divisions are also prominent, with almost half their farms in this lowest class. As a whole, therefore, the South has an unenviable lead in this matter and has about 55 per cent of all Class 3 farms in the nation. The position in the South has greatly improved since the war, but considerable problems remain.

On the brighter side, and at the other extreme, a very high proportion of farms falls into the top sales class in both the Pacific and the North-Eastern regions. For the Pacific division this will come as no surprise. In fact, 22 per cent of all farms here have sales of $40,000 and above, whereas nationally only 7 per cent of all farms fall into this élite class. California, the El Dorado State, in 1964 had more than 16,000 farms, 28 per cent of all its farms, in the $40,000 and above sales class, a situation unrivalled elsewhere in the USA.

The prominence of Class 1 farms in the North-East may be more unexpected, and especially so in New England. The difficulties presented by nature to a productive agriculture here are well documented. A glance at the hilly and stone-littered fields would discourage most prospective farm entrepreneurs, especially in view of

143

the superior physical prospect elsewhere. Erosion of the farm labour force and abandonment of farm land here goes back a century or more, but the modern New England farm population contains amongst its numbers a breed of farmer that even a Californian would grudgingly admire. With his eye set firmly on profitability, he has adjusted his farm economy to both the limitations and the opportunities of the physical and the human environments. This is reflected in the unusually high proportion of New England farms in the top class. Fifteen per cent, in fact, have sales of $40,000 or more; this is second only to the Pacific division. Notable, too, is the relatively small number of farms in the bottom class. The proportion of Class 3 farms in New England is lower than in any other division, another indication of the extent to which the farming has been adjusted to changed conditions.

Figure 24 shows other regional deviations from the 'average' pattern of farm distribution amongst the three sales classes and some interesting contrasts between physical and commercial scale. In the Mountain division, for example, most farm units fall into the middle commercial class, despite their enormous physical size. But enough has probably been said about the divisional variations in these indices of farm activity. One further element with important, and varying, regional effects needs to be mentioned before we outline actual geographical patterns of agricultural production. Federal farm programmes have had no deliberate 'regional policy' but in fact the various programmes have had an uneven geographical impact, impeding change in some areas, promoting it elsewhere. This can be illustrated by specific examples.

Regional Impact of Federal Programmes

Price-support schemes for major crops have been accompanied by acreage allotments based on the geographical patterns of previous years. One effect is to slow down possible changes in the regional balance of production of any given crop. Cotton farming may be taken as an illustration. With the far superior levels of productivity in the South-West the transfer of the main centres of production from the South-East to the newer areas would have progressed farther and faster but for the support programmes and the acreage allotment restrictions. Price supports enabled many sub-standard cotton growers in the South-East to survive, while the western growers had to await the abandonment of quotas held in the South-East before being able to expand their own cotton areas. Beyond a certain point, however, further acreage reductions reduce the permitted area of cultivation on a small farm so drastically that cotton cannot be grown commercially. The farmer may then abandon his quota, which thus becomes available for allotment elsewhere. In essence, however, the Federal programme has slowed down the process of inter-regional adjustment in this crop.

Federal activity has sometimes, by contrast, encouraged change. With their wheat and cotton acreages restricted, for example, farmers have substituted other crops, thus often broadening the range of their economy and benefiting thereby. In this context the very rapid increase in grain sorghum production is worth mention. A new hybrid sorghum with outstanding yields has been developed since the war, and as there was no penalty on feed-grain crops, the output of the new grain sorghum increased rapidly in the major wheat and cotton areas, encouraging an increase of cattle feeding in these same areas. This development is widespread, but is specially important in the rapid expansion of beef herds in the South (most notably in Texas) and in the south-western States.

The land-retirement programmes of 1956 and later years (by which whole or part farms could be retired from crop production) also had uneven geographical effects. No scheme would result in land being retired in equal measure over all regions, but here the programmes were specifically directed towards easing crop surpluses and therefore had their major impact in those regions from which the main surpluses originated. An illustration is the Conservation Reserve Programme, which still had some $9\frac{1}{4}$ million acres under contract in January 1968: over 4 million acres, 44 per cent of the total, were in the tier of States from North Dakota southwards to Texas – all States producing one or more of the most troublesome surpluses (corn, wheat, cotton). Including the contiguous grain lands of eastern Colorado and central and southern Minnesota, over

145

half of the land in the conservation reserve is accounted for. Another concentrated zone of reserve land in 1968 was in Georgia and South Carolina, chiefly on their piedmont areas but also in the Appalachians. By contrast, the amount of conservation-reserve land in the North-East was small, while in the Western region, with 31 per cent of all land in farms, the acreage under contract was under 17 per cent of the total – and most of this hugged the boundaries of the central tier of States mentioned above.

Similarly government price support has been largely directed towards certain major crops – corn, wheat, cotton and tobacco.* Consequently, direct Federal payments to agriculture have been distributed unevenly over the nation, and have depended very much on the structure of regional farm output. Figure 25 illustrates the pattern. The favoured position of the central divisions is manifest. The West North Central and West South Central divisions together received 53 per cent of Federal farm payments in 1967, although they account for under 40 per cent of the total value of farm sales. In the major support crops of corn, wheat and cotton, however, these two divisions together accounted that year for 43, 46 and 53 per cent respectively of total US production. A concentration of cash grain farming in the East North Central and of cotton farming and subsidiary grain and tobacco farming in the East South Central divisions also helps to account for the moderately high proportions of Federal farm payments in these areas. In the latter area the proportion considerably exceeds the proportion of national farm product sales. Cotton and grain farming also takes place in the Pacific and Mountain divisions, but less pervasively; and this is reflected in the relatively low totals of Federal payments. The South Atlantic division is no longer a major producer of cotton, and it is not prominent as a grain producer. The receipt here, therefore, of 8 per cent of Federal farm payments reflects support for tobacco; for this division provided two thirds of national tobacco output in 1967.

* These four, together with rice and peanuts, are treated as 'basic commodities' under mandatory price support. Of the 'non-basic' commodities under mandatory price support, dairy products are by far the most important, but other grains and sugar beets also appear. Of crops under 'non-mandatory' support, soybeans is the most important.

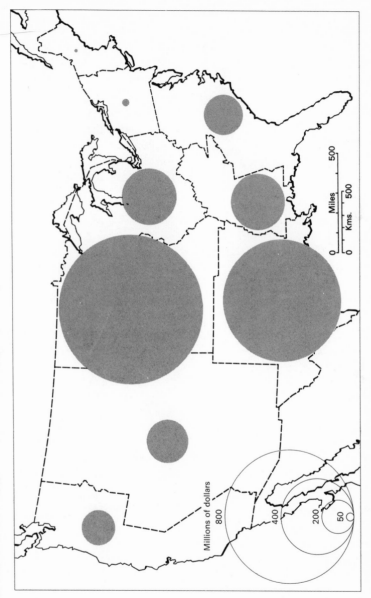

Figure 25. Government Farm Payments, 1967

Here again, however, the proportion of Federal payments falls well below the proportion of total farm sales. A similar situation, but even more accentuated, occurs in the two North-Eastern divisions, which receive a minimal amount of this kind of Federal farm support.

Clearly, therefore, government programmes have a markedly variable impact over the nation as a whole. One could add other examples – the Soil Conservation Service activities, the farm training programmes and special aid for poor farmers in poor areas, and so on. All have a geographical expression, as well as an economic impact on agriculture, and thus help to bring about changes of the kinds described above.

7: Regional Patterns of Agricultural Production

Changes of the kinds described in the previous chapters are naturally reflected in the regional patterns of agricultural production, but are superimposed on other influences (such as local climate and soil conditions, market accessibility and outside competition) which also help to mould the regional character of farm outputs. Figure 26 shows the general patterns of farm activity by divisions, using six categories of farm product. The two largest categories, 'field crops' and 'beef and other livestock products' (i.e. livestock excluding dairy and poultry products), both conceal much important detail, together covering some two thirds of farm sales in 1964. None the less, the national movements outlined in Chapter 5 for these major kinds of product clearly have regional relevance, and Figure 26 provides a suitable starting-point for discussing regional patterns. The position is presented for 1945 and 1964 (both Census years) as an indication of post-war regional adjustments. The patterns of farm output evidently vary greatly and in some areas important changes have occurred. Remember, however, that the figure is based on statistics of final sales, and thus will not accurately reflect the actual patterns of farm operations in different regions. Livestock and product sales, for example, may in one area depend largely on feed bought in, and in another on home-produced feeds. We shall now examine the patterns in each division. The total value of farm sales from 1945 to 1964 rose most in the Western region (+132 per cent), closely followed by the South (+129 per cent). We shall, therefore, consider these two regions first.

The *Western region* showed up well in the various indices of performance discussed above, but its two divisions differ considerably in their patterns of farm activity, and will be discussed separately. Agricultural interests in the *Mountain division* are strikingly domi-

149

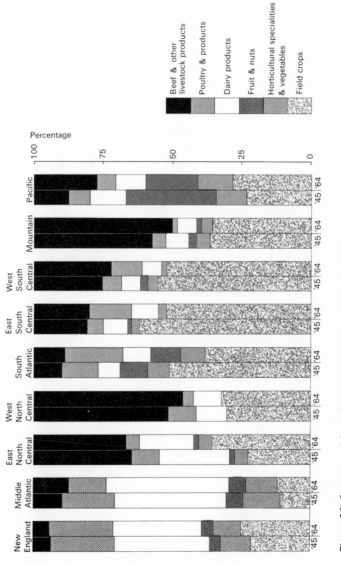

Figure 26. Structure of Farm Output by Division, 1945 and 1964

nated by 'livestock and product' farming. (N.B. The term 'livestock and products' as used here includes chiefly beef cattle and calves, sheep, lambs and hogs; dairy products, poultry and poultry products are classified separately.) This category provides half the total farm sales in the Mountain division. This emphasis is understandable in an area with such water problems, and with huge areas suitable only for extensive livestock grazing (the enormous expanse of public domain in the Mountain States provides well over half the total area grazed). In fact the pattern of farm activity here is imposed by the unsuitability of much of the land for other farm uses. Much other farm production is directly associated with livestock needs; alfalfa and roots, for example, are cultivated as supplementary feed for cattle and sheep. Hay is, in fact, the leading crop by value in four of the eight Mountain States, while beef cattle provide the leading source of farm income in each State. The low carrying capacity of the land is illustrated, however, by the fact that, despite its enormous area, the Mountain division supported in 1968 only 13 per cent of total US cattle not kept for milk, being far out-ranked by the two West Central divisions. Sheep and lambs are also important in Mountain livestock and comprise over a third of the national total of these animals. Both in this division and nationally, however, numbers of sheep and lambs have been greatly reduced since the war.

Field crops form an important source of sales income for Mountain division farmers, but less pervasively. The central Mountain States of Nevada, Utah and Wyoming, for example, sustain little of this type of farming, except in their limited irrigated areas, and hay is the principal crop. In the other Mountain States, field-crop production varies sharply. In the north, in Montana and Idaho, wheat and barley are important, and wheat is a major crop, too, in Colorado. In the south, in Arizona and New Mexico, most crop farms now specialize in cotton. Yields under irrigation in Arizona are over twice the national average and this State has emerged since the war as a high-ranking cotton-producing State. Throughout the Mountain States irrigation is vitally important and, among cash crops other than grain and cotton produced in irrigated areas, sugar beets are prominent, especially in the northern States and Colorado, and so are potatoes in Idaho.

In the whole Mountain division, nearly 13 million acres of farm land were irrigated in 1964, 38 per cent of all cropland used for crops that year; the equivalent national ratio is 11 per cent. (It does not follow that the irrigated land accounted for 38 per cent of the total cropland *actually cropped* in the Mountain States in 1964, but the statistic does indicate the relative significance of water management here.) The irrigated acreage has also expanded since the war (Figure 19, p. 115) but more slowly than before. Irrigation is very costly and increasingly difficult here and, of the 17 million acres of farm land brought under irrigation in the USA between 1944 and 1964, the Mountain division contributed a mere 13 per cent. In 1944 the division contained just over half the irrigated land in farms in the USA, in 1964 just over a third. It appears that the resources, governmental or private, available for this kind of investment can in present circumstances be more effectively applied elsewhere.

Because of water-supply problems, the total area producing field crops for sale in the Mountain States as a whole is limited. Montana provides an important exception. Dry farming is widely practised here, and the State contains about 36 per cent of all Mountain division cropland. Wheat is the major cash crop, but yields remain at about, or below, the national average (28 bushels per acre in 1968), reflecting the fact that these lands are not ideally suited to wheat, but grow it for lack of any equally profitable alternative. In this Montana is very similar to its neighbour, North Dakota, indicating that it is largely a Great Plains rather than a Mountain State. A similar condition exists in Colorado, which has a further 25 per cent of Mountain division cropland. The wheat output here is mainly from the eastern third of the State, but yields are low (20 bushels per acre in 1968), reflecting the deteriorating physical conditions for cropping on the western margins of the Plains. By contrast, in Idaho average wheat yields under irrigation in the upper reaches of the Snake River valley and in the small Idaho extension of the Washington Palouse district are high (46 bushels to the acre).

Together, 'livestock and products' and 'field crops' provide about 85 per cent of farm sales in the Mountain division. Apart from these only dairying needs mention, being usually found, as would be expected, around and near the larger communities. Reflecting the

152

low density of population in this area, the physical conditions and the distance from highly populated centres outside the region, dairy farming is far less important in the Mountain economy than nationally. In sum, farming in this division concentrates chiefly on livestock and products today, as it always has. With the rising demand for beef, this interest has recently become even more specialized. Apart from intensification in this field, little really significant change in the general pattern has occurred since 1945. The very extensive system of farming imposed by physical conditions here is illustrated by farm size. The average for the Mountain division is about 2,000 acres, compared with about 350 acres for the USA. In ranching, 12,000 acres may be considered a small operation, depending on physical conditions. Areas of 50,000 acres and more (including leased Federal grazing land) are sometimes necessary for a viable enterprise. Apart from very expensive further investment in 'oasis cultivation', little can be done to change this. At the Census of 1964, the Mountain division had a quarter of all land in farms in the United States, but only 10 per cent of the cropland and a mere 7 per cent of the total value of farm sales. Developments here, therefore, are interesting, and of some significance, but must not be overrated.

In numerous respects the pattern of farm economy in the *Pacific division* is different, although it does share, over large and important areas, the aridity problems that characterize the Mountain States. For physical, technical and economic reasons, however, the land in the Pacific division can be farmed much more intensively than in the other western States. Thus, from a much smaller total area in farms and in crops, the Pacific division farmer achieves a far greater total output, by value, of a much wider range of farm products. Further, within an overall expansion of farm sales, the Pacific division has experienced the more significant alterations of direction (Figure 26). In particular, the relative contribution of 'livestock and products' has advanced sharply and field-crop production moderately, while fruit production has notably decreased in relative stature. These major themes find echoes throughout, but considerable differences of emphasis exist among the States. Here we shall simply separate the division into northern (Washington and Oregon) and southern

153

(California) components, but California alone accounts for over three quarters of the value of farm products sold by the whole division. In California, too, changes in patterns of production have also been more marked.

In the north the outstanding position of field-crop farming comes principally from wheat, by far the major crop in Washington. Output here has multiplied tenfold since the war, aided by the security afforded by government support programmes, farm-settlement schemes on land newly irrigated by Columbia river waters and by increasing yields, especially in the famous Palouse area of eastern Washington. The average yield in the State, 40 bushels per acre in 1968, is the highest among all major wheat-producing States. In value, hay normally follows wheat in Washington, ranks first in Oregon and second again in California. The high and much increased status of hay obviously reflects the rapid advance of livestock farming. In California, however, the major expanding interest in field-crop production has been cotton. Grown under irrigation, chiefly in the south of the Central Valley, it gives phenomenal yields. In recent years over 1,000 pounds per acre was being achieved *on average* in California – about twice the national yield and matched only in Arizona. In 1945 under 4 per cent of the total US output of cotton originated in California. In 1968 the State supplied 14 per cent, although it had only 2 per cent of the nation's commercial cotton farms and harvested under 7 per cent of the nation's cotton acreage.

While such developments have raised the relative status of field crops in the Pacific division generally, a much sharper increase has been experienced in 'livestock and products' farming which, since the war, has practically doubled its proportional contribution to the total value of farm sales in this division (see Figure 26). Considerable numbers of sheep still graze here, especially in northern California, but, as elsewhere, sheep farming has declined. Beef-cattle production has made the great advance, and cattle sales now provide the largest single source of farm income in both California and Oregon and rank second or third, according to seasonal experiences, in Washington. Cattle *not* kept for milk numbered 3·3 million head in the Pacific division in 1945, but nearly 7 million in 1968, a response to changing market demand, with consequent substantial alteration in the general patterns of farm production.

One important general development in beef farming, in which California has been prominent, has been the growth of large-scale feedlot operations, concentrating on producing 'choice' meat. This development also affects the Mountain States (especially Arizona and Colorado) and other areas of the USA, but may be conveniently treated here. The large-scale feedlot handles over 1,000 head of cattle (some operators have capacities of 15,000 or more) and benefits from the normal economies of scale. Specialization brings advantages of lower labour costs per unit, ability to use advanced high-capacity equipment, the spreading of management and capital overheads, and economies in the purchase of cattle feed. Such cost savings have enabled operators to invade the market at the expense of the more traditional, smaller-scale, farmer-feeder. Thus, by the late 1960s the large-scale feedlot operators accounted for only about 1 per cent of all beef producers in the USA, but for nearly a half of fat cattle sold. California pioneered this type of operation, and offers obvious advantages. Adequate supplies of reasonably priced feedstuffs are vital to such enterprises, and California has such supplies in by-products from cotton, sugar-beet and citrus-fruit farms. This has permitted producers to capitalize upon the avid demand for quality beef which, in California, has had the additional stimulation of rapid population growth.

Within the product mix, room for increasing field crops and livestock and products has been made chiefly by decline in the relative position of fruit and nut farming. The relative status of dairy and poultry products, especially the former, has also declined somewhat. The number of milk cows has diminished in the Pacific division, as in the USA as a whole, but this has been more than offset by increased productivity per animal. Over all, the demand for milk has not risen commensurately with the rise in population, but the population expansion has been enough to prevent dairy products from slipping noticeably in their relative contribution to farm sales. Thus the fruit-farming sector has been the most affected in status by the advances discussed above.

In 1945, fruit and nuts provided one third of all farm sales in the

155

Pacific division, but in 1964 under one fifth. This change, however, is only *relative*. The fruit sector has expanded considerably since the war, but less than the 'livestock and product' or field-crop sectors. California was already the major national source of many kinds of fruits in 1945, and since then US per capita fruit consumption has declined. Neither condition is a good base from which to achieve a startling expansion of output; nevertheless the situation in this division, in which almost one fifth of all farm sales originate in the fruit sector, still has no parallel elsewhere. California, by virtue of its climate, is outstanding. It alone contributed 44 per cent of the value of fruit and nuts sold by US farms in 1964, and currently it ranks first in output of peaches, pears, grapes, plums, prunes and lemons. The northern Pacific States, however, are not negligible in this respect. Washington apples are famous and the State is the largest grower in the nation; Oregon is the largest producer of sweet cherries and is second to California for pears.

Vegetable production, too, is more important in this division than in any other. Over 40 per cent of national farm sales of vegetables originate here. Washington and Oregon have a very large output of broccoli, peas and beans, but California alone accounts for over a third of national vegetable sales. Scientific tomato cultivation is especially prominent, tomatoes coming third after cattle and dairy produce as a source of farm income in the State. California, however, is notable in many other vegetables: out of 29 major vegetable crops California is the leading producer State of no fewer than 16.

Clearly this division has a very wide range of farm activity, a feature contrasting sharply with the pattern for the Mountain division. The common dependence on irrigation, however, needs emphasis. The total irrigated area has advanced considerably since the war (Figure 19, p. 115) and over the whole Pacific division the 10·4 million acres of irrigated land in farms in 1964 comprised 53 per cent of cropland used for crops. While the irrigated lands of Washington and Oregon are of enormous significance to those States, in California the role of irrigation is quite outstanding. At the 1964 Census California was recorded as having some 81,000 farms of all kinds, some 60,000 of which had irrigated land in that year. This implies very heavy investment of both public and private funds. The response is seen in the intensity of farming, in the application of advanced techniques, equipment and managerial expertise, and in the unusually high yields per acre and per man. To summarize the position for the Golden State alone: in 1964 the average Californian farm was valued at $215,000 compared with $51,000 for the US as a whole, and this State, with some 3·3 per cent of all land in farms, accounted for 10 per cent of the national value of farm products sold.

In the *Southern region* the rate of increase in farm sales since 1945 has compared well with that for the West, and considerably surpassed the national average. Yet, under various indices, we have shown the region to be in a relatively poor position. In essence, of course, the superior post-war growth rate rests on the very low levels from which the region began. In 1945 the South had 40 per cent of the nation's land in farms and 48 per cent of farm employment, but provided under 29 per cent of the value of farm products sold. Southern agriculture could, then, go hardly anywhere but up. Twenty years later the proportion of the nation's farm land in the South had fallen to 31 per cent, and the proportion of farm employment to 42 per cent; but the region provided 30 per cent of national farm sales. These figures conceal momentous developments, with massive farm abandonment, millions of jobs lost, and major changes in land use and in social and economic affairs generally. This is inevitably reflected in the agricultural patterns, our immediate concern. Naturally, too, there have been major differences in experience both among and within the three Southern divisions, but here we are considering the broad position, as distinct from local experiences.

Figure 26 shows that in all three Southern divisions, field crops have declined in relative importance, and that all branches of livestock farming have increased, often dramatically. This changed balance marks the most important aspect of the improvements in the use of land and in the farm economy generally. Rotation systems and livestock–crop combinations have become more characteristic of southern farming, and much more land is under grass. More farm land, too, is under forest cover, and this benefits not only the land and drainage systems but, more widely, new industrial development. Ownership patterns have also changed, possession of the land being increasingly vested in the operator. Restrictive tenancy conditions, especially share-cropping, are less common than they were, and 80 per cent of the (albeit far fewer) southern farmers are now owner-operators or part owner-operators. This makes for increasing care for the land being farmed and greater willingness to adopt methods suitable to local physical conditions. Southern agriculture has also, belatedly, become more mechanized. In 1945, for example, there were still 5 million horses and mules working, and needing to be fed, on southern farms. Under half a million tractors were in use, only a fifth of the national total in an area with twice that proportion of the nation's land in farms. By 1964 there were over three times as many (nearly 30 per cent of the US total) working on 10 per cent fewer acres. This has been both effect and cause of the migration of millions from farm communities, a migration undoubtedly beneficial to the farm economy.

Within the diminished role of field crops, a very large decline in cotton acreage and production is most important. This experience is common to every southern State, but variations in the intensity of the experience have produced a major readjustment in the location of important cotton-growing areas. This may be illustrated by dividing the cotton-growing South into eastern, central and western areas. The eastern area (North and South Carolina, Georgia, Alabama) produced 27 per cent of national cotton output before the Second World War, but only 9 per cent in 1967. Over large areas of the old Cotton Belt here, and especially in the Carolinas, it is now difficult to find a field in cotton, and in none of these States did cotton rank, in 1967, among the four principal commodities for farm cash receipts. The central area (Mississippi, Tennessee, Arkansas and Louisiana) now grows cotton chiefly in the vicinity of the Mississippi river and its tributaries. Although in each State (as in all other southern States) total cotton acreages have sharply declined, some new areas have been drained and put under cotton since the war. Such developments, together with improved cotton plants, mechanical methods and better farming practices, have sustained this area in relative importance. Before the war one third of US cotton was grown here. By 1967 the proportion had fallen only mildly to 29 per cent. None the less, as in the east, cotton has been greatly demoted as a source of farm income. Mississippi stands alone here (and in the USA) in having cotton as its largest source of farm income. In none of the remaining three central States does cotton nowadays rank among the top four farm commodities sold. In the western South, by contrast, the industry has advanced in standing – 30 per cent of pre-war national output, 40 per cent in 1967. This area embraces both Texas and Oklahoma, but the latter has also experienced a greater than average rate of decline, leaving Texas, especially the Texas High Plains, responsible for the advancing relative position of the western South. Here, beyond the old cotton belt, cotton is grown under irrigation on very large farms. Yields are moderate, but advanced mechanical and scientific methods make the labour input very small and the crop highly profitable under government-support conditions.

This reference to irrigation in Texas cotton farming leads conveniently to a brief aside on irrigation generally in the post-war South. From 1944 to 1964 total irrigated land in farms in Texas rose by 5 million acres. This represents 30 per cent of the total national increase in irrigated area. Texas now follows California pretty closely in total area of irrigated land (Figure 19, p. 115). The availability of ground water for well irrigation at reasonable cost and the security and aid afforded by the Federal farm programmes have been important elements in this expansion, while a prolonged period of drought increased the desire to tap assured water supplies. Arkansas also solidly, if less strikingly, increased its irrigated area, and the West South Central division as a whole contained 85 per cent of all irrigated land on southern farms in 1964. Obviously, the need is greater in the sub-humid or semi-arid West, but the value of irrigation in more humid conditions is well illustrated by Florida. This State has $1\frac{1}{4}$ million acres under irrigation, 1 million of them having been added since 1944. Fruit and vegetable crops have been shown to benefit greatly here from scientific water management. The effective use of water often also necessitates adequate provision for drainage, and drainage schemes have contributed significantly to improved agricultural practice in many irrigated areas. In addition fertile new acres can sometimes be obtained by draining land subject permanently or sporadically to waterlogging. In the South considerable

159

effort has gone into drainage schemes since the war, and, although detailed statistics have not been gathered, it appears that by 1960 the South had nearly 30 million acres of land in drainage projects – nearly one third of all land drained and used for agriculture in the USA.

The decline of cotton has clearly caused a sharp diminution in the status of field crops in the pattern of farming in the South, but a fair proportion of the land once annually committed to cotton now produces other crops, and field crops as a whole retain a more important place than in other regions (Figure 26). Corn remains important, but less so than formerly. Corn was widely grown in the South as part of the established cotton-based economy, providing food for cotton workers and feed for animals, especially horses and mules. In the late 1930s a third of the national corn acreage harvested was in the South, indicating its significance there, but only a fifth of national corn production was obtained, indicating the poor quality of the farming. Indeed, the method of corn tillage contributed considerably to the grave problems of soil erosion in the region. Since the war, techniques of planting and cultivating have greatly improved and new, more productive, strains of corn are used. Considerably fewer acres, however, are put under this crop, especially in the two South Central divisions, where the output of corn has greatly declined in the past two decades. The South has gained more than most from the decline in the numbers of work horses and mules on the farm.

Corn is often joined by other crops, notably soybeans and hay, in rotation systems connected with livestock farming. The expansion of soybean production has been remarkable in practically every southern State in recent years, and soybean is significant in the farm economy everywhere except in Florida, and in the extreme western States where climate has rather favoured expansion of irrigated sorghum for grain and forage. Numerous crops (e.g. alfalfa, clover, timothy, other grasses, lespedeza and grains) are harvested for hay, many being very beneficial to the soil. Hay production is emphasized in the South Central divisions, where output has risen by over 25 per cent since the war, despite a small decline in acreage.

Another traditional crop still outstandingly important is tobacco.

US tobacco acreages have declined sharply since the war, but the growing of higher-yielding varieties and improvement of farming practices have raised yields equally sharply. Between 1939 and 1967 tobacco acreage was halved and yield per acre doubled. Tobacco is grown widely in the South Atlantic and East South Central divisions, which together produce over 90 per cent of national output, but the really significant producing areas are quite limited. North Carolina and Kentucky alone produced 63 per cent of American tobacco in 1967, and South Carolina, Georgia, Virginia and Tennessee complete the list of major producers. In tobacco, therefore, there has been relatively little change in the traditional geographical patterns, but the advances in technique and yield and the decrease in the damage done to the land by this exhausting crop are noteworthy.

While we have no room for details about all developments of interest and significance, we must mention three other crops, occupying relatively small areas, in which the South possesses a virtual monopoly of production in conterminous USA. In peanuts, often grown in rotation with the major crops discussed above, acreages have dropped from the peak of the late 1940s, but here, too, with more than commensurate advances in yields, production reached record levels by the late 1960s. The major areas of commercial production lie on the coastal plains from south-eastern Virginia to south-eastern Alabama, with Georgia outstanding. In central Texas and southern Oklahoma is another expanding area of peanut cultivation. Rice is another southern speciality, grown in steadily expanding quantities in two major areas, the Gulf Coast on both sides of the Texas–Louisiana border, and the low, irrigated lands west of the Mississippi river in Arkansas. Production is large-scale, highly mechanized, and in many respects similar to that in the only other rice-producing area, in California.

The third and last of these special crops of the South is sugar cane, another traditional southern crop which has grown in significance since the war. Production, understandably in view of climatic requirements, is even more restricted geographically than rice. Louisiana and Florida are the sole producers, with activities in the former confined to the Mississippi delta area and, in the latter, largely to the Everglades area south-east of Tampa. Both the area

161

and the output of sugar cane have risen since the war, chiefly in Florida, where yields are higher and the influx of Cubans has had some influence. The delta area suffers more from climatic problems (especially the occasional 'cold snap'). Despite its high efficiency, however, this industry can exist in the USA only with protection.

The expanded output of several of the field crops mentioned above clearly is connected with the general growth of livestock interests. The large areas of land in farms devoted, wholly or in part, to pasturage also point to the importance of the modern livestock economy. At the 1964 Census, the total area in farms in the South classified as (a) cropland used only for pasture (b) open permanent pasture and (c) pastured forest and woodland amounted to 60 per cent of all land in farms. The comparable proportion for conterminous USA was 57 per cent. The average is, of course, raised by the exceptional position of Texas, with some 78 per cent of farm land pastured, and of Oklahoma and Florida, with two thirds. In every State, however, this use of farm land is important and, in addition, considerable areas of non-farm land are grazed. Not only have individual farmers transferred land from cash crops to pasture. Programmes of road and trackway construction have made large areas of hitherto unused, or under-used, land accessible, while land improvement and reclamation schemes, notably marshland drainage, have further increased the acreages. All such developments have had generous support from Federal sources under the conservation programmes since 1936. On the other hand, considerable areas of poor-quality and eroded pasture land have been put under, or allowed to revert to, woodland.

The impressive expansion of livestock farming in the South shows in the fact that in 1945 the region contributed 18 per cent of total US farm sales of *all* livestock and products (i.e. including dairy and poultry products), but in 1964, 24 per cent. Total US farm sales of these products rose by almost 120 per cent over the period (measured in current dollars); in the South by 190 per cent. Different branches of livestock farming, however, show greatly differing rates of growth. In 1945, for example, the South accounted for a quarter of all sales of poultry and poultry products in the USA, in 1964 more than a half, a remarkable advance. Against this the performance of other branches

162

appears less impressive, but should not be underrated, especially as significant advance had often been made by 1945. By that year, the South accounted for 15 and 17·5 per cent of US farm sales of dairy products and 'other livestock and products' respectively, and this rose further to 19 and 18·5 per cent in 1964. Over all, therefore, the South has made considerable gains and has become a more significant area in US cattle farming.

Within the cattle industry of the South, the emphasis has shifted markedly in favour of beef herds. Total cattle population has risen (26 million head in 1945; 36 million in 1968), but, whereas in 1945 milk cows had been 30 per cent of the total, by 1968 they were a mere 10 per cent, having declined both relatively and absolutely. This decline has been more than offset by increased dairy farming efficiency, so that in 1964 dairy products in the South as a whole provided the same proportion of farm income as in 1945. At the divisional level the situation varies, of course (Figure 26), but everywhere this branch of farming remains less important than in the nation as a whole. The failure to make greater headway is probably attributable to marketing problems. Over great areas this region lacks the very large urban centres that would stimulate demand for fresh dairy produce, while big national surpluses of butter and cheese also help to discourage this side of dairy market development, especially when more lucrative opportunities exist in other branches of livestock farming.

The beef industry, by contrast, has been greatly stimulated by a combination of strong demand and technical advance. The former has already been discussed, but the latter has permitted the South to do better than hold its own in this growing sector of the livestock business. The carrying capacity of southern pastures has been greatly raised by improved grasses and intensive fertilization, while the animal itself has been improved by careful cross-breeding of British and Indian stock. In these ways, beef yield per acre has been more than quadrupled, more beasts being carried and more meat being obtained from each. Between 1945 and 1968 total cattle not kept for milk rose from 18 to 32 million head in the South. This being so, greater increases by 'livestock and products' to the farm sales income of the three Southern divisions might perhaps have been expected (Figure 26). The advance is general in the South, but is nowhere remarkable and nowhere does the contribution of 'livestock and product' sales even approximate to the national average. The issue is clarified by referring to the other forms of livestock in this general category. Sheep and lambs have declined sharply in the USA since the war, but even more markedly in the South. Texas still has the largest flocks of sheep in the USA, but numbers fell by over a half between 1945 and 1968. The numbers of pigs have fluctuated but, generally, less of the national population is found in the Southern divisions than formerly. Such experiences have adversely affected the figures for the 'livestock and products' sector of the farm economy in the South, within which, nevertheless, beef cattle farming has advanced remarkably.

Figure 26 suggests that 'livestock and products' farming increases in significance from east to west. In the South Atlantic division the contribution remains far below the national average. Here the beef industry of central Florida is perhaps noteworthy, deriving useful feed from local citrus-fruit processing plant. Considerable herds are also found in every East South Central State, and livestock now accounts for nearly one fifth of farm sales. Cattle rank among the top three sources of farm income in each State in this division, and the importance to Mississippi and central Alabama of the growth of the industry has often been stressed. In the West South Central division Oklahoma and Texas are outstanding. Indeed Texas continues to run the largest cattle business in the country, having in 1968 over half again as many cattle not kept for milk as the second-ranking State, Iowa. Not surprisingly Texas, too, has developed the very large commercial feedlot, as described for the Pacific division. Government policies to control wheat and cotton acreage left land free for feed-grain production. In Texas this has permitted a great expansion of grain sorghum output, which, with cotton seed cake, provides nutritious feed for the beef herds. Over all, then, but especially in the two South Central divisions, beef cattle farming has made contributions both directly and indirectly to the revolution in southern agriculture.

In growth rates, however, it is the poultry side of the livestock business in the South that has expanded most since the war. Poultry keeping had long been characteristic of southern farming, partly because the local diet had traditionally favoured poultry meat (nowadays Southern Fried Chicken appears on menus throughout the States, and beyond) and partly because chickens could scratch up a living pretty well unaided. Now innumerable specialized chicken houses with scientific aids speed millions of young chicks to an acceptable weight and (more hopefully) flavour. Such highly specialized, large-scale, commercial poultry farming is comparatively new in the southern landscape. By 1964 over half of all US farm sales of poultry and poultry products originated in the South, and this had become a key sector of agriculture over considerable areas. In the South as a whole by 1964 some 15 per cent of total farm cash income was derived from the poultry sector, compared with about 9 per cent in 1945, but there are important differences among the divisions (Figure 26). In the South Atlantic division about one fifth of farm cash income came from poultry, in the West South Central division about one tenth. Within divisions, too, commercial production is remarkably concentrated. The Delmarva peninsula on the northern margins of the South Atlantic division, for example, has a very famous poultry speciality, which has been long established. More recently another, extremely large, poultry area has emerged in northern Georgia, possibly the most intensive areal specialization of this kind in the nation, concentrating chiefly on production of broilers. The South Central divisions also have areas of some considerable concentration, as in northern Alabama and north-western Arkansas, illustrating the widespread significance of poultry to farming in the modern South.

Of other farm product sales identified in Figure 26 we mention only the fruit farming and the vegetable–horticultural specialities in the South Atlantic division. Over one tenth of total cash income of farms here is derived from fruits, and a rather smaller proportion from the vegetable and horticultural specialities. Most of such production is, however, in Florida, with a secondary area of concentration in Delmarva. Even in a broad review of this kind, the special performance of Florida is worth considering, for it has made a profound impression on the markets for such farm products, to the consternation of some Californian farm interests. In fruit production, oranges are outstanding, now providing the largest single source of farm incomes in Florida and by far surpassing the orange output of California. California oranges admittedly make good fresh eating and may fairly claim to have no rival, but this has not been the growing end of the market. Florida oranges are better for processing – canning, concentrating, freezing – and frozen concentrated orange juice has become a most important product in Florida. The post-war output graph began in 1945 at half a million gallons, rose to about 30 millions in 1950 and reached 84 millions in 1960, around which level it has since fluctuated. Florida, again, is by far the largest producer of grapefruit, although, compared with oranges, the crop is small. The State also produces heavily for the fresh vegetable market. Here it ranks second to California, though some distance behind, gaining the market advantage, like California, by producing vegetables which are 'out of season' in the highly populated northern States. Specialities are tomatoes and beans, but others such as sweet corn, cucumbers and water melons are significant locally.

It is clear, then, that changes in southern agriculture have been substantial and far-reaching. This is reflected in the leading commodity in farm cash receipts in each of the sixteen southern States. Whereas in 1945 a field crop (usually cotton or tobacco) provided the largest source of farm income in most States, by 1967 the leading position was taken by cattle in five States, by broiler chickens in three, and by dairy products in two. Tobacco retained its leadership in three, but cotton lint only in Mississippi. The remaining two States had oranges and soybeans as their largest source of farm cash income. While, however, these developments have been so significant as to demand this extensive treatment, the region as a whole nevertheless still remains below standard in its farming. Southern farmers, on average, are less prosperous than farmers elsewhere, as has been demonstrated. Although there is still a large 'poor white' farm population in the South, the regional average is dragged down chiefly by conditions on Negro farms. Reports of the Civil Rights Commission in 1965 showed that the improvements had been pretty well confined to the white farms. In various ways, subtle and unsubtle, accidental and deliberate, the Federal resources available for

166

farm improvement, in the broadest sense, had been channelled chiefly to the whites, thus widening the gap between white and Negro farm families. The increase in average farm size in the South is one sign of improvement. The Commission's *Report* of 1965 showed, however, that while between 1950 and 1959 the average white farm size rose from 175 to 249 acres, the average Negro farm increased only from 42 to 52 acres. Over this period, therefore, the actual gap between the two sectors grew greater, and trends were similar for family income and domestic amenities. This backward and under-privileged sector of the farm community is found over much of the South, but there are also special areas where farming and farm standards of living, both for Negro and for white, are quite grossly below standard. Mississippi, which ranks last among the States by almost any index of material well-being, is an example. In sum, the transformation of southern agriculture as sketched above is a move-ment in progress, rather than a triumph completed.

While the Western and Southern regions have both, for different reasons, experienced growth rates far above average in farm sales since the war, the *North-East region* fell correspondingly far behind. Nationally, the value of farm sales rose by 117 per cent between 1945 and 1964, but in the North-East only by 73 per cent, and the region has continued along a long established trend of decline in the relative significance of its farm activity. The reasons are straightforward. In this region, isolated from the interior of the continent and from Europe, early settlement and agrarian development raised agricul-ture to a relative status appropriate only to a closed economy. Effective competition from the developing interior in the nineteenth century, especially in the staple foods, brought about an early diminution of the status of agriculture and a redirection of activity. The process continued this century and into the post-war years, affecting both staple and non-staple crops, thus applying con-tinuous pressure to north-eastern farmers either to get out of farming there or to seek products in which some advantages still endured. These pressures have been augmented by the expansion of massive urban-industrial interests which have affected farm areas, activities and population, as described above. Inevitably output from farms has not expanded here as rapidly as elsewhere.

The North-East is, therefore, a region which, while housing one quarter of the nation's population at the 1964 Census of Agriculture, accounted for only 7·3 per cent of total farm output by value. To infer that north-eastern agriculture is in a poor condition, however, would be mistaken. Indices introduced earlier showed the average New England farmer, for example, in a rather superior position. The income per commercial farm unit amounted to about $28,000 in 1967, 36 per cent higher than the US average, and exceeded only in the Pacific and Mountain divisions. The North-East in fact uses relatively little of its resources these days for producing foods. Others can do this more effectively. What it does spare for this purpose, however, is in the main pretty intensively used in specialized and profitable ways. The 7·3 per cent of the national value of farm product sales originating in the North-East in 1964 came from under 3 per cent of total farm land.

The high density of population and the presence of large metropolitan complexes give an immediate clue to the appropriate patterns of farm activity for this region, and Figure 26 illustrates the structure of output in both the Middle Atlantic and New England divisions. The livestock side is heavily emphasized, and, of the three major classes of livestock products identified on the diagram, dairy produce is outstanding. No other region shows anything like this intensity of specialization in dairying, and in every State of this region save Maine (where potatoes rank first) dairy produce is the principal commodity sold. Milk cows in the region are normally fed a high proportion of purchased commercial concentrates and yields per cow are everywhere above the national average, rising to 10,300 pounds of milk per cow in New Jersey, compared with 8,500 nationally. The stimulus to the specialization in fluid milk production afforded by the giant metropolitan markets needs no emphasis.

Similar stimulus is afforded to other sections of the livestock business. Poultry and products contribute much more than normally to farm sales. Indeed, in New England their contribution is higher than in any other division. (This high proportional position, however, relates to a relatively small total value of farm output in this division, and the New England poultry industry is, absolutely, only a fraction of the size of that in the South.) Production of broilers has

168

grown, but in 1967 the North-East still provided only 6 per cent of total national broiler production by weight. The north-eastern poultry farmer really specializes in the production of eggs, providing some 14 per cent of national output. Eggs follow dairy produce in cash receipts in five of the nine States of the region.

Further, as befits a farm economy with a huge market on its door-step, the contribution of vegetables and specialities is considerable. Because of the effective post-war challenge in the 'fresh vegetable' sector from California and Florida, emphasis is diverted to local horticultural specialities, which now provide a sizeable proportion of total farm income in several north-eastern States. These products (culinary delicacies, flowers, plants and shrubs) of high value, grown to serve the more affluent sections of the population, can bear the costs of relatively expensive land, of fertilizing soils of low natural fertility and of heavy labour inputs. Such activities, however, are chiefly concentrated on the coastal plains and do not affect large areas.

Finally, the North-East understandably shows less dependence on field crops than any other division. Hay production is a leading interest, connected with dairying. In New England the relative status of field crops is higher than in the Middle Atlantic division, princi-pally because of the large output of potatoes in Maine (second to Idaho in total production) and the tobacco speciality of the lower Connecticut Valley which, with unique conditions and methods, produces a relatively small crop of high-value varieties.

Thus both the relatively low position of farm activity and the pattern of farming in the North-East region today derive from technological advance, which has increased the effectiveness of com-petition in numerous farm commodities from far-distant areas. The pattern that remains, however, is in the main finely adjusted to the unique conditions of urban agglomeration and affluence in this part of the USA. This pattern, more than others, appears commercially sound, requiring little governmental intervention. Whereas in 1967 the Southern region received over 43 per cent of the massive 3 billion dollars of direct government payments to farmers, the North-East received under 2 per cent. Yet the average north-eastern farmer is more prosperous than most. Farm poverty is not unknown in the region, especially on the remoter hill farms of Appalachia and upper New England, but is proportionately less than in the USA generally, which indicates adjustment, at least in commercial terms, to the prevailing situation.

The last analysis of regional patterns of agriculture is of the *North Central region*, the most important of all regions in size and structure of agricultural activity. From 1945 to 1964 farm sales here rose by 111 per cent, slightly below the national rate and not impressive, perhaps, compared with the growth rates in the South and West. Unlike the South, however, farm communities here were not beginning the period from a low base level which could easily be improved upon and, unlike the West, they had little scope for expansion of farm area and the large-scale introduction of new and profitable lines. The stimulus experienced in the West from high population-growth rates was also missing, since there were already very large urban populations in pre-war years. None the less, the North Central region had the largest proportion of total US farm sales in 1964 (42 per cent), as it did in 1945 (43 per cent), and approximately maintaining the relative sales position of the region is itself quite remarkable considering the development potential of other areas of the country.

Over the region as a whole livestock farming ranks high, but is rather less predominant than formerly. In 1945 the sales of 'livestock and products' here amounted to 65 per cent of total US sales, by 1964, 59 per cent. The North Central contribution remains outstanding, but has declined relatively through the expansion of this type of agricultural activity in the West and South. Its relative position in national sales of dairy and poultry products has also declined. The former is a minor change, similar to that for 'livestock and products', but in poultry the region has not materially participated in the post-war rapid national expansion of production. The number of chickens raised on farms has declined much more than in the country as a whole, and the expansion of commercial broiler production has lagged far behind that elsewhere. North Central farmers have settled for a pattern in which the feeds they produce so efficiently are exported to major broiler-production locations, which offer other sets of advantages, and the regional demand for broiler chickens is met chiefly by 'imports'. This approach has affected the field-crop sector, and off-farm sales of field-crop products have risen very sharply. In 1945 the North Central region provided 35 per cent of the total sales of field crops in the USA, in 1964 40 per cent. This indicates the broad change in the balance of production, but patterns of output, and trends, differ greatly within the region itself. The region spans divers identifiable agricultural types and the divisional approach is less satisfactory here than elsewhere. No broad basis of regional division would be entirely satisfactory for this area, however, and we shall comment upon the structure in the East and the West North Central divisions separately.

The East North Central division contains much of the famous Corn Belt area (in western Ohio, Indiana and Illinois) and part of the Dairy Belt. Here all kinds of livestock and livestock products have declined in their proportional contribution to farm sales (Figure 26), to an extent that makes the situation quite remarkable. Field-crop production, by contrast, has risen in status and, by 1964, provided a considerably larger proportion of farm cash receipts than either 'livestock and products' or 'dairy products', the former leaders. Among the grain crops corn is outstanding; acreages harvested for grain have risen since the war. Developments of hybrid corn and in production technique have diminished the need for formerly common crop-rotation patterns, and much of the best land is kept pretty continuously under profitable corn. Production in 1968 was 76 per cent above that of 1945, with outstanding yields achieved in every State. Soybean acreage and production have also risen, especially in Ohio, Indiana and Illinois, chiefly at the expense of oats. Soybeans now normally exceed hay and wheat by value in those States. By such developments the East North Central division has quite remarkably altered the general structure of its farming. This is most striking in Illinois, at the heart of the Corn Belt, and dominating the farm economy of the division by accounting for over one third of all its farm product sales. In Illinois field crops contributed 37 per cent of total farm sales in 1945, in 1964 over a half.

The reasons for this unusual performance are complex. The natural repercussions of developments in other areas, the consequences of technological advance and the influence of Federal farm policies and practices are all involved. The highest returns to the expanding cattle-farming sector have been achieved with large-scale commercial feedlots. The larger such units are, the more profitable they are, and cattle farmers of this new type have, since the war, largely dominated the market. Such large-scale operations, however, have not proved very suitable for mid-western conditions. Land costs are high and the severe winter requires extensive, and expensive, provision of shelter. Thus stock farmers in this division have been under some pressure at a time when meat prices have been falling. On the other hand, various advances have raised yet further the already high crop-production potential of this area. New farming systems, new seeds and new chemical treatments enable the mid-western crop farmer to specialize more intensively and continuously on feed grains for sale. Yields have risen greatly and, as an extra bonus, farmers receive generous Federal payments and the comfort of price supports. So the crop farmer here has been able to raise his output faster than the stock farmer, thus advancing his relative position in the farm economy.

The emphasis on this interesting development must not obscure the tremendous absolute contribution still made by livestock farming in this division. The total value of farm sales is very great and, despite the decline in their relative status within the division, the combined sales value of the 'livestock and product' and 'dairy product' sectors here exceeds the total value of *all* farm sales in four of the remaining eight geographical divisions. Large numbers of cattle are still bred, or purchased for fattening, and the intensity of this activity increases westwards, being especially important in Illinois and Wisconsin. The rearing and fattening of hogs also retains its high significance here. Illinois and Indiana alone had one fifth of the total US pig population in 1968, a rather higher proportion than formerly.

Both Michigan and Wisconsin have usually been considered as major portions of the 'hay and dairy' belt, but it is Wisconsin which nowadays shows the most remarkable concentration, for Michigan, conforming to the regional trend, has placed increased emphasis on grain farming, especially corn and wheat. Milk herds have been halved in Michigan since the war (a rate of decrease paralleling the national average), but have declined by under 20 per cent in Wisconsin. Wisconsin remains, then, by far the largest dairy State, with over 2 million milk cows in 1968, 15 per cent of the US total. The emphasis here is on the milk product rather than on liquid milk sales, by virtue of the distance from major markets and the competition of centres better placed for meeting fresh milk demand. None the less some 55 per cent of the cash receipts of Wisconsin farmers were derived from dairy products in 1964. This percentage was surpassed only by Vermont, where, however, actual production is but a fraction of that in Wisconsin, which can truly call itself the queen of dairy States.

The change in emphasis in farming from east to west in the East North Central division, with 'livestock and products' increasing in significance, continues into the West North Central States. Figure 26 indicates that, in this division as a whole, the contribution of field-crop sales to total farm incomes has only marginally increased but that, contrary to experience in the eastern division, the role of 'livestock and products' has increased sharply. As elsewhere in the region, however, the proportional contribution of poultry and dairy products to total sales has declined. A distinction must here be made between the eastern tier of States (Minnesota, Iowa and Missouri), where 'Corn Belt' farming dominates large areas, and the western tier (the Northern Plains States of North and South Dakota, Nebraska and Kansas), where Corn Belt practices fade gradually into a pattern more suited to the less favourable physical conditions, especially increasing aridity.

In the eastern tier, experiences have been similar in both kind and cause to those described for the East North Central division, if rather less emphatic. Field-crop sales have advanced and livestock-product sales have become less dominant. Cash sales of field crops in these three States in fact rose from 19 per cent of all farm sales in 1945 to 31 per cent in 1964. As in the neighbouring States to the east, corn acreages harvested for grain have risen slightly, chiefly by keeping the best areas continuously under corn. With increasing yields, corn-grain output has risen very steeply and provides the foremost crop in each of the States. Soybeans follow, again having expanded remarkably since the war, and then hay.

The 'livestock and product' and dairy-farming interest, however, remain very large in this part of the West North Central division. Dairying is strongest in Minnesota, in the western margins of which State the old 'hay and dairy' belt terminates. In 1968, with over one million milk cows, Minnesota was still second to Wisconsin in size of dairy herds, and has similar marketing outlets. Minnesota, however, also has large numbers of other cattle which, as in Iowa and Missouri, provide the largest single source of cash income for farmers in the State. Iowa, however, is the outstanding beef and hog State. 'Livestock and product' sales from Iowa alone accounted for 14 per cent of the US total in 1964, a proportion almost twice as high as that for the next-ranking State, Nebraska. In numbers of cattle not kept for milk Iowa follows Texas, but in hogs Iowa excels, having over one quarter of the national total. In this State, then, the modern Corn Belt pattern of farming is seen at its peak of development, although the geographical 'heart' of the Corn Belt also embraces much of neighbouring Illinois. Iowa's very large feeding and fattening interests make cattle and hogs first and second respectively as sources of farm cash income, but its growing output of corn (440 million bushels of grain in 1945, 900 million in 1968) is also reflected in cash sales, so that corn ranks third for cash receipts. The adoption of soybeans as a major Corn Belt crop since the war is also demonstrated here. Output rose from only 35 million bushels in 1945 to 178 million in 1968. This beef, hog, corn, soybean pattern is very much in tune with current patterns of demand, and makes maximum use of the outstanding agricultural potential of this area. (In adjacent Illinois the rank order is corn, hogs, cattle, soybeans; and in Indiana hogs, corn, soybeans, cattle, demonstrating the essential symmetry of the basic Corn Belt pattern.) Not surprisingly, then, Iowa ranks second only to California in total value of output of farm products, but its interests are far more highly specialized.

In the neighbouring western tier of States, the Northern Plains area, the range of important farm products is even less. Dairy and poultry sales accounted for only 7 per cent of farm income in 1964 (14 per cent in 1945); the rest is provided by 'livestock and products' and field crops in an approximate ratio of 6 to 4. This balance again represents a sharp post-war alteration, but of opposite direction to that elsewhere in the North Central region. The contribution of field-crop sales to total farm income fell from 1945 to 1964, whereas the 'livestock and products' contribution rose sharply. Beef cattle have become the prime source of farm income in all the States except North Dakota, where wheat retains leadership. A considerable pig population and the numerous fields under corn are evidence that the Corn Belt does not terminate abruptly at the western boundaries of Iowa and Missouri, and that similar patterns of farming characterize adjacent parts of these Northern Plains States. This is especially true of eastern Nebraska, where the general structure of farming closely resembles that of Iowa. But changing climate and soil conditions gradually assert themselves. Corn yields in these western States are usually below the national average, whereas to the east they are invariably above. Further west, except in irrigated areas, as around the Platte river, increasing aridity forces a change of pattern and range livestock rearing becomes dominant in western Nebraska and South Dakota. To the north and south are the great wheat areas, covering much of Kansas and North Dakota. Wheat remains the crop most likely to produce an acceptable income in these climatic conditions, especially with price support. Dry-farming techniques are widely used, except in the moister eastern margins and in irrigated areas, and crops are usually taken on alternate years. Yields fluctuate considerably from year to year and area to area according to conditions of water supply, but normally fall below the national average. None the less, with large farm units, and very large total wheat acreages, these two States rank first and second respectively as wheat producers. Together in 1968 they supplied 30 per cent of national production. Nebraska and South Dakota together add a further 10 per cent, making this Northern Plains area outstanding for this major food grain.

Clearly, the structure of farming alters considerably as one moves from east to west through the North Central region. Patterns suited to the humid east have less appeal and less validity in the sub-humid or semi-arid west. Farm size also increases steadily towards the west, reflecting the change in physical conditions. Nevertheless the major theme of farming in this region as a whole is feed-grain production and associated livestock feeding. Of the major feed crops of grain corn, oats and soybeans, the North Central region accounted for 88,

86 and 73 per cent respectively of US production in 1968. Among livestock, it contained 43 per cent of all non-dairy cattle, and 78 per cent of hogs. Additionally, 56 per cent of all wheat, and large proportions of other farm products ignored in this survey, are also generated here. Clearly, the role of this area in United States agriculture is outstanding.

Conclusion

This analysis of regional patterns of agriculture has obvious weaknesses. Some result from our dealing only with major features and trends. Thus many facets of farming in sub-regions and smaller areas have been ignored, and readers desiring a profounder study of regional agriculture should consult the recommendations for further reading. Other defects arise from using Census divisions instead of agricultural regions, for Census division boundaries do not fit well the boundaries of validly defined agricultural regions. The geographical divisions used, however, do embrace large areas within which the patterns, problems and opportunities of agriculture present a basis for coherent discussion. The major exception, although a very important one, was the North Central region, which contains the whole or part of several of the most prominent agricultural regions, specifically defined. The whole Corn Belt, much of the hay and dairy belt, most of the spring and the winter wheat belts, parts of the general farming region, and several smaller agricultural areas, such as the fruit, truck and speciality areas east of Lake Michigan and south of Lake Erie: all are found within the East and the West North Central divisions. This clearly presents serious obstacles to such a brief analysis as we have attempted.

It seems appropriate, therefore, to close this treatment of the agricultural sector by referring to the major types of farming regions, as currently recognized by the US Department of Agriculture (Figure 27). The map of these regions is well known to students of geography. In general it closely resembles O. E. Baker's map compiled in the 1920s, despite fundamental changes in the character and organization of the industry and in the regional structures of

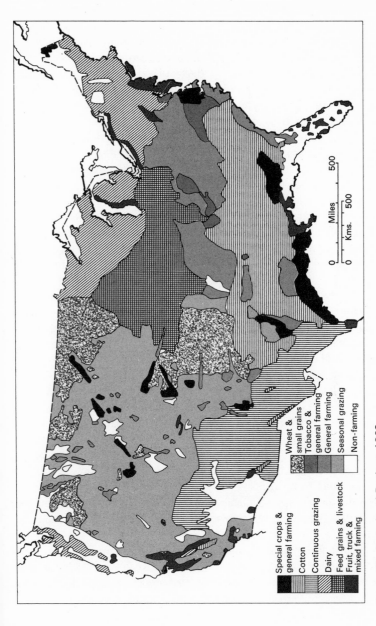

Special crops &
general farming

Cotton

Continuous grazing

Dairy

Feed grains & livestock

Fruit, truck &
mixed farming

Wheat &
small grains

Tobacco &
general farming

General farming

Seasonal grazing

Non-farming

Miles

Kms.

0   500

0   500

Figure 27. Agricultural Regions, 1968

farm activity since that time. The broad patterns at the time of Baker's major study bore definite and tested relationships both to physical constraints and possibilities and to economic opportunities. Major adjustments to earlier patterns of agricultural land use had already been made and, although serious maladjustment still existed in places, the broad regions of Baker's time were the end result of long decades of trial and error. Marion Clawson has identified a threefold, though overlapping, sequence in the development of agricultural land use in the United States:* extension of area, sorting of uses, intensification of activity. The third phase has generally been in progress since the First World War, and we might thus expect broad similarities of pattern to remain. None the less the type and the structure of farming have changed in many vital ways, following developments in production systems and mechanisms, marketing methods, patterns of demand and governmental intervention. Thus the situation in an 'intensification' phase remains dynamic and, within the broad fields of agricultural 'specialization' (which permits the defining of regions), it is clear that continuity does not prohibit change.

The specialization that gives a name to most major types of farming region, of course, rarely has been a consequence of one-product farming. The classification represents an attempt to summarize the chief characteristics of farming in the area concerned. Profitable farm operation, which involves the fullest utilization of labour, machinery and equipment, favours, where possible, a certain diversity of activity, and such diversity at the farm level is reflected in overall regional patterns. Any superior opportunities offered by one or two specific lines of activity in a given area, however, must also be reflected in a regional emphasis illustrated by the statistics, enabling a valid label to be attached. Even at the broad divisional level, the differing emphases of farming activity in different parts of the country was evident, but so also was the real complexity of the total pattern.

The foregoing analysis showed that established regional patterns are not inviolable, but gradually evolve. Regional specializations themselves may change, although the process is slow because of

* See *Land for Americans*, 1963, pp. 61 ff.

established interests, investments, contacts and culture. Geographical inertia characterizes agrarian, as well as manufacturing, regions. Historical studies show, however, that regional specialization has changed in the past, and the process continues, if for rather different reasons. One major current illustration, mentioned above, is the Cotton Belt. Traditional patterns of cotton cultivation here have undergone erosion for three decades or more. The process is not yet complete but Baker's Belt has been irreparably broken. New forms of activity are represented on the map by the expanded area of 'truck and special crops' and 'general farming', and there are other local specializations, as in the poultry area of northern Georgia, not shown. Such developments, and the changing balance of production of other commercial farms, with cotton playing a decreasing role, have shrunk the specialist cotton areas. The term 'Cotton Belt' is no longer really valid for this part of the country, although its use draws attention to the region's special problems. What term can replace it is less certain. The evolutionary processes in US agriculture appear to be generally towards patterns of increasing diversity and complexity rather than towards specialized monocultures. Already in many parts the pattern is so complex, embracing so many intermediate systems and end products that it defies labelling, and becomes 'general farming' in the classificatory system. As such conditions spread, which they will, new methods and forms of agricultural regionalization will have to be found. At present, however, there still remains enough inter-regional distinctiveness to permit a classification of types of farming regions based on one or more major end products.

Despite the facts of increasing complexity and diversity of agricultural patterns, highly specialized forms of agriculture may be practised by farms and by geographical areas. Poultry farming provides an illustration. Most modern poultry-meat producers concentrate their activity in broiler houses which, although producing scores of thousands of broilers, cover relatively small areas. They buy in much, if not all, of their poultry feed, and market with big, brand-named firms – which may also provide the chicks. Such individual units are obviously very highly specialized. Similar farm-unit specialization is demonstrated by the large-scale commercial

179

feedlot discussed earlier. Over relatively small geographical areas, too, the activities of numerous farms may create a highly specialized kind of farm activity. Salad-vegetable production in the Delmarva area, large-scale fruit farming as in parts of California and Florida and cranberry production on Cape Cod are good examples. The localities concerned greatly favour one type of production, for various reasons, and the organization and investment involved is highly specific, not applicable to other types of farm activity. So local areas of intensive specialization arise and persist. By and large, however, multiple-product farming has become increasingly significant, but with a marked regional flavouring which enables a series of major types of farming regions still to be delimited, fairly satisfactorily, on the ground.

8: Minerals and Mining

It would be difficult to overstress the significance of the contribution of the mineral industry to the modern economic growth of the nation and the current role of minerals in supporting the affluent society. For a century or more the growing population has enjoyed a rising standard of living, largely because of the expanding use of minerals and mineral products, and the development of techniques for their discovery and exploitation. Industrial developments, transport, energy, agriculture and all forms of construction depend upon minerals, and the effective functioning of the economy thus depends upon a sustained and adequate supply.

It may therefore seem paradoxical that mining and the mineral industries appear to make a small and decreasing contribution to the economy both in employment and in value of products. With nineteenth-century economic development, and especially after the Civil War, numbers engaged in mining rose steadily. Large settlements were created solely to exploit local mineral resources, as in Appalachia. Elsewhere the existence of, or rumours of, precious metals attracted thousands of newcomers to remote places, and mining communities played a notable part in the evolution of patterns of settlement and economy. The total numbers engaged in mining rose pretty steadily to about $1\frac{1}{4}$ millions in 1920. Since then employment has fluctuated with economic or strategic circumstances, but from a 1948 peak of just under one million the number has declined fairly continuously to about 600,000. At the same time there has been a clear change in the status of mining in the structure of employment. In the early 1900s mining provided over 3 per cent of all jobs in the USA, but the rapid expansion of other sectors of the economy, and the sharp absolute decline in mining employment in the past two decades, has reduced the proportion to under 1 per cent. The income originating in mining has also risen relatively slowly, so that the contribution of mining to national income, in 1940 already very low at 2·4 per cent of the total, had fallen to little over 1 per cent by 1970.

This performance needs to be set in proper perspective. The records of employment and the trends they show are not the sole criterion of the health of differing sectors of the economy. This has already been stressed for agriculture, and the situation in mining is somewhat similar. Outstandingly significant, again, are the great advances in productivity. Employment certainly is important, but we must not confuse changes in numbers employed with the well-being of the industries concerned. Occasionally the volumes of employment and output in an industry may move broadly in step in the same direction. More normally in America they move at different speeds, and sometimes in opposite directions, with employment rising slowly, or even declining, while output rapidly increases. Thus, in mining as a whole, output has risen steadily while employment has declined. In 1969 the volume of all mineral production was some 39 per cent above the average for 1957–9, but employment had fallen by 15 per cent. Dollar values, and the size of the contribution to the national income, may also prove an unreliable index of the condition of an industry. Immediately relevant here is the increased efficiency of discovery, extraction, transport and utilization of many minerals, so that much more is accomplished nowadays with a relatively smaller input of national resources.

Geographical Effects of Minerals Production

Having said this, we may now re-emphasize the critical importance of the mineral industries. There is no field of modern economy in which minerals do not make a contribution, and often it is a major one. The geographical distribution of mineral deposits and the varying conditions of extraction, transport and use have consequently played a significant role in forming the economic geography of the nation. This role was, of course, more direct in the nineteenth century than today. The attractions of a coalfield for manufacturing activity before the First World War need no elaboration, and the relative cheapness of moving iron ores via the Great Lakes to coalfields obviously helped the development of the north-eastern States as the major centre of industry and of population in the country. Elsewhere, too, mineral deposits were the motive for settlement. The metallic ores of the Mountain division, for example, attracted a population which would hardly otherwise have settled in this region, and this was reflected in the employment structure. In the 1870s mining employed over a quarter of the labour force engaged in this division, against under 2 per cent for the nation. In Montana and Idaho approximately a half and three quarters respectively of the relatively small working population were miners in 1870. Life was not easy, and the labour demanded high reward. Such was the demand for these minerals, however, that high prices were readily paid, and per capita incomes in the Mountain division were, for a time, very high indeed. Apart from some preliminary treatment of certain extracted ores to improve their transportability, however, little industrial activity resulted from mining in the Mountain region. Nevertheless the mineral deposits stimulated development of transport and commercial contacts, and also a certain amount of settlement and agricultural activity, often with permanent effect.

The attractions of mineral resources to other forms of economic development appear, for various reasons, to have diminished in the present century. For one thing, there is now a greater range of important minerals in demand for various purposes. Often these are used in combination, while some are substitutes for others, so that the locational attractions of any *one* are likely to have been diminished. Enormous economies, too, have been achieved in mineral utilization by industry, and great advances made in transport (including improvements in the transportability of minerals by various on-site processing techniques). Moreover, growth in recent decades has been most rapid in industries which use relatively small inputs of minerals, or mineral products, per unit of output. In such circumstances the attractive powers of mineral locations *per se* were bound to shrink. The consequences of earlier conditions are, however, witnessed in the form of major established industrial areas or centres of population concentration, while the ability of certain mineral occurrences still to attract major industrial investment is demonstrated by recent developments along the Gulf Coast. Here

the generous endowment of the basic elements of chemicals manufacture (natural gas, oil, salt and sulphur) has stimulated the rapid
growth of a highly important chemicals complex. Employment in
the chemicals and allied products industry in Texas and Louisiana
has almost trebled since the war, supported by a massive expansion
of local mineral output. While mining employment nationally fell
sharply after 1949, that in Texas grew strongly until the early 1960s
and remains much above pre-war levels, while in Louisiana the
numbers are still expanding.

Changing Geography of Minerals Output

That the geography of minerals production will be a changing study
is obvious from the nature of the industry. Adjustments among
producing areas necessarily follow from changes in supply and
demand conditions, and the results from 1940 onwards are demonstrated for employment and value of output in Figure 28. Over the
period employment in mining fell by almost a third, but those
divisions exploiting Appalachian mineral resources (i.e. the Middle
Atlantic, South Atlantic and East South Central divisions) show
much higher contraction rates. The Middle Atlantic experience,
concentrated particularly on the coalmining communities of
Pennsylvania, has been unprecedentedly severe. At the other extreme
the West South Central division (chiefly in Texas and Louisiana as
noted above) has had considerable growth in mining employment.

Thus, measured by employment, major mining areas show a
dramatic shift in relative significance. In 1940 the Middle Atlantic
division provided one quarter of all mining jobs in the nation, the
West South Central 14 per cent. By 1968 only 8 per cent of all mining
jobs remained in the former division, while the latter had almost one
third. Other changes of position, as recorded in Figure 28, strengthened the relative stature in mining activities of divisions west of the
Mississippi, which altogether provided 32 per cent of US mining
employment in 1940, but 57 per cent in 1968.

Measured by value of minerals produced, inter-regional developments become more complex. The changing production and demand

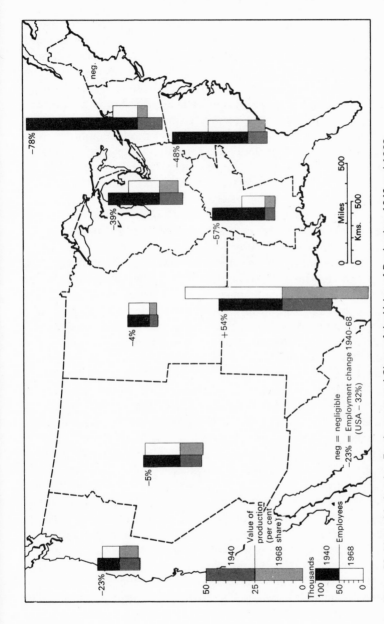

Figure 28. Mineral Industries, Employment and Share of the Value of Production, 1940 and 1968

situation that employment data represent is complicated by the differing values of the minerals produced in different areas. Moreover, while the dollar value of mineral output represented in Figure 28 has risen everywhere, actual physical output has not necessarily risen. In brief, the share of the total value of national minerals output fell most sharply in the Middle Atlantic division and rose most sharply in the West South Central division, thus resembling the shifts in employment. The massive expansion of production in the West South Central division dominates the pattern, however, and the use of proportional share calculations, as in Figure 28, conceals other significant growth performances. Measured in current dollars the national output of minerals rose fivefold over the period. The Mountain division as well as the West South Central division exceeded that growth rate, and the West North Central and East South Central divisions came close to it.

The types of minerals produced are important in explaining these experiences. This may be illustrated from the East South Central division, which has maintained a constant share of national mineral output by value, despite an extremely sharp decline in employment. In fact, the product mix of this division has changed significantly, with the relatively labour-intensive production of coal and iron ore declining, and the high-value output of natural gas, and to a lesser extent oil, increasing. Product mix affects the situation similarly in other divisions. In sum, areas west of the Mississippi (where high-value minerals such as oil, natural gas and non-ferrous metals have greater relative significance) are increasingly prominent in the national pattern of mineral production, whereas the relative stature of the eastern divisions has been steadily undermined by the demand–supply situation in coal, historically the major mineral interest.

Apart from physical depletion of reserves, and consequent rise in comparative costs, substitution among minerals, economies in use, business depression and advances in mining technology may all affect mineral output and employment, with a geographically variable impact. The consequent adjustments in centres of production may clearly have important effects on population and levels of economic activity in areas concerned, for mining activities, while contributing little to *national* employment and income, still dominate

186

the economic life of many communities. If such specialized centres are in relatively isolated locations (as often happens), serious problems can result from decline of output or employment. Sometimes the deterioration of the competitive position of a producing area can be long foreseen and, if the community involved is small, the hardship for individuals and the harmful multiplier effects have few regional repercussions. By contrast, a rapid and relatively unexpected decline will always bring unpleasant consequences, but especially to communities which are both highly specialized and of moderate to large size. The loss of local export income will have drastic repercussions throughout the economy, from which neighbouring communities cannot be entirely insulated. Examples of this process are numerous, and provide a major cause of the massive problems of Appalachia (although other elements contribute to the lamentable conditions in much of that unfortunate region).

The Changing Structure of Mineral Production

For further analysis we must distinguish more carefully between minerals of different kinds. While consumption of minerals has grown very rapidly (on a constant dollar basis per capita consumption more than doubled between 1940 and 1970), not all minerals have enjoyed buoyant markets, and the demand for each varies in volume, reliability and secular trends, as well as in spatial distribution. Supply, for its part, is affected by varying physical and geographical conditions, such as the extent of known mineral bodies, their quality and disposition in the country rock, the generosity or parsimony of nature in distributing them over the country, and the conditions governing their access to centres of demand. For our immediate purpose we may distinguish three broad groups, metals, non-metals and fuels, and Figure 29 traces the physical volume of production from 1940 to 1968 in each of these classes. The average situation for all minerals combined is also presented, showing that the physical volume of production, overall, more than doubled over the period. (It should be noted that Figure 29 shows data at five-year intervals, thus ironing out many sharp annual fluctuations.)

187

Figure 29. Physical Volume of Mineral Production, 1940 to 1968

The outstanding performance is that of the *non-metallic minerals* (excluding the fuels), with a practically fourfold expansion of output. For several minerals within this group the rate of growth of demand has been very high – for instance, in those used in construction or the chemicals industry. Consequently, employment in non-metallic mining operations has, against the general experience, risen fairly steadily, by about 50 per cent since 1940, despite considerable advances in techniques and machinery. The *mineral fuels* have also experienced rapid expansion of demand, and output has risen at a rate closely corresponding to that for 'all minerals' over the period. Within the fuel group, however, the demand for coal fell off during

188

the 1950s and early 1960s, so that only recently has coal production surpassed the 1940 level. Employment in coalmining thus fell very sharply from the early 1940s and, because of outstanding advances in productivity, remains far below those levels, despite the recent recovery of demand. In oil and gas extraction, too, employment has declined somewhat from a peak in the mid 1950s, so that employment in the mineral-fuels sector over all is very much less than in former years, and continuing decline is expected. For the *metallic minerals* overall, volume of output has remained fairly static, fluctuating around a level similar to that of 1940. Within this group, again, output has risen for some products (e.g. copper) but been less buoyant for others, such as iron, in which the market has been affected by economies in use, by substitution and by increasing imports. Over all, the maintenance of a relatively stable volume of output at a time of improving mining technology has meant a fairly sharp contraction in metal-mining jobs. Again, in general, employment prospects are not good, but do vary among the different metals. Clearly, then, adequate generalizing is difficult, even at the level of the three groups of minerals identified in Figure 29, and we shall examine each group in greater detail. In this chapter the non-metallic minerals and the metals will be discussed, with a special case study of iron ore. Mineral fuels will be discussed in the next chapter.

Foreign Trade in Minerals

We must here introduce international trade as another important element affecting the general minerals situation: trends in domestic output may be unreliable guides to the consumption patterns of any mineral. The changing conditions of mining in any area, the discovery and development of newer, richer deposits, policy decisions at different levels (both public and private); all may create changes in geographical patterns of supply which may involve an increase in imports. Of course, exploitable indigenous reserves of some minerals may not exist, but even where domestic output is large and growing rapidly it may still be insufficient for the needs of industrial and other consumers. Thus the U S A is a major importer of minerals, as well as a major producer. Imports have climbed rapidly in both volume and value since the Second World War, and have occasionally had important internal geographical consequences. Among the major imported mineral ores and concentrates are bauxite, iron ore, copper and lead. In all except bauxite, the US is also a major world producer. The ferro alloys (chromite, manganese and nickel) are in short supply domestically, and thus also figure prominently as imports, as does tin, in which domestic production is negligible. The largest mineral import, by volume or value, however, is crude petroleum. Imports have quadrupled since 1950, in spite of a quota system enforced by the Federal government.

The USA also figures prominently in mineral export lists. The export of bituminous coal, which has grown in size and significance since the Second World War, has been outstanding; and many Appalachian communities must be grateful for this. Other mineral exports fall far behind in value, but sulphur and potash merit identification because of significant post-war expansion. Copper exports are also quite large, but chiefly as refined ingots and bars, which themselves contain, on average, something over one third imported copper, so the export situation here is less clear-cut than in the former commodities. Essentially, therefore, minerals are significant items in US trade, but more especially as imports. This gives some concern to government and business interests. Steps have been taken to increase domestic production, for example, by making Federal loans available for prospecting and developing internal resources, or by restricting overseas investment (normally a balance-of-payments measure which can have not entirely unintended effects on overseas mineral developments by US interests). Such policies, however, seem likely only to limit the rate of growth of imports, and the country will continue to rank among the largest mineral importers in the world.

Non-metal Minerals

The rapid physical growth in this class of minerals production was illustrated in Figure 29, and briefly commented on above. The literature on minerals so often ignores this branch that the high and growing monetary value of the business is worth emphasizing here. Compared with the metals, for example, the value per ton of most non-metals is low, yet, even in 1940, the total value of output approximately equalled that of the metals, and by the late 1960s had become twice that of the metal group.

Outstanding in this group are portland cement, stone, sand and gravel. Together these account for almost two thirds by value of non-metallic mineral output. They supply building and construction industries, and the great expansion of construction since the war (roads, dams, public buildings, airports, industrial and commercial plant and so on) accounts for the outstanding growth of this sector of the minerals industry. National expenditure on construction work in the 1960s was more than twice as high (on a constant dollar basis) as before the Second World War – itself a period of unusually high activity because of New Deal construction projects.

The growth in output of the major mineral requirements for chemicals manufacture, quite apart from natural gas and oil, has been equally impressive. Lime, salt and sulphur production has multiplied several times in volume since 1940 to support the massive expansion of the nation's chemicals industry. Connected with chemicals manufacture, too, but more directly with fertilizer production, is the output of phosphate rock and potassium salts. Responding to the tremendous rise in demand for farm fertilizer, output of these minerals has risen tenfold in volume since 1940. But other chemical demands for elemental phosphorus and phosphoric acid are also large and growing, while the chemical applications of potassium compounds have expanded rapidly. In sum, this small group of minerals makes a vital and growing contribution to the national economy, and its output has risen notably.

These non-metals account for all but about 14 per cent of the total value of output of minerals in this class. The remainder includes over a score of products, which cannot be examined separately here. By far the largest in total value of output are the clays, of multiple types and uses; but several others, including asbestos, boron minerals, mica and feldspar, are produced in greater tonnages. Some, like boron, magnesium compounds and fluorspar, also find uses in the chemicals industry, but have larger applications elsewhere. Little can be said of this group as a whole except that, as with the other non-metals, output has increased rapidly in recent decades.

The non-metallic mineral industry is distinctive in its geographical patterns (Figure 30) as well as in growth rates. Significant production is found in every State, which has no parallel in the mineral fuels and metals categories. In fact, non-metallic mineral production corresponds broadly to the geographical distribution of population and economic activity. Thus the largest current producer of these minerals is California, the most populous State, while other very large centres of production occur in Texas and Florida, which have experienced rapid growth, and in the highly populated, economically busy States of the Manufacturing Belt. Half the total output, by value, of the non-metals is provided by eight States which also contain 48 per cent of total population. At the other end of the scale, in the remoter and less populous States, such as the Dakotas, Montana and Wyoming, production is commensurately low. An important exception is New Mexico, which practically monopolizes the output of potassium salts.

Clearly, within the non-metallic group conditions of demand and supply for the constructional minerals explain the ubiquity of activity. Sand and gravel are produced in every State, while exploitable deposits occur in almost every county, although the quality (and thus the suitability for specific uses) varies. Every State also contributes to the total output of stone, though again type, quality and end uses differ and affect the detailed geographical patterns of operations. Crushed and broken stone, for example (the 'growth' sector of the stone business, used chiefly for roadstone and concrete), is produced everywhere. Dimension stone (for buildings, memorials etc.) is less widely produced, despite wide distribution of reserves. Slate output is largely concentrated in four Appalachian States.

Cement production is also practically ubiquitous. All but six or seven States (chiefly small north-eastern States, such as those of New England, which fall within economic supply range of large workings in neighbouring States) are recorded as producing portland cement. Clearly, then, for 'construction' minerals as a whole there exist rather special conditions of widespread supply and widespread

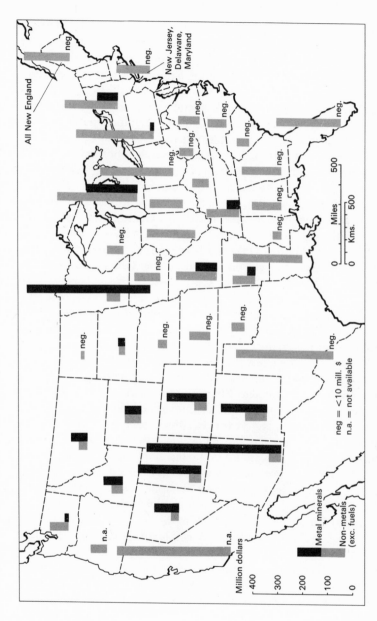

Figure 30. Output, by Value, of Metal and Non-metal Minerals, 1968

All New England

New Jersey, Delaware, Maryland

neg.

neg.

neg. = <10 mill. $
n.a. = not available

Million dollars

400
300
200
100
0

Metal minerals

Non-metals
(exc. fuels)

n.a.

Miles
Kms.

0   500
0   500

demand. The bulky products are also of low value per unit of weight, not economically transportable over long distances. Such conditions promote a pattern of dispersed production, although major concentrations of industry and population naturally attract major concentrations of output.

Other non-metallic minerals operate under a different combination of controls, and exhibit differing geographical patterns. Common salt deposits, for example, are widespread in the USA, but, unlike the constructional materials, several important regions are without commercially exploitable reserves. New England and other eastern coastal areas are examples, together with the Pacific North-West. However, very large, virtually inexhaustible reserves occur elsewhere. The most notable include the great Silurian salt beds of the north-eastern States, stretching through New York, Pennsylvania, West Virginia, Ohio and Michigan, and forming one of the most extensive salt fields in the world. The Gulf Coast area, with hundreds of massive Jurassic salt domes, is also outstanding. An enormous Permian basin containing huge reserves of salt occurs in the central-southern States of Kansas, Colorado, Oklahoma, Texas and New Mexico; and yet another very large deposit has recently been found underlying North Dakota and neighbouring areas. In addition, there are many smaller deposits in other States. On distribution of reserves alone, therefore, widespread production is possible. In fact seventeen States produce common salt, but about 47 per cent of the total output in 1968 originated in the Gulf Coast States of Louisiana and Texas, and 43 per cent in the north-eastern States of Ohio, New York, Michigan and West Virginia. Elsewhere only California and Kansas are significant producers. Thus production tends to be sporadic rather than widespread, and this reflects both the geographical conditions of supply, as just described, and the nature of the demand, which is chiefly from the chemicals industry. The north-eastern and Gulf States named above provide more than two fifths of all US employment in basic chemicals manufacture.

Finally, contrasting completely with the ubiquitous output of construction materials are examples of very highly concentrated working of non-metals which are either rare in nature or in com-

194

paratively small demand. Boron is a good example. The entire US output comes from California. One or two other western States are known to have deposits, but the demand is adequately met from the Californian workings, despite high transport costs. The case of abrasive garnet is similar. Production is restricted to New York and Idaho, and, though there are other known reserves, these two are capable of meeting all foreseeable demand.

In detail, therefore, the non-metals present a complex system of production patterns but, as a group, are distinguished by their wide-spread distribution and the attractions offered to many producers by major concentrations of population and economic activity. This latter characteristic presents the enterprises chiefly concerned (e.g. stone, sand and gravel producers) with problems which are not so consistently present in other branches of the minerals industry. By its nature most mineral-extraction activity is unpleasant, noisy and dirty, and destructive of the landscape. This is especially so when the operations are carried out almost entirely (as is the case here) over large surface areas, by means of strip mining or open-pit quarrying. This is the special dilemma of this industry. Economic construction of roads and buildings demands huge quantities of materials from local resources (sands and gravels can rarely stand the cost of moving more than thirty miles from source). Thus the heaviest demands are made on these resources in just those areas where competition from other forms of land use and the need to preserve environmental quality are greatest. The growth of urban areas, while providing the market for the mineral producers, thus also brings problems. Land prices rise as urban uses advance, and huge volumes of quality reserves are sterilized either by the local adoption of restrictive zoning ordinances or, more permanently, by covering the ground with roads and buildings. The extractor also faces increased pressure to render his remaining workings less unsightly and less intrusive, and to restore the land after extraction – a costly process. The non-metallic mineral producer is not alone, of course, in facing such problems. A major theme of politics in America in the 1970s will be that of environmental quality, in which all mineral extraction, as well as other economic activities, will be involved. But, because of their unusually close physical ties with areas of greatest population, the producers of the low-value constructional materials face problems of special urgency. Sand, gravel and stone workings are currently responsible for one third of all the land disturbed by surface mineral operations in the USA. Not a single State or metropolitan area is free of the environmental problems that follow, and such problems will certainly increase as demand for these minerals expands yet further.

The Metallic Minerals

We have seen that these minerals as a whole have a relatively unimpressive output record for recent decades, but some further explanation is desirable. Certain minerals within this group have been affected by greatly increased efficiency in utilization, by the competition of substitutes in major markets and by rising supply from secondary sources, i.e. the recovery of materials from industrial and domestic scrap. In addition, policy decisions and changing domestic-supply conditions have sometimes led to large increases in imports. Thus, a given mineral could be maintaining, or even increasing, its importance to the economy, yet be static, or even declining, in domestic production. Several metal ores have been affected in one or other of these ways, but perhaps the most significant example is that of iron. More will be said of this below. To take another illustration, the high and rising supply of scrap lead (especially from car batteries) and increased imports helped to depress the primary domestic output of this mineral until the 1960s.

The contrast between the geographical patterns of output of these minerals and those of the non-metals is evident from Figure 30. Arizona and Minnesota alone produce 40 per cent of US metallic minerals output, and only Utah need be added to account for a half. Yet these three States have little over 3 per cent of the US population. For the non-metallic sector the three leading States produce only 22 per cent of total output and have almost precisely that proportion of the nation's population. Thus, the production of metal ores is much more highly concentrated, with no essential locational connection with major centres of population and economic activity. The significance of employment trends is immediately apparent. In 1967 employment in metal mining was one third (some 37,000 jobs) lower than in 1940, and a fairly rapid rate of decline is continuing. With activity mainly in rather remote locations, alternative jobs will not be readily available for redundant personnel and serious economic problems can arise in areas of major concentration.

Of course, both national and regional trends will vary with the types of metal ores produced. National output is dominated by copper and iron, which together normally account for about 70 per cent by value of total metal-ore production, and rather less of total metal-mining employment. Among the numerous remaining metals, uranium, zinc and molybdenum are distinguished by high value of output. Others are of considerable economic significance (e.g. gold and silver, lead, tungsten) but together account for only one tenth of the output of the class.

Among these minerals, supply and demand conditions and employment and output trends often vary markedly, as one or two examples will show. With a few notable exceptions, the dominant producers of metal ores are the Mountain States. Over 90 per cent of copper-mine production, for example, comes from this area. The total output of copper has risen sharply and, in contrast to the other important metals, employment has remained fairly stable over the past two decades. The technological advances in the treatment of copper ores, resulting in a decrease in the copper content of an ore considered 'economic', are notable. A copper content of only about a half of one per cent is now considered adequate, compared with 2 per cent earlier this century and 1·2 per cent as recently as 1940. This has greatly increased the workable copper-ore reserve in the USA, and done much, together with the development of surface mining machinery, to increase the domestic output of this mineral. But while domestic production has been high and growing, demand has expanded even faster, so that the USA has become a major net importer. This raises policy issues which affect several minerals, and which will be taken up below. The outstanding centre of domestic copper production is Arizona, where output has more than doubled since 1940 and which has for a decade or more contributed over half of the nation's output. Neighbouring Utah accounts for another fifth, and other considerable producers are also found among the Mountain States. East of the Rockies, only Michigan (the major nineteenth-century source of copper) is notable, nowadays accounting for about 5 per cent of national output.

The Mountain division also possesses enough reserves of uranium ores to place it high among world producers. Secular expansion of demand for this mineral seems assured as nuclear-power programmes advance throughout the world. New Mexico, Wyoming, Colorado and Utah are currently the major uranium-producing States. In molybdenum, too (of which the US has about 70 per cent of world production), mining is concentrated in the Mountain States (especially Colorado) which also figure predominantly in gold, silver, tungsten, vanadium, and other metal-ore output.

Zinc and lead are important exceptions to the general dominance of the Mountain division in metal-mining activity – together with iron ore, of which more is said below. Zinc-ore production is more widespread than that of other leading metals, and the Mountain States supply under a third of total domestic output. Tennessee and New York are the leading producers. Lead mining is concentrated chiefly in Missouri. Production here has expanded considerably since the war and Missouri contributes some 60 per cent of domestic production. But most of the remaining output comes from the Mountain division. In both zinc and lead total domestic production has declined since the Second World War, and imports are large. This again raises policy issues, which we now outline in relation to the base metals.

In every base metal of which the USA remains a large producer (i.e. copper, lead and zinc) demand has greatly outrun domestic supply and imports have risen. The different strands of this situation give rise to opposing policy implications in which the government has inevitably become involved. Undoubtedly, though indigenous resources remain very large, the best domestic reserves of these ores have been consumed. Imported ores are of higher grade, and sometimes also cheaper because of lower labour costs in the supplying areas. In such circumstances consumers of these metals often favour increased imports – a mood which may be shared by those US producers (as in copper mining) who also have large investments in

198

overseas workings. Imports are further favoured by the need to conserve remaining indigenous reserves. Clearly the economy faces the future more securely when large and accessible domestic reserves are available.

But, by the same criteria, the case for maintaining a large and active indigenous capacity, aided where necessary by government support, is strong. A run-down and technically backward minerals sector could not quickly respond to emergency demands, and strategic considerations demand maintenance of production at fairly high levels, despite the relative expense. Moreover, a strong domestic industry can provide a useful lever in price negotiations with overseas suppliers while imports put additional pressure on the balance of payments. In the event, the government appears to have accepted the case for preserving domestic capacity, and, while applying no clear and consistent minerals policy, has supported in various ways the uneconomic domestic production of the minerals concerned. The reasons for such intervention are not solely strategic, but nowadays include the desire to maintain employment in distressed areas. Tariffs, quotas, stockpiles, tax incentives, special subsidies and assistance with exploration costs have all been invoked on occasion. Lead and zinc mining have received protection and aid in all these ways, and since 1961 direct subsidies have been available for small enterprises in an attempt to ease the run-down of employment. Copper mining, where the reserve situation is fairly satisfactory, has been helped in opening up new workings in times of crisis (e.g. during the Korean war), in stockpile support and in loans for exploration. Many other minerals participate in strategic stockpile programmes, and government funds are also available for research and development programmes related to minerals supply and use. More recently, too, the Federal government has become concerned with problems of environment and the deleterious effects of mineral working. There is certain to be increasing government activity and commitment of resources in this field. Certain aspects of the energy economy have also stimulated government action, as discussed in the following chapter. For the moment we will turn to consider iron ore as a final case study in the present context.

Iron ore merits special treatment not only because of its fundamental significance in a modern economy, but also because it illustrates admirably the changing circumstances of supply and use currently affecting the geography of the USA minerals industry. Since the development of the modern iron and steel industry from about the mid nineteenth century, enormous quantities of iron ore have been extracted from indigenous resources. Exploitation had, naturally, been concentrated on the highest quality and most accessible ores, with little concern, until comparatively recently, about the adequacy of the reserves. During the Second World War and the years immediately after, however, extremely heavy extraction made the industry uncomfortably aware that the known reserves of good ores had been seriously depleted. In particular, the abundant Lake Superior ores, on which most American steel manufacturing had been based, were reported as approaching exhaustion. The future situation, it was feared, would involve an increasingly heavy dependence on overseas supplies. This might well produce a general rise of iron-ore prices and seriously affect costs, especially in the major middle-western iron and steel locations, which had flourished on the excellent conditions of access afforded by geography to the Superior ores. Moreover, heavy dependence on foreign sources would be as undesirable for iron as for other strategic minerals. The mood was therefore one of concern, if not of pessimism.

In the event, this concern was not entirely justified; but undoubtedly serious supply and cost problems failed to materialize only because of the vigorous measures it prompted. The problems were to ensure an adequate, low-cost, reliable supply, and to achieve improved conservation in developing and using the remaining domestic resources, while retaining an indigenous iron ore producing capacity of appreciable size and good heart. The chief solutions were to prosecute more vigorously the search for and development of new sources of supply in politically 'safe' areas overseas; to probe more intensively the iron-ore resources of the US itself (in particular, to increase them by developing methods of utilizing the abundant lower grade ores); and, finally, to achieve greater economy in the use of iron ore in the blast furnace. Each merits brief discussion.

Before the Second World War, foreign trade in iron ore was of little concern to the American consumer. Small quantities, mainly of special kinds of ore (1 or 2 million tons per year) were imported, and rather smaller quantities were exported, chiefly to Canada. After 1945 the situation changed. Exports of ore rose to about 5 or 6 million tons per year in the late 1960s, chiefly still to Canada but also to Japan. Far more significant, however, was the rise in imports, depicted in Figure 31. At first, the quantities drawn from developed overseas sources, e.g. Chile and Sweden, were modestly increased. Supplies from Canada from a new source opened up in the early 1940s at Steep Rock, near the western end of Lake Superior, also increased somewhat. Meanwhile intensive prospecting, proving and developing activity in various promising, and politically reliable, areas of the Western Hemisphere proved fruitful, especially in the confirmation of the Cerro Bolivar and El Pao reserves of eastern Venezuela and the Quebec–Labrador deposits of Canada. The first shipments from both areas were made in the early 1950s, and thereafter imports rose swiftly. Thus, whereas in 1945, iron-ore imports had provided only about 1 per cent of total supply, since the middle 1960s they have provided about one third. The major current source is Canada, which supplies about half the total, followed by Venezuela with a quarter. Most of the balance comes from other Western Hemisphere sources, Liberia being the only significant example, so far, of American development of iron-ore resources outside that hemisphere.

Clearly the prospect is of even greater use of overseas supplies. Fears of world shortage have receded, following a series of very large discoveries and the virtual certainty of more. World production in 1970 was well over three times that of 1940 and under no great pressure. The present condition is rather one of surplus capacity and relatively low prices. Movement, too, is more economical with the increasing use of giant ocean ore-carriers. But imported ores are not only abundant and low in price; they are also richer in iron than the best ores currently worked in the USA, and often less contaminated by impurities (such as silica) which raise processing costs. This applies especially to the Venezuelan ores, which therefore offer additional cost advantages to suitably located

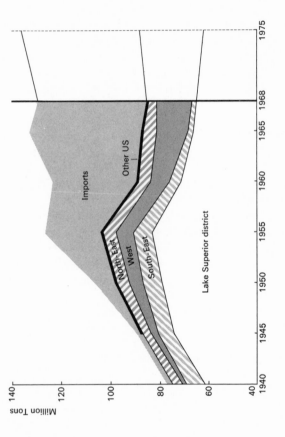

Figure 31. Usable Iron Ore Production and Imports

American iron and steel manufacturers. Over all, then, the venture into the wider world, undertaken in the late 1940s, has proved profitable. Before the end of the 1970s foreign ore will probably be meeting at least half the national requirement, and subsequently the proportion is likely to continue to rise.

Such increased use of imported ores inevitably had internal repercussions, not least on location decisions in iron and steel manufacture. Low-cost foreign ores at eastern tidewater played a considerable role in attracting new post-war investment to eastern coastal locations, where the advantages of market proximity were already very strong. Capacity at Bethlehem Steel's Sparrows Point plant, near Baltimore, was enormously increased, creating probably the largest integrated iron- and steel-producing unit in the world. A new integrated works was built by US Steel at Fairless Hills on the Delaware, while capacity was expanded at other coastal region sites, including Bethlehem itself. Some of these works use some domestic ore from eastern mines, but the imported supplies are of the greatest significance. Thus almost half of total US iron-ore imports enter the country through Philadelphia and Baltimore, and the advantages of the ore itself, and the low costs of its movement to the Delaware and Chesapeake Bays, permit it to penetrate the Appalachians and serve blast furnaces in the Pittsburgh, Wheeling and Youngstown areas as well as the coastal furnaces. Movement inland has more recently been further facilitated by the introduction of enormous unit trains, each comprising some 300 ore wagons and hauling some 30,000 tons of high-grade ore. The eastern margins of the Middle West have therefore become areas of competition between imported ore brought from the east coast, ores from Lake Superior and, via the St Lawrence Seaway, from the Quebec–Labrador deposits.

Improved access to foreign ore supplies (especially from eastern Canada) became of major concern in the post-war years to existing iron and steel manufacture in the Middle West. Opening up the Quebec–Labrador deposits could hardly benefit the competitive position of the giant steel mills between Buffalo and Chicago unless the ore could be cheaply moved to them. This fact put the considerable weight of the steel lobby behind the St Lawrence Seaway project. This important project had been a political shuttlecock

203

A Modern Geography of the United States

between the US and Canada since the early years of the century and, perhaps understandably in the circumstances, the steel industry had earlier been supremely indifferent. In the changed situation the steel lobby's powerful support helped to overcome the final hesitations of Congress, heavily pressed by north-eastern interests demanding the electrical power the project would provide, and worried by the declared determination of Canada to go ahead alone if the US hesitated any longer. Construction began in 1954 (the year of the first ore shipment from Seven Islands) and the opening of the Seaway in 1959 improved immeasurably the access of the mid-western steel centres to the ores they needed. By 1968 some 19 million tons of imported ore were being received by American ports on the Great Lakes (over 40 per cent of total US imports), compared with under 8 million tons in 1960. This was vital in the large expansion of steel-producing capacity in the Middle West, where imports now compete directly with supplies from the major indigenous centres of production. Iron-ore prices have in fact tended to decline in the late 1960s, and this, of course, puts further pressure on the domestic ore-producing industry, to which we will now turn.

The indigenous iron-ore resources of the USA are far from approaching exhaustion, but the best ores have been severely depleted during almost a century of exploitation. By 1970 about 4,000 million tons of iron ore had been extracted, for example, from the Lake Superior district alone, and over the years the quality of the available ore had diminished. Early this century the average iron content of the major Minnesota ores was between 60 and 70 per cent. Nowadays the best reserves still have a natural iron content of about 57 per cent, but probably less than 500 million tons of such ores remain in the whole Lake Superior area. In these circumstances, the possibility of using materials of lower grade and different structure – materials which would not have been properly considered as 'ores' in earlier years – had to be considered. When these materials are included, the resource picture alters remarkably. The Lake Superior district alone is estimated to have over (possibly well over) 100,000 million tons of taconite and jaspilite, containing, in general, between 22 and 30 per cent of iron. How much of this can become effective reserve remains to be seen, but other large quantities, often of rather

204

better quality ores, are known to exist elsewhere. The search continues, sometimes successfully. Late in 1969, for example, US Steel announced an 'extensive' discovery in western Nevada, variously estimated to contain 250 million to 1,000 million tons of 'good-quality' ore. At various times since 1950 Federal assistance has been available for exploring and developing iron-ore deposits, and rapid tax amortization provision for new or expanded iron-ore production facilities has given extra incentive to the search.

The domestic resource situation is therefore far from depressing. But much depends upon technical advances to convert the potential into actual, exploitable reserves. The taconites and jaspilites, for example, pose problems so far only partially solved at acceptable cost. The pressure to solve these problems, however, remains considerable, despite the success of the overseas ventures. Superficially it may seem strange that the American steel industry continues to invest very large sums in developing and applying techniques for using low-grade, high-cost domestic ores, when better, cheaper, ores are available in ample quantity from overseas. But security of supply requires an adequate domestic reserve and an active producing capacity, and in the long run work on these indigenous deposits could pay off well, even in economic terms. Thus the great mining companies (in which the steel corporations normally have dominant shareholdings) have invested enormous sums in developing these new sources.

Most significant has been the increasing use of the Lake Superior taconites. These occur in massive quantity in and around the famous Mesabi range in Minnesota. They (or the similar jaspilites) are also known in Michigan, Wisconsin and other parts of the country. So far, the major impact of their development has been felt in Minnesota and, to a much smaller extent, in Michigan. Taconite is an extremely tough rock, with its iron content dispersed in fine grains throughout the material. It has presented very serious technical problems for mining and treatment, and only since the war has it been thought worth while to tackle them vigorously. The material is now mined by flame drilling and blasting. The fragments are crushed and the iron grains concentrated magnetically. The grains are finally agglomerated into pellets of iron ore, with a 63 per cent iron content.

The magnetic concentration is a key process, and unfortunately some of the iron in the rock now being mined does not respond to the technique, and much of the known deposit of taconite is also 'non-magnetic'. Some two thirds of the known taconite formations are not economically amenable to any method of concentration yet known.

The first commercial taconite concentrating plant was opened at Silver Bay, Lake Superior, in 1956, but growth was impeded by an uncertain legal and tax situation in Minnesota. In 1964, however, a tax structure favourable to the industry was guaranteed for twenty-five years and the steel companies then undertook a massive investment programme. By 1970, taconite pelletizing capacity was some 50 million tons (chiefly in Minnesota), with 70 million tons expected by 1975. This capacity will probably not be fully used. Costs of these pellets are higher than for overseas supplies, although somewhat offset by certain advantages. The pellets are, for example, higher in grade and cheaper to handle and transport than conventional 'direct shipping' ore. They also resist freezing which, in a conventional ore, sometimes means that the material has to be 'mined' again out of stock. Moreover, they constitute a superior blast-furnace charge, requiring less smelting fuel and greatly increasing blast-furnace capacity. Most of these advantages, of course, also apply to other beneficiated ores. Beneficiation includes washing, roasting, grading, sizing, blending and sintering of ores, and plant for this has been installed rapidly since the war. Naturally, the cost advantages are greatest if the ores are beneficiated in the mining area before shipment. Only 17 per cent of the ore had been improved before movement in 1940, but by 1969 almost 90 per cent. Increased use of beneficiation has enabled the American iron and steel industry to economize significantly in its use of iron ore. Clearly, then, considerable advance has been made in the use of leaner home ores, improving their workability, transportability and value in use. Enormous sums have been invested, but the product still remains relatively high cost.

The organization and techniques of domestic iron mining have also changed considerably. The large investment required for mining and treating the leaner ores has raised the scale of efficient operation and forced many smaller mines out of business. In 1953 the domestic output of usable ore* reached its peak of 118 million tons. To obtain that amount, 157 million tons of crude ore were produced from 325 mines. By 1968 usable output had fallen to 85 million tons, but 192 million tons of crude ore had to be mined to produce it. Even so, the number of operating mines fell to 109, with the biggest thirty alone providing about 70 per cent of the total output in 1966. The closing of mines has continued to the present.

Underground mining, with production costs up to four times those of surface workings, has suffered most from post-war developments. Underground operations can rarely compete unless they produce a high-grade, direct-shipping ore, and open-pit workings now provide well over 90 per cent of all production. Thus areas of important underground operations have experienced a sharp decline. Output in Wisconsin, for example, which was almost entirely from underground workings, had probably ceased by 1970. In Alabama, too, where underground mines were very important, output has greatly diminished. The relative advantages offered by surface operations are obvious, but the decline in the quality of the material mined and recent advances in machinery and technique emphasize them. The capacity of earth-moving machinery, for example, has greatly increased, making a much greater amount of overburden economically removable. In 1954, for example, the Bureau of Mines' *Yearbook* reported the use of a mechanical shovel of 30 cubic yards' capacity. By 1960 the largest mechanical shovel capacity had risen to 85 cubic yards. The newest monster now claims 200 cubic yards in a single bite (but its economic application is so far rather limited). Trucks shifting the ore to the beneficiation plant now carry 150 tons in a single load, and new designs will raise this to above 200 tons. But such machinery is expensive, needs large undertakings for efficient operation and thus raises the effective scale of enterprise and reduces the number of mines in business. All of this has implications

---

* 'Usable ore' is ore shipped from the mine to the consumer. Part of it may be 'direct shipping' ore, i.e. crude ore of higher grade, shipped without prior treatment; the rest will be ore that has been treated in some way to improve its grade, structure and transportability.

for employment, to which we shall return after a review of the current geography of production.

Amid all this change, one major element of stability lies in the internal geography of production. Figure 31 shows the output of usable ore from the major districts since 1940 at five-yearly intervals, which avoid the complications of large annual fluctuations. The continued dominance of the Lake Superior district is clear. The changing conditions of production within this region are, however, illustrated by the fact that in the early 1940s over 80 per cent of the crude ore was shipped direct from the mines to consumers, whereas by the late 1960s less than one tenth comprised 'direct-shipping' ores. We should note that Minnesota alone accounts for 60 per cent of all usable ore shipped from US mines. Nearly all still comes from the Mesabi range, where the new era is proclaimed by the ever larger quarries and by the new taconite processing plants. The last underground mine in Minnesota closed in 1967. Michigan remains the second producing State, with about 16 per cent of national usable ore shipments from its Marquette and Menominee ranges. Gogebic range mining, however, ended in 1967, after eighty-four years of active life, and Wisconsin no longer produces significant quantities of iron ore.

Other producing districts have experienced varying fortunes, as Figure 31 suggests. Output from the South-East (Alabama and Georgia), once the second-ranking district, declined sharply after the mid 1950s. The grade of ore is low, production costs are high, and crude ore output per man-shift is one third or more below the US average. The Birmingham iron and steel industry, the 'natural' market of the area, is increasingly using imports from Venezuela, via Mobile, and unless the situation changes, significant production in this area could well cease in the 1970s.

Meanwhile, the 'western' district (which includes all areas west of the Mississippi except Minnesota) has increased production considerably. Details are not available because the statistics for California, Texas and Arizona are withheld from publication under the disclosure rule. Estimates, however, put total western production at about 13 million tons by the late 1960s. The largest identified producing States are Wyoming, Utah, Missouri and Montana, each

208

producing between 1 and 2 million tons of usable ore. Large low-grade reserves are known to exist, and more are being proved. Labour productivity is high (only Missouri has any significant underground activity), and output from the area will probably expand further. Growing quantities are being exported from the Eagle Mountain deposits of California to Japan.

Finally, in the north-eastern district, output has remained fairly stable from workings in northern New York (the Adirondacks), New Jersey and eastern Pennsylvania. Production costs are high (several underground mines still operate) and crude ore production per man-shift is over all only half the US average. All the crude ore produced is beneficiated, and an agglomerate with 63–4 per cent iron content obtained. The price of this agglomerate is considerably higher than the US average, but the consuming blast furnaces, to which the mines are usually financially linked, are relatively close by.

Changing ore supply patterns and developments in techniques of production have profoundly affected employment. According to Bureau of Labor Statistics data, 40,000 workers were engaged in iron-ore mining (including beneficiation processes) in 1953, the peak production year. The average employment per mine was 123 workers. By 1967, 26,000 were employed in many fewer mines, the average per mine being now 200 workers. The actual number of jobs lost might not appear to present an unmanageable problem, but most operations are in areas where alternative opportunities for employment are limited, and the impact of developments is felt in other local sections of activity, notably transport. Thus the total loss of earning power may be considerable, and have grave local multiplier effects.

Since the main producing areas are in the Upper Lakes region, the situation there, and especially in north-eastern Minnesota where nearly half the industry's national work force is engaged, is worth outlining. While iron-ore production is not the sole economic activity here, it does make a large contribution to economic life, and the changing situation has created special problems. The area is physically difficult, not because of strong relief, but because of poor soils, poor drainage and harsh winter climate, which diminishes production and raises construction and operating costs. It is remote

209

from the main centres of economic activity in the north-eastern USA, especially in winter, when lake movement is halted. Road communications are also poor, and, because of its location, the area has not significantly benefited from the great inter-State highway construction programme of the 1960s. The chief settlement attractions had been the ore and the forest resources, both now past their peak. Apart from Duluth, few sizeable urban areas have grown to provide a wider range of employment opportunities. Employment in metal mining (chiefly iron ore) in Minnesota fell from 19,000 to 13,000 between 1953 and 1969 and (although only partly resulting from developments in ore production and movement) the transport services dropped some 11,000 workers. These are State-wide figures but most of their impact has been in the Lake Superior area.

In consequence, population growth in north-eastern Minnesota has been only one third of the national average since 1950, as people have moved away. Even in the Duluth–Superior metropolitan area, employment has grown relatively sluggishly; manufacturing has declined and the largest expansion is in government employment. Since the 1960 Census the metropolitan area has, in fact, lost population. Inland from the lakeside settlements conditions worsen. Unemployment rates have long been well above the national level and there is much poverty. Given the current trends in the iron-ore business, employment in primary activities will hardly expand, and to retain a large population in the area requires new job opportunities. The remoteness from large markets make the outlook unpromising, however. Private capital could certainly find better prospects elsewhere.

Here, then, is an area of difficulty. Under the Area Redevelopment Act of 1961, all the counties of north-eastern Minnesota were designated Redevelopment Areas, eligible to receive various forms of Federal aid. Comment on this Federal programme will be made later. The Act was replaced in 1965 by the Public Works and Economic Development Act, under which development planning could be encouraged over broader areas, and even by unified programmes reaching across State lines. The Minnesota areas of difficulty have, under this dispensation, been joined with similar areas of difficulty in northern Wisconsin and northern Michigan to form the Upper Great Lakes Economic Development Region, whose problems are now being reviewed by a special Regional Commission. The strategy of the economic development programme is still under consideration, but with Federal resources, financial and technical, available there may be new ground for hope.

Table 11: Material Handled in Iron-Ore Mines, 1959 and 1968
(million tons)

	Surface workings		Underground mines		Total	
	1959	1968	1959	1968	1959	1968
Crude ore	96	202	19	14	115	216
Waste	118	155	2	3	120	158
Total	214	357	21	17	235	374

Source: Minerals Yearbook, 1960 and 1968

The final theme in this context is the environmental effects of iron-ore working. Figures of material handled at iron-ore mines in 1959 and 1968 (Table 11) may be used to illustrate the increasing problems of waste disposal. Of a total increase of 139 million tons in volume of materials handled, crude ore contributed 101 million tons, waste the remaining 38 million. The Table shows that the ratio of waste to crude ore production is much less for underground operations (21 per cent in 1968) than for surface workings (77 per cent), but over 90 per cent of total production is nowadays from surface operations, whose command of mammoth earth-moving machinery has been noted. Further, the quality of the crude ore is much lower than formerly. In 1959 the ratio of crude to usable ore production was 1·70 to 1; by 1968 it was 2·30 to 1. Thus the crude ore itself contains a rising quantity of waste, and ore producers face a huge and increasing problem of waste disposal.

The workings themselves also create environmental damage and hazards. The open pits are often more than 1,200 feet deep, because the ore occurs in thick beds. For working, this is a favourable situation. Large quantities of ore are won from relatively small surface areas; the works have a long life and the damage done to surface area per ton of output is minimized. Such pits, however, are often dangerous, impede the movement both of people and wildlife, and disrupt drainage. They also produce enormous waste piles to disfigure the landscape. Fortunately, the waste is usually chemically inert, and, given flat terrain (as in the Lake Superior area), no major water pollution problem results. The eventual landscape impact could, however, be striking. An official report* suggests, for example, that if the present practice continues, the Mesabi range, 120 miles long and 3 miles wide, will eventually become a gigantic lake. Such open-pit working accounts for over three quarters of all land disturbed by surface iron-ore mining in the USA. The alternative 'area-strip' technique, however, does considerably more damage per ton of ore produced. This technique is used for shallow working of low-grade ore over a large area. It leaves parallel waste piles, 50 feet or more high and 50–100 feet apart, which obviously do grave damage to landscape and environment.

Compared with coal, sand and gravel, and most other minerals, the damage done by iron-ore operations has, so far, been small. The total area involved (164,000 acres reported in 1965) is only 5 per cent of all land disturbed by surface mining operations, and presents less urgent problems than those left by the working of sands, gravels and coals. The damage done in iron-ore working is also much more concentrated geographically than that of other minerals. Almost three quarters of the total is found in Minnesota and Alabama alone. It is also often in areas remote from major population concentrations. The amount of surface damage done by iron-ore mining is, however, bound to rise. This follows from the techniques used, the increasing volume of waste being mined, the lower grades of ore produced, and the determination of the steel interests to maintain, or even increase, domestic capacity. The geographical concentration of activity is consequently an advantage from a national point of view – but not to those States immediately concerned. Land disturbed by iron-ore workings is already 60 per cent of all disturbed land in Minnesota and 40 per cent in Alabama. The environmental problems created by iron-ore extraction will, therefore, be serious in these, and other large producing States, in the 1970s.

* US Department of the Interior, *Surface Mining and Our Environment*, 1967.

9: Coal and the Energy Economy

Energy has long been used lavishly in the United States, and consumption continues to expand sharply (Figure 32). This reflects not simply the growth of population and economy, but also the continuously rising demand per capita for energy. In 1910 each American consumed 160 million British thermal units (BTU) of energy, in 1940 180 million BTU, and in 1969 almost 300 million BTU, despite increased efficiency in production and use. This is many times the per capita consumption in other advanced economies and as an index reflects the affluence, vast productive potential and voracious appetite for resources of the American economy.

Together with this increase has gone a major transformation of energy sources, illustrated in Figure 32. Early this century, coal still provided 85–90 per cent of total demand. Its volume of output has since fluctuated considerably but, relatively, coal has continuously lost ground. Up to 1940 oil made the greatest advance, but subsequently natural gas has expanded most rapidly. Currently a new competitor, the atom, is establishing its base· for a considerable advance. Such changes have many consequences for the economic and social conditions of large areas of the country. A review of the energy economy which adequately embraced each of these major sectors would need to be of great length. Here we must be selective and, because of the tremendous geographical and social implications of its recent history, coal will receive special emphasis. Other energy sources will be treated chiefly in regard to their relationships with coal.

Coal

During the nineteenth century the coal industry grew rapidly in both output and numbers employed. Methods were labour-intensive and

213

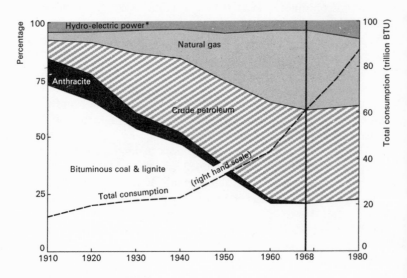

*Includes nuclear power from 1960

Figure 32. Consumption of Fuels and Energy by Source

employment generally grew faster than output. Employment and output expansion continued into this century. By 1920, when 660 million tons of coal were produced, some 785,000 miners were employed and numerous communities of appreciable size had grown on the major coalfields, their economic life centred on the production and transport of coal. Some larger centres (such as Johnstown, Wheeling, Youngstown, Charleston and Pittsburgh) attracted major coal-using industries and other urban functions, thus providing a wider range of employment. But numerous other places had little to support them except their mining interests. The dangers of this situation are clear. During the depression years the bread line was an everyday feature of life in many coalfield communities, and, although coal output recovered from the depths reached in the early 1930s, employment continued to decline. In appraising the changing circumstances of this industry in recent decades, we must, however, distinguish between anthracite and bituminous coal. The former will be treated first, and comparatively briefly.

Anthracite production has been highly concentrated in eastern Pennsylvania, at such centres as Carbondale, Scranton, Hazleton and Pottsville. Difficult physical conditions hindering mechanization and productivity, and problems of mine drainage and water control, result in high costs of production. Thus anthracite has always been higher priced than the other coals, but its value for steam-raising helped it to remain important in the energy economy, as Figure 32 shows, in the early decades of the century. Between the wars, however, its competitive status deteriorated rapidly, and the process has since accelerated as the area served by natural-gas supplies broadened, undermining the major remaining market for anthracite in space heating.

At its peak during the First World War, anthracite production hovered near 100 million tons per annum, and 150,000 or more men were employed on the East Pennsylvania coalfield. In 1969 about 11 million tons were produced, and only 6,000 men were employed. The problems so created have proved difficult, for they are confined to a relatively small geographical area and the pace of contraction has been very severe, especially since 1950. Lucerne County, for instance, at the heart of the anthracite area, contains the cities of

215

Wilkes Barre and Hazleton, and other quite large communities such as Kingston, Nanticoke and Pittston. In 1950 the population of this county was 392,000. Employment in mining had begun to fall back in the 1920s, but in 1950 some 39,000 jobs still remained (28 per cent of all employment). Ten years later only 6,000 mining jobs were left, and the county's total non-agricultural labour force had fallen by a quarter. Throughout the 1950s, therefore, the Wilkes Barre–Hazleton 'labour-market area' (Lucerne County) was one of the nation's 'chronic labour surplus areas'. Unemployment rates were regularly some two or three times the national level, and reached 17 per cent, the highest in the nation, in 1958. Local development bodies made great efforts to attract new industries with some success, especially in the 1960s, when a buoyant national economy and new schemes of Federal support aided them. Manufacturing employment rose by nearly 12,000 between 1960 and 1969, and small gains were made in other non-agricultural sectors. The number of mining jobs was halved again, but unemployment rates nevertheless fell from 12 per cent in 1960 to only 3·9 per cent in 1969 (still above the US average, but much improved). Total employment, however, remains below the 1950 level, and the improvement in part reflects the out-migration of labour. By 1968 the population of the county had fallen to 340,000, and, with per capita incomes almost 20 per cent below the US average, continued decline looks inevitable. Moreover, the new jobs have been largely for women, in clothing, food processing and light assembly work, for example. The traditional roles of men and women have thus often been reversed, the woman going out to work and the man doing the domestic chores.

The figures given above certainly indicate an improved productivity in the remaining mines. Underground operations have been largely mechanized, while two thirds of the output is now won by surface methods. Strip mining today covers large areas and reaches depths of 800 feet or more in working the contorted and irregular seams. Considerable quantities are also obtained comparatively cheaply from the waste of earlier mining – dug out of tips ('culm banks') or dredged from river beds. None the less, the relative cost position of the industry has not improved and output per man-day is below 40 per cent of that achieved in the bituminous sector. In sum, the price of anthracite remains high relative to other coals and other fuels, and its markets have consequently declined catastrophically.

The fall in anthracite production may well continue to virtual extinction, but can do little further damage to the economy of the coalfield area since the numbers involved are now so small. The problem now is how to attract a wider range of new industries to districts with poor social capital, in an environment afflicted by the damaging labours of generations of miners.

The record of *bituminous coal* differs in many important respects from that of anthracite. The statistical highlights are presented in Table 12 for selected years from 1900, on which a few comments follow. (The figures for bituminous coal include lignite production, but lignite output totals under 4 million tons a year, and is therefore ignored in this treatment.) Bituminous coal production grew strongly

Table 12: Bituminous Coal: Salient Statistics, Selected Years, 1900–1968

	Production (million tons)	Employment (thousands)	% of underground production mechanically loaded	% mined by stripping	Productivity (tons per man-day over all)
1900	212	304	n.a.	n.a.	2·98
1918	579	615	n.a.	1·4	3·78
1923	565	705	0·3	2·1	4·47
1932	310	406	12·3	6·3	5·22
1940	461	439	35·4	9·2	5·19
1947	631	419	60·7	22·1	6·42
1954	392	227	84·0	25·1	9·47
1961	403	150	86·3	30·3	13·87
1968	545	128	95·7	34·1	19·37

Source: Minerals Yearbooks

in the early twentieth century, reaching a pre-1940 peak in 1918. Employment attained its all-time peak in 1923. Throughout the twenties output fluctuated sharply, but the secular trend was downwards, and the trough of production for the inter-war period came in 1932. Recovery was then maintained through the 1940s, and output attained record levels in 1947 – 50 million tons above the 1918 peak and, most significantly, achieved with almost 200,000 fewer workers. Increased mechanization underground (represented in the Table by mechanical loading practices) and the growth of strip mining had raised productivity greatly, but the achievement to that time was completely overshadowed by later advance.

The fall from the 1947 pinnacle was severe and with output fluctuating considerably, the industry entered a very difficult period from which it began to emerge only in the 1960s. Production in 1961 was little higher than in the trough of 1954, but has risen considerably since, and the decade ended on a remarkable note of optimism about the future for coal. This optimism does not extend to the employment of a large labour force, however. The 40 per cent increase in production between 1954 and 1968 was accompanied by a further *decrease* of some 42 per cent in employment. Obviously it is this productivity achievement that is responsible for improving the competitiveness of coal energy. Equally clearly, the process has brought hardship to hundreds of thousands of ex-miners and their families.

Productivity in Coalmining

The figures in Table 12 indicate the spectacular gains in productivity since the mid 1950s. The proud overall achievement at that time of ten tons per man-day (unmatched by any other major world producer) was dwarfed as twenty tons per man-day were approached in the later 1960s. Closing down higher-cost workings, concentrating underground mining where physical conditions favoured mechanization, rapidly increasing surface operations, all helped the trend. Perhaps most important, because of the influence on employment and its destructive impact on landscape and environment, were the developments in surface operations. By 1966 over one third of bituminous coal was mined by stripping and a further 3 per cent by auger techniques. In that year the output per man-day achieved by these methods averaged 34 tons and 44 tons respectively, compared with a prodigious, yet relatively unimpressive, 15 tons per man-day underground. All these figures represent a very considerable advance, and one which has subsequently been maintained.

We have already noted the development of earth-moving machinery of gigantic capacity, able to excavate increasing depths of overburdens to reach promising seams. In the mid 1940s an average of 32 feet of overburden was being excavated at strip mines in the US to exploit an average five-foot seam. By 1965 an average of 50 feet was being removed to reach similar seams. Where conditions are favourable and seams are thicker, the depth of overburden removed rises to several times this average. Even so, the strippers are still skimming the cream, and much greater depths of working are in store. 'Strippable reserves' are currently defined as coal 18 inches or more thick with overburden of up to 150 feet. So far, it appears, we have witnessed only the overture; the full score has yet to be played. But, in view of the rising conservation movement, the programme may have to be changed. Up to now, however, stripping has proved highly attractive to the industry. Every producing State, except Utah, has strip capacity, although its relative significance varies with local conditions. Among the large producing States the proportion produced by surface mining varies from about 90 per cent in Indiana and 70 per cent in Ohio to less than 10 per cent in West Virginia, where physical conditions are not so favourable. In the very small producing States, such as Kansas, Missouri and Oklahoma, virtually all the output is from strip mines.

Augering as yet contributes only a small proportion of coal output, but advanced in the 1960s in several major areas. Because of the high productivity achieved, it will certainly be more widely adopted where adequately thick and horizontal seams are found. The method usually follows strip (or 'contour') mining in hilly country. 'Contouring' leaves a cliff face at the point where further cutting into the hillside becomes uneconomic. A giant auger (eight feet or so in diameter) is then bored into the seam, extracting the coal at very low cost. So far the chief fields are in Kentucky and West Virginia, but other Appalachian coalfield areas, such as Ohio and Virginia, have increasing auger output.

Meanwhile important developments have also affected underground operations. Mechanical loading, one of such developments, has long been advancing (see Table 12), while continuous mining techniques have made headway more recently. Even in the late 1950s only a quarter of coal mined underground was won by continuous mining methods; ten years later about half was being obtained in this way, bringing a major improvement in productivity. Underground mines still contribute above 60 per cent of total coal production, and the competitiveness of coal thus depends considerably on the productivity achieved. The importance of underground operations in different coalfields, however, varies with the physical conditions of occurrence and the types of coal produced. Underground mines, with relatively high cost structures, usually produce the better quality coals and coals for special uses (e.g. metallurgy). But these are not the growing sectors of the market, and it is in providing cheap coal for power stations that the outstandingly productive surface-mining operations have proved most effective.

Geography of Production

The area underlain by bituminous coal or lignite deposits is very extensive, but significant production is found in relatively few States. Figure 33 shows the pattern of production of the three major mineral fuels. The Appalachian and Eastern Interior coalfields (the latter embracing Indiana, Illinois and the western counties of Kentucky) together supply about 95 per cent of total coal output so that, nationally, other producing areas are insignificant. These two major coalfields contain about 30 per cent of the total remaining recoverable coal reserves of some 800 billion tons,* and virtually all coals in these fields are bituminous. Elsewhere, nearly three quarters of the reserves are sub-bituminous or lignitic. The Appalachian coals are of especially high quality and have long monopolized the market for high-grade coking and gas varieties.

In contrast to conditions in the anthracite area, physical conditions of occurrence have favoured low-cost production of bituminous coals, both by underground and by surface methods. In the major

* Estimates for 1960. 'Recoverable' reserves represent half the total estimated reserve to allow for various losses.

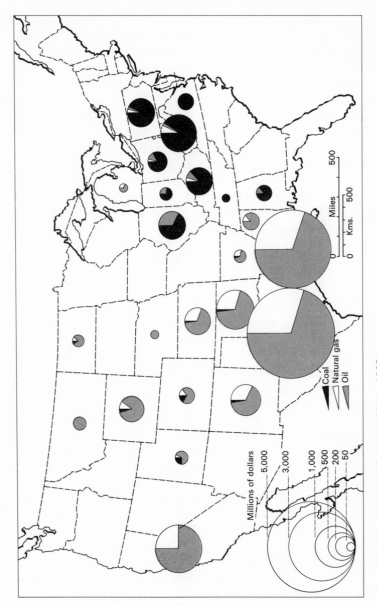

Figure 33. Energy Mineral Output by Value, 1968

producing States of West Virginia, Pennsylvania and Kentucky, for example, coal seams average $4\frac{1}{2}$ to $5\frac{1}{2}$ feet thick, are in general horizontal and uniform with favourable roof, floor and drainage conditions. Such circumstances permit the highest degree of mechanization, and productivity has continuously responded to new investment in more advanced techniques.

In examining the production patterns of bituminous coal in Appalachia, the field may conveniently be divided into northern, central and southern sections. Northern Appalachia (Pennsylvania and Ohio) has sunk considerably in relative stature as a coal producer, chiefly through the decline in rank of Pennsylvania. Up to 1930 Pennsylvania was the major coal-producing State, and more coal has still been produced from this State than from any other. The 'Pittsburgh seam', now much depleted, was especially famous. Some six feet thick, almost horizontal, of huge extent, normally less than 500 feet below the surface and often accessible from valley-side adits, it helped to lay the foundations of the great iron and steel complex of western Pennsylvania. But the peak year of Pennsylvanian production came in 1918, and output has since steadily declined. West Virginia took first place among coal-producing States in 1931. None the less, Pennsylvania is still a major producer. Deep-mine production remains important, but by the late 1960s surface operations supplied about 40 per cent of total output.

Within northern Appalachia, mining moved westward in the nineteenth century, to enter Ohio. Coal producers here also faced difficulties in the inter-war years, but gradually found that conditions greatly favoured surface-mining methods. Low-cost strip operations have thus become very important and Ohio has the highest overall productivity of the Appalachian coalfield States. Consequently, total output in Ohio was stable even through the 1940s and 1950s, and expanded in the 1960s. Recently over 70 per cent of the coal mined has been from strip pits. The product is of lower quality and suitable chiefly for power-station use, but this is a growing market. By contrast, much of the Pennsylvanian coal is of higher quality, commands a higher price, and is used for special purposes by industrial consumers whose demands have not been expanding greatly. Pittsburgh remains the natural centre for this part of the Appalachian coalfield, surrounded by famous or evocative names like Connellsville and Uniontown, Black Lick, Cokeburg and Coal Bluff. But in coal production the area is a shadow of its former self, and the changing patterns have brought difficult times to many districts.

The Central Appalachian coalfield lies in West Virginia and Virginia, east Kentucky and a small area of Maryland. West Virginia became the largest coal-producing State in 1931 and ever since has provided a quarter or more of national output. Early in this century, the chief centres were in the north of the State, adjacent to Pennsylvania, serving the Pittsburgh industrial region via the Monongahela river. Gradually, however, the southern areas around the Big Sandy and Kanawha rivers and their tributaries developed, and have long been the largest centres of production. Underground mining conditions favour very high productivity, but the very rugged terrain has rather discouraged surface operations, which remain less important than in any other major producing State. The relatively limited contour mining does much physical damage, however, and is normally followed by highly productive auger working. None the less about 85 per cent of West Virginia coal still comes from underground mines. As in Pennsylvania, good-quality coals are produced in large quantity, but the market for such coals has not been buoyant and West Virginia producers have been relatively slow to develop their power-station markets.

Much of this State was opened up to intensive settlement only in this century, with the coming of the mines. Numerous communities were settled in remote and difficult situations with no *raison d'être* apart from their coal output. Recent developments have therefore had serious repercussions over wide areas. In 1948 total mining employment reached a post-war peak here of 138,000. By 1969 it was a mere 47,000 and West Virginia had long been one of the most depressed States of the Union. Even in 1968, when unemployment nationally was at its lowest level for twenty years (3·6 per cent), eleven West Virginia counties had rates above 10 per cent while the State average was 5·7 per cent. Coal industry problems, though not the only cause of such poor conditions, bear a large share of the responsibility. A similar history and similar problems of unemployment, depression and poverty affect the neighbouring coalfield areas

223

of east Kentucky. Here, the background to development and the appalling conditions of life and environment have been eloquently recounted by H. Caudill in *Night Comes to the Cumberlands*.

The remaining large central Appalachian coal-producing State, Virginia, has an unusual history. Before the war this State was a minor producer, with output hovering around 10–12 million tons per annum, rising to about 20 million in the early war years. In the 1950s, however, while the industry elsewhere was in difficulties, output expanded steadily and by 1968 reached 37 million tons. Uncommonly, too, a large proportion of this rising output (above 80 per cent in the late 1960s) is obtained from deep mines. This reflects the influence of position. Virginia, with relatively easy access to Atlantic ports, has increased its coal production by expanding exports. Southern West Virginia and east Kentucky areas have also benefited from this trade, but not so greatly as their eastern neighbour, whose rising output has sustained mining employment at early 1950s levels, despite increasing productivity.

Production in southern Appalachia (Alabama and Tennessee) has never been outstanding. Tennessee was always a minor producer and, at its peak in 1926, Alabama produced only 21 million tons. Conditions underground are generally inferior to those experienced further north. Seams are thinner and more irregular, and continuous mining techniques have made little headway. Productivity is therefore comparatively low. The quantity produced by surface working has grown, but the output per man-hour falls short of the national average. Here again, therefore, we find the familiar theme in the coal-industry record, an area in difficulty. In 1947 about 24,000 coal miners were employed in Alabama. Twenty years later only 5,000 remained.

Beyond the barren Cincinnati anticline lies the second most productive American coalfield, the Eastern Interior. This field, extending from Illinois into Indiana and west Kentucky, occurs in a basin covered with glacial materials, with coal outcropping sporadically around the periphery of the field and along the valleys. The disposition of the coals is highly favourable, and short-shaft mines in Illinois, at the heart of the field, reach down to seams some $7\frac{1}{2}$ feet thick. Here the physical conditions are reflected in the very high

224

productivity of underground workings; over twenty tons per man-day were achieved in the late 1960s, the highest level in the nation. But the conditions generally favour stripping, which is prominent everywhere. Over two thirds of the Eastern Interior output is obtained by stripping, and the productivity of the whole field is notable even by US standards.

The Eastern Interior coals are all bituminous but not of the high qualities of the northern and central Appalachian areas. Coking-quality coals, for example, are pretty limited, and even these normally have to be mixed with Appalachian coal to produce a satisfactory coke-oven charge. The field possesses a considerable advantage, however, in its proximity to the huge mid-western market. This consumes considerable tonnages of coal in industrial uses, while power-station demand is very large and growing strongly. Thus the field has been increasing its share of national output since the war. Employment, however, has experienced the normal downward trend.

Outside the Appalachian and Eastern Interior fields interest in coal is small and scattered. Huge reserves of bituminous coals and lignites lie virtually untouched in the West Central and the Mountain divisions. Production is only locally of significance, and normally, so far, as a fuel for power stations, as in Colorado, Wyoming and New Mexico. But coking coal is produced in Utah and Colorado and this has been useful in aiding the establishment of iron and steel works in those States and in California. Understandably, however, energy demands in all areas removed from the major producing coalfields are oriented to sources other than coal. Plans for very large coal-fired power stations were being laid in these areas in the late 1960s and long-term contracts for coal from the western fields have been signed. This may indicate a revival of interest in the enormous coal reserves west of the Mississippi, but much must depend on what nuclear power achieves and on the solution of current environmental problems of coal-fired stations.

Oil and Gas

By contrast with the unsettled situation in coal, the oil and natural gas industries have enjoyed continuous growth. Statistics of production for 1940 to 1968 are in Table 13. These show the very rapid rate of expansion in natural gas and the steady growth of crude oil

Table 13: Crude Petroleum, Natural Gas and Natural Gas Liquids: Domestic Production 1940–68

	1940	1950	1960	1968
Crude petroleum (million barrels)	1,353	1,974	2,575	3,329
Natural gas (marketed production; billion cubic feet)	2,660	6,282	12,771	19,322
Natural gas liquids (million barrels)	56	182	340	550

Source: Statistical Abstract, 1969

output. Oil imports have considerably boosted domestic *consumption* of petroleum products since the war, but, even including these imports, natural gas and gas liquids have grown far more impressively (Figure 32). From 1940 to 1968 natural gas and gas liquids raised their contribution to total US energy consumption from 12 per cent to 35 per cent, whereas oil moved from 31 per cent in 1940 to 42 per cent in 1960, but moved back to 40 per cent by 1968.

The future of both minerals is assured, but the position of domestic producers is more uncertain, for the domestic reserve and production cost position is not entirely satisfactory in either. For example, the reserve to production (R–P) ratio in 1960 for crude petroleum was 12; but by 1967 it had fallen to under 10, and has remained at this level. Certainly there is enough petroleum lying in the ground, unproved, for many years' supply. But there is some question about whether it can be located and produced at competitive prices. US domestic oil sells in a protected market at rates normally considerably above the world average, yet exploration has fallen off, and producers complain about very high costs of exploration and recovery. The situation is intimately affected by import policy, which is discussed below. Another imponderable is the Alaskan reserves, as yet not clearly known,* and for which wildly varying estimates of costs of production and movement have been made. It seems inevitable, however, that imports will be increasingly needed to meet the demand for oil.

For natural gas the R–P ratio in 1960 was 21, but by 1969 had declined to 13. This partly reflects the regulation of the price of inter-State shipments by the Federal Power Commission, for it is claimed that they have not given adequate incentive for exploration work. Early in 1970 an official report described natural gas reserves as 'critically low'. Estimates of 'potential reserves' are very high, but proving them (an essential, but costly, part of the business) has been insufficiently pursued in recent years. It is considered that production may fall short of demand by the mid 1970s, in which case natural gas imports from Canada and Mexico, or liquefied natural gas imports from other areas, could become substantial.

Geography of Production

The geographical patterns of domestic oil and natural gas supply differ significantly from that of the coals. Figure 33 shows little coincidence of the major producing areas for coal on the one hand and for gas and oil on the other. Crude petroleum and natural gas production is heavily concentrated in Texas and Louisiana, together accounting for 60 per cent of oil and 70 per cent of natural gas. Far behind these two, although they are large producers, come California and Oklahoma, while most other States with significant output are also west of the Mississippi. In fact, under 5 per cent of the total US output of these minerals originates east of that river – in complete contrast to coal production. Rarely, then, does a significant output of coal coincide geographically with that of oil or gas. Among the

* Standard Oil of New Jersey in 1970 estimated North Slope reserves at 20 billion barrels, of which Prudhoe Bay accounted for 10 billion. Other estimates go twice or more above these figures. In 1969, before the Alaskan discoveries, total US proved reserves were estimated at 30 billion barrels.

major coal States, only Illinois has any notable interest in crude oil. Other north-eastern States have thousands of wells, which often are pumped only intermittently and produce on average only a fraction of a barrel of (high-quality) oil per day. Similarly, several eastern coalfield States appear as natural gas producers but only West Virginia achieves anything like significant production.

Such geographical variations have important implications, not only for fuel production and marketing, but also for the energy economies of different areas and for regional economic structure and performance. The uncertain production and poor employment record of the coal industry has affected chiefly States in the difficult Appalachian region. The possession and development of great coal resources has been a mixed blessing for the area, and the populations attracted by them. Meanwhile, oil and gas production has risen and relatively high levels of employment have been maintained. In 1940 about 203,000 persons were employed in extracting oil and natural gas. In 1969, some 282,000 were so employed – less, it is true, than a 344,000 peak in 1957, but not disastrously so. Moreover, increasing output of these minerals has presented opportunities for employment in associated activities such as field services, transport, refining and chemicals manufacturing, all of which have expanded in the major producing areas as output has risen. Thus the leading oil and gas States continue to benefit greatly from their endowment of these minerals.

Demand–Supply Relationships

The decline in the relative contribution of coal to the national energy supply is related both to the technical requirements of fossil-fuel consumers and to changes in consumer preferences. Technical needs dictate the type of fuel for some major consuming sectors, thus limiting the area of effective competition. This is chiefly true of transport, in which petroleum products currently have a virtual monopoly. Outside such specific uses, the choice available among possible primary sources has increased. Important developments of this kind took place before 1940, but since the war oil and natural

228

gas have penetrated all major consuming areas. Thus most primary-fuel consumers can choose among the three fossil fuels on grounds of technical superiority, convenience or price. In this competition coal lost ground substantially and continuously, first to oil products and later to natural gas, in what had been important markets. But

Table 14: Primary Energy Consumption by Major Markets, 1947–68 (per cent)*

Market		Coal	Natural gas	Petro-leum†	Hydro-power	Total input (trillion BTU)
Household	1947	50	17	33	—	6,800
and	1962	9	44	48	—	11,000
commercial	1968	4	47	48	—	13,600
Industrial	1947	58	23	20	—	12,700
	1962	31	44	25	—	15,400
	1968	29	48	23	—	19,300
Transport	1947	35	neg.	66		8,800
	1962	neg.	4	97		11,400
	1968	neg.	4	96		15,100
Electrical	1947	47	9	11	33	4,400
utilities	1962	51	23	6	20	9,100
	1968‡	51	23	8	17	14,000

* Rounded to nearest whole number
† Including natural gas liquids
‡ Nuclear Power 1 per cent

Source: Minerals Yearbook, 1963, 1968

gas has also won markets in which oil had for a while enjoyed a preferential position, while coal has recently shown renewed competitive strength in certain uses. Thus the situation is not always clear cut. Figure 34 illustrates the changing structure of the market for coal, and Table 14 the changing preferences of the four major consuming sectors.

In transport, while oil has long dominated road and shipping

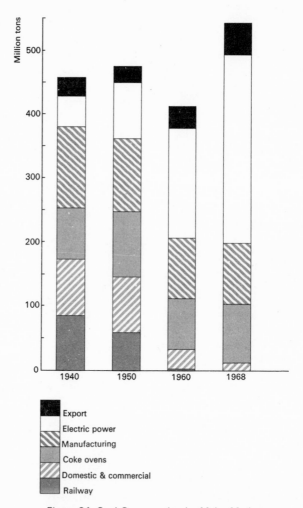

Figure 34. Coal Consumption by Major Markets

markets, coal remained a large contributor to the railways until the 1950s. In 1940 the railways consumed almost one fifth of total US coal supply and were the coal industry's largest single customer. But coal was already feeling the competition of oil, and after 1944 (when the railways consumed a record 132 million tons of coal) sales to this market declined. By the early 1960s they were entirely negligible. Meanwhile oil industry sales were increasingly concentrated on the transport sector, in which demand grew steadily. Since the war a continuously expanding proportion of the rising US refinery output has gone into transport uses and the balance of refinery production has thus been substantially altered. In 1950, for example, petrol and jet fuel accounted for 46 per cent of the volume of output of US refineries, by 1968 56 per cent of a much larger total output. Moreover, a rising proportion of distillate fuel oil output has also gone, as diesel oils, to transport uses, which now consume almost two thirds of US refinery output. The domestic production of residual fuel oils consequently has fallen, relatively and absolutely. The total US *consumption* of residual fuel oil, however, has not declined and imports of residuals have become heavy at certain coastal locations. But, clearly, the trend in US refinery operation has been to up-grade domestic crude supplies to obtain greater yields of the high-value lighter products demanded by transport uses.

Competition for the three remaining classes of consumption is more interesting. In the rapidly growing *household and commercial sector*, where demand is chiefly for space-heating, the remarkable post-war expansion of natural gas is indicated in Table 14. This expansion is chiefly at the expense of coal, another market in which once very large coal sales have shrunk to negligible levels (Figure 34). But without the geographical extension of the area served by natural gas, oil would certainly have captured a much larger share of this market. In fact, as the gas pipelines extended their geographical coverage, the rate of growth in oil sales to domestic and commercial consumers declined so that, in the later part of the period covered in the Table, sales of natural gas were increasing at over twice the rate for oil, and gas seems set to become the largest supplier to this market. The pace of growth of natural gas here, however, is levelling off, as domestic and commercial consumer preferences change yet again, now in favour of electricity, of which development more is said below.

The *industrial sector* shows a relatively sluggish rate of growth in demand for mineral fuels, but none the less remains the largest single consuming sector (Table 14). The fossil fuels are here not only a source of energy but also, for some industries, a raw material. The petrochemical industry provides the most obvious example, but coke in blast furnaces is a raw material of the process as well as a medium for heat. The precise allocation of fossil fuels to industrial energy or raw material uses is, however, too complex to be developed here, and the statistics refer to the total supply of these minerals to industry. In the manufacturing industries, coal has experienced mixed fortunes (Figure 34). Coke has still no effective competitor in blast-furnace uses, but coal sales to coke ovens have both fluctuated with the fortunes of the iron and steel industry, and been affected by the economies achieved in the coke ovens themselves and in the use of coke in blast furnaces. Sales of coal to coke ovens have therefore remained pretty stable, despite the substantial secular rise in iron production. Technical advance and economy in use, too, as well as substitution by oil, have kept coal sales to the expanding steel works static for some years, after rapid decline in the first post-war decade. Sales to cement mills, however, have risen steadily with the great increase in construction activity, but the amount involved is relatively small. Other manufacturing markets have, on average, reduced their purchases of raw coal, despite an advance in total energy consumption, which sums up what has happened to the market for coal in the manufacturing sector as a whole.

Oil and gas, by contrast, are meeting more of industry's fuel needs (Table 14). Both initially advanced at the expense of coal, capitalizing on their relative virtues of cleanliness, ease and cheapness of movement, certain technical considerations and, for natural gas, the relief from holding stocks. Recently, however, as in other sectors, gas has advanced more slowly and at the expense of oil, which has been affected by rising prices and the policy of concentration on transport fuels. Coal still commands some 30 per cent of the industrial market and now appears to stand relatively well, because of the proximity of coal-supply areas to major industrial centres. In industry, however, as in the domestic and commercial markets, the energy input is increasingly being taken in the form of electricity. Electricity already dominates the industrial need for a source of motive power, and has long been used for heat in electrometallurgical and electrochemical industries, which are very large consumers. Increasingly, however, industrial users requiring small-energy inputs, apart from power, are attracted by the advantages electricity offers – in plant heating or air conditioning, for example. Thus the industrial demand for electricity has grown rapidly. Since the same is true for the domestic and commercial markets, expansion in total demand for energy in the form of electricity has been very great indeed.

In 1940 the installed *electrical generating capacity* in the United States totalled 51 million kilowatts, by 1968 over 300 million. Such an expansion was bound to affect the available primary sources, here including hydro-power alongside oil, natural gas and coal. Absolutely, all have contributed towards this very large increase in capacity, but their relative status has changed considerably. This is true of hydro-power, for example. Capacity increased from 11 million kilowatts to about 50 million from 1940 to 1968, but the contribution to total electric power supply nevertheless fell from 33 to 17 per cent. Most parts of the country still have untapped hydro-electrical potential, but its development in most locations is currently uneconomic. New hydro capacity tends to be designed for peak load operation, for which it is well suited. The base load is more efficiently and economically met from very large, modern, thermal stations, in supplying which the fossil fuels compete with one another, and in future will face growing competition from the atom.

Among the fossil fuels available for power station consumption, no *one* possesses an overwhelming advantage technically (as, for example, petrol in motor vehicle transport) or in convenience (as, for example, natural gas for domestic space heating). Thus price becomes the arbiter for most decisions in this context, and location relative to fuel sources or transport networks is an important element in the choice of fuel. At the national level, coal is the cheapest fuel for steam-power generation but only marginally cheaper than natural gas. Oil is considerably more expensive – on a BTU basis more than 30 per cent dearer per unit in recent years than the competing fuels.

233

Of course, the national average situation means little here, since so much depends on the actual location of consumption *vis-à-vis* supplies. None the less, because of its generally high relative cost, fuel oil has made only a limited advance in the power-station market, and that chiefly at coastal locations on imports of residual fuel oil. Thus about 80 per cent of oil consumed in electricity generation is consumed in the five coastal States of Florida, New York, New Jersey, Massachusetts and California. The major indigenous oil-producing States of Texas and Louisiana together consume only about 1 per cent of all oil used nationally in electricity generation. Over all, in 1968 under 8 per cent of total US generating capacity was fired by oil – down from a peak of above 10 per cent in the late 1940s.

The demand by power utilities for natural gas has, by contrast, risen rapidly. In the major producing areas gas has been a far cheaper source of electricity generation than oil or coal. But in serving distant markets for power generation (as, for example, in the industrial North-East) natural gas faces transport costs which normally rule it out of low-value uses like electricity generation. Thus natural gas is an important fuel source for power stations over a relatively limited geographical area. The West South Central division and California alone account for above two thirds of all the gas consumed in this way. Other smaller gas-producing States, such as Kansas, also rely on gas-fired power utilities to a greater than normal extent. Elsewhere at present such plant is often provided in low-capacity units for 'stand-by' duty. Such gas-fired units are relatively expensive in both capital and operating cost (and thus per unit of power generated), but they are very flexible and available for use at short notice. They can thus meet peak requirements or temporary shortages better than coal-fired stations. Natural gas has therefore advanced considerably in the field of electricity generation, supplying about 23 per cent of the nation's power production in 1968, compared with 9 per cent in 1940. Further relative expansion, however, is unlikely, and the rate of growth in sales to this market fell sharply in the 1960s. The price of gas has risen in recent years, and the physical returns to new investment in natural gas supply are diminishing. Prices must rise further, and gas will probably be increasingly confined to its higher-

234

value uses as in heating and as a chemical raw material. Its share of the power-station market will probably fall in the 1970s, unless the clamour for clean air gives it a reprieve as the cleanest burning fuel available.

Experience since the war indicates that base load requirements over much of the USA are best met by large modern coal-fired power stations, especially east of the Mississippi, where the largest total demand for electricity is found. In 1968, over half of all American power was produced in coal-fired stations, compared with 47 per cent in 1947. Since this has been a time of enormous investment in new generating plant, and fresh decisions on type of plant were continuously being made, coal must have offered important cost advantages in a very large number of cases. Sales of coal have thus increased spectacularly from about 50 million tons in 1940 to almost 300 million in 1968. Several factors help to explain this situation. Firstly, technical advances have achieved significant economies in coal consumption. In 1940, the electrical utilities consumed on average 1·34 pounds of coal per kilowatt hour (kwh) produced. By 1968 it was 0·87 pounds. The pace of advance in this field has slowed in the past decade, but the efficiency of coal use in power stations is none the less much higher than in the early post-war years.

Coupled with economies in coal use have been economies in coal movement to power stations. This matters greatly since, on average, rail freight adds upwards of 75 per cent to the minehead cost of coal. In an interesting experiment in 1957 coal was moved in a slurry by pipeline 108 miles from a mine in eastern Ohio to a power station in Cleveland. Its success startled the railway companies into improving their coal transport facilities and sharply decreasing their rates. The pipe was put on a 'stand-by' basis in 1963, but an important reduction in cost of coal movement in the North-East had been achieved. Among the advances has been the introduction of the 'unit train' system which has sometimes made a saving of up to $1·50 per ton – about a third of the minehead value of the coal. Coal movement by very large road truck over shorter distances and increased use of river transport have also achieved substantial economies.

Finally, siting power stations at, or close to, the mine has offered obvious cost savings. This has been facilitated by improved transmission technology. Extra high voltage transmission lines can transport electric current economically over long distances to major centres of demand. This enhances the value of coalfield sites for power stations since it reduces coal-supply and transport costs. For such reasons, therefore, the market for coal in power generation has grown very rapidly. In 1940 just over a tenth of domestic coal sales in the USA went to power stations. By 1968 this market absorbed over half of considerably higher total sales. Power stations should remain the major market for coal in the future, with purchases of more than 600 million tons per annum in prospect according to some observers, despite further economies in use. Some major producers already have long-term contracts (twenty or more years) for very large quantities. But much will depend on the sustained growth of demand for power (which appears pretty certain) and on the role of nuclear plant, which is more uncertain. So far its contribution has been negligible. (A separate review of the nuclear sector is made below.) Another imponderable concerns the possible impact of the campaign against air pollution on coal-burning in electricity generation.

The structure of energy consumption as represented in Table 14 is, of course, an average of highly varied regional situations. There is no more a single energy economy representative of all parts of the USA than there is a typical agricultural economy. Rather there are numerous energy systems reflecting local resources, access, costs of movement, structure of demand, and so on. The generalized national situation provides a useful peg on which to hang discussion, but Figure 35 emphasizes the varied regional structure of demand for the fossil fuels in the 'competitive' uses. The demand represented here comprises the household, commercial, industrial and electric utility sectors. Consumption in transport uses has been excluded, since everywhere this sector is dominated by oil products. This competitive market for the fossil fuels is shared by coal, oil and gas in the national proportion of 35, 20, 45, respectively; but the regional structures clearly differ enormously from this average pattern. The significant markets for coal lie largely east of the Mississippi (excluding New England), where the very large industrial and electric utility demand draws heavily on coal. With transport uses excluded, the relative

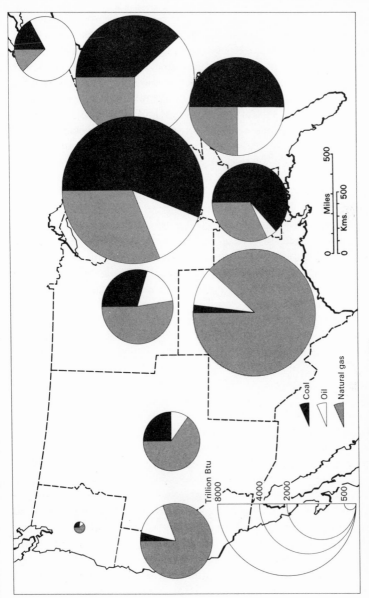

Figure 35. Patterns of Fossil Fuel Consumption, 1965

standing of oil in the energy economy is, of course, greatly decreased. Significantly, however, it makes a major contribution to the 'competitive' market in eastern coastal areas, where oil imports have been growing. Oil is the dominant source of energy in New England, but the Middle Atlantic division consumes a greater volume than any other. Elsewhere, expensive indigenous oil is limited in its penetration of non-transport markets, and even in the major oil-producing West South Central areas it barely accounts for 10 per cent of fossil fuel consumption. Natural gas, by contrast, has important markets of one sort or another everywhere except in the extreme North-East (New England) and North-West (Washington and Oregon). Understandably, however, the biggest single market area is in the enlarged West South Central division (here including Kansas and New Mexico), where gas use, especially by industry, is very great indeed. In several western areas it should be noted that hydro-electric power provides an important proportion of energy supply, not represented on the map. This is especially true of Washington and Oregon, where some three quarters of all energy used is derived from hydro sources. But this brief review of regional energy systems has been highly oversimplified, since its object is merely to indicate the regional variety subsumed within the national average patterns discussed above.

Trade in the Mineral Fuels

The mineral fuels have an important place in US external trade and all three major minerals are involved. Natural gas imports, however (from Canada and Mexico), have so far been relatively small. They are important in the receiving areas, of course, and their significance seems certain to increase. Discussion here will, however, be confined to coal and oil, which figure prominently in present trade patterns. Exports have provided a very important market outlet for the coal industry since the war. Annual shipments have fluctuated with economic conditions in importing areas, international emergencies and other variables. Assisted by the secular decline in ocean freight rates and the very high productivity in US mines, however, the industry has found important and apparently permanent markets in several overseas areas, while supplying growing quantities to Canada. Japan and Italy are the major overseas destinations, but other European countries (some with important domestic coalmining industries, like Germany and Belgium) have found it profitable to purchase coals from the USA. In Britain such imports, greatly desired by certain large consuming interests like iron and steel, have been prevented by government intervention. Thus US coal exports have recently maintained a healthy annual total of about 50 million tons, and further growth is likely. The trade has benefited the Hampton Roads area of the east coast, where most of the overseas exports are handled, and the coal industry of Virginia which, as was shown above, has expanded significantly in consequence.

Trade in oil has been far less straightforward, and we can here afford only a brief outline of a highly complex situation. Before the Second World War the US was a small net exporter of oil. Subsequently, with domestic demand increasing sharply, imports of crude oil and refined products (notably residual fuel oil) rose swiftly, too, and the US became the world's largest importer. These imports now account for a fifth of total domestic consumption, but they would undoubtedly have grown much more but for Federal government intervention. The cheapness of foreign oil delivered at coastal locations greatly enhanced its attractions for consumers in areas remote from the major US fields and, between 1950 and 1956, crude oil imports doubled. In 1957, under pressure from domestic producers, the government introduced a 'voluntary' system of control for crude imports. Thereupon consumers increased their imports of refined products, which rose by about 60 per cent between 1956 and 1959. In 1959, therefore, the government introduced a mandatory system of oil import quotas, which with modifications is still in force. Imports have continued to grow, but at a rate related to the increase in domestic production. Overseas imports in areas east of the Rockies have been restricted to 12·2 per cent of the crude oil and natural gas liquids produced in these areas. (Overland imports from Canada and Mexico have nominally been exempt, but are in practice controlled less formally.) West of the Rockies the system recognizes the costs of moving oil across the mountain zone, and overseas imports are permitted to make up the difference between domestic supply and demand, once overland imports have been taken into account.

The justification for Federal intervention has been that an uncontrolled inflow of cheap foreign oil would seriously damage the domestic industry and thus affect national security. It is argued that many oil producers (especially smaller ones, with no overseas investments to supplement internal operations) would be driven out of business; domestic production would decline to dangerously low levels; exploration for domestic resources would be further curtailed; and the economy would come to depend upon foreign supplies, which could be interrupted in emergencies. Against this case are many large oil consumers (who have had to pay relatively high prices) and certain major consuming areas remote from domestic oil and gas supplies (such as New England), which have been forced to subordinate their interests in cheap energy to those of the domestic producers of oil on security grounds they consider unsubstantiated. 'Vulnerable' imports from the Middle East, never very large, have recently declined. The major foreign suppliers remain Venezuela and Canada, the latter growing rapidly. These are considered 'safe' sources, with little prospect of interruption for political reasons.

Such a conflict of views has no simple solution. What is clear is that the policy is expensive. American crude oil prices have long been above world prices. Early in 1970 the world average price of crude oil was about $2 per barrel, the US average about $3·30.* With domestic consumption exceeding 4,000 million barrels per year in the later 1960s, the price of the import quota system is obviously high. Not all US domestic producers have such high costs, of course, and thus not all would be driven out of the market in freely competitive circumstances. Again, if the US market was thrown open to international trade, world prices would certainly rise. There are many other ramifications, too, both of maintaining the present controls and of dismantling them. The system has become increasingly complex, with special quotas, exemptions and other ad hoc arrangements affecting the interests of individuals, companies or geo-

---

* Price relationships are not stable. Because of special problems in the Middle East, import prices were above the domestic level in mid 1970. The normal situation is, however, as reported in the text.

graphical areas. A precise balance sheet is thus not easily computed, but an official Cabinet review of the system, published early in 1970, set the costs to the American economy at between $4·5 billion and $5·5 billion per annum, a large bill for debatable gains in 'national security'. The Cabinet 'task force' itself remained divided over the issue, and its majority recommendation that a tariff should replace the quota system has been ignored. (A small duty is, in fact, already imposed.) The dilemma is not easy to resolve, and the promised arrival of Alaskan oil will probably have only a marginal effect. Delays in building the Trans-Alaska pipeline, brought about by technical problems and the issues of environment and conservation, probably mean that oil supplies from this source will not reach appreciable size until the mid 1970s at the earliest. Even then, they are considered unlikely to serve more than about 5 per cent of total demand. The fact of, and the need for, large oil imports thus remains, with its many economic, political and geographical implications. In these circumstances, restrictions on Canadian oil (already nominal) will probably be set aside.

The Impact of the Atom

At various times since the early 1950s nuclear power has been reported to be on the verge of becoming a competitive supplier of electricity, at least in locations with high-cost conventional power. Each time it failed to achieve these expectations – partly because it was chasing a moving target in conventional power-station costs, where considerable economies have been achieved. So it was perhaps not entirely unexpected that the much-publicized 'breakthrough' of the late 1960s, like its predecessors, fell short of expectations. The important difference on this occasion was that it persuaded the utility companies in the USA to embark upon a major programme of investment in nuclear facilities, so that by the end of 1969, 48 large stations were being built and 32 more were on order. Fifteen were already in operation, but many of these were small experimental stations and the nuclear contribution to power supply in 1969 remained only about 1 per cent of the total.

In the middle 1960s, General Electric (a major nuclear power-station construction company) quoted a guaranteed price for a nuclear plant at Oyster Creek, NJ, which would have enabled electricity to be produced at under 4 mills per kilowatt hour, at that time a most competitive price (N.B. One mill is a thousandth of a dollar). As anticipated by the builders, more orders followed, the flow becoming a flood after the Tennessee Valley Association (in an area quite close to low-cost coal supplies) ordered two nuclear plants in 1966. The quote for Oyster Creek was, in fact, a 'turnkey' project – a fixed-price contract undertaken by the builder to get into the business and to stimulate new orders. Not surprisingly, the low cost claimed in 1964 for the production of power from Oyster Creek was not achieved. The station came into operation late in 1969, two years behind schedule, and, although the operators are protected by the 'turnkey' quote, the true price of its power is substantially above the early estimate. In the important TVA contracts, other unusual circumstances seem to have operated. As a Federal body, the TVA can borrow money at very favourable rates and it has lower tax liabilities. Moreover, in its cost calculations the TVA apparently assumed a longer than normal life for its plant. The cost calculations, therefore, were based on special conditions; but a bandwagon had been set rolling, to be partially the cause of subsequent difficulties. In 1966 24 large nuclear plants were ordered (in addition to 6 already on the books), and in 1967 a further 31, as utility companies hastened to 'look modern'. Thereafter new orders fell to 14 in 1968 and only 7 in 1969, while several earlier orders were cancelled. The rush to 'go nuclear' had exposed weaknesses in the capability of the nuclear power-station builders. Huge and costly bottlenecks occurred in the manufacturing sector; skilled labour, for manufacturing and construction, became difficult to obtain; legal obstacles and site-acquisition problems multiplied. Thus, costs steadily rose and delivery dates receded. In 1967, for example, the estimate for construction cost per kilowatt hour of capacity for a large nuclear station averaged $130. In 1968 the estimate was revised to $150, and in 1969 revised again to about $200. Meanwhile, delivery dates had stretched from four years to seven years or more, and some supply companies had to invest hurriedly in conventional capacity to meet their growing demands. In 1969 more than 40 large conventional stations were ordered, representing over 85 per cent of the new capacity ordered that year.

The situation at the opening of the new decade, therefore, is little clearer than it was in the 1960s. The nuclear power industry has again failed to attain expected targets, but the gap between nuclear costs and conventional steam-plant costs cannot now be great in high-cost locations such as New England. Little can be said confidently on these matters, as the variables are numerous and changing. The true cost of nuclear power will in fact remain unknown until the large new stations have operated for some years. The quantity of power supplied from nuclear stations will, however, rise substantially. By 1975, on current schedules, about 90 nuclear units should be operating, with a total capacity of 64,000 megawatts, or about 13 per cent of estimated national capacity at that time. Thereafter the guesses grow more hazardous, but the USA Atomic Energy Commission considers that in 1980 a nuclear capacity of about 150,000 megawatts is most likely – just over one fifth of an estimated total generating capacity of about 700,000 megawatts. Since the nuclear plants will operate as base-load stations, they will provide a rather higher proportion (AEC estimates about 28 per cent) of actual power supply.

Figure 36 shows the location of the nuclear plants operating or being built in 1969. The pattern is fairly predictable. The major concentration occurs in the North-East manufacturing belt on both sides of Appalachia. This belt accounts for over 40 per cent of all electricity sales in the USA. Following this belt in size of electricity sales come the South Atlantic and Pacific divisions, also represented quite strongly on the nuclear map. The Great Plains and Mountain States have little to show, and the West South Central division, the major oil- and gas-producing area, currently has no nuclear plant under way, although one is planned for Arkansas. Appalachia, too, apart from the TVA projects in northern Alabama and the small experimental plant in western Pennsylvania, is understandably investing little in nuclear facilities. It should be noted that the map does not distinguish between plant sizes. Seven of the fifteen stations operating in 1969 were small – of less than 100 megawatt capacity;

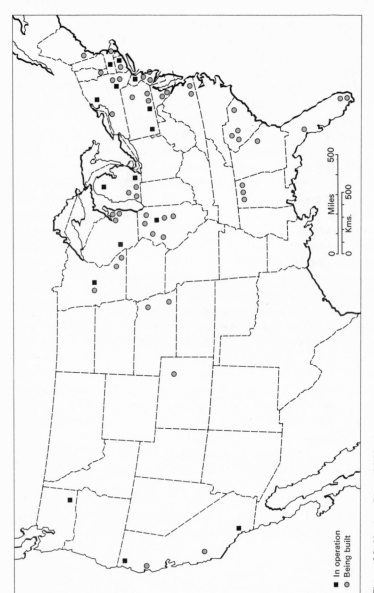

In operation ■
Being built ●

Figure 36. Nuclear Plant, 1969

while some plants under construction are rated at over 1,000 mega-watts. The map does not, therefore, reflect the real nuclear power capacity, actual or potential, of the various States.

The development of nuclear power clearly has implications for the future of coal. The greatest expansion in the demand for energy has come in the electric power sector – a trend certain to continue, and even accelerate – and among the fossil fuels coal has remained the outstanding source of electricity generation. Difficulties in natural gas supply and cost seemed indeed likely to make coal more com-petitive over even larger areas of the market. In default of a major change in government policy, therefore, to permit much larger imports of cheap fuel oils, coal's position among the fossil fuels would have further improved. As this became clear in the middle 1960s, optimistic forecasts were made about the future for coal. In 1965, for example, estimates of coal requirements in power stations by 1980 were hovering between 600 and 700 million tons, and a total demand for coal of over 900 million tons was predicted – a new 'golden age' for coal. The atomic attack on the energy market, though itself blunted, has moderated such ebullience, but the utility market is expanding so fast that the demand for coal will nevertheless grow steadily, if not as rapidly as recently forecast. After the great rush to get on the nuclear bandwagon, the utility companies are becoming more discriminating. Nuclear plant will offer a considerable advant-age in one type of situation, and fossil fuel in another, while in some neither will offer a clear advantage and the choice will be more open. In sum, despite the entry of nuclear power in substantial quantity, the demand for coal in power stations will rise steadily. Although coal's *share* of this market will decline, the expansion of demand for electricity will be so great that sales to utilities will (saving some new and major technological advance) probably continue to grow for the remainder of this century. We must return, however, to the imponderables of environmental preservation and improvement, which could affect the overall situation quite substantially.

The Environmental Problem

One cloud on the horizon for utility companies is the increased public concern over environment and pollution. This is only one part of a major national issue which touches life and the economy at every point. An outline of the problem in the context of the energy sector provides a suitable final theme for this chapter. Every stage in the production, transport and consumption of energy is inevitably accompanied by some sort of physical impact, but some results are actively harmful rather than 'passive' in their impact on landscape and environment, and are increasingly criticized. Coalmining, for example, has caused massive damage to the physical and ecological environment of many areas; oil leaks from underwater wells have polluted lake and seaboard areas; surface pipelines and transmission cables have intruded in areas of great beauty; energy consumers have grievously polluted the atmosphere. Such harm is preventable, but prevention is often costly. The current mood of the articulate in America is that the price should be paid. One or two examples of the issues will be mentioned here, first in relation to the power-supply situation discussed above.

The concern over the conventional coal- or oil-burning utilities is chiefly about their discharge of smoke containing solids or chemicals, which are injurious to health, to land and its productivity, to buildings and to other property. It was estimated in 1967 that power utilities dispersed about 16 million tons of pollutants annually, about 13 per cent of the total weight of atmospheric pollutants.* Power stations are the largest single source of noxious oxides of sulphur, and a very large producer of particulate matter, which at worst is toxic and at best grossly unpleasant. In some areas, such as New York, these power stations, as the largest single source of atmospheric pollution, are the prime target of attack. Utilities anxious to provide new conventional capacity to keep pace with demand for power face increasing difficulty in finding suitable sites without involving themselves in prolonged and costly litigation. The demand for the use of

* The prime air polluter is transport, which accounted for 60 per cent; followed by manufacturing with 19 per cent.

pollution-control techniques and mechanisms will have to be met, but the processes, as they are expensive, will certainly affect the price of electricity produced in conventional plant. This was one advantage claimed by the nuclear interests in their competition with the fossil fuels in the mid 1960s, and it undoubtedly helped them then to win orders in major electrical supply systems like that for New York.

The nuclear stations, however, have themselves since been assailed by the 'environmentalists', and public concern about possible hazards is growing. In 1969 the US Atomic Energy Commission thought it advisable, for the first time, to include sections on 'Public Concern' and 'Environment' in their annual report. As the number of nuclear plants has grown, so has anxiety about various possible consequences. The hazards of radiation, the problems of radioactive wastes, the effects of thermal pollution on river or marine life, the possible consequences of a major accident in a plant, have all received increasing attention. The last of these is, at present, the most easily countered. The safety record so far is excellent, and the problem should dispose of itself in time. The same cannot be said of the other issues. All nuclear plants are allowed to discharge small volumes of radioactive materials, and controversy centres on the amount of radioactivity that human beings can safely tolerate. In truth, nobody really knows, and this will remain an active area of dispute. The long-term effects of thermal pollution of water bodies are also uncertain, and this issue, too, will not be resolved quickly. So the nuclear development programme is being impeded, while proposals for overcoming some of the problems would greatly increase the costs of power.

The present dilemma of the power industry is thus acute. Demand for electricity is, at the least, doubling every decade, yet provision of the capacity to meet the demand is in many areas being actively opposed on environmental grounds. Consolidated Edison of New York City, the nation's largest power company, recently proposed to build a nuclear plant at Montrose on the Hudson. This project was so fiercely opposed that it was abandoned; while extension of the existing Indian Point nuclear plant has been delayed over a dispute about the damage being done by hot water currently discharged into the Hudson river. The Company consequently decided to meet its urgent needs for new capacity by building oil-fired stations, but this plan has in turn come under attack from New York City's clean-air protagonists. Life will not be easy in the power-supply business in the 1970s, and the Federal Power Commission has urged the passage of local, State and Federal laws to set legal standards in these environmental matters so that the utility companies will at least know where they stand and be able to plan accordingly.

At the mineral-producing end, the environmental issues centre chiefly on coalmining, and the damage it does to land, water and wildlife. Oil and gas mining (especially oil, with its seepage problems in underwater operations) present some problems, but, compared with coal, they are so far small in scale and local in character. In coalmining, too, deep mines, while normally disfiguring the land-scape and damaging soil and water with spoil tips and drainage arrangements, are not a major contributor to the environmental problem. In relation to the quantities of coal extracted, deep mines use surface areas fairly economically. Such a tolerant view is, how-ever, tenable only because of the enormous dimensions of the problem created by the rapid post-war expansion of surface mining. Rising public concern with environmental matters led to the institution, under the Appalachian Regional Development Act of 1965, of an official inquiry into the nature, extent and effects of surface mining. The subsequent publication of the Bureau of Mines Report *Surface Mining and Our Environment* (1967) was a landmark in the history of conservation, providing the first authoritative estimates of the areas affected. The area of land 'disturbed' by surface mining of all relevant minerals had, by 1965, reached the extraordinary total of 3·2 million acres, of which surface mining of coal accounted for 1·3 million acres, or 41 per cent – by far the largest single contribution.

Both major surface techniques of contour mining in hilly areas (often followed by auger extraction) and area stripping in level terrain do great damage to environment and often, too, to man. Mile upon mile of contour bench and associated 'highwall' isolate large tracts of hill-top areas, while the huge volume of waste thrown down the hillside destroys more vegetation. Valuable top soil is thrown away or buried. Land slides block streams and roads, and waters are heavily polluted by acid and sediment. Square miles of land are turned over to depths of 100 feet or more, and abandoned in hill and dale formations. Surface and sub-surface drainage is disrupted and the land rendered economically useless, with any aesthetic value it had possessed also destroyed. The effects reach far beyond the limits of the 'disturbed' acres. Fish and wildlife miles away can be poisoned; lakes are created which affect water flows elsewhere, and the flood danger in mountain areas is increased by the destruction of vegetation in mined areas upstream. All of this profoundly affects the mental attitudes of people who live in the afflicted areas – usually, too, they have no control over the disruption of their lands and lives or even, sometimes, the destruction of their property.

Figure 37 illustrates the geographical pattern of this disturbance. The pattern for all commodities is presented, so that coal may be seen in context and the general regional incidence of surface damage assessed. The largest totals of disturbed land are in Pennsylvania, Ohio and West Virginia, and in each coal is by far the greatest contributor. In Appalachia some 800,000 acres – a quarter of the national total – have been disturbed, and the use of one million more acres has been impaired. It is estimated that Appalachia alone has over 20,000 miles of highwalls created by coalmining, and often entire mountains have been circumscribed and rendered inaccessible.

This legacy cannot effectively be tackled by private interests. The scale of the damage is too great and the costs involved too high. Here again, therefore, increased governmental action must come. Government intervention will not only grow, however, in the treatment of existing despoiled areas. The area now being disturbed by surface mining is estimated at over 150,000 acres per year. Without required standards of practice for extraction and restoration, compulsory for all operators, the worst kinds of damage described above will continue. So far Federal regulations have applied only to the public lands, but wider Federal involvement to establish standards and requirements and to pursue research was recommended in *Surface Mining and Our Environment*, mentioned above. Federal programmes to repair past damage and minimize future damage might stimulate stronger efforts by State and local governments. Several States where the impact of surface mining has been great, such as Kentucky, West

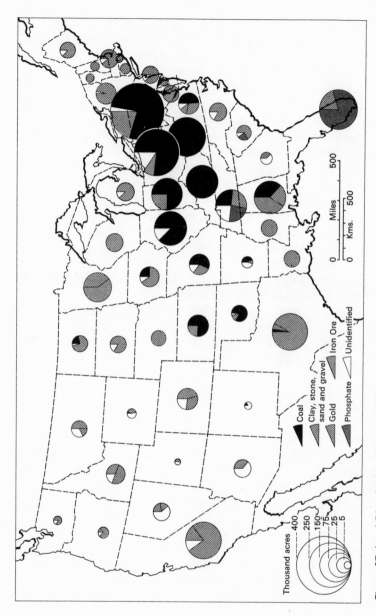

Figure 37. Land Disturbed by Mining, 1965

Virginia and Illinois, already have laws designed to control undesirable after-effects. The laws, however, often lack bite and, in any case, are not rigorously enforced. Strict enforcement is clearly difficult in a free-market situation in which certain competing districts may get a cost advantage by the absence of controls over working and reclamation. Moreover, this dubiously effective intervention aims at limiting future despoliation. The existing areas of destruction are unlikely to be dealt with at this level, if only because the financial requirement would be too great.

The need, then, is for the universal standards, the practical enforcement and the financial resources that only the Federal authorities can provide. In this, as in associated fields such as air and water pollution, however, legislation in the 1960s, although abundant, gave Washington limited powers, leaving the major role in initiating and implementing programmes to the State and local governments. The commitment of resources was also rather meagre. In a related issue of great significance, however, the Federal government has been automatically involved. The proposed eight-hundred-mile Trans-Alaska pipeline will have important environmental effects. Its mere presence will interfere with wildlife behaviour, while a major oil spill could have dreadful consequences. The controversy between oil interests and environmentalists here required Federal intervention. The national need for oil will doubtless ensure that the pipeline is built; but the government will insist on costly provisions which will limit its immediate environmental impact and guard against the worst possibilities. The Federal role as guardian of the national estate now seems well established, therefore, and the new Environmental Protection Agency may well serve to strengthen Federal influence in these matters in the 1970s.

10: Some Characteristics of Modern Manufacturing

The role of manufacturing is crucial in the American economy. Directly, it employs massive numbers, and indirectly it supports much other employment. The attitudes and techniques of the manufacturer pervade all sectors of society, with consequences upon the style and quality of life which a Jeffersonian would deplore, but which have enormously raised national standards of material well-being. The manufacturer's needs for capital and labour, for material supplies and markets, have, implicitly or explicitly, dominated economic research in recent decades. The problems of the manufacturer and of a manufacturing economy are a prime concern of politicians and administrators, and have greatly changed political attitudes even in this most 'conservative' of countries.

Table 15: Employment and Income in Manufacturing: Selected Years, 1869–1969

	Employment (million)	% of all employment*	% of national income*
1869	2·1	17·5	14·5
1899	5·4	20·0	17·5
1919	10·6	25·0	23·0
1937	10·7	22·5	26·5
1947	15·4	26·5	30·0
1958	16·3	25·5	29·5
1963	17·4	25·5	30·0
1969	20·1	26·0	30·0

* Rounded to nearest 0·5 per cent

Sources: Long-Term Economic Growth and Statistical Abstracts of the United States

This predominance of manufacturing is none the less not fully reflected in its record of employment. With great expansion in population and economic activity, the numbers engaged in manufacturing have naturally risen, but since the war the rate of new job formation has fallen well behind the increase of population and employment generally. Table 15 shows the record, for selected years from 1869. Up to 1919 expansion was very fast, and manufacturing considerably increased its proportion of all employment to reach a quarter of the total by 1919. The inter-war slump shook the numbers down to only 6·75 million in 1932, but economic recovery in the late 1930s and wartime requirements, raised the total in the 1940s. Since the war, although manufacturing employment has fluctuated, there has happily been nothing to compare even remotely with the massive disruption of the early 1930s. Thus the employment statistics for the years 1947 to 1969 give a reasonably correct view of secular expansion. Even so, the manufacturing sector has not raised its relative position and for twenty years or so has provided approximately 26 per cent of all jobs, a proportion very similar to that of 1919.

This plateau does not imply a static situation in manufacturing. As in the other goods-producing activities discussed earlier, labour productivity has risen greatly. On a constant 1929 dollar basis, for example, manufacturing output per man-hour has been computed at over three times as high in 1957 as in 1919. From 1947 to 1969 the index of manufacturing output per man-hour rose from 72 to 143 (1957–9 = 100). This largely reflects continuous heavy investment in manufacturing. The real net value of structures and equipment in manufacturing rose from $33 billion to $92 billion between 1940 and 1968 (1958 dollar values). In sum, the slowly expanding labour force has commanded a rapidly expanding capacity to produce, a capacity that underpins the affluence of the American economy.

In discussing the significance of manufacturing, we should also note the contribution of this sector to the national income. Up to the inter-war period American manufacturing was relatively labour-intensive, providing more, proportionately, of the national employment than of the national income (Table 15). Since then, the positions have been reversed and manufacturing has provided some 26 per cent of all employment, but about 30 per cent of the national income.

This serves to emphasize its basic role. The next largest contributors to national income are government and governmental enterprises and wholesale and retail trade (about 15 per cent each in 1968). Given the tremendous rise in government-generated income, and in the services category generally, it is remarkable that manufacturing has maintained its proportional position so consistently. This again illustrates the enormous advance in producing capacity, as well as the widening range of manufactured products introduced into the market in the past two decades.

Within the secular expansion of manufacturing have been some highly significant developments. The structure of output has changed as once-dominant industries have declined and new processes and products have superseded them. Partly because of this, types of employment available in manufacturing have changed. Again, too, partly through changes in the structure of output, but also for other reasons, the geographical distribution of manufacturing has altered. These major themes will be examined in this and the following chapters.

Changes in the Labour Force

Labour employed in manufacturing has changed significantly in character since the war. Some of these changes, and their implications (e.g. the rising female component) were discussed in Chapter 4. Here attention is directed to a major shift in the relative positions of 'production' and 'non-production' personnel. Production workers broadly include all employees on the shop floor up to and including the 'working' foreman; non-production workers include supervisory and administrative personnel, sales and service employees and professional and technical staff. Post-war developments have steadily increased the importance of the latter, with economic, social and locational implications. Table 16 shows that not only has non-production employment grown at a rate about eight times that of production employment (this very high ratio is partly a consequence of the low 1947 base figure), but also that it has experienced a considerably greater *absolute* rise, contributing, in fact, about 60 per

Table 16: Production and Non-production Workers in Manufacturing, 1947 and 1969

	1947 (million)	1969 (million)	Increase 1947–69 Absolute (million)	%
All manufacturing	15·5	20·1	4·6	29·7
Production workers	13·0	14·7	1·7	13·1
Non-production workers	2·6	5·4	2·8	107·7

Source: Employment and Earnings Statistics for the United States, 1909–1969
Department of Labour Bulletin 1312–6 and 1370–7

cent of the total addition to the labour force in the twenty-two years. Thus non-production employees now provide about 27 per cent of the manufacturing work force, compared with 16 per cent in 1947. Moreover, production workers' employment has advanced erratically. In the cyclical trough of 1958, for example, production workers' jobs in manufacturing were more than two million below those of the cyclical peak year of 1953. Such fluctuations mean hardship for individuals and for the more exposed regions. Meanwhile, non-production employment has advanced continuously ever since the war.

Such experiences reflect the changing character and technology of manufacturing. New styles of production and marketing have been introduced in every branch but, in addition, industries with high proportions of 'white-collar' employment have advanced in relative standing. The research, development and testing functions are significant among such operations. Employment of these workers has increased in practically all manufacturing, but especially in the more technologically advanced branches. The latter have provided the major growth points for industry in recent times, and this reinforces cumulatively the roles of technicians and research workers. This is further discussed below.

Implications of Labour-force Trends

These trends have several consequences for labour and for regional development. Employees in non-production occupations have in general higher incomes than those on the shop floor. Details of their earnings are not published, but the scale of the differential is suggested by the fact that the average earnings in 1968 for *all employees* in manufacturing were approximately $7,300, but for production workers $6,200, only 85 per cent of the overall average. Moreover, the evidence is that the gap has widened since the war. Areas with large shares of the growing non-production functions are thus favoured in their income structures. This introduces another important aspect of the general trend, which concerns location.

One large sector of the non-production labour force is the managerial, clerical and sales personnel. These employees are not always, or even mainly, employed at the manufacturing plant locations. They are often, especially headquarters staff, concentrated in large cities. Easy contact with other enterprises ranks high among the many reasons for this. Representatives of other similar firms and of suppliers and customers are normally available, and there is easy personal access to advertising agencies, lawyers, insurance brokers and so on. Especially attractive are cities regarded nationally or internationally as prestige headquarter cities, either in general (New York), or for particular industries (Pittsburgh for steel and aluminium or Detroit for motor vehicles). Again, the fast-growing research, development and testing functions in manufacturing are also often performed in locations separate from the manufacturing plant, especially at sites in suburban areas, which can provide the spacious layout, the good communications and pleasant working conditions calculated to attract first-rate R & D personnel. Such sites are particularly sought in areas with good higher educational facilities, and where research, development and testing *services*, qualified consultants and specialists in relevant fields, are readily available. All of this has obvious regional significance.

Finally, the wider implications examined on a broader national level in Chapter 4 should be recalled here. The non-production jobs in manufacturing normally require (or, at least, employers demand) a better education than do most production jobs. Thus people with low educational qualifications are experiencing increasing difficulty in obtaining satisfactory employment in manufacturing. These include the millions of rural migrants to the cities, both white and Negro. Earlier this century, untutored migrants to the great manufacturing cities found many kinds of jobs open to them. Employment in manufacturing was then expanding more rapidly than recently and lack of education was not a complete impediment to employment. But openings for production workers are decreasing relatively throughout manufacturing, while some industries show an absolute decline in such jobs. The poorly educated are clearly in jeopardy in such a situation. Indeed, they are in double jeopardy, for the tasks performed by many production workers require considerable skills and flexibility. Thus in this sector, too, the demands for well-educated, trainable and adaptable labour are growing, as production techniques become more sophisticated.

The Structure of Manufacturing Activity

These developments in the labour force have largely been a function of the changing product mix of manufacturing, brought about over recent decades by several elements in combination. In the first place, the pattern of market demand altered as the population increased in size, as per capita real incomes rose and tastes and fashions changed. At the same time technical progress has produced a wide range of new goods for mass-market consumption and a lowering of production costs for certain established products, thus altering demand–supply relationships. Further, some industries of early 'maturity' no longer have the same impulse to growth as the successful 'infant' industries, and must therefore lose ground as new industries expand. Again, some have been affected, not only by internal changes in demand and competitive conditions, but also by rising imports; while government activity has favoured some kinds of industry, protecting them against competition or stimulating them by government programmes and purchases. Thus, while most

257

industries have expanded in absolute size (especially if measured by output rather than employment) at a time of rapid population and income growth, they have expanded at differing rates, and their relative positions have changed considerably. In 1900, for example, the food-product, textiles, clothing and leather-product industries together contributed one third of the national value added by manufacturing. Incomes were comparatively low (and thus spent to a great degree on 'essentials') and many products now important were not invented or were in the expensive early stages of development. By the mid 1930s, however, this group of industries accounted for only just over a quarter of all value added and, with a rapidly increasing range of products on the market and an equally rapid increase in real incomes since the war, their proportion of all value added in manufacture is now only one sixth.

The US Standard Industrial Classification system identifies twenty-one 'major industry groups' (called the 'two-digit' industries) in manufacturing. We cannot examine all of these, but by grouping them according to their 'growth' experience some generalizations can be made about the characteristics of modern manufacturing. We must, however, be aware of the shortcomings of this approach. The two-digit industries are themselves each composed of several kinds of manufacturing activity. These have strong affinities, but it must not be assumed that each kind of manufacturing embraced in one major industry group has the same kind of history, problems or prospects as others in the group. Thus, the proposed 'grouping of groups' has special dangers, and the generalizations suggested below could sometimes, perhaps, be invalidated in a more detailed analysis.

'Growth' and 'Laggard' Industries Defined

The major industry groups can be arranged in rank order according to a variety of different criteria involving absolute and relative change in employment and productive activity. Such an arrangement can then be used to provide a 'score' for each industry, on the basis of which the total array can be ranked by 'growth type'. For this study the criteria used were rate of employment growth, size of employment growth, rate of growth of value added and the index of industrial production. The base and terminal years were 1947 and 1967, both Census of Manufactures years. With the Miscellaneous and the Tobacco Manufactures groups excluded from the analysis, the nineteen remaining industry groups arrange themselves over a ten-point scale as shown in Table 17. In this arrangement, three categories of manufacturing are distinguishable. The first group has scores of 7·1 to 9·2 and contains the top performers in American manufacturing activity. These are the 'growth' or A-type industries. (This category includes ordnance and accessories manufacture, for which full information is not available but which, from various lines of evidence, almost certainly takes first place.) At the opposite end of the scale a group of industries scores 3·2 or less. This group embraces the chief 'laggard' industries, the X-type category. The group occupying the middle ground in 'growth' performance is the O-type category. Positioning the lines between the categories is a somewhat arbitrary process. The nineteen groups have been divided into roughly equal compartments, but there is in practice no sharp division between the industries that fall near the lines. There is, however, a remarkable consistency, using all pertinent criteria, in the rank order of industries within each group, and various other methods produce no significant alteration of rank.

It is important to remember that membership of the A-type category does not presuppose a monopoly of technical skill, efficiency and so on, while membership of the X-type category does not necessarily imply that the industry is 'backward' in a technical or managerial sense. The allocation to the classes depends purely on growth experience in employment and output over the two decades. Clearly, this is very important in itself and vital in regional economic development. A high rate of new job creation and a rapid increase in output imply growing prosperity for the areas concerned. The converse indicates a likely problem situation. However, this is only one view of a complex matter. Some technologically advanced, or advancing, industries, and ones with high rates of new investment, can also have uninspiring records, or even be 'laggards' on the 'growth' criteria used above.

This being understood, the 'growth' records of the A- and X-type

Table 17: Rank of Industry Groups by 'Growth Type' (score out of 10)

A-type	Score	O-type	Score	X-type	Score
Ordnance and accessories*	n.a.	Printing and publishing	6·0	Primary metal manufacture	3·2
Electrical equipment	9·2	Fabricated metal products	5·8	Petroleum and coal products	2·4
Transport equipment	8·5	Paper and allied products	5·4	Food and kindred products	2·4
Chemicals and allied products	8·2	Stone, clay and glass products	4·4	Leather and products	1·0
Rubber and plastics products	7·8	Furniture and fixtures	4·4	Textile mill products	0·8
Instruments and related products	7·6	Apparel and related products	3·8	Lumber and wood products	0·7
Machinery manufacture	7·1				

* Full details not available (see text)

categories as a whole can be compared. While aggregate employment in A-type industries grew by nearly two thirds between 1947 and 1967, that in X-type fell by 11 per cent. In value added both A- and X-type sectors show growth, with rising output and inflation, but the record of the A-type industries is far superior; their value added has expanded by 370 per cent over the period, compared with 160 per cent for the X-type category. Viewed in another way, the seven industry groups in the A-type sector provided 83 per cent of all new jobs in manufacturing over the period and even without the ordnance group, for which full value added data is not available, contributed half the total US increase in value added in manufacture. We must probe reasons for this great disparity of performance to see if any particular characteristics attach to these extremes.

The Durable and Non-durable Product Balance

A traditional division of manufacturing is into durable and non-durable product classes, a division which provides a simple means of introducing a discussion and also has intrinsic economic significance. Durable manufactures have a life span normally of years – say three, four or more. They include both producer goods (machinery and equipment for manufacturing) and consumer goods such as cars, refrigerators, television sets and furniture. Non-durable manufactures have a relatively short life span and must, therefore, be more frequently replaced by the consumer. Clothing and footwear, foodstuffs and paper are examples. Figure 38 shows the official division of the major industry groups into these categories,* and the employment record for 1947 and 1968. This classification, like most classifications, has rather woolly edges and some anomalies. However, it is clear that the secular trend of growth over several decades has decidedly favoured the durable goods industries, taken as a whole.

In the earlier stages of US industrial growth, non-durable pro-

* The 'Miscellaneous' category (which here includes the 'Tobacco and products' industry group) is placed in the non-durable column to balance the graph. It contains both durable and non-durable products and for statistical purposes its employment has been equally allocated to each.

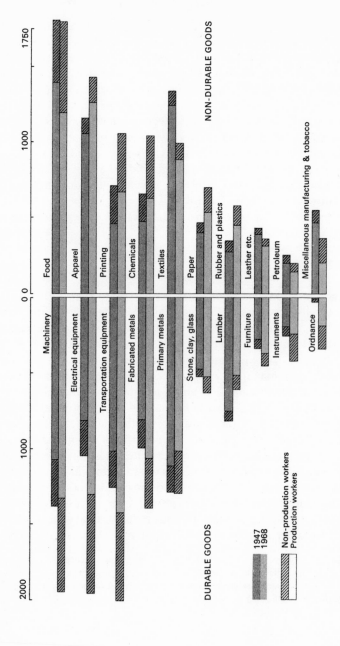

Figure 38. Employees on Manufacturing Payrolls by Major Groups, 1947 and 1968

ducts dominated output, because of levels of income, tastes and technology. Even as recently as 1940, over half of all manufacturing employment remained in the non-durable sector. Since the war, however, manufacture of durable goods has expanded very markedly. Between 1947 and 1968 employment on the durables side grew from 8·2 million to 11·4 million, in non-durables only from 7·4 million to 8·4 million. Durable goods production thus now provides 58 per cent or more of all employment in manufacturing, and this faster rate of expansion seems certain to continue through the 1970s.

In detail this change has been more complex than the broad figures suggest. Certainly, five of the seven major industries in the A-type category are durable goods industries, and four of the six X-type industries produce non-durable goods, which supports the major theme. But the employment record for each major group (Figure 38) shows that the poor performance of the non-durables derives chiefly from the textile, leather and food product groups, in which numbers engaged fell in total by almost 400,000 over the period. In contrast, several other non-durable groups experienced considerable expansion. Outstanding among these has been the growth of the chemicals industries and rubber and plastics products,* both of which rank with the A-type industries; but printing and publishing and paper manufacture also have impressive post-war records and rank high in the O-type category (Table 17). Together these four non-durable industry groups added 1·2 million jobs between 1947 and 1968.

The durable goods industries, too, despite the general advance, do not all fully share the experience of growth. The electrical equipment, transport equipment and machinery groups, together accounting for over half the total post-war increase in the nation's manufacturing labour force, have made large gains. Smaller absolute, but *very* impressive relative, growth came in the instruments and ordnance groups. On the other hand, furniture manufacture and stone, clay and glass product manufacture have mediocre records, while the lumber and wood products group languishes at the very foot of the ranking (Table 17). Over all, therefore, the expansion in durable goods manufacture is primarily by the metal-based industries. Fur-

* Full title 'Rubber and Miscellaneous Plastic Products'. The production of plastics materials is included in the 'Chemicals and Allied Products' group.

ther, within this category developments have strengthened the metal-*using* rather than the metal-*making* groups, and primary metal manufacture itself falls into the X-type category. The relatively slow growth of this latter industry group results partly from improved use of primary metals (a given quantity going further than before), partly from the rapid growth of industries in which the metals used provide little of the final value of the product, partly from the inroads of substitutes (plastics, concrete and even paper) in certain end uses, and partly from increasing imports. Productivity has improved through very large investment, but market conditions have not been buoyant and the growth of output has over all been sluggish. In sharp contrast, the metal-*using* industries have moved from strength to strength, and now dominate the pattern of US manufacturing. In 1968, transport-equipment manufacture became the first major industry group ever to employ, in peacetime conditions, more than two million workers,* and the electrical equipment and machinery groups, close behind (Figure 38), passed the two-million mark in 1969.

The durable/non-durable product distinction has significance apart from growth rates. The two classes of manufacture respond differently to short-term business fluctuations. Durable goods purchases can be more easily postponed, promoting more violent cyclical fluctuations in their production and employment. Areas specializing in such types of production thus experience a rather volatile employment situation, and the economic slow-down at the beginning of the 1970s will undoubtedly bring employment in the leading durable goods industries well below the peaks they reached during the sustained growth of the 1960s. Some areas will consequently experience relatively high unemployment. Meanwhile, the effects of a minor recession on the non-durable goods industries will, on past experience, be relatively mild. The secular trend will, however, eventually reassert itself, and will remain decidedly favourable

* During the Second World War, employment in this group rose to above 3·5 million, largely because of the expansion of military aircraft manufacture. Current levels of employment are partly attributable to the military requirements of Vietnam, but the economy as a whole is on a 'peacetime' footing rather than, as in the 1940s, geared up for a flat-out war effort.

to the durables. The durables are also prominent in income considerations. Average hourly earnings on the shop floor in durable goods industries considerably exceed the average in non-durables. Further, the durable goods industries employ larger numbers of white-collar personnel, thus reinforcing their incomes advantages. This point will be taken up again below in a broader context. Now it leads into a consideration of other relevant matters in the A- and X-type industry dichotomy and, firstly, their differing structures of employment.

The Role of Non-production Workers

The general structure of the labour force in manufacturing was discussed above. Now the generalities can be brought down to cases. Figure 38 divides employment in each major industry group into its 'production' and 'non-production' components. Compared with the 1968 average of 27 per cent of all manufacturing employment in non-production occupations, very high ratios (above 40 per cent) occur in the ordnance and chemicals groups, and high ratios (29 per cent and above) in the instruments, electrical equipment, machinery and transport equipment groups. Of the seven A-type industries, only the rubber and plastics products group (with 23 per cent non-production workers) falls below the average for all manufacturing. At the other end of the scale the textile, leather, and lumber and wood product groups have the lowest ratios of non-production workers (11 per cent to 14 per cent). A broad connection between such ratios and growth performance seems to be implied. We have seen that non-production occupations have shown the greatest employment growth in manufacturing since the war, and in the first two post-war decades the A-type industries provided 62 per cent of all the new non-production jobs, the O-type industries a further 25 per cent, and the X-type (with 38 per cent of all manufacturing employment in 1947) a mere 14 per cent.

The relationship is not hard and fast, of course. Two industry groups with non-production ratios above 30 per cent (food products and petroleum and coal products) are X-type industries. Both have

265

experienced post-war decline in employment, but this has been concentrated on production workers. Increasing mechanization (or 'automation') has allowed both to increase output despite a fall in production employment. The stability of their non-production work force, however, has created high non-production ratios. Even among X-type industries with low non-production levels, however, the ratios have markedly improved since the war. While the number of production workers has fallen, 'white-collar' employment has risen modestly. Textile mill production workers, for example, fell from 1·2 million in 1947 to 0·87 million in 1968. Non-production employment, however, rose from 79,000 to 112,000 over that period. The lumber and the leather groups had similar experiences. Clearly, no industry can be completely isolated from a trend so pervasive. None the less, this development is heavily biased toward the growth-industry end of the spectrum. Currently over half the non-production workers in US manufacturing are in the seven A-type industries, and we proceed to examine one important element contributing to this notable situation.

Research and Development

Research and development have been outstandingly significant in the changing post-war structure of US manufacturing. National expenditure on R & D by Federal and private agencies has risen greatly, both absolutely and as a proportion of the Gross National Product. Comparable figures are not available back to the 1940s, but in 1955 total R & D expenditure amounted to $6·3 billion, 1·6 per cent of the GNP. By 1970 the total had reached over $27 billion, 3 per cent of the GNP. Most of this expenditure (70 per cent in 1970) has been applied to industrial R & D, and the Federal government contribution has long been vital. The application of private funds has recently increased more rapidly, but the Federal contribution amounted to over half the total until 1968 and stood at 44 per cent in 1970.

Application of R & D funds on this scale has had a major impact on manufacturing and, since the funds have not been dispersed

Table 18: Distribution of Funds for Industrial R & D

Industry	% of total funds			% from Federal sources	
	1958	1965	1968	1958	1968
Aircraft and missiles	31·8	35·9	32·4	85·5	80·0
Electrical equipment	23·5	22·3	23·1	67·9	56·3
Chemicals and allied products	9·5	9·8	9·4	15·9	12·3
Machinery	9·3	7·9	9·3	43·9	26·0
Transport equipment (excludes aircraft and missiles)	9·9	8·6	8·4	35·6	27·1
Petroleum refining and extraction	2·9	3·1	3·1	5·0	13·9
Professional and scientific instruments	3·5	2·7	3·4	46·6	36·3
Primary metal	1·4	1·5	1·4	12·6	3·6
Rubber products	1·1	1·2	1·3	23·6	17·9
Food and kindred products	1·0	1·1	1·0	7·2	0·6
Fabricated metal products	1·6	1·0	1·0	42·9	6·4
Stone, clay and glass products	0·9	0·8	1·0	n.a.	3·0
Paper and allied products	0·5	0·5	0·5	nil	nil
Textiles and apparel	0·2	0·3	0·3	nil	n.a.
Lumber and wood products and furniture	0·1	0·1	0·1	nil	nil
Others	2·8	3·1	3·9	59·5	n.a.
Total (per cent)	100·0	100·0	100·0	56·9	
Actual ($ billion)	8·4	14·2	17·4	4·8	

Source: Statistical Abstracts
n.a. = not available

equally among the various industry groups (Table 18), this has contributed significantly to the changing structure of output. Understandably, the national interest in aeronautical development (civil and military) and missile and space programmes makes the aircraft and missiles sector outstanding in both the magnitude of R & D effort and the contribution from Federal funds. Close behind, however, comes the electrical equipment group in which the electronics and communications sectors have also been heavily involved in military and space programmes. Some other research and development efforts are small only by comparison with the two leaders. In each of the chemicals, machinery and transport sectors over a billion dollars has been expended in R & D work every year since the mid 1960s. The record for the chemicals group is especially impressive, given the relatively small Federal contribution. Among the smaller spenders the instruments industry has a large total in relation to its size. Here again, however, the Federal interest is manifest.

Not surprisingly, the industries with the most notable R & D records fall into the A-type category. The combined total expenditure for such industries accounted for 87 per cent of all industrial R & D expenditure in 1968, a proportion practically identical to that of 1958 and 1965. This situation separates out the A-type industries more emphatically than any other index; and on this rest the favourable predictions for these industries. Of a total of about 1·1 million scientists, engineers and technicians employed in private manufacturing enterprises in 1967, approximately 900,000 were in the A-type industries. Not only does this explain the growth records of the recent past, but it also appears to ensure the future expansion of the industries concerned.

An element of uncertainty must, however, accompany the large Federal contribution to the R & D effort of these major industries, and the very great Federal purchasing contracts which follow. Procurement for defence purposes fluctuates with the tenor of international affairs, and programmes such as that for space research are liable to alteration and interruption as the economic situation, or the goals of politicians, change. Federal outlay for space research and technology, for example, rose from $0·4 billion in 1960 to a peak of $5·9 billion in 1966,* but fell to an estimated $3·2 billion for 1970. Space R & D contracts and production facilities are consequently being run down, and scores of thousands of people have lost their jobs. Serious consequences may follow in certain areas. At Cocoa Beach, Florida, for example, the population rose from about 25,000 to a quarter of a million between 1950 and the late 1960s as a direct consequence of space programme requirements. The recent loss of several thousand jobs at the Cape Kennedy launch centre, therefore, is having a seriously adverse local multiplier effect. By contrast, Federal outlays for defence rose throughout the decade

* N.B. Not all of such monies are directed into the private sector, or into the manufacturing industry.

1960–70, but are equally liable to be reduced, given favourable international developments, or redirected within the manufacturing sector as military requirements change. Thus the A-type industries chiefly affected have their problems. But R & D potential can be directed to different ends, and military or space discoveries do sometimes have civilian applications. Thus, although the future may not be completely untroubled for such industries, prospects for the longer term appear good.

Such characteristics of the A-type industries normally mean that they bring higher incomes to the people they employ and, conse-quently, to those areas where they are concentrated. Scientific, engineering, technical and other 'white-collar' personnel normally command higher pay rates than shop-floor personnel. Further, in such industries, where innovation is the order of the day and mass production techniques are not always well established, production workers, too, often receive higher than average rates. Thus, for many years the average hourly earnings of production workers in five of the seven A-type industries have exceeded the national average for all manufacturing, whereas in four of the six X-type industries they have consistently been below that level. The 'growth' industries command a high, and rising, proportion of the total wage payments in US manufacturing. In 1967 they accounted for 42 per cent of all manufacturing jobs but 48 per cent of the national production workers' payroll.

Capital Investment

Given the need to provide much new capacity in the main 'growth' industries, one might expect the A-type industries to dominate the pattern of new investment in manufacturing (for plant and equip-ment) as emphatically as they dominate R & D expenditures. In fact, while there is indeed a very high level of investment in the major growth industries, it is not remarkably high in relation to investment elsewhere. In 1967, for example, the A-type industries accounted for 44 per cent of new capital expenditure in manufacturing. This is not notably superior to their proportions of all employment and value

269

added. The X-type industries accounted for 33 per cent of new investment, a ratio significantly improving on their relative position in employment and value added. This situation merits discussion, for it illustrates the point made above that some 'laggard' industries can experience rapid *technical* advance.

In this matter no year, or period of years, gives a 'typical' pattern of investment activity among industries. Various circumstances cause investment plans in general, or particular industries, to fluctuate. Petroleum refining companies, for example, invested heavily in the early 1950s, but the growth of demand disappointed expectations and up to about 1967 the industry suffered from over capacity. New capital expenditure, much of which was for replacement purposes only, thus became relatively low. By 1967, however, growth of demand justified additional plant, and new investment turned sharply upwards. Thus selecting a period to give a true picture of the relative investment performance of this, or any other, industry is difficult. None the less, certain major groups appear consistently among the big spenders. From 1965 to 1968, for example, seven groups invested more than $1 billion each year. These investment leaders are identified by growth type in Table 19, which also shows their proportion of total investment in new plant and equipment for manufacturing over the four years.

Table 19: New Capital Investment by Leading Industry Groups
(% of U S total manufacturing 1965–8)

Industry	% of total	Growth type
Primary metal manufacture	14·2	X
Chemicals and allied products	14·0	A
Transport equipment	9·0	A
Food and kindred products	8·4	X
Machinery	8·4	A
Electrical equipment	6·9	A
Paper and allied products	6·8	O
	67·7	

Source: Statistical Abstracts

Some Characteristics of Modern Manufacturing

The appearance of four A-type industries among the seven leaders is not surprising, given the definition of these industries, but the appearance of two X-type industries is, perhaps, less expected. The primary metal and food product groups are, however, mature industries of great size and, despite their weak 'growth' records, they need continuous investment to replace or modernize capacity. Despite sluggish growth in demand, competition for the market continues and new techniques and mechanisms must be adopted to remain competitive. In iron and steel, for example, a belated start was made in the early 1960s on a programme of investment in the new basic oxygen techniques. Basic oxygen capacity rose from 3 million tons in 1960 to 70 million tons in 1970. With the slow growth of the market for steel and increasing competition from imports this new capacity is mostly replacement for obsolete open-hearth furnaces. Thus the huge investment outlays have not produced a great output expansion, nor a large employment growth, for labour productivity is improved by the basic oxygen technique. Similarly, the large food product group, experiencing slowly rising overall demand, is becoming increasingly mechanized and therefore needs great investment. Both these 'laggard' industry groups, too, have their 'growth' sectors, which undertake much new investment to increase capacity. The food group, for example, has experienced a great expansion in output, employment and investment in frozen fruits, juices and vegetables while the primary metal group has seen similar rapid growth in non-ferrous wire drawing.

The very large capital expenditures of these primary metal and food product groups lift the total investment in the X-type industries to the relatively high levels mentioned above. Other slowly growing industries have less incentive and, because of their technology, less need for heavy investment programmes. This is shown by their record. The lumber and wood product, textile mill, leather and leather product and apparel groups, for example, together provided 17 per cent of the nation's manufacturing employment in 1967, but under 8 per cent of total expenditure on new plant and equipment between 1965 and 1968. These are, of course, labour-intensive industries, but their investment effort, though relatively small, is none the less vital to their competitive ability.

Moreover, in all industries it is not merely how much investment but where it takes place that is geographically significant. New investment in process favourably affects the economy of the area in which it is undertaken and, once completed, normally contributes jobs and incomes over many years. Over time, too, the sum of investment decisions decides the regional distribution of industry and produces changes in location patterns. Much of the limited post-war investment in lumber and wood product manufacture, for example, has been in the South and, within this group, the investment in softwood plywood plant has recently been relatively large. Only one such plant existed in the whole of the South in 1964 but, by 1968, 32 were operating. This process will eventually have notable repercussions in the location pattern of this industry, currently dominated by the West. In another slow growth industry the direction of new investment, despite its small total, has already had important geographical consequences. The manufacture of clothing has long been concentrated in New York, but is losing ground there and growing elsewhere, especially in the South. Thus, between 1947 and 1969 employment in the apparel trades in New York City fell from 349,000 to 224,000, while in Alabama it rose from 8,000 to 45,000, in Tennessee from 20,000 to 67,000 and in Mississippi from 12,000 to 39,000. Such developments have greatly changed the geographical pattern of this industry.

Another consequence of new investment is often a rising scale of operations, both in the leading growth industries and among the laggards. In the lumber and wood products group, for example, the small unit still dominates. In 1968, 81 per cent of operating plants employed under nineteen persons and 96 per cent employed under a hundred, both considerably greater proportions than in any other industry group. The number of plants employing under a hundred persons, however, has in fact fallen steadily, whilst the number employing over a hundred has grown. Thus, despite the poor post-war growth record, the larger establishments are providing an increasing share of total output. Similar trends are found in US manufacturing as a whole, and a discussion of the characteristics of scale follows immediately.

Considerations of Scale

Scale considerations are significant to industrial operations on two levels, the individual producing unit, or factory plant, and the commercial control or legal organization of the business. Both have geographical relevance. At the plant level, American manufacturing has long tended towards the largest practicable scale of operations, thereby securing internal economies of scale of kinds that need no description here. These economies have, in general, been augmented by recent technological and organizational advances in making and moving goods, and further favoured by the great increase in effective domestic demand. This trend, common throughout manufacturing, is reflected in the growing proportion of manufacturing workers employed in large or very large plants. Figure 39 shows both the distribution of plants according to employment size and the associated distribution of employment. Small plants, with under twenty employees, dominate the pattern in numbers but provide a tiny proportion of manufacturing employment. The reverse is true for units employing 500 or more, and the trend is strongly in favour of this group. Employment data do not always fully reflect this phenomenon of rising scale, larger units being often more capital-intensive. Census details are not yet available for 1967, but the 1963 Census showed establishments employing 500 or more then accounting for 43 per cent of employees but 50 per cent of value added in manufacturing. Furthermore, within this group, those employing 2,500 or more have achieved the greatest expansion. Value added in these very large units rose by 227 per cent between 1947 and 1963, compared with the overall increase of 159 per cent in all manufacturing. All other size groups increased their value added at under the national average rate, the rate of increase in fact falling consistently with decreasing size of plant.

Among the two-digit industries, the identity of the groups with the greatest and the least concentrations of activity in large plants is interesting. Nationally, 46 per cent of manufacturing employment in 1968 was in plants with 500 or more employees, but the ordnance and accessories group had 93 per cent, the transport equipment group 83

273

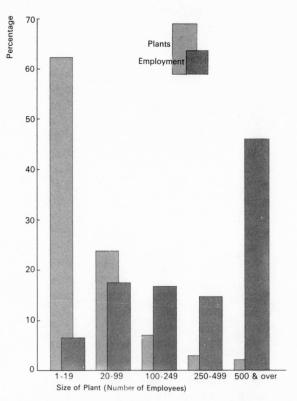

Figure 39. Distribution of Manufacturing Employment by Size of Plant, 1968

per cent and the electrical equipment group 68 per cent. These will be remembered as the nation's leading growth industries. In addition, the instruments, chemicals and machinery groups have above 50 per cent of their employment in these large units and, of the seven A-type industries, only rubber and plastics products has a proportion even as low as the national average. Details for plants above the 500 employee size also show that of 222 manufacturing plants employing 5,000 persons or more in 1968, over three quarters were in A-type industries. The industry groups with the lowest proportions of their employment in large plants are lumber and wood products (9 per

274

cent in plants employing 500 or more in 1968), apparel and related products (16 per cent), food and kindred products (23 per cent) and leather and leather products (22 per cent). Interestingly, each of these is a laggard or a very slowly growing industry, sharply contrasting with the top-ranking 'large-scale' industries.

There is, however, no necessary causal relationship between scale of production and rate of growth. The primary metals group, for example, an X-type industry, had 67 per cent of its employees in plants employing 500 or more, and 32 plants employing 5,000 or more in 1968, a number exceeded only by the transport equipment and electrical equipment groups. In another laggard industry group, petroleum and coal products, the proportion of labour employed in large plants also appreciably exceeds the national average. Further, in the O-type category several bright growth records have occurred in industries where the large plant is not at all dominant, as in printing and publishing (only 29 per cent of employment in plants of 500 or more) and fabricated metal products (also 29 per cent). But while no essential association exists between scale of production and rate of growth, past rates of growth and current scales of activity clearly have some connection. In providing new or replacing old capacity, most industries adopt new methods and new machinery which, in recent decades, has normally raised the scale of plant operation. The consequences are accordingly most evident in the rapidly growing industries, where new plant provides a larger proportion of total capacity.

The nation's leading growing industries, therefore, are industries with large size of operating unit, whereas in many less buoyant industries the smaller scales of production remain dominant. While the trend towards larger scale of operations is pervasive, however, it affects some industries more than others. The nature of the product or the market, or of the materials supply, or other considerations may set a practical limit on size in some industries which is well below what is *technically* feasible. Certain food products, fashion fabrics and lumber products manufacture provide examples. Moreover the technical optimum (i.e. the best scale of operations in view of equipment capacities and production techniques) differs from industry to industry, and even from firm to firm within the same industry. Thus,

275

even in the A-type industries, with large plants dominating, numerous small establishments efficiently and profitably supplement and complement the output of their larger fellows in the same broad industry group.

In the US the virtues of either large- or small-scale activity are often extolled and the achievements of the other decried. Large units are thus sometimes described as 'typically American', and responsible for most, if not all, major innovations and advances. Small units are extolled by others as the guardians of free enterprise. In fact, no magical quality attaches to either; both have strengths and weaknesses, and both are essential in the structure of American manufacturing. Technical, market and other relevant considerations permitting, large-scale operations bring numerous advantages, with significant cost reductions. Increasing size, however, even at plant level, brings increasing problems, especially perhaps in relation to labour. Smaller-scale operations often have greater flexibility (e.g. in accommodating changes in demand), greater ease of introducing new ideas, especially those not requiring large capital outlays, and better opportunities of involving the workers, in generating their enthusiasm and concern. Small plants face higher unit costs, of course, and also perhaps (e.g. in a single-plant firm) difficulty in raising adequate capital or securing an appropriate share of Federal contracts. The latter difficulties are less for the multi-plant company, and we now briefly consider the company size aspect of scale.

The trend towards large-scale commercial organization is well established in American manufacturing. In 1947 the fifty largest companies in US manufacturing already accounted for 17 per cent of all value added in manufacturing, by 1966, 25 per cent. Very large companies offer attractive advantages of diversification, control of large assets, ability to obtain very large Federal research, development and production contracts, and so on. Some of these companies confine their operations to a single industry, like IBM in computers; others form great 'conglomerates', serving many markets at the same time. Some industries have become remarkably concentrated in this way. In 1966 in at least a dozen industries half or more of the national value of output came from the four largest companies. Among these are telephone and telegraph apparatus (94 per cent of output from the four largest companies), cigarettes (81 per cent), motor vehicles and parts (79 per cent), soap and other detergents (72 per cent) and tyres and inner tubes, and metal cans (both 71 per cent). Such giant bodies have clearly brought many benefits, but, equally clearly, such size brings power which can be abused. The Federal government is interested at both ends of the scale. The anti-trust laws are designed, hopefully, to prevent the abuse of monopoly, or oligopoly, power. Indirectly, too, this legislation reflects a desire to protect small enterprise. Small enterprise, however, has also been directly fostered by Federal assistance, especially by the establishment in 1958 of the Small Business Administration. Its aim is to 'render aid and assistance to small business concerns' and it has powers to give financial and technical assistance and to see that the small firms get their share of government contracts. The problem of defining the limits of 'small business', however, has not been resolved, and neat devices have permitted very large firms, like American Motors, to be designated 'small' for certain purposes. The record of the SBA is, not surprisingly, a mixed one.

The geographical effects of concentration of ownership are uncertain. It has been suggested that heavy concentration inhibits industrial movement as giant companies seek to protect existing investment. This could obstruct the emergence of new industrial areas. The record of the iron and steel industry in the early twentieth century appears to support this view. V. R. Fuchs, in an exhaustive analysis, however, found that the opposite was in general more likely to be true. His most 'mobile' industries were those with highest concentration of ownership.* Plant size, for its part, has direct locational implications. As the units of production grow in capacity fewer are needed to serve a market of given size. Thus in industries with plants of outstanding size (as in aircraft manufacture) significant locations are few. For smaller-sized plants locational patterns differ. Some, as in much food product manufacture, are distributed broadly as the population they serve. Others, as in the lumber and wood product group, affected by material supplies, concentrate in certain favoured regions. Yet others gain from the clustering of numerous small plants, and concentrate in major metropolitan areas. The women's clothing

* *Changes in the Location of Manufacturing in the United States since 1929.*

trade is a good example. Finally, efficient production at very large scale implies good access to a sufficiently large market. Even the large and affluent domestic US markets may still be insufficient to absorb the entire output of the largest modern plants where several firms are in the business, and international trade becomes essential.

International Trade

Internal considerations of income, tastes, technology, competition and so on, as we have seen, are not themselves sufficient to explain the changing positions of manufacturing industries. For some the great economies of large-scale production coupled with domestic competition make it advantageous, even essential, to develop markets outside the USA. The massive and affluent American market is, in turn, attractive to foreign manufacturers, who sometimes possess cost advantages enabling them to invade that market. Thus the USA is a major exporter and importer of manufactured goods. In 1968 such exports were valued at $23·8 billion, and about 7 per cent of all manufacturing employment was attributable to exports. Imports of manufactures totalled $20·6 billion and, while the number of jobs will be reduced in certain industries by these imports, there seems little doubt that, on balance, more jobs are created than lost by international exchange in manufactures. We cannot examine the complex issues in detail, but in some industries the positive or negative balance of trade is large enough to have important internal consequences. Attention will be briefly directed to this.

Table 20 gives the value of the export and import trade in selected manufactures in 1968. The general implications are clear. The A-type industries listed here had exports valued at $18·4 billion (77 per cent of all manufactured exports). Imports of the same classes of commodity were $9·4 billion. Such overall figures conceal important detail. In the transport equipment group, for example, the 1968 trade in new automobiles was highly adverse to the USA (exports $0·97 billion; imports $2·78 billion), in aircraft and parts highly favourable (exports $2·31 billion, imports $0·29 billion). Similar examples occur

Some Characteristics of Modern Manufacturing

Table 20: Exports and Imports of Selected Manufactured Production, 1968

	Exports ($ billion)	Imports ($ billion)
Machinery	6·57	2·28
Transport equipment	5·61	4·22
Chemicals	3·29	1·14
Electrical appliances	2·29	1·50
Metals and manufactures	2·12	4·65
Instruments	0·67	0·29
Textiles	0·52	0·96
Clothing	0·18	0·86
Total ($ billion)	21·25	15·90
% of US total	89	77

Source: Statistical Abstracts

elsewhere among the major exporters. Over all, however, these 'growth' industry groups clearly benefit from a favourable balance of trade.

In contrast are those industries adversely affected by the trade situation. In 'metals and manufacturers', for example, domestic producers of iron and steel face both a slowly growing internal demand and also increasing competition from imports. Exports of iron and steel mill products were valued at $0·58 billion in 1968, somewhat lower than earlier 1960 levels. Imports reached $1·96 billion, however, having increased steadily throughout the 1960s. In textile manufactures, too, imports rose considerably in the 1960s, and the balance of trade became increasingly unfavourable in both general textile products and clothing (Table 20). Among the mill products, synthetic and woollen fabrics provide the largest single kind of imports by value, but in other sectors imports now provide a large proportion of total domestic supply. Carpets and rugs, scouring and combing mill products and cordage and twine (where imports amount to a quarter or more of domestic supply in all) are instances. Undoubtedly, in industries such as iron and steel and textiles, therefore, imports have restricted the growth rates of the domestic industry.

Other industries in the X-type category are similar. Imports of

279

leather and leather products have risen sharply and by the late 1960s had reached above five times the value of exports, which have been fairly static. Most of the imports, by value, are of footwear but elsewhere in the leather business imports of relatively small total value (such as leather gloves) have come to dominate the internal market, to the distress of domestic producers. In lumber and wood products, too, imports greatly exceed exports, and in some sections (hardwood plywood and hardwood veneer, for example) measure a quarter or more of domestic shipments. Clearly, for these industries, the balance of trade is a serious matter. But restrictive policies on trade would probably not greatly change conditions in such industries in the longer term, or benefit the country in general. Trade is reciprocal and a protectionist policy of high tariffs and low quotas might result in losses of exports from other sectors of US industry. Moreover, import competition stimulates technical advance in both 'laggard' and 'growth' industries. The recent massive investment by the iron and steel industry in the basic oxygen process was partly stimulated by the technical superiority of overseas competitors who had adopted it. Restrictionist policies may thus bring temporary or localized relief to the protected interest, but the wider and longer-term benefits are doubtful.

Inter-industry Relationships

This discussion has necessarily relied chiefly upon data for the major industry groups. In the Standard Industrial Classification, however, the 21 major (two-digit) groups (e.g. group 22, textile mill products) are subdivided, first into over 130 three-digit groups (e.g. 225 knitting mills) and then into about 420 four-digit industries (e.g. 2,253 knit outer-wear mills). The two-digit grouping thus includes data from industries which may have little in common. This degree of aggregation presents problems essentially insurmountable in a study as broad as this. Some examples were given above of conditions at more discriminate levels which illustrate the different experiences possible within, as well as between, major groups. It is hoped that these sufficiently reinforce the point.

Another weakness so far has been discussion of the industry groups in isolation, with little account of the possible relationships between them. Yet a most important characteristic of modern manufacturing is the high degree of interdependence among the various classes of activity. These relationships are demonstrated most clearly in 'input–output' analyses; the most recent for the USA refering to 1963.* Such input–output tables show the complete structure of purchases by each identified industry, and set out the pattern of sales of each, both to other identified industries and to 'final demand'. Naturally, the range of industries involved in purchase or sales transactions varies greatly. Some industries sell much of their output to the final consumer. For the ordnance, footwear, household furniture and apparel industries, for example, 90, 88, 80 and 78 per cent of output respectively went to final demand in 1963. Only 3 per cent, however, of the primary iron and steel output, 10 per cent of plastic and synthetic materials, and 18 per cent of chemicals plants output went to final demand. For the latter, and indeed for most manufacturing, the 'intermediate' market is of the greatest significance and embraces numerous purchasers in both manufacturing and non-manufacturing sectors. The summary tables of the 1963 input–output study identify 52 classes of manufacturing. The primary iron and steel industry made sales to at least 44 of them (only sales over $0·5 million are tabulated). Understandably, the highest value of such sales was to metal-using industries (especially the fabricated metal products industries and the motor-vehicle group), but the wide spread is perhaps surprising, and certainly important. Similarly, the plastics and synthetic materials industry made sales to 36 of the 52 identified manufacturing industries, and the chemicals industry to 50. These are random examples from the industries which have low proportions of their output going to final demand.

A wide spread of sales destinations implies a wide spread of purchasing requirements, or inputs, among industries. Most manufacturing industries identified in the 1963 tables receive inputs from 20 or more other manufacturing industries. Among the examples

* *Input–Output Structure of the U.S. Economy: 1963*, 3 vols., U S Department of Commerce, Office of Business Economics, 1969.

cited above, primary iron and steel manufacturers bought from 38 other manufacturing industries, plastics and synthetic materials from 24 and chemicals from 35. Industries oriented strongly to final demand must also obtain their own input requirements from other industries. The footwear, furniture and apparel industries, for example, call on 23, 31 and 22 other manufacturing industries, respectively, for supplies. These inter-relationships are not confined to flows of goods between manufacturing concerns, but also intertwine manufacturing with other sectors of economic life. The chemicals industry drew inputs from 73 of the 87 identified industries (primary, secondary and tertiary) in 1963, and the primary iron and steel industry from 59.

Further illustrations are unnecessary. The fact is that the Standard Industrial Classification does not provide a listing of separate activities pursued in isolation from each other. Manufacturing today is a complex function, requiring close links with other manufacturers (as suppliers and customers) and with services of many kinds. These linkages, to function effectively, may have to be reflected on the ground and in location patterns. No hard and fast rules can be laid down, of course. Some intermediate products and some services are economically transportable over thousands of miles without causing problems of higher costs or possible dislocation of the production flow. But many are not so transportable, because, for example, of the transfer costs, or of the needs for close interchange between supplier and purchaser or for keeping inventories low. Important geographical consequences follow, cost advantages, for example, accruing to locations at or near the great concentrations of activity. Modern mobility of people and goods makes crude transfer costs less significant to manufacturing today than formerly, thus making dispersal of activity more possible. The increasing interdependence of different enterprises, however, relying upon the smooth interchange of services and materials, parts, components and subassemblies, seems in some respects to operate in the opposite direction. Concentrations of activity now offer many new advantages and, while the geographical area over which economies of concentration can effectively operate has greatly widened, such concentrations are still evident on the map and on the ground. This inter-relationship of industries is another highly important characteristic of modern manufacturing in the United States with direct implications for the regional patterns of manufacturing, as will be shown in the following chapters.

Conclusions

The US manufacturing economy comprises industries which, although often interdependent, have widely differing characteristics. These differences have been discussed chiefly in the context of a division of the manufacturing sector into 'growth' and 'laggard' categories. This approach has not permitted an assessment of all the important characteristics of American manufacturing. Further analysis must, however, be foregone, and this chapter ends with a brief summary of the characteristics of growth and laggard industries, industries of intermediate type being assumed to partake in various degrees of the character of each extreme. The laggard, or declining, industries seem to be mainly old-established industries, catering to those sections of market demand which, despite rising affluence, are expanding slowly. Some suffer from competition from substitutes or from growing imports. Although they are not technically backward, they have low levels of research and development activity. They are not often or deeply involved in national programmes which stimulate the flow of Federal R & D funds and lucrative government contracts. Production-line wage rates are low, and opportunities for non-production employment sparser than in the 'growth' sector.

The converse holds, in the main, for the rapidly advancing industries. They contain the chief centres of innovation, and often produce goods of a kind unknown before the war. They are research and development oriented but, with notable exceptions, as in chemicals, they depend heavily on Federal funds. Their products appeal greatly to a sophisticated and affluent internal market whose demand for the 'essentials' is virtually sated. Vigorous exporting is characteristic. They pay high wages on the production floor, and offer far greater opportunities than the 'laggards' in white-collar occupations. Given

283

the buoyant conditions of their markets, new investment in plant and machinery is consistently high. Since the patterns of industrial structure differ considerably from region to region, all of this has important implications for regional economic growth and welfare, and this theme is pursued in the following chapter.

11: The Geography of Manufacturing: The Manufacturing Belt

The growth of new industries and the decline of old is inevitably reflected in changing geographical patterns of activity. The newer industries have markedly different locational needs, arising from their different structure of inputs and the changing nature of the product. In the nineteenth century many areas became highly specialized in particular types of manufacturing for which they offered special advantages, but the new products and processes of the twentieth century would not necessarily be attracted to the same locations. Moreover, while the structure of demand for manufactured products altered, great changes were also made in other ways relevant to location decisions and to regional patterns of development. The more important ones were discussed in Chapter 4, and we need here recall only the chief elements and their particular impact in this context.

In transport, technical advances and changes in pricing practices have clearly been very significant and have, other things being equal, favoured locations with access to large market areas. In fuel and power and raw material supply overall, greater efficiency in production, transport and use has decreased the locational attraction of the primary sources. Advances in production technology have, among other things, altered the costs structures of industries and the desirable scale of operations, while increased governmental concern about strategic industries, defence needs and economic and social problems generally has also had important locational effects. Further, the changing regional distribution of the increasingly affluent population has altered quite fundamentally the regional patterns of markets and labour supply. While such major elements in the general process of geographical change can be identified, however, the subject is in detail extraordinarily complex. Decisions on location are taken by innumerable individuals, or numerous corporate enterprises, for whom motives and ultimate objectives may differ, while the factors considered most important in location vary to some extent, even for similar types of manufacture. Thus no theory has yet fully explained the processes of differential regional growth, but the facts themselves remain. These are, in sum, that developments in the twentieth century have created new conditions in the location of manufacturing industry and that manufacturing operates in a totally different setting in volume of demand, tastes, efficiency of production, servicing and movement and the geographical distribution of labour and markets. In this context, major changes in geographical patterns must be expected.

While our chief concern is to examine trends in the past two or three decades, it will be useful to set these geographical developments into a deeper historical context, since events during and since the Second World War have often extended and underlined

Table 21: Distribution of Employment in Manufacturing by Geographical Division, 1870–1969

	(per cent)*			
	1870	1910	1940	1969
New England	21·5	13·5	11·0	7·5
Middle Atlantic	35·0	31·5	29·5	21·5
East North Central	20·5	22·5	28·0	26·5
West North Central	6·5	8·5	5·0	6·5
South Atlantic	8·0	9·0	11·5	14·0
East South Central	4·0	4·0	4·0	6·0
West South Central	2·0	4·0	3·5	6·0
Mountain	0·5	2·0	1·0	2·0
Pacific	2·0	5·0	6·0	10·5
US total manufactur-ing employment (thousands)	2,640	10,660	10,980	21,100

* Rounded to nearest 0·5 per cent

Source: H. S. Perloff *et al., Regions, Resources and Economic Growth (Statistical Appendix) for 1870 and 1910,* US Department of Labor; *Employment and Earnings; States and Areas* for 1940 and 1969

trends initiated much earlier. Table 21 therefore presents calculations of the proportional distribution of employment in manufacturing amongst the nine divisions from 1870 to 1969. The data are not fully comparable throughout this period, for the classification of manufacturing activity and methods of collecting and processing data have changed; but the broad patterns suggested in the Table are undoubtedly accurate. The background is one of rising employment in manufacturing, both generally and (with some exceptions for the period 1910 to 1940) in each division. The varying *rates* of growth are, however, shown clearly by the regional shares of jobs. The broad conclusion is that the geographical balance of manufacturing has undergone steady alteration throughout the century covered by the figures, and that important new centres of manufacturing have emerged or are emerging.

Figure 40 also portrays the trends in manufacturing employment, but for 1940 to 1969, using both absolute and relative growth data. One major theme, differentiating the three north-eastern divisions (New England, Middle Atlantic and East North Central) from those elsewhere, is immediately apparent. Employment growth rates in manufacturing in these three divisions have, except for the East North Central between 1940 and 1950, been regularly below the national average. Elsewhere, except for the South Atlantic division between 1940 and 1950, they have been regularly above. In other words, the three north-eastern divisions have experienced relative decline, illustrated in Figure 40 by the representation of the percentage of total US manufacturing found in each division. None the less, the massive size of manufacturing employment remaining in the North-East is also evident, and in 1969 these three divisions still possessed 56 per cent of the nation's manufacturing jobs. This treatment, therefore, is in two major parts, one dealing with the north-eastern area, the other with the developments elsewhere.

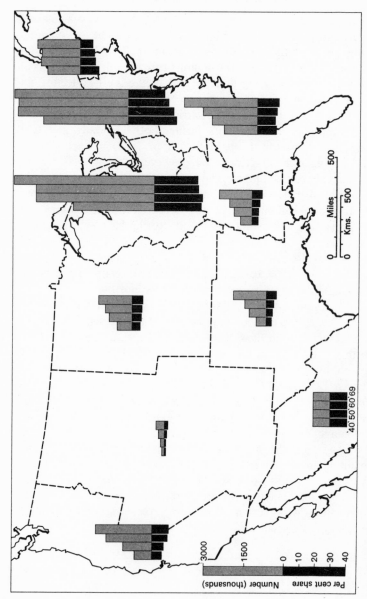

Figure 40. Employment in Manufacturing, 1940—69

The Manufacturing Belt, Concept and Past Development

In essence, the three north-eastern divisions comprise that part of the North American continent known as the 'Manufacturing Belt'. The Belt in detail does not coincide exactly with these three Census divisions. It excludes, for example, northern parts of New England, Michigan and Wisconsin and north-eastern New York, and includes parts of Maryland, West Virginia, Iowa and Missouri and has an international extension into Ontario. The three divisions, however, contain the heart of the Belt and we may conveniently use them to represent the Belt in its entirety. Some geographers consider that the concept of the Manufacturing Belt no longer has much relevance in evaluating the economic geography of the country; others regard it as an important 'intellectual convenience'; yet others view it as still a major fact of economic life. A brief review of the concept of the Belt and its place in the literature thus seems appropriate.

Certainly, as a regional concept, the Manufacturing Belt is to some extent unusual. In its natural endowments and physical structure there is no unifying base. This is not itself a major impediment to regional definition, but human and economic criteria also present certain problems. For example, the various parts of this enormous area can be clearly recognized either as distinctive regions in their own right, or as important parts of other major human regions. Nor can the emphasis on manufacturing activity and continuity suggested by the name be properly taken to imply an unbroken and unrelieved extension of urban-industrial complexes throughout the 'Belt'. Manufacturing activity occurs sporadically rather than continuously and there are very large tracts of farm, forest and open space. A journey from New York to Chicago could be very disappointing if it were expected to confirm the mental image the term 'Manufacturing Belt' conjures up. The industrial potential of the Belt appears as highlights in New York and its satellites; the Trenton–Philadelphia–Baltimore axis; the Greater Boston and western Connecticut areas; the Mohawk Valley complex and the developments at and around Buffalo, Pittsburgh and the Erie Lake shore cities; Detroit, Cincinnati and Chicago and, on the western margins, St Louis. These and numerous smaller intervening centres are linked together, not by a continuous sprawl of housing and industry, but by the characteristics of their economic life (i.e. a common concentration on, or dependence on, manufacturing activities), and also functionally by providing each other with industrial materials, components, parts and services, and markets for final manufactures. It is this great series of inter-trading centres, so concentrated in this north-eastern area, that gives the region its special character, permitting a Manufacturing Belt to be defined and regarded as the 'core area' or 'economic heartland' of the United States. This area emerged in the late nineteenth and early twentieth centuries as the most densely populated part of the country; as the most highly urbanized and industrialized part; and as the wealthiest section of the nation. Here developed a pattern of regional activity still without parallel in magnitude, style, functions and material rewards, which is physically, as well as conceptually, distinct from other areas of significant industrial development in the country.

The term 'Manufacturing Belt' was introduced by Sten de Geer in 1927, drawing on, and developing, the concept of an industrial 'quadrilateral' that had emerged earlier.* He defined the area on the distribution of manufacturing wage-earners in towns with populations of more than 10,000, and in towns and cities with at least 1,000 wage-earners in manufacturing. On several grounds his definition might be considered unsatisfactory, but the area he out-lined closely resembles those delimited by later researchers using different criteria, and shows an impressive similarity with a map of 1958 data by Pred.† During the inter-war years several researchers developed the concept in direct analyses, while others did so indirectly in work on the delimitation of manufacturing regions in the USA as a whole. Since the war the Manufacturing Belt has been frequently used as a tool in analysing changing industrial

* Sten de Geer, 'The American Manufacturing Belt', *Geografiska Annaler*, Vol. 9, 1927.

† A. Pred, 'The Concentration of High-Value-Added Manufacturing', *Economic Geography*, April 1965.

patterns, giving rise, incidentally, to considerable disagreement on the implications of wartime and post-war developments in diminishing the stature of the Belt and, given these developments, on the validity and usefulness of the concept itself. The early pre-eminence of the Belt, however, can be emphasized statistically, and some reasons for its emergence suggested.

Using data for the New England, Middle Atlantic and East North Central divisions as a whole, Table 21 indicates that in 1870 about 77 per cent of the nation's manufacturing workers were employed in the Belt, while 56 per cent of the total population lived in these divisions. By 1910, when total manufacturing employment had multiplied fourfold, the share of the Belt was about 68 per cent. Since, however, the region's share of the total population had also fallen, to 48 per cent, the ratio of percentage of manufacturing employment to percentage of total population for the Belt had risen from 1·38 to 1·42, indicating that the Belt had increased its per capita share of manufacturing activity. Thereafter, until 1940, the relative position of the Manufacturing Belt remained almost precisely the same as in 1910, for both employment and population.

Thus a quite extraordinary geographical pattern had persisted over many decades. Such a phenomenon can have no simple explanation, but must result from the interaction of numerous variables. The early settlement and development of industrial interests in parts of the north-eastern coastal areas had undoubtedly had permanent effects, and population movement and development of transport facilities in the early nineteenth century took industrial contacts and traditions westward to the interior of the Belt. Here the natural resource endowment was exceptionally favourable, including timber, iron ores, salt, copper ores, petroleum and, above all, coal. Natural waterways, when improved, provided economical access to the resources of other areas, especially the great iron-ore ranges of the Lake Superior district. The region, thus favoured, attracted tremendous capital investment in transport services, settlements, basic industries (mining, iron and steel and other metals, chemicals and so forth) and secondary manufactures. The population grew rapidly and the labour force acquired considerable expertise; very large industrial complexes with intricate

291

webs of interconnected activity emerged, and, with high per capita income prevailing over large areas of the Belt, the area had tremendous market potential. This catalogue of advantages offered or opportunities taken could be extended. Some initial attractions have diminished, others have been created or have acquired greater significance. What is clear is that none of these elements in isolation explains the phenomenon of the Manufacturing Belt: 'circular and cumulative causation' has manifestly operated here, although in highly favourable circumstances, to arrive at this unique, highly complex end product.

Many of the same conditions as those promoting the emergence of the Manufacturing Belt as the nation's pre-eminent region of industrial activity also help to explain developments within the Belt itself. While the relative standing of the whole Belt remained virtually unchanged from 1910 to 1940 (with about 68 per cent of the nation's manufacturing employment in both years), the geographical balance within the region altered significantly (Table 21). Consequent on the Great Depression, total national employment in manufacturing in 1940 was approximately the same as in 1910; but the eastern divisions of the Belt had faced special difficulties not only from the depression itself, but also from important structural changes. Manufacturing employment in 1940 was thus considerably below the 1910 figures in both the New England and the Middle Atlantic divisions. These divisions retained numerous advantages both natural (e.g. access to major world shipping routes) and acquired (e.g. large populations and centres of academic and technical excellence) to support renewed expansion of manufacturing after 1940, but the secular trend strongly favoured areas west of the Appalachians. Naturally, around the turn of the century the 'Middle West', being more recently developed, had faster growth rates than the old-established eastern centres. But the general conditions for manufacturing growth were outstanding, and highly favourable for the continuous expansion of the new industries. Thus, although this part of the Belt also suffered from the depression, the favourable effects of structure were sufficient, over all, to counter the cyclical decline. Manufacturing employment in the East North Central division grew by over a quarter even between 1910 and 1940.

The division thus advanced greatly in relative standing, so that by 1940 the balance of advantage within the Belt had moved strongly to areas west of the Appalachians.

The Present Character of the Manufacturing Belt

Since 1940 the Belt has lost ground relative to the national growth of manufacturing activity (Figure 40). Nationally, employment in manufacturing rose by 83 per cent between 1940 and 1969. The New England and Middle Atlantic divisions expanded their employment, but only by 25 and 35 per cent respectively. After 1950 the East North Central division, too, assumed for a while a below-average growth posture, so that its twenty-nine-year overall increase was some 72 per cent. By 1969, therefore, the Belt as a whole provided 56 per cent of the nation's manufacturing jobs, compared with 68 per cent in 1940. The regional proportion of total population had also fallen, however, to 44 per cent so that the ratio of percentage of US employment in manufacturing to percentage of US population had fallen only to 1·27, reflecting the still notable concentration of manufacturing activity in the Belt.

The continuing pre-eminence of the Belt can be demonstrated in several possible ways. Figure 41 expresses the situation by value added in manufacturing per head of the population in each State. The pattern is remarkable. Nationally the value added per capita in 1967 was approximately $1,300. Seven States achieved levels 30 per cent or more above that, all in the Belt; and no State belonging truly to the Manufacturing Belt* had below the national average of per capita value added. Outside the Belt, no State equals the national average. Even California, of which more might have been expected, fell 7 per cent below the national level and, clearly, the Manufacturing Belt sets a pace in intensity of manufacturing activity which other regions cannot yet match.

Another striking visual expression of the dominance of the Manufacturing Belt is presented in Figure 42, which maps the thirty metropolitan areas of the USA with over one million

* I.e. excluding Maine and Vermont which would not qualify in a precise definition.

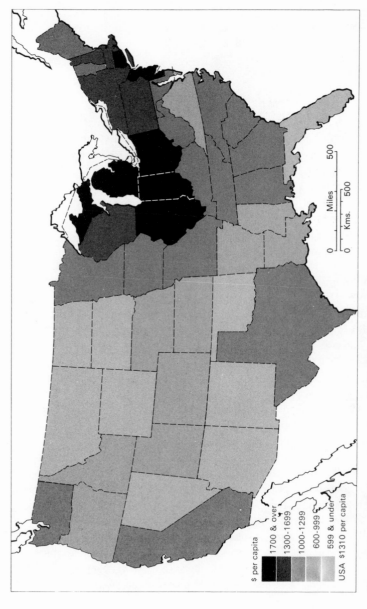

Figure 41. Value Added in Manufacturing Per Capita by State, 1967

$ per capita

1700 & over
1300-1699
1000-1299
600-999
599 & under

USA $1310 per capita

Miles
0   500
Kms.
0   500

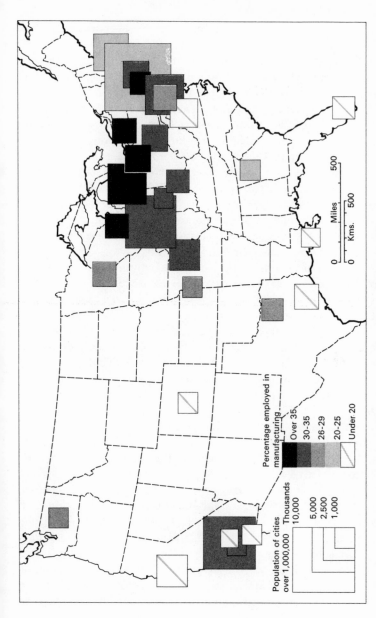

Figure 42. Large SMSAs by Proportion of Employment in Manufacturing, 1969

Percentage employed in manufacturing

Over 35
30-35
26-29
20-25
Under 20

Population of cities over 1,000,000   Thousands

10,000
5,000
2,500
1,000

Miles
500

Kms.
500

inhabitants in 1969, showing for each the proportion of total employment in manufacturing. These thirty areas contain 38 per cent of the nation's population and, because of the attractiveness to industry of the large metropolitan area and its facilities, a rather higher share, 43 per cent, of the nation's employment in manufacturing. The concentration of these great metropolises within the Manufacturing Belt is itself very impressive, but even more remarkable is the intensity of their interest in manufacturing. Nationally, 29 per cent of all non-agricultural employment was in manufacturing in 1969, but in twelve of these great north-eastern cities the proportion was above this, in five considerably above. Outside the Belt only two metropolitan areas of this size have an interest in manufacturing reaching the second degree of intensity identified in the map. In the Belt only two of these great metropolitan areas have proportions in manufacturing below the national average. These are New York (24 per cent of all employment in manufacturing) and Boston (25 per cent). Both are special cases, having trade, finance or other services of such magnitude that manufacturing employment, although very large (in New York, by far the largest in the nation) is relatively low. Such cases apart, in most cities of the Belt, of whatever size, manufacturing employment has significance seldom found elsewhere. This is reflected in the employment structure of the Manufacturing Belt where, over all in 1969, 34 per cent of all non-agricultural employment was in manufacturing (USA 29 per cent).

Another aspect of the great cities' functions has relevance here, namely management, whose day-to-day decisions determine the course of economic affairs throughout the nation and influence the location patterns of economic activity. Since such decisions are chiefly made by people living and working in the largest centres, there is inevitably a significant fall-out effect on other functions and operations in those areas themselves. New York is the prime management centre in the USA, and this must have a beneficial effect on other activities, including manufacturing activities, in this area of the country. There are other significant management centres, of course, and W. Goodwin has ranked these centres in order of the value of assets they control – an index he considers the best measure of relative importance.* He discovered thirty-one cities in which managerial operations commanded assets of $1 billion or more. No fewer than twenty-one of these were in the Manufacturing Belt, compared with seven in the South and only three in the West. This puts the dominance of the Belt into a broader commercial context.

The presence in the Manufacturing Belt of these great metropolises, and numerous other urban-industrial entities of considerable size, implies another condition supporting the special status of this area of the country. This is the enormous market potential here. The per capita personal income in the New England, Middle Atlantic and East North Central divisions in 1969 amounted to 10, 13 and 7 per cent respectively above the national average of about $3,700. Given the large population, this implies an enormous concentration of purchasing power in this area, a matter of continuing significance in location decisions for industries serving final consumer demand, and consequently for others. This enviable income status is itself largely due to the high average earnings in manufacturing (Figure 43). The hourly earnings of production workers are above the national average in all relevant States except Pennsylvania (which stands on the average), Massachusetts and Rhode Island. This position of the north-eastern States owes much to a favourable structure of industry, to which we return below. The map emphasizes the present unrivalled earnings potential (and, therefore, purchasing potential) of the Belt. Other areas of high average earnings occur, notably along the southern and western fringes of the Belt, where beneficial spread effects are felt. Nowhere else is there an equivalent agglomeration of people whose earnings in manufacturing are consistently above the national average. The Pacific States have high averages but the industrial centres concerned are often far apart and the total number of people involved is but a fraction of that in the Belt.

The market for manufactured products, however, is not only, or even mainly, with the final consumer. The interchange of parts, sub-assemblies and semi-manufactures is a vital element of an efficient production system. In providing for such interchange the

* W. Goodwin, 'The Management Center in the U.S.A.', *Geographical Review*, Jan. 1965.

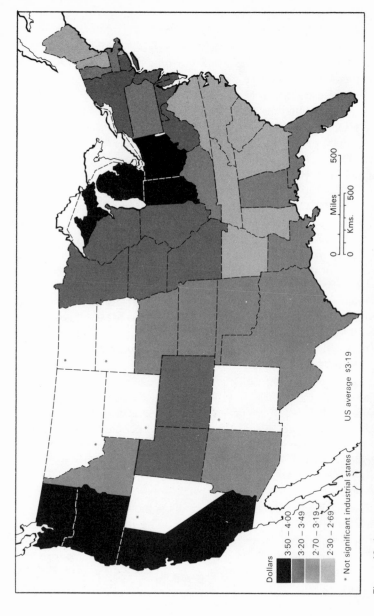

Figure 43. Average Hourly Earnings of Production Workers in Manufacturing, 1969

Dollars

3·50 – 4·00
3·20 – 3·49
2·70 – 3·19
2·30 – 2·69

* Not significant industrial states

US average $3·19

Miles
0   500

Kms.
0   500

Manufacturing Belt possesses unique strength. We noted in Chapter 10 the complexity of inter-industry linkages as displayed in input–output tables. Such linkages have special implications for manufacturing in the Belt, helping further to explain its concentration of major industries. The situation can be illustrated from the five metal-making or metal-using industry groups shown in Table 22, using data drawn from the 1963 Input–Output Study of the US Office of Business Economics. The Table does not represent a closed system, since data for both non-manufacturing and final demand are omitted. Thus the outputs of industries and the inputs to industries shown here do not balance. Nor have the transactions between 'other manufacturing industries' been computed in detail, but merely as they impinge on the five selected groups. The degree of inter-manufacturing trading by each of the five groups varies considerably, as the final column of the Table indicates. For the primary metal group, transactions within the manufacturing sector comprise 84 per cent of all output, but the proportion falls to 33 per cent for the transport equipment group, which has a much greater relative volume of sales outside manufacturing, especially to final demand. None the less, inter-manufacturing sales are very important for each of these industries.

In output (read along the rows in the Table), two 'extreme' patterns of inter-manufacturing trading appear, for the transport equipment group on the one hand and the fabricated metal product group on the other. In the former, 81 per cent of total sales to the manufacturing sector are within the group itself. This situation is to be expected, for the manufacture of parts, components, sub-assemblies and so on to be sold to the final assembly plants is classed together with those plants in the transport equipment group. This condition itself has important geographical implications, but sales to other manufacturing industries are also very large, amounting to $3·8 billion in 1963. In the fabricated metal product group, by contrast, only one ninth of all inter-manufacturing sales is within the group itself. Over half its sales are to the other metal-based industries and over a third to 'other manufacturing'. Again, this is not unexpected. The group has a varied output of items such as containers, metal shapes, nuts, bolts and screws which are

Table 22: Input–Output Table: Five Major Industry Groups, 1963

Columns represent inputs for each group. Rows represent output of each group	Primary metal	Fabricated metal	Machinery	Electrical equipment	Transport equipment	Other manufacturing	Inter-manufacturing total	Inter-manufacturing transactions as % of total transactions
				(million dollars)				
Primary metal	10,444	7,472	4,188	2,655	5,634	2,393	32,796	84
Fabricated metal	696	1,522	1,748	1,500	3,284	4,604	13,354	53
Machinery	756	747	5,941	1,017	3,207	895	12,563	36
Electrical equipment	291	296	1,885	5,902	1,884	1,233	11,491	34
Transport equipment	148	352	744	428	15,944	2,108	19,724	33
Other manufacturing	1,304	1,721	1,518	2,995	3,258	—	—	—
Total manufacturing	13,639	12,110	16,024	14,497	33,238	—	—	—

Inputs and outputs do not balance since this table omits data for non-manufacturing and final demand

Source: Input–Output Structure of the US Economy, 1963, Department of Commerce, Office of Business Economics, 1969

obviously needed by all manufacturing enterprises. The remaining metal-based industries share the characteristics of both the transport and fabricated metal groups. They have a large internal trade and trade with other manufacturing industry – but most especially with the other metal industries, so that the interconnections here are, in total, very strong indeed.

The output transactions of one industry group are the input transactions of others, and Table 22 thus shows (in the columns) the interconnections of these metal-based industries from the input side. The magnitude and depth of these interconnections are immediately impressive. Again, two extreme patterns present themselves. The primary metal group provides over three quarters of its own inputs, but the fabricated metal group only 13 per cent, depending fundamentally on inputs from the primary group. The other identified groups fall between these two. Apart from their very significant internal transactions, all draw heavily from the primary metal group, as would be expected, but invariably one fifth or more of total inputs from manufacturing sources comes from the other metal-based industries. Over all, therefore, the Table exposes an enormous volume of inter-trading among these five metal-based industries. But this pattern of inter-relationships at the industry level reflects only the tip of an iceberg. Beneath lies a multitude of additional contacts between firms and individual plants. Such conditions have strong implications for location and for the Manufacturing Belt.

In 1968 the Belt provided very high proportions of the nation's employment in each of these five major industry groups: in primary metal, 73 per cent; fabricated metal, 66 per cent; machinery, 69 per cent; electrical equipment, 65 per cent; and transport equipment, 55 per cent. Each of these percentages greatly exceeds the region's proportion of the nation's population (44 per cent in 1968) and, except for transport equipment, considerably exceeds the region's proportion of all manufacturing employment (56 per cent). It cannot be entirely fortuitous that these groups, whose internal trade and exchanges with one another are so great, share such a preference for locations within the Belt. It is not suggested here that inter-industry linkages are the sole, or even the major, cause of

301

such persistent concentration. The matter is extraordinarily complex, as has been emphasized, and the roles of final demand, of labour supply and quality, of established connections and reputations, of invested capital, and so on remain considerable. Industrial linkages, however, rank high among the causes of such concentrations, and provide another reason for the enduring strength of manufacturing activity in this area.

Structure of Manufacturing in the Belt

For whatever combination of causes, the Manufacturing Belt has, despite its relatively slow *rate* of growth since 1940, attracted much new employment in numerous industries and processes. The domination of the region in certain major industry groups has just been illustrated, and we may now look at the structure of industry in the broad context of the 'growth' and 'laggard' groups identified in Chapter 10. Nationally, in 1968, about 40 per cent of all manufacturing employment was in the A-type industries and 25 per cent in the X-type. In the Manufacturing Belt the proportions were 43 and 20 per cent respectively, indicating a better than average structural situation, over all. Within the Belt, however, there is considerable diversity of experience (Figure 44).

Developments in New England have been of unusual significance. The region's chief X-type industries (textiles, shoe and leather product manufacture) have, as is well known, greatly declined from their historical position as major staples. Meanwhile vigorous expansion has occurred in each of the seven A-type industries, most notably in the electrical and transport equipment groups. Thus the structure of the region's manufacturing has been revolutionized. In Massachusetts, in 1947, for example, some 40 per cent of all manufacturing employment was in X-type industries, and 32 per cent in A-type, but by 1968 the proportions had been changed to 20 and 43 per cent respectively. This transformation was accompanied by considerable hardship, and several Massachusetts cities have been classified as areas of 'chronic labour surplus' for twenty years or more. Even today, total manufacturing employment

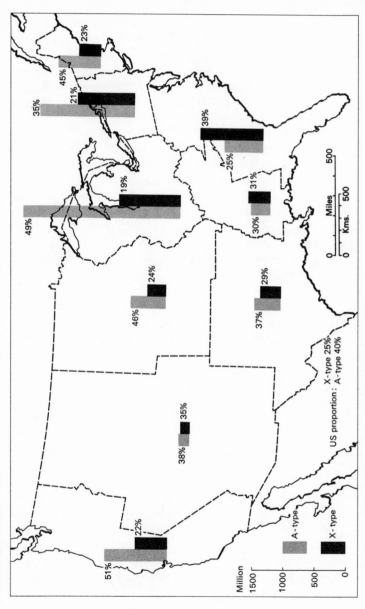

Figure 44. Employment in A- and X-type Manufacturing, 1968

remains slightly below the 1947 level. In the State as a whole, however, the change has been both remarkable and beneficial, and Massachusetts, as the largest manufacturing State in the region, contributes strongly to the generally favourable present structure of New England industry. Maine, New Hampshire and Rhode Island have lower than US average proportions in A-type industries and higher than average in X-type, and remain to some extent areas of difficulty within the region. Over all, however, they are swamped by the situation in Massachusetts and Connecticut. In Connecticut, the structure of manufacturing has long been strong in the growth sectors and total employment has risen considerably since the war. By 1968 it was unique in having 61 per cent of its manufacturing jobs in A-type industries and only 11 per cent in X-type sectors. In New England as a whole, therefore, employment in growth industries has moved from 32 per cent of the total in 1947 to 45 per cent in 1968, whereas for the laggard groups the proportion has dropped from 38 to 23 per cent.

Very largely this transformation has been associated with the research and development capabilities of the region. Since the war New England's university, corporate and private research facilities have bent much of their great expertise to defence equipment, missiles and aerospace demands, for which huge Federal contracts have been available. Figure 45 shows that expenditure on industrial R & D in New England in 1968 reached approximately 10 per cent of the national total, although the region had under 8 per cent of US manufacturing employment. Since research and development work often earns production contracts, the importance of industrial R & D to New England is clear. Almost half the total expenditure came from Federal sources in 1968, however; a degree of dependence which could prove unhealthy.

At the western end of the Manufacturing Belt the States of the East North Central division have a uniformly favourable structure. For the whole division, practically half the manufacturing employment was in A-type industries in 1968, and under one fifth in the laggard sectors. This very favourable situation is strongly reflected in the maps of value added per capita (Figure 41) and hourly earnings in manufacture (Figure 43), and has been reflected, too,

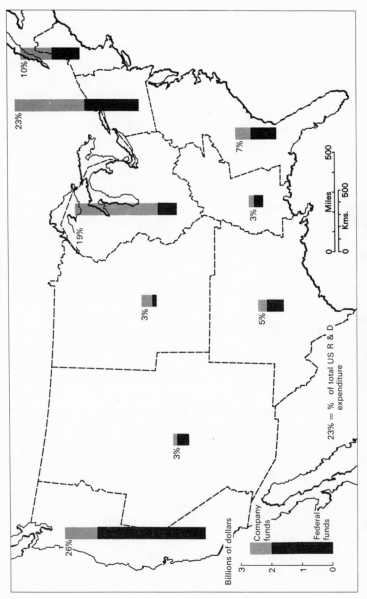

Figure 45. Expenditure on Industrial Research and Development by Division and Source of Funds, 1968

in the rising relative importance of this part of the Belt as employment grew at rates far above those in New England and the Middle Atlantic division. Moreover, while growth *rates* for the East North Central division have recently been below the national average the actual increases in employment in manufacturing have been very large. Thus between 1940 and 1969 manufacturing employment in the East North Central division as a whole grew by 2·1 million. The increment in the Pacific division was only 1·4 million, although it grew three times as fast.

All of the A-type industries, except the ordnance group, are represented strongly in the East North Central area. The division had about 26 per cent of all the nation's manufacturing employment in 1968, with slightly lower proportions of the nation's chemicals and instruments industries, but much higher proportions of electrical equipment, rubber and plastic products, transport equipment and machinery industries. We have little space for detail, but in machinery manufacture the ENC division alone has over 40 per cent of national employment, with massive capacity in metal working and general industrial machinery, construction equipment, farm machinery, engines and turbines. Transport equipment manufacture here also employs some 37 per cent of the national total, and the concentration on motor vehicle production is universally known. Despite expansion of facilities elsewhere, this division still employs over two thirds of the nation's motor industry workers, the State of Michigan alone about 40 per cent.

The X-type industries as a group have relatively small stature in the industry of the East North Central division, but their chief representatives here, food product and primary metal manufacture, do have an important role and attain considerable size. Food-product industries benefit greatly not only from the proximity of a large population, but also from the great and productive agrarian interests of this area. Thus about a fifth of the nation's total employment in this industry is in this division. Primary metal manufacture has close connections, as shown above, with the other metal-based industries of the region, which are of enormous size. Consequently the division employs some two fifths of the national labour force in primary metal manufacture. This industry group, although legitimately designated 'laggard' industry, adds immensely by its capacity here to the attractions of this division to the leading 'growth' industries. The area is without rival as the heartland of American industry.

Curiously, the division receives rather less than its 'share' of industrial research and development expenditure (Figure 45). This is chiefly because it has attracted only a minor portion of the Federal funds available for this purpose. For a time, at least, Federal requirements moved away from the kinds of military hardware this division was most adept at providing, into missiles and aerospace products, for which the area was relatively less well equipped. Thus only 5 per cent of Federal resources put into industrial R & D in 1968 went to the East North Central area. For company funds, however, the situation is very different. Year by year, more company R & D funds are attracted to the ENC division than to any other. In essence this may be a safer long-run situation than that in, for example, California where most R & D monies come from the government. The power of the ENC division is therefore seen in the 32 per cent of total company R & D funds it attracted in 1968 for this reflects the shrewd assessments of private interests in pursuit of profits and is perhaps, therefore, a more reliable guide.

The Middle Atlantic division follows the East North Central as the nation's second largest centre of manufacturing. The growth rate of employment has been sluggish here, however. The absolute increase in manufacturing employment between 1940 and 1969 was little over half that in the East North Central area, and also fell below that in two divisions (Pacific and South Atlantic) outside the Belt. This unimpressive performance has chiefly reflected the relatively poor structure of manufacturing in the division. In 1947 almost a third of total employment was in X-type industries, which proceeded to shed a third of a million jobs by 1968, chiefly from the primary metal and textile groups. In addition an 'intermediate' activity, apparel manufacture, also experienced drastic decline in New York State, losing 135,000 jobs, only partly offset by a modest expansion in Pennsylvania. Following the national trends, all of the A-type industries expanded in the division, with the machinery

307

and electrical equipment groups making outstanding gains. Thus, in total, the growth industries added more than half a million jobs between 1947 and 1968, but the rapid contraction of all the X-type interests, and of clothing manufacture, balanced these gains so that total manufacturing employment in the division in 1968 was practically identical with that of 1947.

Such adjustments have, however, considerably improved the structure of industry in the division (Figure 44). Even so, the structure remains unusual. Below-average proportions of total employment are found in both A- and X-type categories. In this division, that is to say, intermediate type industries assume a greater than normal significance. In this category the apparel industry, despite its considerable contraction, remains of great size, providing some two fifths of all apparel trade jobs in the nation. Printing and publishing also reaches its national peak of development here, with New York State alone providing almost one fifth of US employment. Among the three States of this division, Pennsylvania remains weakest in industrial structure, with 30 per cent of its employment in both the A-type and the X-type categories. This represents some advance (in 1947, 42 per cent of manufacturing jobs were in the laggard industries, 25 per cent in the growth categories), but the adjustment here, as in Massachusetts, has been accomplished with difficulty. High rates of unemployment have been common in Pennsylvania, where several large cities have been long classified as areas of chronic labour surplus. Although all the seven growth industries have expanded here, only the rubber and plastics group has expanded notably, and it remains relatively small in absolute size. Among the X-type industries Pennsylvania retains an unusually large interest in primary metal manufacture (almost one fifth of total national employment in 1968), but here this nationally slow-growing industry has experienced a sharp absolute employment decline.

In industrial R & D expenditure, the Middle Atlantic division has not done badly. In 1968, for example, it accounted for approximately the same proportion of such expenditure in the USA as it did of employment, and over all did considerably better than the neighbouring East North Central division (Figure 45). About 40 per cent of the total came from Federal funds, on which the usual reservations might be expressed, but the division also attracted a large share (27 per cent) of private company R & D funds and came close to the corresponding total in the ENC division. Clearly, therefore, the research and development potential of this division is very great and, unusually, attracts large resources from both Federal and private funds. This 'best of both worlds' situation indicates that the structure of manufacturing in this division will continue to improve and that the area will soon throw off its current label as the slowest growing division in the nation.

The Manufacturing Belt: Final Observations

In the total manufacturing potential of this area of north-eastern USA we have an impressive geographical phenomenon, which has sustained itself remarkably, despite the inevitable, sometimes very rapid, recent growth of manufacturing elsewhere. Probably, too, this pattern will continue to dominate the geography of manufacturing through the foreseeable future. In so far as current research and development activity underpins future growth prospects, the geographical pattern shown for 1968 in Figure 45 (which well represents recent experience) is a good augury. The Belt attracts about half of all industrial R & D funds; but, still better, within that total it attracts an even larger share (70 per cent or so) of private company R & D expenditure. The region's capacity in R & D is naturally reflected in current location decisions. Despite its enormous existing body of capital investment (normally implying that less extra investment is required than elsewhere to achieve the same result), about half the nation's expenditure on new plant and equipment in manufacturing is made in the Belt (Figure 46). Such considerations, together with those outlined earlier, seem to justify the view of the region's future expressed above.

Up to at least the early 1960s the long-term trends in regional growth had prompted concern among some economists and politicians about the future in the Manufacturing Belt. A period of great

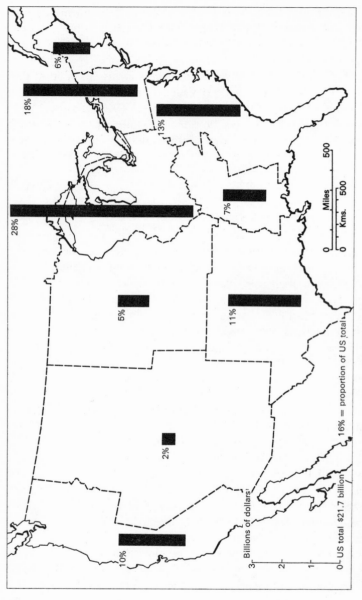

Figure 46. Expenditure for New Plant and Equipment in Manufacturing, 1967

difficulty was foreseen in large parts of the region as the attractions of the South and West continue to drain industrial enterprises from the Belt. In fact, the expanding relative stature of such outside areas has derived from differential growth rates in manufacturing activities, rather than from the actual migration of industries. Certainly, parts of the Manufacturing Belt have experienced, and still experience, considerable hardship. Several large, and many small, communities in New England and Pennsylvania, for example, have been in difficulties for years, but in essence these are the natural consequences of economic adjustment in mature industrial areas. The essential strengths of the Belt as a whole remain, to assert themselves over the longer term. Preliminary data on employment for 1963–7 (Census of Manufactures) in fact suggest that the phase of most rapid relative loss has already ended. Employment growth in the Belt as a whole was little short of the national average rate, while the East North Central division exceeded the national rate so that here increase in relative stature has again begun.

This industrial heartland, concentrating manufacturing capacity and the wealth that flows from it, has had profound effects upon other regions. On the Myrdal model of regional development, both 'backwash' and 'spread' effects have been experienced in regions outside the Belt. Through the late nineteenth and early twentieth centuries the heartland's development creamed off the capital, entrepreneurial and skilled labour resources of other areas, for few offered so firm a promise of adequate returns. Moreover, as the capacity of the Belt expanded, as economies of scale and concentration were achieved and as transport networks improved, manufacturers in the Belt sought markets throughout the nation. This often undermined small-scale local industries in other regions. The protection previously given them by distance was overcome by northern efficiency in production and marketing and by transport and commodity pricing practices. The description of a late nineteenth-century Georgia funeral, quoted by Smith and Phillips,* in which the South provided only the body and the hole, speaks eloquently of northern industrial pre-eminence at the time, and would have applied to many other southern areas. The relationship

* J. C. Smith and M. O. Phillips, *North America*, 1942, p. 329.

311

of the Manufacturing Belt to other regions was largely that of creditor to debtor.

Beneficial 'spread' effects, however, were also felt, with increasing impact. The needs of the North-East for foods and raw materials stimulated in the 'back-country' the output of farms, forests and mines. These demands sometimes encouraged the preliminary processing of the materials, and as population grew so did markets and employment in activities required to service them. Further, the search of some northern industrialists for cheaper or more docile labour led to considerable direct northern investment in manufacturing beyond the Belt, although at first chiefly close at hand in the northern States of the South Atlantic division. Such processes, however, gradually developed centres of manufacturing outside the Belt.

'Backwash' and 'spread' effects run counter to each other and in sum these 'natural' economic processes had but a limited effect on the general geographical pattern of manufacturing before the Second World War. Between 1910 and 1940 the major national development was the strengthening, within the Belt, of the East North Central division (Table 21). Beyond it notable growth occurred only in the South Atlantic division, while some other areas actually lost ground. With the war, however, came a new stage in the regional development process. The search for 'safe' locations and for surplus labour brought investment in community infrastructure and manufacturing capability to many areas outside the Belt, and often began a self-reinforcing process of industrial growth and population growth which is still continuing. We examine this development below, but would emphasize one further point here. The influence of the Manufacturing Belt in its evolution is still perceptible, not only in its own current position, but also in the regional structures of activity elsewhere. As the manufacturing centre *par excellence* it had gathered to itself the élite among industrial processes, the most rewarding tasks. Other growing centres would, largely, perform the simpler operations, especially the early processing of the materials they supplied. The Belt's capacity could best be used, its enterprise most rewarded, in the finer tasks of fabricating, finishing and assembling. This flavour remains today.

312

Six out of every ten American workers in A-type industries (the sophisticated, modern industries) are in the Manufacturing Belt. In the less glamorous and less rewarding activities such as textiles and lumber and wood products manufacture, however, the Belt has yielded pride of place to other regions.

12: The Geography of Manufacturing: Other Regional Developments

Some observations on the development of manufacturing in areas outside the Manufacturing Belt were made in the previous chapter. Often these have emphasized the primacy of the 'heartland' area and less than justice may consequently have been done to the size and character of industrial development elsewhere. If so, the following discussion should help to improve the perspective. Unique and important as the Manufacturing Belt is, the growth of industry elsewhere has singular significance both for the regions concerned and for the nation as a whole. Table 21 (p. 286) shows that areas outside the Belt increased their proportion of the nation's manufacturing employment from 31 to 45 per cent from 1940 to 1969; an absolute increase of 5·5 million persons. Figure 40 (p. 288) shows the distribution of this increment over the country, and attention will be directed first to the South, which has attracted over half of these 5·5 million jobs.

The South

In 1940 the South (i.e. the South Atlantic, East South Central and West South Central divisions) possessed under one fifth of the US work force in manufacturing, but nearly one third of the nation's population. By 1969, while the population percentage remained roughly the same, that for manufacturing employment had risen to a quarter. It would be difficult to overstress the significance of this. A massive decline in farm employment accompanied the great, and often beneficial, changes in agriculture in this period, so that the regional problems of employment and income remained very serious. Military and other Federal government spending have certainly

314

helped to create new sources of income, but the basis for a lasting advance of the Southern economy lies fundamentally with efficient exploitation of the region's natural resources and the establishment of a large and competitive manufacturing sector. The current ratio of the region's share of US manufacturing employment to its share of US population (0·8) indicates a still serious deficiency in the main income-generating activity. Not every region, of course, should necessarily have the same share of manufacturing employment as of population. This would be almost a denial of the value of inter-regional trade. In general, however, the returns accruing to the primary economic activities (agriculture, forestry and mining) are small and declining relatively. Partially because of its greater than normal dependence on such activities the South is a poor region which cannot, from its own resources of income, sustain large tertiary employment. So, improved standards depend upon manufacturing (and associated primary production), in which the South is still relatively deficient. Figure 41 (p. 294) demonstrates its comparatively low intensity of manufacturing activity, in sharp contrast with conditions in the Manufacturing Belt. Moreover, not only in size, but also in character and distribution, the development of manufacturing in the South, while improving, so far leaves something to be desired.

In the first instance, the structure of manufacturing is poor, X-type industries (Figure 44, p. 303) and the slower-growing 'intermediate' industries, such as clothing and furniture manufacture, preponderating. In 1968, about 35 per cent of manufacturing employment in the South was in X-type industries, compared with the national average of 25 per cent. With clothing and furniture manufacture added, about half the South's industrial employment is in the nation's most slowly-growing industries, though in this region the laggards have in fact been 'growth' industries.* The economic environment in the South has attracted industries which, for various reasons, have lost favour in the more sophisticated industrial areas. For example, the textile industry since the war has lost employment in the USA as a whole. In 1947

* The sole exception is the lumber and wood-product group, where there has been a slow decline.

almost 1,300,000 were employed, in 1968 only 985,000. Against this, textile employment in the South actually rose, from 620,000 to 690,000 so that about 70 per cent of all employment in this nationally declining industry is now in the southern region, and there chiefly in the South Atlantic division. In a slow-growing 'intermediate' industry, apparel manufacture, developments have also been interesting. Outside the South, employment in the clothing trades has declined since the war, but the expansion in the South (from 142,000 to 496,000 between 1947 and 1968) has more than offset this, so that over all the industry, nationally, has grown modestly. There are other similar instances, and we may now examine possible explanations.

One fact immediately apparent is that southern manufacturing is heavily oriented towards low-wage industries. Average hourly earnings in 1968 in the textile, apparel, food, lumber and furniture groups in the USA were $2·21, $2·21, $2·80, $2·56, and $2·47 respectively. The average for 'all manufacturing' was $3·01, and the shortfall is thus sizeable in each case. Yet these five industries provide more than two fifths of manufacturing employment in the South. Moreover, southern earnings tend to fall below the national average in every industry. In North Carolina in 1968, for example, the average hourly earnings in the five industries named above were $2·13, $1·85, $2·00, $1·99, and $2·14 respectively, and North Carolina is not unusual. It is not simply that, within the range of operations of each industry group, the lower-paid are concentrated in the South but that, with a few exceptions, wages paid for the same class of work in the same industry are lower in the South than elsewhere. This attracts industries in which a high proportion of total costs are attributable to labour, in which labour-cost differences are the chief geographical variable in the cost structure, and in which a lack of advanced labour skills is not a major impediment. The industries named above are in this category, and thus the South has advanced absolutely and relatively in these nationally declining or slow-growing groups.

While such developments have brought jobs to areas where they were desperately needed, significant consequences follow from such a heavily weighted industrial structure. Figure 43 (p. 298), which shows the hourly earnings in all manufacturing by State, highlights the relative weakness of the South. From Virginia and Kentucky southwards and westwards to Texas and Oklahoma, inclusive, thirteen southern States have an average earning power in manufacturing below the national average and, in seven cases, far below. This geographical phenomenon, like the concentration of high earning power in the Manufacturing Belt, is unique, and has equally important, though uniformly less favourable, consequences. With Delaware, Maryland and the District of Columbia (belonging more to the north-east coastal megalopolis than to the South) excluded, the per capita personal income in even the wealthiest southern State in 1969 fell 10 per cent below the national average, while in nine States the per capita personal income fell 20 per cent or more below the national figure. The implications for market demand, and thus for certain classes of manufacturing, are direct and obvious.

The average hourly earnings differential between the South and other parts of the USA, however, has decreased in recent decades, for several reasons. Firstly, the growing industrial development and increasing sophistication of the work force makes it less possible to maintain rates of pay wildly out of line with those elsewhere, while some large national companies, building branches in the South, have paid the same rates there as elsewhere. Union activity and Federal Minimum Wages legislation in certain industries may also have played a part. Labour supply has continued to be abundant, however, especially for the lower-skilled and unskilled jobs, and this has a depressive effect on wages. The high rates of population growth, despite large migrations, and the continued flow of labour from agriculture are chiefly responsible. Thus, relative hourly earnings have advanced, but only slowly and uncertainly, and they remain well below the US norm.

Wage rates, however, are only part of the total labour-cost situation, which is also affected by labour skills, trainability, adaptability and attitudes, and by fringe-benefit practices. In labour skill, the South has offered little for manufacturing. The relative weakness of its educational system is reflected in the lower ability of its native labour force, which is in turn reflected in the historical

317

emphasis on industries requiring simple skills and low levels of labour training. The higher skills – of manager, supervisor, technician and so on – have generally had to be 'imported'. Such 'imported' labour, unlike native southern labour, often secured incomes in the South equal, or superior, to those elsewhere. Such problems become less acute as an industrial tradition is created, however, and, in favoured areas of the South, a growing proportion of the higher grades of labour is being met from 'local' resources. On labour efficiency, it has been argued that the low wage rates in the South have been offset by the lower productivity of an unsophisticated labour force. If this was ever generally true, it is less so now. Calculations of labour 'productivity' in major industries show the South to compare favourably with other regions in this respect. Labour attitudes are often better, more cooperative and accompanied by lower turnover and absentee rates than elsewhere, all factors which help productivity.

· A further element augmenting the labour-cost advantages of the South is the relatively low level of the fringe benefits, which add very considerably (perhaps a quarter or more) to the earnings of the average US manufacturing worker. These benefits include employer contributions to various welfare programmes, facilities at the factory and so on and, most important, the number and length of paid holidays and vacations. In general, they are less generous in southern industry, which adds further to the relative attractions of a southern location to industries of several kinds.

Several of these features of the southern labour market may owe their magnitude (or, indeed, their continued existence) to the lack of union influence in the region. It could be argued that southern labour is being 'exploited', to the detriment of its own standards and, by extension, of those elsewhere. No doubt the aims of the labour unions would be to raise both the direct wage payments and the indirect benefits to workers in the South. On the other hand, of course, these elements of the southern economic landscape have attracted the jobs the South so desperately needed. Successful union activity might thus only undermine one of the region's major attractions for industry and inhibit, not advance, industrial expansion. Attitudes to unionization are, therefore, somewhat ambivalent.

318

The difference in the relative intensity of labour-union activity between the southern States and industrialized States elsewhere, however, remains considerable (Figure 47). In every southern State except West Virginia and Kentucky (which have large numbers employed in the strongly unionized coalmining industry) labour-union membership, as a proportion of all non-agricultural employment, is below the national average, and often very far below. By contrast, in the Manufacturing Belt union activity is almost invariably more intense than it is nationally. It may fairly be assumed that this contrast has played a part in location decisions. Southern communities, advertising in the northern media for industry, often stress their low levels of unionization, assuming that this will be interpreted as meaning a tractable and relatively untroublesome labour force. They have certainly achieved some success. So far, however, the attractions of the South have proved most seductive to the low-wage, high labour-cost industries, which, while contributing significantly to the 'industrialization' of the South, will not achieve the increase in income required to lift living standards in the South to the national level.

So far we have concentrated on the labour-cost situation, which has undoubtedly been a leading element in the pace and the style of southern industrial development. Another feature, however, has been a heavy emphasis on industries connected with the early processing of materials from farm, forest, and mine, rather than with the later stages in the fabrication or assembly of intricate modern products. In part this was a consequence of the dominating position of the Manufacturing Belt and its command of capital and technical resources. The South, however, has possessed and does possess considerable attractions for processing industry in its endowment of raw materials. Thus, although cotton farming is much less important than it was, cotton production did play some part in the evolution of the southern textile industry, while the increasing range of produce from the new agriculture in the region has stimulated southern food product manufacture. One cannot accurately separate the 'materials-processing' from the 'product-fabricating' industries, especially within the limits imposed by the major industry groups, but we can list those industries in which the

319

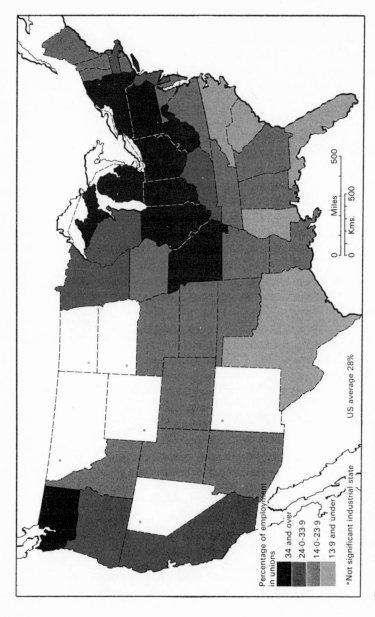

Percentage of employment
in unions

34 and over

24·0-33·9

14·0-23·9

13·9 and under

*Not significant industrial state

US average 28%

Figure 47. Labour Union Membership, 1968

Miles   500   500

0

Kms.   500   500

0

South accounts for more of national employment than it does of manufacturing employment generally (i.e. 25 per cent). These, in descending order, are: textiles, lumber and wood products; furniture and fixtures; chemicals and allied products; apparel and related products; food and kindred products; stone, clay and glass products; and (marginally) paper and allied products. The appellation 'materials processing' applies to several of these and makes our point. This characteristic of southern manufacturing is not confined (as was the low-wage character) to the nationally laggard or slow-growing industries. The presence of the chemicals industries is especially significant, and suggests an examination of the A-type industries in the region.

In general, the nation's 'growth' industries remain quite meagrely developed in the South (Figure 44, p. 303), providing only 29 per cent of manufacturing employment in 1968. To put it starkly, the South, with 31 per cent of the nation's population, has 25 per cent of the US labour force in manufacturing and under 18 per cent of its workers in 'growth' industries. The question is 'Why?' Several types of manufacture in this class have high or very high labour costs and are affected in location matters by possible geographical variations in these costs. The New England experience demonstrates this, for that region, as a 'low-wage' area in the high-wage industries, has attracted much new capacity in advanced industries such as electronics. Clearly, the southern environment must lack some other ingredients essential for the successful growth of many modern industries. The picture must not, however, be overpainted. All seven A-type industry groups have expanded their employment in the South. In some, although growth rates have been high, the actual employment gains remain quite small. The instruments, ordnance and rubber and plastic product groups are examples. In others, however, although the industries concerned remain fairly small in the South relative to their development elsewhere, sizeable absolute gains have been made. This is true of the machinery, electrical equipment and transport equipment groups. In addition there is chemicals manufacture, here in a class by itself for growth, so that the South has emerged as a major national centre for this industry.

Two principal reasons may be suggested for these advances, which are of great importance to the South, despite their limited impact so far on the total regional situation. Firstly, there is the attraction of southern resources, especially for chemicals manufacture, mentioned above. The abundant natural gas, oil, salt, sulphur and phosphate deposits, especially in the Gulf region, have attracted a huge capital investment to support a major southern interest in a fast-growing industry. The South currently possesses two fifths of the nation's employment in chemicals manufacture, and, despite its highly capital-intensive nature, the industry provides a quarter of all southern employment in A-type industry. Secondly, government programmes and requirements during and since the Second World War have been influential, attracted by southern resources of land space, climate (in the western South), remoteness from existing major military targets and labour surpluses. The wartime needs for military equipment and supplies, and the attractions offered by the South for their production, stimulated investment not only in plant and equipment, but also in community infrastructure and labour training which had permanent effects. The continuing demand for military aircraft since the war, and the great development of the space programme, especially in the 1960s, have caused billions of government dollars to be expended in the South, and the famous Space Triangle emerged, centring on Houston (Texas), Huntsville (Alabama) and Cape Kennedy (Florida), all of which have expanded dramatically in population and economic activity. The South has greatly benefited, both materially and psychologically, from these developments which not only brought in capital, but also promoted the expansion of the A-type industries mentioned above. These interests, however, remain heavily geared to Federal spending and in this matter the influence of senior southern congressmen, who chair important Government committees, has been considerable. In the last analysis, however, southern aerospace projects are supported more by contractors, subcontractors and services from *outside* the South than from within the region. Chemicals apart, there is little evidence of the A-type industries in general having found some *raison d'être* for a southern location outside the special stimulation of Federal programmes. Some possible reasons can readily be seen from the contrast with conditions in the Manufacturing Belt.

One major difference is in the quality of the labour force, and in the size of the pool of skilled labour. Despite the emerging industrial tradition and the influx of talented experts, the South remains deficient in these respects. A general improvement in labour-force characteristics is impeded by poor education over much of the region. Most southern children complete far less than the national average number of years in school, and the quality of that shorter period of education is often low. The relatively weak base of the educational pyramid is reflected at higher levels. Fewer Southerners find their way to institutes of higher education, and few of such institutes in the South have yet built reputations for science and technology which match those of, say, the north-eastern and Californian colleges. Such conditions must affect the types and structure of industrial employment in the South. In 1968 the region (excluding Maryland and Delaware) had under one fifth of all scientists then in employment in the USA, and, of these, over a quarter were concentrated in Texas, where chemistry, space and marine scientists are in strong demand. This situation reflects, and is reflected in, the size of expenditure on industrial research and development in the South. Figure 45 (p. 305) shows that such expenditure reached only 15 per cent of the US total in 1968 – far less than the region's shares of population and manufacturing employment, and significantly less, too, than its share of A-type industries. The region shows up better for Federal money for these purposes (18 per cent of the US total), but the attitude of private companies is shown in the mere 12 per cent of their national R & D expenditure applied in the South. Most of this, too, is concentrated in those megalopolitan extensions of Maryland and Delaware.

Another relative, and associated, deficiency in the South lies in markets. We have seen that per capita income here remains comparatively low. None the less, it has advanced slowly and, because of the very large population, the total purchasing power is sizeable – sufficient to attract activities strongly affected by final demand. The prime deficiency in this respect is thus in intermediate flows, i.e. the poor potential for inter-industry trading and servicing (or industrial linkages) of the kinds so highly significant in the northern States. This is not merely a matter of the smaller total capacity of manufacturing in the South, but also – and more significantly – its geographical distribution.

The South lacks the large industrial complexes in which modern industries thrive. The differences between the circumstances in the South and the Manufacturing Belt can be seen first in Figure 42 (p. 295), which shows not only that the South is short of major cities, but also that those which do exist are not essentially 'manufacturing cities' and are widely separated. Further, with Baltimore excluded, as part of Megalopolis, of fourteen US metropolitan areas having manufacturing employment of 200,000 or more in 1968, not one was in the South. Dallas, the largest southern manufacturing centre, employed 160,000, ranking only twentieth in size in the nation. The five major southern cities shown on the map have only one tenth of the region's manufacturing employment, and the rest is not notably concentrated even in manufacturing centres of moderate size. The fifteen metropolitan areas in the South (including the five major cities) which employed 50,000 or more in manufacturing in 1968 together accounted for only 25 per cent of the region's manufacturing employment. The contrast with the Manufacturing Belt is emphatic. In the Belt there were forty-one such metropolitan areas in 1968, and they accounted for 77 per cent of the region's employment. Moreover, each of these areas lies in close proximity to others. In the South many of these 'larger' manufacturing centres stand in virtual isolation (e.g. the expanding Dallas–Fort Worth area is over 200 miles from Houston, its nearest large neighbour), while most manufacturing employment is scattered through scores of smaller cities and rural townships. Such industries as lumber and wood products, food products, textile mills, clothing and furniture manufacture may lend themselves to such a geographical pattern, but this is manifestly not the case for most 'growth' industry. The South still lacks those complex concentrations of large 'parent' industries with auxiliary industries and services which a modern industrial economy requires, and, until the appropriate kind of environment becomes more general in the South, the expansion of the newer, technically advanced and high-paying industries will remain rather sporadic and uncertainly based.

One notable exception to these conditions appears along the Gulf Coast, centring on Houston, Texas, and spilling into Louisiana. Here a very large complex of petroleum refining and organic and inorganic chemicals manufacture has emerged, promoting the intricate web of inter-industry trade and servicing which marks the truly modern industrial area. The rewards are commensurate. In Texas, for example, chemical industry employment rose from 21,000 to 62,000 between 1947 and 1968, and earnings are very high. The average hourly earnings of production workers in the Texas chemicals industry in 1968 were $3·68, 28 per cent above the State average for all manufacturing, and considerably higher, too, than the national average for chemicals workers. The benefits to this part of the South need no emphasis and in detailed maps of income by county, based on 1960 Population Census data, the area Freeport–Houston–Lake Charles stands as an island of high income and relative lack of poverty. Another noticeable concentration of industrial activity in the South is on the Appalachian Piedmont, chiefly in the Carolinas. This embraces numerous small industrial centres, beginning with Danville in southern Virginia and running through Burlington, Concord and Spartanburg to Anderson and Augusta on the south-western border of South Carolina. This comprises a highly intensive development of textile manufacture, with a considerable inter-trading of filaments, yarns, cloths and so on, and connections with machinery and clothing manufacture and other activities in the area, which gives it something of the character of the modern industrial complex. It lacks, however, the scientific base, the buoyant market conditions and the high incomes of the Houston-centred complex. Nevertheless the area stands out on an income map from the veritable sea of poor counties surrounding it.

In preceding paragraphs we have considered why the nation's major 'growth' industries have not achieved considerably greater status in the South. We have not diagnosed a fatal illness but a relative weakness. Poor industrial structure brings problems that are not necessarily insurmountable. Manufacturing has in fact expanded strongly in the South since 1940, and the region has many advantages to offer certain types of activity. Especially in the South Atlantic division (where significant industrial development began in the late nineteenth century), but now in other southern areas also, there is an established industrial tradition and numerous towns and cities anxious to welcome new industry and able to support it. This anxiety often finds expression in inducements of various kinds (grants, tax concessions, advance factory building and so on) by local authorities. The long-term effects of such promotional efforts are not certain, and many communities outside the South have followed suit – either out of their own needs for new employment or as a defensive measure against inducements offered elsewhere. What is certain, however, is that this widespread practice illustrates the general appreciation in the South of the need for industrial development, and leads to the provision of industrial services and facilities of kinds not generally available a decade or two ago. Moreover, material and power supplies are good, water problems often less serious than elsewhere and transport connections throughout the South (and between the South and other regions) have been greatly improved.

Such attractions, augmented by the labour-cost advantages discussed above, have led to relatively heavy industrial investment in the region. Figure 46 (p. 310) shows that, in 1967, 31 per cent of all new expenditure for new plant and equipment in the USA went into the South. Much has been for small-scale industry in dispersed locations, and the efficiency of such capital investment is often lower than that of a similar size of investment in larger-scale projects in big industrial centres elsewhere. The overall quantity, however, clearly reflects the attractions of southern locations to numerous entrepreneurs and to branch establishments of large national companies. The relative weakness in the A-type industries, therefore, means that the South has a poor industrial structure, oriented to industries unlikely to expand rapidly in the future, which generally pay low wages, with all that that implies for regional prosperity. But the expansion of the X-type industries and certain other of the national slower-growth activities has brought its own kinds of benefit to the region, not least in taking jobs to numerous small towns and rural centres where there was grievous need.

The Geography of Manufacturing: Other Regional Developments

The Pacific Coast

To epitomize the character of recent developments in the Far West, most people would select the term 'growth' and, in most contexts, it would be very appropriate. The recent history of population expansion and economic development in the Pacific division undoubtedly presents a remarkable record. It reflects chiefly the astonishingly rapid advance of California to primacy among States in population and to second place, following New York, in its total labour force and numbers employed in manufacturing. In Washington and Oregon growth has been far less notable, so that California *is*, to many people, the Far West and has, understandably, come to dominate the post-war literature dealing with this part of the nation. In this treatment, however, the division will normally be regarded as a unit.

The growth of manufacturing here has certainly been extremely rapid, but economic development has embraced a diversity of activities so that manufacturing is less significant in the employment structure than it is in the nation as a whole (24 per cent of non-agricultural employment here, 29 per cent nationally). Moreover, while manufacturing has attained large dimensions, the divisional share of US manufacturing employment (10·6 per cent in 1968) remains below its share of population (12·3 per cent). None the less, the division has lately advanced rapidly in national significance (Table 21, p. 286). As recently as 1940 the area was relatively unexceptional in its manufacturing sector, and had advanced little since 1910. Since 1940, however, expansion has been continuous (Figure 40, p. 288) so that by 1969 the division had raised its manufacturing employment by 220 per cent (US average +83 per cent) and achieved notable status in manufacturing activity.

In structure and character this development shows sharp contrasts with the southern region. Being remote, the Far West was less affected in its formative years by the 'backwash' of the cumulative advance of the Manufacturing Belt, and its relative isolation proved an eventual source of strength. While Far Western lumber and mineral resources, agricultural produce and fisheries were, to the

327

region's benefit, increasingly drawn upon by the Belt, its development of manufacturing was not so greatly inhibited. The considerable protection afforded by distance from north-eastern manufacturers stimulated both the processing of local products for export and the manufacture of various consumer goods for which, as population grew, the regional market offered profitable opportunities. Again, more recently, the great expansion of manufacturing in the West, especially in California, has owed much to the large immigration of educated adults, normally skilled in various ways, so that expanding labour force, incomes and market potential have interplayed as cause and effect of industrial growth. Manufacturing has grown with the economy, with no impediments from existing interests or established patterns. In the South, by contrast, development of manufacturing necessitated alteration or adaptation of existing economic, social and geographical structures and patterns. Moreover, far from being aided by a massive inflow of skills and trained labour, the southern region has faced problems associated with a large natural increase of a poor and relatively unskilled population and the absorption of huge numbers released from other sectors of economic activity, problems sharply emphasized by racial issues. Such contrasts are reflected in other ways, as will be shown.

The excellent growth record in the Pacific division rests on a favourable industrial structure. In 1968, A-type industries comprised over half of all manufacturing employment, and X-type only 22 per cent (Figure 44, p. 303). Only the great East North Central division has as satisfactory a position. The A-type expansion in the Far West, however, is rather abnormal. More than anywhere else, its growth has depended upon Federal expenditure, especially on government programmes for military development and space exploration. The fact that Californians are vocal exponents of the virtues of free enterprise and self-reliance is thus not without irony. Aircraft production in the region was given a tremendous boost during the Second World War and, although employment has since fluctuated in accord with government purchases, it has regularly supplied one eighth or more of the divisional totals in manufacturing, and one third or more of national employment in the aircraft industry. Moreover, with the development of military missiles and space exploration, the industry has entered an 'aero-space' rather than simply a conventional aircraft phase and now embraces the missile-production sections of other industries. An official publication in 1970 estimated that 42 per cent of national employment in aerospace activity is currently in the Pacific division; by any standards a notable concentration. Moreover, the demand of the major aerospace companies for parts and components, accessories and sub-assemblies, and for numerous industrial services, including research and development, has strongly affected other sectors of manufacturing industry.

A remarkably strong and consistent expansion among the A-type industries has thus occurred in the electrical equipment group. Employment multiplied tenfold between 1947 and 1968, and the industry now ranks second in size to aircraft manufacture. Within this group, however, it is communications equipment and electronic components that have gained most, and the connections with aerospace activity, though not exclusive, are direct and obvious. Similarly, instruments manufacture is not a major industry, but it has grown rapidly since the war, and again has strong connections with aerospace. Thus the small, highly specialized, manufacture of optical instruments and lenses has expanded so that the Pacific division now provides over one third of national employment. Much larger absolutely, and growing even faster, however, is the ordnance and accessories division, which, according to County Business Patterns data, became the third-ranking industry in California in 1968, following transport equipment and electrical equipment manufacture. This is another extraordinary concentration: 40 per cent of the national work force in this industry in a single State. The connection, again, both with Federal contracts and with the aerospace industry is manifest, for this industry group now includes the manufacture of guided missiles.

Thus manufacturing in the Far West is strongly oriented to products for which Federal expenditure is critical. These products indeed fall into the A-type category and have notable records of expansion in this division, but nowhere else is there as much dependence upon such types of manufacture and a single major purchaser. Figure 48 compares the pattern of A-type industry

329

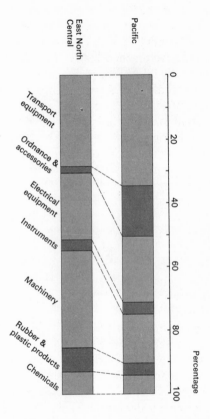

Figure 48. Employment in A-type Manufacturing, Pacific and East North Central Divisions, 1968

employment in the Pacific and East North Central divisions. (Total A-type employment in the latter is two and a half times that in the Pacific division.) The differences, obvious even at the industry-group level shown on the Figure, become yet more profound within the groups. Thus, transport equipment manufacture in the Pacific division is overwhelmingly for aircraft production, which is in turn oriented chiefly to government demands. In the E N C division, motor vehicle manufacture takes first place, and is oriented chiefly to private final demand. The comparative status of ordnance and accessories manufacture requires little comment. The E N C division has small strength in types of equipment important in current military buying, while in the Far West the size and importance of this activity has already been stressed. The transport equipment and ordnance groups together provide half the A-type employment in the Pacific region, but vastly less in the E N C area. Electrical equipment manufacture achieves identical stature in both divisions, but in the Pacific area is heavily geared to aerospace requirements, while in the E N C division interest is widely spread in numerous branches, serving all classes of intermediate and final demand. Outside these industry groups, the East North Central division is also considerably more diversified in its 'growth' activities. Machinery ranks very high, embracing an enormously varied output, while the chemical and rubber and plastic product groups are also much more significant than in the Pacific division.

This special character of 'growth-industry' development in the Far West supports (and is supported by) an unusually large research and development commitment. A process of circular and cumulative causation has again been operating. Chiefly for climatic reasons (although strategic considerations, the need for open space as well as favourable climate, and the prior interest in aircraft manufacture were also considerations) the Federal government supported massive development of aircraft manufacture in the Pacific division, especially in southern California, during the Second World War. The associated research and development needs attracted scientists and other R & D workers – all the more readily because of the much-publicized physical attractions of the area as a place to live. The growing research, development and production potential naturally attracted more R&D contracts and the process has continued. Today, California employs more qualified scientists than any other State: 13·7 per cent of the US total in 1968, compared with 10·5 per cent and 5·5 per cent in New York and Pennsylvania, respectively the second- and third-ranking States. For physicists and mathematicians California leads even more markedly, with above 15 per cent of the national total.

The Pacific division has obviously commanded a very large share of national R & D expenditure since the war. In 1968, 26 per cent of this expenditure went into this division (Figure 45, p. 305), a proportion similar to that for earlier years and far beyond the region's share of either population or manufacturing activity. The dependence on Federal funds, however, is heavy. Three quarters of the total expenditure normally comes from Federal sources, and no other division approaches the Pacific in the size of the Federal commitment. The application of private-company R & D funds here is relatively small, falling far behind the totals in both the East North Central and Middle Atlantic divisions. But research and development work for the Federal government is often followed by the allocation of defence contracts. Thus the Pacific division was awarded contracts worth over $7 billion in 1968, 17 per cent of the national total. The 'prime contractors' involved directly in these awards may subcontract work outside their own geographical area, of course, and the final destination of the large sums involved is not accurately computable. Probably, however, the Pacific division gets more than its 'share' of subcontracts and, on balance, must do unusually well out of these defence awards. In 1968 over half a million workers in the Pacific division were employed directly in defence-generated jobs.

The unusually heavy dependence on government decisions and budgets inevitably introduces an element of uncertainty into the future of industrial development in the Far West. So far, the close involvement with Federal programmes has, on the whole, been beneficial, but there is no guarantee that these programmes will continue at present levels or in the same direction. The possible effects of changed Federal needs or policies, the likely speed of a run-down of existing programmes if this were decided upon, the possibilities of redirecting Federal funds into other activities which could use the existing research, development and production potential of the division, are all matters of conjecture. In the future the division may have to face the severe frictional problems of a major industrial adjustment and already by early 1970 the reduction of space expenditure was having serious effects in places.

The X-type industries in this division, although comparatively small in total (Figure 44, p. 303), contain three notable sectors, in two of which local resources have been of great importance. The lumber and wood product group has about 28 per cent of national employment, and jobs have declined only slightly since the war. Virgin timber stands in Washington, Oregon and northern California are greater than elsewhere and nearly four in ten of US lumber camp workers are found here. Not only does this activity serve the growing divisional market (for example, furniture production has increased sharply since the war), but it retains the national significance it achieved earlier in the century.

The food-product industry is somewhat similar, and remains a very large employer. Many branches of this industry are market-oriented, and the division has its proper share of dairy and bakery products and beverage manufacture, for example. In canned and frozen foods, however, it serves a national market and in this branch of food production the Far West employs about a third of the national labour force. While in this activity, as in lumber and wood products, raw material attractions are strong, the third notable X-type industry in the Pacific division, primary metal manufacture, is relatively poorly served for raw materials. Wartime needs, however, proved sufficient to overcome cost difficulties, and the group has since been sustained by the rapid local advance of the various metal-using industries. The region's first, and only, integrated iron and steel plant was constructed at Fontana, California, with Federal aid, during the war, its ore coming from Eagle Mountain in the south of the State and its coal from 250 miles away in Utah. This far from ideal situation was supported by strategic necessity during the war, but has subsequently benefited from the region's growing demands for steel. Market demand has also stimulated expansion of steel-rolling, and the production and rolling of non-ferrous metals, especially aluminium. Thus, while the region still draws various types of steel from large East-Coast plants, employment in the primary metal industries has, contrary to national experience, expanded fairly strongly. Nationally, however, the region remains a minor centre of primary metal activity.

Expansion of regional demand is also chiefly responsible for growth in other sectors of manufacturing. Not only has there been the rapid increase of the total population, but also the impressive, and rising, affluence of the division as a whole. The dominant A-type industries give high average hourly earnings in manufacturing (Figure 43, p. 298) and very large total earnings in manufacturing, contributing strongly to very high per capita income. Indeed, for the division as a whole, the per capita income ranks with the Middle Atlantic division as the highest among the nine geographical divisions. Among the States, California follows closely behind Connecticut, New York, Illinois and New Jersey. This affects the magnitude and style of regional demand, and the location of many industrial enterprises. Thus in California employment in printing and publishing has doubled since 1947 and in paper and paper products more than trebled. The manufacture of clothing, especially women's clothing and sportswear, has also sharply expanded. Such experiences are primarily responses to regional demand but themselves affect numerous other activities serving final, or intermediate, demand both within and beyond the region.

The growth and structure of manufacturing in the Pacific division have been sketched, and we may now consider its geographical pattern. This is again unusual, providing another impressive contrast with the southern region. Figure 42 (p. 295) shows that the Pacific division has six metropolitan areas with a population above 1 million. These six account for 71 per cent of manufacturing employment, and industrial areas of small, or even moderate, size are scarce. Further, the map distinguishes three Pacific metropolises as 'industrial cities' (here we include Seattle, which had the national average proportion of manufacturing employment in 1969), and these three alone have 56 per cent of the region's manufacturing jobs. This is the reverse of the situation in the South. There, the five great metropolises, none of them a 'manufacturing city' in the sense used here, together provided less than one in ten of southern jobs in manufacturing. The contrast epitomizes the differing conditions for, and differing structures of, industrial activity in the two regions. The Pacific concentration is, indeed, even more emphatic than the figures quoted suggest. Three of the million-plus metropolitan areas (Los Angeles–Long Beach, San Bernardino–Riverside–Ontario, and Anaheim Santa Ana–Garden Grove, to give them their full titles) are contiguous and form, in effect, a single manufacturing area. Industrial employment here has grown even more rapidly than in the division as a whole. With just over a million employed in 1968, this small area contains half the region's total manufacturing labour force. Within the United States it is outranked only by the New York–north-eastern New Jersey complex, which embraces $1\frac{3}{4}$ million manufacturing workers. Even the consolidated Chicago–north-western Indiana area, with just under a million in manufacturing, falls behind this southern Californian concentration, which is thus one of the greatest industrial complexes in the world.

The pace of advance of the Pacific division in the post-war decades could not continue indefinitely and in fact the *rate* of growth has fallen steadily over each period shown in Figure 40 (p. 288). In part, the outstanding growth rates of the 1940s and early 1950s reflected low industrial employment in the base years. Equivalent absolute gains made now give lower proportional results. But the Pacific division is also nowadays taking a smaller share of the national increment to manufacturing employment. To take the record for post-war Census of Manufactures years, in 1947 the division had only 6·3 per cent of total US employment in manufacturing, but accounted for 26 per cent of the national expansion between 1947 and 1954. This good performance continued through the difficult economic period to 1958 with manufacturing employment still growing quite strongly at a time of national decline. Between 1958 and 1963, the Pacific division commanded 22 per cent of the national rise in manufacturing employment and by 1963 had 10·3 per cent of the US total. From 1963 to 1967 (the most recent inter-censal period), however, the region attracted only 9 per cent of the nation's new manufacturing jobs. These figures.

335

should not be overemphasized, for the hectic advance of the earlier years simply could not be maintained. But the size, kinds and location of existing industrial development has brought problems to which national attention is increasingly being directed, and which may be reflected in future growth.

The issue of Federal dependency has already been stressed, and became serious in 1970 with the sharp cut-back in aerospace spending. The leading industrial corporations are striving to diversify their activities, with some success, but too many eggs remain in this one basket and the transition to a more balanced structure must be long and painful. This situation will discourage further large inflows of scientists, technologists and engineers, on whose skills the region's upward economic spiral has rested. In other ways, too, development bids fair to destroy some of the delights of living in this area which have proved so attractive to millions of migrants. These are well-rehearsed matters. The characteristic low density urban-industrial sprawl has devoured huge areas of land, and introduced complex difficulties of adequate servicing and efficient movement. The growth of great centres of population and industry, and the unique position of the motor vehicle in patterns of life and economic activity, have produced very serious air pollution. The recreational and scenic delights are overcrowded with cars and people. These are not new problems in modern industrial society; but they are not what many migrants come to this region to find.

Most of the foregoing is concerned with California, where 78 per cent of the division's population and employment in manufacturing are found. The divisional basis of treatment proves much less satisfactory here than in the Manufacturing Belt or, despite its internal diversity, the South. There are few affinities between the northern and southern parts of this Pacific division and few generalizations of wide validity. Manufacturing in the Pacific North-West does indeed show something of the divisional emphasis on aerospace. In the Seattle–Everett metropolitan area, 60 per cent of all manufacturing jobs are in aircraft and parts production. This large concentration naturally colours the picture for the North-West as a whole, but the major manufacturing interest is in fact in lumber and wood products. In geographical patterns, too, the North-West, like California, shows heavy concentration. Four fifths of Washington manufacturing employment is in Seattle–Everett, and half the Oregon total in Portland. These considerations apart, however, the northern and southern parts of this division share little except a common position, fronting the Pacific Ocean.

Moreover, even California shows sharp distinctions between north and south, and not a few clashes of interest. In northern counties, such manufacturing as there is resembles that in Oregon – lumber and wood and food product manufacture. Southward, San Francisco–Oakland provides a kind of overture to the great industrial complex 350 miles away, beyond the San Rafael mountains. Industry around the Golden Gate, however, remains smaller in scale and much more diversified. Food-product manufacture provides the biggest single activity, reflecting the intensive agriculture of the Great Valley. Apart from this there are numerous industries of metal-using and other types, while aerospace and associated R & D activities have become important. But it is to coastal southern California that this discussion has mainly referred. Here is the major centre of industrial activity and here are all the problems outlined above, but emphasized by serious water-supply difficulties. On water supply, the conflict between the conservationists of the north (increasingly concerned with potential repercussions in central California of supplying yet more water to the desert areas) and the developers of the south (whose livelihood is geared to the continuation of urban-industrial growth) are most acute.

This division, therefore, stands on an intriguing watershed. Not all the fruits of the great industrial growth in southern California are attractive, and serious problems remain to be resolved. As the image changes, what will happen to the traditional population movement west? The northern parts of this division lack many difficulties currently faced in the south. They also lack the climate and, with that handicap, seem unlikely to provide a major new focus for the 'go-west' urge as the lustre of California diminishes.

Other Locational Developments

The geographical areas already covered embrace 92 per cent of the nation's manufacturing potential. The two remaining divisions have vast geographical territory, but significant manufacturing occurs only in limited areas, mostly in the West North Central division. In this latter division manufacturing activity experienced a sharp decline, partly at least due to changes in industrial classification, between 1910 and 1940 (Table 21, p. 286), but has advanced steadily since then (Figure 40, p. 288). Most of the growth is really, however, an 'overflow' from the Manufacturing Belt. Four fifths of manufacturing employment in the division lies in the eastern tier of States (Minnesota, Iowa, Missouri), and half of that in the St Louis and Minneapolis–St Paul metropolitan areas. In character, too, there are close links with the East North Central division. The major metal-using industries figure very strongly and, although food product manufacture retains a large interest, the overall structure of industry is favourable (Figure 44, p. 303). The affinities of the eastern States of this division with the Manufacturing Belt show clearly in the maps of average hourly earnings in manufacturing (Figure 43, p. 298) and labour-union membership (Figure 47, p. 320). The transitional character of these same States, however, appears equally emphatically in the map of value added per head (Figure 41, p. 294).

This last map helps also to put industrial development in the Mountain division into focus. From 1940 to 1969, manufacturing employment grew faster here than in any other division, but total employment and value added remain insignificant (see also Figure 40, p. 288). In employment structure, A- and X-types approximately balance. Of the latter, food products lead, and lumber and wood products follow at some distance. Neither is surprising. Less expected, perhaps, would be the 10 per cent of manufacturing employment in the primary metals group, but the division's large metal-mining interests are often associated with preliminary processing. Integrated iron and steel works are also found, at Pueblo, Colorado, and Geneva, Utah. The latter, a wartime Federal government establishment, was sold to private enterprise after the war. Its location relative to demand is probably better than that of Pueblo, which has not done well in recent years. Among the A-types, the electrical equipment and machinery groups are most prominent and there is some aircraft and parts manufacture. So far, however, only Colorado has manufacturing employment exceeding 100,000, with a concentration in Denver. In Arizona, Phoenix has registered a rapid increase in manufacturing (8,000 in 1949, 67,000 in 1968, chiefly in electrical equipment and machinery), but this is prominent only because of its isolation. Like the rest of Mountain division manufacturing, it is tiny in the national context. The Mountain division possesses no industrial complex of significant size and commands only a tiny fraction of national research and development expenditure (Figure 45, p. 305). New industrial investment is also small (Figure 46, p. 310), but while population grows, so will manufacturing industry, as cause or effect. Arizona, particularly, promises to continue increasing its industrial capacity impressively. In general, however, the manufacturing potential of the Mountain division will remain small, reflecting the absence of large population concentrations and associated economies of scale and agglomeration so well provided elsewhere. The entrepreneur guided solely by profits could nearly always find better prospects elsewhere.

The regional changes in the distribution of manufacturing reviewed here have been chiefly brought about by differential regional growth. Regions previously deficient in industrial potential have moved some way, at least, towards closing the gap. The types of manufacturing involved, and the geographical patterns, vary with regional or local influences, but always government activity in some form has played a part. The results so far are a rather more even distribution of the nation's manufacturing potential over its various populated parts, and an improving balance among regions in per capita income. None the less, considerable disparities persist in both manufacturing capacity and income, and these will not quickly be removed. The evidence for recent years suggests that the speed of this geographical adjustment is diminishing, but also that most industrializing regions are slowly broadening their range of manufacturing interests. Thus, while regional industrial structures will

339

never become identical, the grosser variations that have long persisted will be to some extent diminished, normally to the benefit of the regions concerned.

One final, and very important, element in the changing geography of American manufacturing concerns a more local level of redistribution. Manufacturing activities have always been attracted to cities, and especially to the larger cities. Through most of the nineteenth century the central areas of the emerging metropolises were magnets for industrial entrepreneurs large and small. The orientation of transport facilities, chiefly rail, and the large and growing working populations of these centres afforded great advantages. In the later nineteenth and the early twentieth century suburban population growth and technical advances in industry and transport encouraged a spread of manufacturing into the suburbs, but manufacturing employment continued to expand in both types of location. This process continued until shortly after the Second World War. Cyclical fluctuations apart, manufacturing jobs grew in number both in the major cities and in their surrounding areas, although faster in the latter, so that the central city share of the total declined. More recently, however, the number of manufacturing jobs in central cities has declined absolutely as well as relatively, introducing a new, and highly unwelcome, fact into the general pattern.

These themes have provided the basis of studies by Creamer, from which illustrative data can be drawn.* In 1929 about 59 per cent of manufacturing employment in the USA was located in thirty-five 'principal industrial areas' (i.e. broadly what are now Standard Metropolitan Statistical Areas), illustrating the great attractions of the larger centres. In 1954 the proportion in these areas was about 61 per cent, since when, although actual numbers have risen, their relative attractions have lessened. By 1966 forty-one such 'principal industrial areas' accounted for 57 per cent of all manufacturing employment, still a very large, but diminished, share. For some types of production a location in a smaller city or

* D. Creamer, *Changing Location of Manufacturing Employment (1963)*, and *Manufacturing Employment by Type of Location: An Examination of Recent Trends (1969)*, The Conference Board, Studies in Business Economics, Numbers 83 and 106.

town was evidently thought to offer advantage. (Often, of course, such smaller centres would still be within easy contact range of a major city.) More significant, however, have been the changes within the principal industrial areas themselves. Of the total manufacturing employment in these areas in 1929, 63 per cent was in the principal (or 'central') cities and 37 per cent in the peripheral areas and satellite cities. Employment expansion to about 1954 was in all parts of these industrial areas, but more rapidly in the peripheries and satellites. Thus, in 1954 the central cities contained 55 per cent of the total manufacturing jobs in the industrial areas of which they were the 'capital'. Since then, however, they have lost ground absolutely, shedding almost three quarters of a million manufacturing jobs between 1954 and 1963. By 1963 they provided only 49 per cent of the total industrial employment in their areas.

These are national average figures and the situation varies in intensity from one region to another. The process is understandably most advanced in the old industrial areas of the Manufacturing Belt, New York, Boston and Pittsburgh, for example. Even in the more recently industrializing regions, however, the trend is firmly established, and, while the central cities may still be expanding in absolute terms, their share of all manufacturing employment in their industrial areas is normally declining. There are straightforward reasons. The conditions of transport created by the motor vehicle and modern road networks, and the changed preferences in styles of living, have favoured low-density suburban housing developments. Many modern industries, released from ties to railways, have sought benefit, in suburban locations, from modern layout of plant and site (requiring large areas for plant and parking space) and from the mobile and expanding suburban labour force. The consequences for the central city are grave. One illustration will suffice. In 1947, New York City employed 1,073,000 in manufacturing, 54 per cent of all such employment in New York State. In 1968 the number employed in the city was only 845,000, 45 per cent of total State manufacturing employment. The loss of a quarter of a million jobs has been disastrous for the central areas. Not only have the earnings of city dwellers fallen, and their employment opportunities diminished, but the removal of manufacturing establishments has sharply eroded the city's tax base, and made it less able to remedy the deficiencies that may have influenced the decision to relocate in the first place. New York is not exceptional, and this is but one type of problem which central cities in the United States, by and large, currently face. The situation is in some respects explosive, and the chief elements are examined in greater detail in the following chapter.

13: Urban Growth and Change

An important consequence of the productivity revolution in agriculture, changing conditions in the minerals industry, growth and change in manufacturing and expansion of tertiary activities, is the increasing urbanization of the American people. Either as cause or as effect of the interplay of such adjustments, American society has become one of the most urbanized in the world. To some, this remains undesirable. To an extraordinary degree the Jeffersonian myth, the 'agrarian ideal' with virtue safeguarded only in 'those who labour in the earth', has persisted. To Jefferson, writing in the very early days of the Republic, 'the mobs of great cities add just so much to the support of pure government as sores do to the strength of the human body'. 'Generally speaking', he wrote, 'the proportion which the aggregate of the other classes of citizens bears in any State to that of its husbandmen, is the proportion of its unsound to its healthy parts.' This attitude, rather unhelpful even when he wrote, has coloured the approach of many Americans to this day. It is sometimes suggested that the suburban sprawl that now characterizes the American scene is itself a product of this attitude of mind. Thus, while seeking the advantages of city life, Americans have tried to introduce a 'rural style' of living (i.e. an essentially low-density style) into the urban context. The big cities continued to grow, it is suggested, while they still catered for this need; i.e., until the inter-war period. 'The decline of the big cities began when the problems of population density and congestion seriously cut into the possibilities for maintaining an agrarian-influenced life style within them. So long as city life was able to offer most of the amenities of rural-style living as well as the economic, social and cultural advantages of the city . . . the expansion of cities as cities

343

continued.'* Once this was no longer so, smaller settlements and suburban areas in separate political jurisdictions became paramount in urban growth.

There is undoubtedly much truth in this assessment, and the agrarian myth remains one to be reckoned with. However, the expansion of suburbia, the nature of that expansion, and the consequent problems of the central city are not simply to be explained in these terms, and other motives can be adduced. In the first instance the post-war Federal housing programme offered the advantages of easy home purchase to many millions who had previously rented accommodation in the city. This greatly stimulated the building of homes for sale in the suburbs. Again, a Federal court decision in 1954 ordered the desegregation of schools and, rather than send their children to racially mixed schools in central areas, very many whites moved out to the unmixed suburbs. This largely explains the expansion by above 80 per cent of the white population of the 'urban fringes' of urbanized areas between 1950 and 1960 (US population + 18·5 per cent). For many, too, this rapid growth of suburbia itself provided the motive for moving, in the economic opportunities it offered. In such cases the 'rural life style' has not been a prime consideration but an additional bonus. Moreover, however strong this rural life appetite may be, it is normally less powerful than the desire to achieve high material standards. The true test of the current power of the yeoman tradition would be the magnitude of the sacrifices Americans were prepared to make to achieve it. In essence they would make very little. Most move to suburbia because they feel that life there offers them more in numerous ways – better schools, lower taxes, nicer neighbours, less traffic, less noise, less crime, fresher air, more space. Only some of these have rural connections. The average American suburbanite seeks comfort in an environment as far removed from the harsh realities of nature as can be afforded. In other words, it is the *urban* life that is essential rather than the rural.

In fact, Americans, being human, would like the best of all worlds. Grass and trees, space and fresh air are good, and if they can be

* D. J. Elazar in R. A. Goldwin (ed.), *A Nation of Cities*, 1967, pp. 104–5.

dovetailed into the economic, social and cultural opportunities that only urban living can offer to most people, so much the better. But the suburban vista in the USA seldom captures much of what is precious in a rural environment. Most rural qualities simply cannot be captured in towns of any great size, and the danger of the agrarian myth lies in belief in the fallacy that rural life is rural because densities are low. As millions of Americans, then, seek rurality in low-density suburbia (if they do so consciously) they inevitably destroy what they are seeking. More of this will emerge in the following discussion. A cautionary note may appropriately be made here. In attempting a brief over-view of the urban situation, numerous generalizations have to be made about the character and problems of American cities. However valid they may be, they remain only generalizations, concealing in fact much of the great variety in patterns and experience to which no short essay can do justice.

The Pace of Urban Growth

In Chapter 2 the changing rural-urban balance of the population was outlined. The problem of definition, then mentioned, may now be briefly discussed. Before 1950, the official US definition of 'urban' applied only to incorporated (i.e. self-governing) settlements with a population of 2,500 or more. Large numbers of truly 'urban' folk were omitted (and consequently counted as 'rural') because they lived in unincorporated settlements or in places with population of less than 2,500, even though such places were, perhaps, on the very fringe of a large city and therefore truly urban. For the 1950 Population Census, however, all places (incorporated or not) with a population of 2,500 or more were recognized as 'urban' and the concept of the 'urbanized area' was introduced. Under this, the urban fringe areas of cities with 50,000 population or more were mapped according to a formula taking account of contiguity, density and function, and their populations included in the urban category. Such adjustments to the definition altered the figures considerably. In 1950, under the previous definition, the

345

urban population was around 90 million, under the new definition, 97 million. The new procedure is still not ideal, for all definitions involve value judgements and arbitrary dividing-lines and, while the statistics based on them may look impressively accurate, they must be treated with normal suspicion.

The pattern of urban and rural population growth (Figure 8, p. 32) suggests that urbanization has proceeded rapidly throughout this century. In 1900 about 40 per cent of the total population could be classified as urban, by 1960, 70 per cent. Because of the special difficulties involved in inter-censal estimates of the urban–rural breakdown, no further official data will be available until the 1970 Census results are published, but the trend has certainly continued. It is estimated that between 1960 and 1969 the US population increased by 21·8 millions, of which 16·3 millions were in the official metropolitan areas and only 5·5 millions outside them. A reasonable assumption is that most, or even all, of this non-metropolitan growth has been urban in character, the farm population having continued its decline. Thus the entire increment in population can be added to the urban total for 1960, to give a current urban proportion of nearly 75 per cent of the population.

Growth by Size of Urban Places

This continued expansion of the urban population introduces important questions. One is on the size of the urban areas which are growing most, on which different kinds of data provide somewhat conflicting evidence. According to data for the officially designated 'urban places' (here the evidence available terminates with the 1960 Census) the most 'popular' cities are those of small to moderate size. The proportion of urban population living in urban places of over one million on the one hand and below 10,000 on the other has decreased this century, but in places of between 10,000 and 50,000 has increased sharply (places of 25,000 to 50,000 most sharply of all). This is sometimes quoted to support the contention that Americans remain strongly attached to the rural way of life and often, though forced by economic developments to

346

live in urban places, compromise by settling in areas of only moderate size. Undoubtedly growth has been impressive in communities in this size range, especially from 1950 to 1960 when they raised their proportion of total urban population from 21 per cent to 26 per cent, and their numbers by 12 million. In the same period, however, the population of urban places above 50,000 also increased by 12 million, though the size of the increment decreases as the urban places become larger so that there was no significant change in the numbers living in urban places of one million population or more.

The Standard Metropolitan Statistical Area

These data are somewhat misleading, however. Many rapidly growing urban places of up to 50,000 population are in fact located close to other centres of equal or greater size. Functionally, several such places may together form a single urban entity. This is the reasoning behind the identification of the Standard Metropolitan Statistical Area. This is defined as: 'A county or contiguous group of counties which contain at least one central city of 50,000 population or more; or "twin cities" with a combined population of 50,000 or more; plus other contiguous counties which are essentially metropolitan in character and are socially and economically integrated with the central city.' In essence, therefore, but using whole county areas as the 'building blocks',* the SMSA formula embraces size, contiguity and integration of functions which make it an acceptable, or even essential, unit of analysis in urban affairs. On recent evidence, most population growth is taking place in the SMSAs rather than in the 'free-standing' urban places of small or intermediate size. Thus, in 1950 some 59 per cent of US population lived in metropolitan areas, in 1960 63 per cent, and by 1969, 65 per cent. Moreover, within the SMSAs the largest gains in population are in areas with populations of over a quarter of a million. For example, between 1960 and 1966 the 110 such areas added

* An exception is in New England where townships, rather than counties, are the basic units.

A Modern Geography of the United States

about 12 million people, whereas the 120 with populations of less than a quarter of a million added about $1\frac{1}{2}$ million.

For more detailed evidence on size and growth rates we must again rely on 1960 Census data (Table 23). In 1950 and 1960 there

Table 23: *SMSA Population Change 1950–60 by Size of SMSA**

Size of SMSA (million)	Number of SMSAs		Total population change (million)	% change	Total population in 1960 (million)
	1950	1960			
>3	5	5	6·0	23	31·8
1–3	10	19	13·2	79	29·8
0·5 to 1	21	29	4·8	33	19·2
0·25 to 0·5	44	48	0·6	4	15·8
0·1 to 0·25	89	89	0·5	3	14·5
<0·1	43	22	−1·4	−44	1·8
All SMSAs	212	212	23·6	26	112·9

* Areas as defined for 1960

Source: Census of Population

were 212 metropolitan areas, which increased their total population by 26 per cent over the decade. There were, however, considerable differences in the growth rates of SMSAs of different sizes. Both absolutely and relatively, areas with populations of one to three million grew most. Less 'popular' were areas with less than half a million people, and least 'popular' were areas in the lowest class of SMSA with populations of less than 100,000. But the growth in each size class was much affected by the changing number of areas in the class. Over the decade, while the number of designated SMSAs remained the same, many moved up into a different size category. The number of areas in the 1–3 million group rose by 9, whereas the number in the 100,000 and below class fell by 21. None the less, the fact that emerges is that metropolitan areas of very large size (i.e. with populations of more than 1 million) have proved the most attractive. The 24 areas with more than a million people in

348

1960 alone accounted for 85 per cent of the entire metropolitan population growth between 1950 and 1960, and no later evidence suggests any remarkable change in pattern since then. Probably, within the boundaries of the metropolitan areas, the small- or intermediate-sized political units (either suburbs or satellite cities) have grown most rapidly, as the evidence for urban places suggests. None the less the relevant functional unit is the metropolis, and the search for a satisfying life style must for most people take place within the limits imposed by economic requirements in ordering the efficient spatial arrangement of production processes.

The Mechanics of Urban Population Growth

The population of urban areas is fed from three major sources, natural increase, net migration and area redefinition. The last refers to the reclassification of rural territory as urban when it attains the necessary size or character. This is done on Census data, and can contribute considerably to the total. Thus about 60 per cent of total urban growth between 1950 and 1960 was attributable to area reclassification, which reflects the strong suburban growth of the period. This is a straightforward statistical adjustment. The dynamic elements of urban population growth are natural increase and net migration, the latter being of tremendous moment in recent decades.

Migrants to any urban area comprise two major groups, those moving from one urban area to another and those who are essentially newcomers to city life. The former are indeed very large in number. We have seen that Americans are mobile, and inter-metropolitan movement forms part of the general search for better conditions and opportunities. In 1967, about 40 per cent of persons aged fourteen years and more living in urban areas had moved there from other urban areas. Many of these are relatively well-to-do or, as they are well-educated, have reasonable prospects. Thus, unless they happen to be black, they raise few special problems by their movement.

The newcomers to American cities are a different case. Some are foreign migrants, who chiefly settle in the large cities. Generally,

349

again, since their flow is controlled in numbers and skills, and they are usually from urban backgrounds in their own countries, their arrival in the cities raises few unmanageable difficulties. Most, however, have been people moving from rural or small town areas with a background normally providing a poor preparation for big city life. We have recorded that the American farm population fell from about 30 million in 1940 to under 10 million in 1969. Not all of the millions who lost their farms, or farm jobs, migrated to urban areas, of course, but many did, and the rate of migration has quite steadily increased. From 1950 to 1955 the farm population migrated at an average annual rate of 5·4 per cent, totalling over 1 million persons per year. The rate fell slightly from 1955 to 1960, probably because of the economic difficulties in that period, but rose to 5·7 per cent for 1960–65 and to 6·3 per cent for 1965–8. The problems which flowed in in the wake of this massive influx of people oriented to rural jobs and ways of life, and often inadequately educated to compete for the better jobs, or any jobs, in American cities, were immense. In 1967, one out of every five urban Americans had rural childhood origins, and over one third (or, if they were black, two thirds) of the migrants from rural to urban areas were living in the official 'poverty areas' of central cities.

The peak of these migrations has probably now passed. Although the *rate* of farm population migration continued to rise in the 1960s, that population has been so reduced that fewer individuals are involved. Thus, while 1·1 million on average left the farms for the cities annually from 1950 to 1955, the number fell steadily to an average of 0·7 million between 1965 and 1968. The potential for further large-scale migration from farm to city is nowadays much less, and the recurring problems arising from this particular source should become less acute. Natural increase, of course, remains the major source of urban population growth. For metropolitan areas as a whole, natural increase provided 72 per cent of total growth between 1960 and 1964 and, with decreasing migration, 77 per cent between 1964 and 1969. But the situation varies so greatly from city to city that few valid generalizations are possible. A few cases suggest the range of experience.

Between 1960 and 1967, Baltimore had a natural increase of

350

170,000 and a net migration gain of 16,000. Clearly, natural increase is dominant here, with some net migration gain. In Chicago, however, there was a net migration loss of 32,000 over the period. The increase in population of 550,000 came entirely from a more-than-offsetting natural increase of 582,000. On the other hand, net migration can be the larger, or even the dominant, element in metropolitan growth. In Washington, DC, between 1960 and 1967, for example, a natural increase of 286,000 was accompanied by a net migration gain of 355,000. In Anaheim–Santa Ana (California), over the same period, net migration provided no less than 77 per cent of population growth; and in Miami 64 per cent.

Metropolitan areas in the USA have thus had widely differing experiences. Among the 100 largest metropolitan areas, forty-three had a net migration loss between 1960 and 1967, and in five this loss exceeded the natural increase, so that total population fell. These five are Pittsburgh, Johnstown and Wilkes Barre–Hazleton in Pennsylvania, Duluth–Superior (Minn.–Wis.) and Spokane (Wash.). By contrast, the highest growth rates, largely from high net migration gains, came in Anaheim–Santa Ana, San Jose (California) and Fort Lauderdale–Hollywood (Florida). The geographical distribution of the areas at the extremes is significant, and their experiences have great effect on the regional differences in metropolitan growth. Naturally, the 'older' industrial areas, where metropolitan development came early, have comparatively low growth rates, and conversely. Moreover, given the adjustments in regional economic structures, growth in new areas is sometimes greater absolutely as well as relatively. Thus the West and the South have experienced the larger expansion of metropolitan populations in recent decades. None the less, the biggest total metropolitan populations remain in the Manufacturing Belt.

Intra-metropolitan Patterns

A well-known feature of metropolitan development in advanced countries is the differential growth rates of cities and their suburbs. In the United States this difference possesses unusual significance,

A Modern Geography of the United States

for it adds racial problems to the general difficulties of great cities everywhere. The general pattern for 1950–69 (Table 24) is quite straightforward. Suburban* population has throughout expanded

Table 24: Population Distribution within SMSAs, 1950–69

	Metropolitan areas		Central cities		Suburbs	
	million	% increase	million	% increase	million	% increase
1950	89·2	—	52·2	—	37·0	—
1960	112·9	27	57·8	11	55·1	49
1969*	129·2	14	58·6	1	70·6	28

* Estimates

Source: Current Population Reports

much more rapidly than that of the central cities. From 1960 to 1969, the total population of the latter was practically at a standstill and, indeed, sample surveys for 1964–9 indicate that the total has begun to decline. As recently as 1960, more people still lived in central cities than in suburbs, but by 1969 the suburbs contained by far the larger populations. The national figures, as usual, conceal much variety. For instance, the record varies according to the sizes of the areas concerned. In the 1960 Census detail for areas in the size ranges used in Table 23, one finds a consistent pattern. Some central areas of large metropolises have, in fact, been losing population for some time but, over all, areas in the larger classes have smaller increases in their central cities and larger increases in their suburbs than areas in the smaller classes. For example, in SMSAs with populations of 1 to 3 million the central population increased by only 6 per cent between 1950 and 1960, but their suburban population rose by 45 per cent. At the lower end, SMSAs with populations of less than 100,000 experienced a rise of 29 per cent in central-city population but only 11 per cent in the suburban.

* 'Suburb' here relates to that portion of the official metropolitan area which lies outside the central city. Such areas often contain small cities and open country, in addition to the spread of residential areas commonly referred to as 'suburbs'. In the Census tables these areas are termed 'outside central cities'.

This one would expect. The smaller areas often have greater opportunity (e.g. in space available) for raising their central populations, and are working towards the higher densities of resident population common in central areas of large metropolises. The possibilities are indicated by comparing the existing densities of central cities of different size. Smaller cities such as Mobile (Ala.) and Austin (Tex.) had population densities of 1,300 and 4,100 per square mile respectively in 1960. Among the larger cities Cleveland, Ohio, had 11,500 and Chicago 16,000. In a class by itself is New York City with 26,000 per square mile and, in Manhattan, 75,000. The smaller, younger, metropolises are unlikely to wish, or need, to match the densities of a Chicago or a Cleveland, but powerful forces operate to push them above existing levels, and their central city populations can be expected to increase for some time.

Generalizations from Table 24 conceal not only variations among metropolitan areas of different size, but also variations between regions. In part such differences are themselves related to size, for the number of metropolises in the various size classes differs from region to region. Thus, most million-plus metropolitan areas are in the Manufacturing Belt. These have very slow-growing, or even declining, central-city populations. Of the five SMSAs with over 3 million population only one (Los Angeles) increased its central population between 1950 and 1960. New York, Philadelphia, Chicago and Detroit all had net losses. Such experiences colour the pattern for the Manufacturing Belt, where the latest estimates show central-city populations, over all, declining. Elsewhere they still grow, although less rapidly since 1960. One generalization does hold good throughout, however: everywhere, suburban populations continue to expand.

Of the greatest importance, within these general adjustments of metropolitan area populations, are the experiences of the Negro population, touched upon briefly in Chapter 2. Table 25 shows the broad patterns for white and Negro populations of metropolitan areas for the years 1950 to 1969. The statistics need little reinforcement. The major population increase in metropolitan areas over the nineteen years was white (+32 million, or nearly two thirds of the total metropolitan area rise), yet, over all, the white population

Table 25: Distribution of White and Negro Population within Metropolitan Areas, 1950–69

| | 1950 | | | | 1960 | | | | 1969* | | | |
| | White | | Negro | | White | | Negro | | White | | Negro | |
	mill.	% of total	mill.	% of total	mill.	% of total	mill.	% of total	mill.	% of total	mill.	% of total
SMSAs total	80·2	100	8·3	100	99·7	100	12·2	100	112·0	100	15·7	100
Central cities	45·3	56	6·4	77	47·4	48	9·7	80	45·3	40	12·4	79
Suburbs	34·9	44	1·9	23	52·3	52	2·5	20	66·7	60	3·3	21

* Estimates

Source: Current Population Reports

of central cities did not increase at all. Between 1950 and 1960 there was a small rise, but since 1960 the number has declined absolutely. In 1950, central cities housed 56 per cent of the white populations of metropolitan areas, but by 1969 only 40 per cent, and the suburbs had experienced enormous growth. For the blacks, metropolitan numbers rose by 7·4 million between 1950 and 1969, which is almost precisely the number by which the Negro population of the country grew over the nineteen years. Six million, or over four fifths of the total increase in the black population, however, were added to the population of central cities.

Within the central cities, too, millions of Negroes are crowded together in segregated quarters, sharply distinguished from their white fellow Americans in patterns, prospects and quality of life. They sometimes live at astonishingly high densities. According to one observer, Negroes living in Harlem, New York, are crowded in at nearly 4,000 per *block*; at this density the entire 1960 population of the USA could be domiciled within the five boroughs of New York City.* Ghetto conditions are well documented and readers wishing further details should refer to the 1968 *Report* of the National Advisory Commission on Civil Disorders, a Commission established by President Johnson following the major riots of the summer of 1967, which paints the picture with horrifying clarity.

The Commission asked itself why Negroes have generally failed to escape from poverty and the ghetto, unlike the hordes of European immigrants who came to the cities before 1920. The answer is that the situation was then essentially different. In particular there is today a great shortage of unskilled jobs such as the European migrants obtained in their hundreds of thousands. Moreover the Negro, because of his colour, faces a constant prejudice of a kind that the European minorities in time escaped from. Again, unlike most Europeans, consistent pressures have kept the black, and often even the successful black, firmly ensconsed in recognized Negro neighbourhoods. The cities themselves, too, have grown greatly in size and complexity and their political organizations are no longer so capable of solving minority problems. Even when the Negro population comes to outnumber the white

* R. A. Dentler, *Major American Social Problems*, 1967, p. 170.

(as in Washington, D C, and Newark) or when Negro mayors are elected by a combination of black and white liberal voters (as in Gary and Cleveland), few startling changes can be made because of the changed economic and social structure of the metropolitan area and the diminished status, especially financial, of the central city. Finally, many European migrants were already 'urbanized' and were settling in urban areas which we should now consider moderate or small. The Negro migrants have been chiefly from rural or small-town environments in the South, moving into gigantic and complex metropolitan areas for life in which they were totally unprepared. Thus in 1967 two thirds of the black rural-urban migrants were living in the 'poverty areas' of the central cities. In short, most Negroes have traded a rural slum for a ghetto slum in a sea of concrete, and their condition has not uniformly improved with the exchange.

The situation may, however, be changing in some important respects. Firstly, the migration of Negroes from the South may be diminishing in size. Between 1940 and 1950 non-white migration from the South averaged 160,000 net per annum. For 1950–60 the rate was 146,000 per annum, and estimates for 1960–69 suggest an annual average of about 90,000. If such estimates prove correct, the influx of 'fresh' migrants to central cities will have decreased, with consequent benefits since the black population growth rate in these areas will have been sharply diminished. Secondly, the black population of suburban areas has been growing slowly, despite pressures to contain them in the central areas. This growth has not so far kept pace with the expansion of the total Negro population of metropolitan areas. In 1950, suburban Negroes accounted for 23 per cent of the total metropolitan Negro population, in 1969, 21 per cent. Estimates for 1964–9, however, indicate that, for the first time, the *rate* of Negro population growth in suburbs was higher than for whites (4 per cent compared with 2·5 per cent). Admittedly, the black growth is on a very small base, could be partially explained by a sampling error in the estimates, and may sometimes represent only an extension of the Negro ghetto across an arbitrary dividing-line between city and suburb. Moreover, such a growth rate would need many years to make any

356

meaningful impact on the current position. But perhaps the straws are in the wind. Further, a recent study of Negro movements in Michigan shows that in large northern cities black people, whose entry to the suburbs is opposed by white home-owners, are sometimes escaping from the ghetto by moving beyond the suburbs to small, formerly agricultural, settlements.* Difficulties of access to employment, services and so on must arise but, in certain conditions, this phenomenon could become common before the end of the century and provide one useful channel out of present difficulties. More will be said below on the problems of central cities and suburbs. At present a review of the effects of urban growth on land use appears appropriate.

Urban Land Use

In reviewing land use in Chapter 3, the problems of the inadequacy of the statistical base and of attitudes to land resources loomed large. They must now be re-emphasized. According to Table 5 (p. 64) the 1960 estimate of area of land covered by incorporated cities of 2,500 or more was 21 million acres. This was undoubtedly an underestimate of the area of land in all urban uses, but any reasonable extension of the figure still leaves the total a minute proportion of the national area. A new estimate for 1964,† embracing areas occupied by incorporated and unincorporated places of 1,000 or more population, gave a total of 29·3 million acres. While no doubt inaccurate, and not distinguishing between different classes of urban use, the figures show clearly that the area of land covered by urban developments remains under 2 per cent of the national total.

For this reason it sometimes proves difficult to view the growing urban area in proper perspective. Even doubling the total by the year 2000 (which is not unlikely) will still leave less than one acre in twenty-five 'urbanized'. The significance of the urbanized areas,

* J. O. Wheeler and S. D. Brunn, 'Negro Migration into Rural Southwestern Michigan', *Geographical Review*, April 1968.

† *Major Uses of Land and Water in the United States, 1964*, Agricultural Economic Report No. 149, Economic Research Service, US Department of Agriculture, 1968.

however, is out of all proportion to their size. They house three quarters of the population and most new Americans born between now and AD 2000 will live in them or their extensions. They are, as Clawson has pointed out, 'the most strategically located lands of the nation', and the unimproved value of these urban lands 'is greater than the value of all other land in the nation'.* Moreover, much of the rest of the land area is devoted, directly or indirectly, to serving urban requirements for food, materials, recreational space and water. These last two make particularly heavy and urgent direct demands on land in the immediate vicinity of urban areas. Watersheds and reservoirs, parks and open spaces beyond the urban boundary thus belong in a real sense to the true 'urbanized area'. Further, there is the geographical distribution of this urban demand on land, which lifts the problem far above the level of urgency which the figures quoted above suggest.

It is clear that large areas have been absorbed by the growth of urban, and suburban, populations in the present century. The estimates in Table 5 credit cities of 2,500 or more with 6 million acres in 1900. By 1960, the total was at least 350 per cent greater, while population had increased by about 130 per cent. However crude the figures, they disclose a much more than proportional expansion of urban areas. That 60 per cent of urban population growth between 1950 and 1960 was due to area reclassification indicates the magnitude of the problem in the post-war years, for these suburban populations almost invariably live at very low densities. For the decade 1950–60 it has been calculated that, over all, the expansion of the urbanized area exceeded the growth of population by a ratio of 8 : 3.† Housing, schools, shopping areas, roads, car parks, churches and all the space-devouring penumbra of modern suburbia have multiplied. Hot-dog and hamburger bars, milk-shake and ice-cream parlours, dining saloons, second-hand car lots, motels, cut-price retailing businesses and the rest project ribbons of commercial activity for miles along roads in every direction from every sizeable town. Such development considerably

* M. Clawson, *Land for Americans*, R.F.F., 1963, p. 18.
† C. A. Doxiadis, *Emergence and Growth of an Urban Region: The Developing Urban Detroit Area*, Vol. I, pp. 58–9.

impedes the effective use of other land in the vicinity, and results in complete idleness for large areas. Much land stands derelict in the hands of land speculators, in hope of future urban expansion. Clawson estimates that the area of such idle land in, or on the fringes of, urban areas actually equals the used area. Some such land available for development is essential but around US urban centres it typically 'represents the requirement for from twenty to fifty years of growth'. This is 'far in excess of a reasonable amount, and . . . great economies could be achieved in its better use'.*

The passion for low-density development is not only wasteful of land but tends to reduce the quality of urban life for many people. Access to unspoiled country becomes increasingly difficult, especially from the inner areas of large cities and for poorer citizens generally. The journey to work also often imposes obvious penalties, while providing roads and parking facilities for increasing numbers of car-driving commuters is costly.† Providing adequate services and amenities for a scattered suburban population is also very expensive.

The current rate of loss of land to urban growth is not easily computed. The best estimate is probably that of the Department of Agriculture report for 1964, quoted above. This suggested that about one million acres were being built over each year, with slightly under half the total going to direct urban uses. Again, given the size of the country, the total land involved seems negligible. At the present rate an area equivalent to the size of England could be built over before the end of the century, but still give a total urban acreage of not much above 3 per cent of the nation's surface. Since builders and home-owners prefer level, fertile areas, most of this land will be of good agricultural potential, but this is not normally regarded as a cause for anxiety. More significant is the likely geographical location of this new urban territory. Currently one fifth of the

---

* M. Clawson, *Land for Americans*, p. 16 and, with R. B. Held and C. H. Stoddard, *Land for the Future*, p. 95.

† For New York City the capital outlay required to cater for each car-driving commuter has been estimated at $21,000; and for Washington $23,000. Department of Agriculture, *Communities of Tomorrow*, 1967, p. 5.

entire urbanized area of the United States is in the north-east coastal States from Massachusetts to Maryland, and a further 16 per cent is in Michigan, Ohio, Indiana and Illinois, chiefly in an area embraced by a line joining Cleveland, Detroit, Chicago and Cincinnati; 10 per cent is in California alone, and chiefly in the southern part of the State. Add southern and eastern Florida and half the urban area of the nation is accounted for. These are also the areas where suburbs and satellites will expand most rapidly and, as separate urban centres grow, they will eventually coalesce to form new megalopolitan areas to rival the existing megalopolis of the North-East.

The speed of the process and the character of the resulting development will depend upon the attitudes of those involved and the willingness to cooperate and ability to cope of numerous planning agencies. Decisions taken now on town form and densities, functional organization, transport networks, recreational provision and so on, will be very important both for the economical use of land resources and for the efficiency and satisfaction of urban life in the later decades of the century. Local authorities have quite considerable powers over land use in zoning and subdivision procedures and in their rights of eminent domain (Chapter 3). Moreover, since as much as a third of any built-up area may be publicly owned (roads, parks, public buildings and so on), local policy on these matters can powerfully influence general dispositions and standards. While powers seem adequate, however, the ability and willingness to use them are suspect. A critical deficiency occurs in the financial resources available for planning activities. The chief defect, however, lies in administrative structure, which is discussed below.

The Modern Metropolis: Planning and Federal Involvement

The processes of centralization and decentralization that characterize the modern metropolis, a strange amalgam of centripetal and centrifugal forces, have many consequences, beneficial to some people, interests and areas, harmful to others. We cannot examine here the detailed range of metropolitan problems, their causes and effects. Most are well known and some have been touched upon already. Suffice to say that the increasing affluence of the majority and the use of the motor car have over the years changed the distribution of people and jobs and have, for better and for worse, transformed the life and the pattern of organization of metropolitan areas. 'Downtown', problems of slums, ghettos, traffic congestion, noise, dirt, unemployment, poverty, crime – none new to cities – have reached a new scale and intensity. Meanwhile the incomes of city administrations have (although the cities themselves remain the source of much of the nation's wealth) failed to increase sufficiently to cope with demands for slum clearance, traffic management, crime prevention, education, welfare services and the rest. In the suburbs, too, life is not always the combination of rural and urban delights suggested as the reason for their phenomenal growth. Loss of family ties, loneliness, long and crowded journeys to work, inadequate services and rising taxes often take the gilt off the gingerbread. City and suburb alike suffer from problems of movement: congestion on roads, pollution of atmosphere and the decline of public transport systems that isolates both individuals (especially the poor, the aged, the infirm and the young) and communities.

There is, of course, a danger, in such a recitation of problems, of creating an impression of a metropolitan America beset by unpleasantness and crisis. This is, happily, far from the truth. Conditions vary greatly from city to city, area to area and almost from person to person. In part, too, the problems of the city arise out of its very success. Certainly, for example, the incidence of poverty in metropolitan America is far below that elsewhere. But its very success in this respect attracts more poor migrants who, by their concentration, tend to worsen their own conditions and attract more attention to their plight. Perspective, therefore, is essential. Americans live in metropolitan areas by and large because they choose to. Whatever the difficulties, these areas offer, for most, opportunities for work, education, cultural pursuits and entertainment of kinds that are not available elsewhere. None the less, the dilemmas are real enough, and closely related to their resolution is the matter of city-area planning.

Although equipped with various effective techniques for achieving an ordered use of land and, therefore, some control over the functioning of the metropolitan system, city planning in America faces several difficulties. Forward planning of land use and urban distributions is not compulsory, as it is in the UK; many Americans remain unconvinced that any benefits could be derived from such planning; and financial resources are often too slender to permit a planning department to operate efficiently or to implement plans. Beyond these, however, is the problem of the administrative fragmentation of the metropolitan area. The 110 SMSAs with populations of over 250,000 share 16,045 local governments, 85 per cent of which have powers to tax. The 123 smaller SMSAs have 4,653 governments, again with 85 per cent of them possessing powers to tax. The complexity in some major areas is illustrated by metropolitan Chicago, which embraces 1,113 government units, of which 93 per cent can levy a tax on property; metropolitan Philadelphia, 876 units, 66 per cent with taxing powers; and metropolitan New York, 551 units, 99 per cent with taxing powers. Some of the units concerned are enormous, with gigantic budgets. New York City Council, for example, has a budget (inadequate for its needs, of course) which would put many countries of the world into the shade. Others are tiny local jurisdictions with responsibility for separate and very limited functions such as education, water, fire services or mosquito control.

This pattern of local government may have an impeccable pedigree, but its implications in the present context are clear. The metropolitan area is in many ways a single functioning system, with numerous sub-systems it is true, but in which the whole is greater than the sum of the parts. This must be so, or the modern metropolis would be a nonsensical creation and its emergence and continued growth inexplicable. Thus the functions of one district have effects in all; the problems of one district pervade the entire area; the plans for one area have immediate consequences in others, serving them or depending upon their cooperation. Illustrations are not hard to find. The construction of an intra-urban expressway, or the improvement of existing roads, alters traffic flows over wide areas, not simply in the vicinity of the construction. Slum clearance displaces numerous families, to be accommodated elsewhere. Open-space or recreational provision in one area benefits users from other local jurisdictions. Clean-air programmes in one part of a city are pointless unless other parts cooperate, and so on.

All of this indicates a fundamental need for close cooperation throughout a metropolitan system, difficult enough with only a handful of authorities concerned, but almost insuperable where scores or hundreds of petty local jurisdictions exist. It is not being suggested that the creation of a more appropriate pattern of local government areas would provide a panacea, but it *is* being suggested that the current Balkanization of American city areas is in a class by itself as an impediment to programmes for alleviating their problems. This is no new discovery. The facts have long been evident, and deplored, at many levels (and defended at others). The situation, however, seems too deeply entrenched for remedy. The solution probably lies in promoting better cooperation among the important administrative entities in any area, and this thought leads into a review of the role of the Federal government.

The difficulty of raising sufficient revenue to meet requirements has been a pervading problem of metropolitan areas, but especially for the central cities of the large SMSAs. Many authorities have, over the years, run heavily into debt, and the servicing of past loans has itself become a major drain on resources. Increasing local taxes provides no remedy, for it often induces a further exodus of tax-paying business. The cities have, perforce, looked elsewhere for aid. State governments have, in general, not proved responsive. The position is complex but, in essence, State legislatures have often been dominated by rural interests, have been jealous of the city's power and often, too, have lacked the funds themselves. Thus the cities have turned especially to the Federal government, which alone commands adequate resources. Over the years, therefore, Washington has become heavily involved in urban affairs, subsidizing roads, slum clearance, public transport schemes and, recently, 'model-city' plans. Until the middle 1960s little Federal control existed over the effectiveness of spending under various programmes. Washington provided the funds, the local authorities spent them, but little seemed to be accomplished.

One reason for the poor results has been that metropolitan area problems were tackled in bits and pieces, by numerous Federal agencies. The departments of Housing, Health, Education and Welfare, Commerce, Labor and Transport, the Office of Economic Opportunity, and others, administered the many schemes which had congressional approval and financial support. Some of these schemes overlapped, or attempted to serve opposing ends, and separate government agencies are not noted for cooperation in administering programmes for which they have responsibility. Further, over time, a maze of legislation has been enacted, so that few local authorities are really aware of the range of sources of funds at their disposal for various purposes. In 1969 about five hundred separate schemes and programmes existed from which urban areas were entitled to benefit. Such division of responsibility and multiplicity of enactments must reduce the effectiveness of the Federal contribution.

Powerful Federal intervention in urban affairs is still fairly new, however, and its character and organization are changing with experience. Like most such activity it is regarded with suspicion, and hostility by many. None the less, the Federal government has the only purse capable of providing sufficient resources. With this fact of life becoming more generally appreciated, Washington appears to be entering on an increasingly important role. Minor Federal intervention in urban affairs occurred before the Second World War, concerned with low-rent public housing and associated programmes. Significant legislation is, however, a post-war product. In the late 1940s and the 1950s, for example, legislation made Federal funds available to assist home purchase, urban renewal or rehabilitation programmes, slum clearance and, in a minor way, open-space provision and mass transit systems. An important legal decision of 1954 established the rights of local authorities to purchase private property compulsorily for redevelopment by private interests.

In the 1960s the scope of the legislation widened considerably. In 1964 an Urban Mass Transportation Act made Federal grants for new equipment available to public systems in financial difficulties. In 1965 the Department of Housing and Urban Development (HUD) was established, to bring under a single authority many programmes and functions previously administered by separate agencies, and to administer all new urban measures. Finally, in 1966, the Model Cities programme was established as a major development, to use selected cities as 'laboratories' in which all available resources were to be concentrated in designated areas to demonstrate the benefits to be obtained from comprehensive planning and cooperative effort. Originally intended to embrace a mere handful of cities, political and other pressures pushed the number of candidates up to almost 200, without a corresponding increase in resources. By 1968, 75 cities had been awarded planning grants. Cooperative problem analysis, establishment of goals and drawing up of plans have gone ahead in many cities, but numerous difficulties have arisen. Clashes of interests within the cities, inter-departmental conflicts in Washington and difficulty in obtaining adequate funds have impeded progress, and the movement seems to have lost momentum. So far, only Atlanta has gone beyond the planning stage, and the demonstration project has confirmed again how difficult it is to achieve orderly planning and development in metropolitan areas, given the great diversity of interests and fragmentation of responsibility.

This latter problem, however, continues to receive attention in Federal programmes. Increasing emphasis is being placed on the need for programmes and plans for whole cities or whole metro-politan areas. Loans and grants available under various Federal schemes become contingent upon the production of such plans and evidence of local cooperation. Various supplementary grants are available in areas showing willingness and ability to cooperate in these ways. By late 1968, often in direct response to such provisions, 171 SMSAs had established 'area-wide' planning agencies. Their value in practice remains to be tested but, while Washington has no power to force the hands of local authorities, the hope is that the financial carrots will persuade many to sink their differences, rivalries and jealousies, and work together for effective solutions to those difficulties which are amenable to proper area planning.

Critics of Federal activities have suggested that intervention has so far hardly helped, and has often worsened the difficulties, as when loans or grants for urban renewal have been used to replace slums with high-priced city apartments, leaving the displaced poor to fend for themselves and, in the event, to increase overcrowding in other slum areas. Certainly, much that has been done with Federal funds has been self-defeating. The hope is that the lessons are being learned, and the direction of legislation in the 1960s indicates that they are. It seems certain that in this field, as in others, the Federal role, already large, will grow larger, especially as the reapportionment of congressional seats allocates more places in the legislature to politicians with urban problems and interests uppermost in their minds.

14: Geographical Dimensions of Federal Government Activities

At numerous points in this work, mention has been made of Federal concern with, or involvement in, economic and social affairs. The theme has been pervasive and it appears desirable to end the book with a specific discussion of the geographical implications of government activities. That governments now play a major role in the conduct of affairs and have immense influence over economic activities, under all political systems, is a truism, and the USA is no exception. In its control of budget, tax and economic policy, in the passing of laws and the making of national rules and regulations for business, in the purchasing of massive supplies of goods and services and the employment of great numbers of people, in providing huge sums for research and development work and so on, the Federal authority wields tremendous power.

It is not easy to indicate briefly the full measure of the direct power and influence of the central government in modern times, much less the manifold indirect consequences of its operations. Some measure of the magnitude of its spending activities alone, however, is given by the fact that in 1969 Federal purchases of goods and services amounted to no less than one hundred thousand million dollars – 11 per cent of the Gross National Product. As recently as 1950 the total was a mere $18 thousand million – 6 per cent of GNP. The pace of growth, as well as the absolute amount involved, is quite spectacular. National defence, of course, takes above three quarters of the total, but this still leaves vast funds for other Federal purchases. Total employment, both in government itself (but excluding military personnel) and in private industry, resulting from these purchases was put at about 7 millions in 1969.

It is not simply the magnitude and pervasiveness of Federal activities which is significant here, but also their differential geographical effect. This has already been noted for Federally-sponsored industrial research and development, and the award of military contracts. Such programmes inevitably favour the advanced and wealthy areas. A different aspect of Federal money programmes may be illustrated from the disposition of Federal aid to State, local governments and individuals in 1968. The total sum so expended exceeded $25 billion, and Figure 49 shows the per capita distribution of this aid by State. Against a national average of $126 per capita, receipts are very high in many central and Mountain States and in Mississippi (highest North Dakota, $357), low or very low in the Manufacturing Belt, certain other eastern States and California (lowest New Jersey, $71). This aid is given under various programmes of which public assistance, highways and education and agricultural conservation, extension and research work are the largest, covering two thirds of the total. The geographical impact is naturally affected by the nature of these programmes but, in sum, it obviously varies greatly and, since the areas with the lowest per capita aid are often also the wealthiest areas which provide much Federal tax income, a notable redistribution of income is achieved.

Many other Federal operations – in agricultural support programmes, the conduct of military affairs, transport subsidies, urban renewal, aid to small business, regulation of mineral industries, control of oil imports and so on – also have geographical implications. Some have been mentioned earlier, and must suffice as examples. Here we direct attention to programmes and policies dealing specifically with areal problems of unemployment and poverty, and regions of economic difficulty.

Distressed Areas and Government Involvement

Economically distressed areas can be created by any of a number of possible causes, can be local in character or embrace entire regions, and can represent either temporary difficulties or major problems of structural change and adaptation. Cyclical fluctuations in manufacturing, for example, have produced serious problems of localized

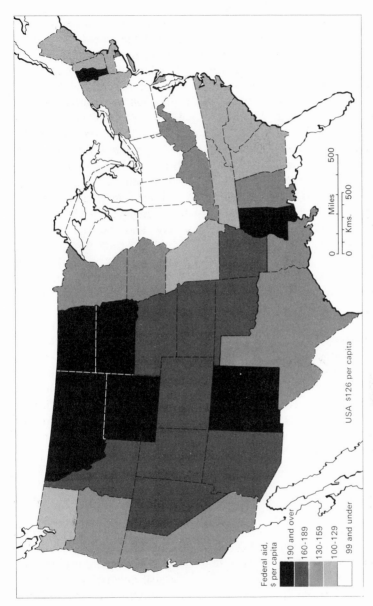

**Federal aid,
$ per capita**

190 and over

160-189

130-159

100-129

99 and under

USA $126 per capita

Miles 500

Kms. 500

0

Figure 49. Federal Aid to States, Local Governments and Individuals, 1968

unemployment on several occasions since the war. Thus mid-western motor vehicle-producing centres have had periodical difficulties which have brought serious unemployment and considerable distress. In Detroit, for example, unemployment reached 16 per cent in 1958, the worst of several bad post-war years for the motor vehicle capital. While this situation included an element of structural adjustment, as the geographical distribution of auto assembly plants changed, however, these problems of the Mid West were essentially temporary. Lost jobs in motor vehicle production have been either recovered or replaced by growth in other industries. In Detroit between 1958 and 1969 total manufacturing employment rose from 474,000 to 602,000, and unemployment dropped from very high rates in 1958 and 1961 to about national average proportions in the later 1960s.

More disturbing, therefore, are the effects of major secular changes in technology, market conditions or geographical location. Far-reaching developments in the techniques of iron and steel manufacture, for example, reinforced by changing type and distribution of demand, have seriously affected established steel centres, especially in western Pennsylvania. Secular change in markets (especially the growth of substitutes and changes of consumer preference) have, together with advancing techniques of production, destroyed many thousands of jobs in coalmining and in woollens manufacture, again with devastating effects of the areas specialized in these types of production in Appalachia and New England. The complex farm problem has resulted over large areas in low and relatively static incomes at a time when costs and prices have been rising rapidly. Areas thus affected usually present widely ranging symptoms of economic backwardness or stress. Unemployment, underemployment, low incomes, out-migration, poor education, poor health and medical services, low local government revenues, run-down public services, poor quality leadership, poor psychological attitudes, sub-standard physical environment, are examples. Not all are present in each distressed area, of course, but each has sufficient symptoms to warrant general concern.

It was seen in Chapter 4 that, in a free-market situation (on Myrdal's theory), once marked differences appear between separate regions in economic conditions, from whatever cause, the 'natural' forces of economic development tend to reinforce the successful region, often to the detriment of others. This theory of cumulative causation, and its possible backwash effects, has powerful empirical support. Certainly in the shorter term, and probably in the longer term too, regional inequalities persist, and even become greater, failing any powerful enough countervailing force. In modern conditions this force must normally be governmental intervention.

The development of attitudes favourable to greater government involvement in the affairs of distressed communities and areas, and in problems of unemployment and poverty generally, came late in the USA. The general tendency, still not wholly abandoned, was to cling to the belief that the benevolent working of a free-enterprise economy would of itself, sooner or later, abolish problem areas and give satisfactory conditions to all except the idle and the thriftless. In this climate of opinion, government intervention was expected to be minimal – unless powerful sectional interests were involved. There also have been in the USA conditions which make Federal intervention in matters of employment, poverty and area distress especially difficult and tricky. Among these are the sheer size of the country and the complexities of economic structure and regional interchange, so that programmes intended to alleviate one problem may create, or exacerbate, others. Moreover the structure of government divides powers between Federal and State authorities and, at lower levels, gives autonomy in many functions to thousands of local government units. At, and between, all these levels, there is fruitful ground for suspicion, jealousy and friction.

None the less, it gradually became manifest (between the wars if not earlier) that the problems of modern economic growth and of stress and change in sectors and regions, could not be resolved by *laissez-faire* methods and were too great and all-embracing to be handled by local or State governments in isolation. Important national issues demanded more direct Federal action, while the more serious and persistent local problems required the co-ordinated approach and the financial and other resources that only Federal government involvement could ensure.

As in the UK, the first major impetus to a much deeper government intervention in the affairs of industries and regions came in the 1930s from the appalling depression of that time, with the national *average* unemployment rate reaching 25 per cent of the labour force in 1933. The relationships between business and government were drastically changed by the New Deal legislation of that period, and have never returned to their former condition. Moreover, heavy Federal expenditure on relief projects and public works, and the establishment of the TVA, began a new era in the involvement of Washington with economic affairs and, in a tentative way, with regional problems. The great activity and high employment that followed during the 1940s had the effect of diminishing the urgency of the problem. None the less, sufficient fear of the possible return of 1930s conditions remained in 1946 for Congress to pass its Employment Act. This has become a landmark in the history of the reorientation of attitudes to, and ideas on, the government's role in economic affairs and, specifically, in ensuring sufficient employment.

The Act declared it a 'continuing policy and responsibility of the Federal Government to use all practical means . . . to foster and promote conditions under which there will be offered useful employment opportunities . . . for those able, willing and seeking for work . . . and to promote maximum employment, production and purchasing power'. To assist the President in meeting this new charge, the Act established a small, but important, body, the Council of Economic Advisers, whose annual reports and regular advice have had great influence. But the Act itself gave no clear guidance on how the new responsibility was to be met, and failed to provide for the needs of areas of major economic distress. Nevertheless, the fact that the government accepted this share of responsibility both for the performance of the economy and for individuals seeking work was, as President Johnson put it in his 1966 Economic Report, 'an essential and revolutionary declaration', laying the foundation for the later development of principles and practice.

Post-war Experience and Action

As things transpired, national unemployment rates for the first twelve post-war years (1945–57) were exceptionally low. In eight of these years, the rate was below 4·5 per cent (then considered by some economists as 'full employment') and the median level for the twelve years was 4·3 per cent. Compared with the inter-war years, this was extraordinarily good, and it is not surprising that many Americans lost interest in the problem, which ceased to be a live national political issue until the late 1950s. Even in the first post-war decade, however, the national averages concealed considerable regional disparity. Many centres, some of moderate to large size, were enduring considerable hardship. Thus in 1954, when a mild recession took the national unemployment rate to 5 per cent, ten 'major labour market areas' (i.e., broadly, metropolitan areas with a central city of 50,000 or more) had rates above 10 per cent (the highest being 24 per cent in Lawrence, Mass.), and eighteen above 8 per cent. Numerous smaller cities suffered similar, or worse, conditions, while the general malaise of unemployment, underemployment, low incomes and poverty afflicted hundreds of rural counties.

The problems of such areas of difficulty in a generally buoyant and expanding economy were not completely ignored at this time. Several aid programmes were established and several attempts made in Congress to pass legislation to permit a larger and more direct Federal involvement. The programmes of aid began in 1949 with the classification of areas of 'very substantial labour surplus'. Classified areas had priority in the award of government procurement and construction contracts and, in the early fifties, of military contracts (provided there was no increase in costs to the government). Certain tax privileges were also offered to business, and special technical aid was made available. These efforts were small in scale, backed by very limited resources, and had little effect. Priority in Federal purchasing meant little when the areas concerned had not the means of fulfilling a government contract, especially for military equipment of increasing sophistication. Moreover, no

373

distinction was made between areas where profound structural changes were bringing long-term problems of maladjustment and those temporarily afflicted by some cyclical or other short-term fluctuation. Attempts from the middle fifties to take bolder steps to help the 'depressed areas' were also abortive. Bills acceptable to Congress were vetoed by the President and one drawn up in the late 1950s by the President was not accepted by Congress.

It cannot therefore be said that the period was one of total unconcern in this matter; but neither was it one of really serious and determined purpose. It was widely considered that the depressed areas could best be aided by the Federal government's use of its powers to stimulate economic activity nationally, and thus raise general employment to steadily higher levels. In a buoyant national situation, free-market forces would improve conditions in areas of difficulty, or induce a movement of resources away from such areas to places where they could find employment. There is much truth in this contention. If government efforts achieved conditions in which the national economy grew vigorously, all parts of the country must benefit in some way or another. Post-war experience in the United States and elsewhere, however, indicates that this 'aggregative strategy', by itself, will not cure the problem areas. While conditions in such areas certainly improve in a prolonged period of national growth, with its heavy demand for labour and other resources, they remain throughout less favourable than elsewhere, and swiftly revert to more unfavourable levels when national growth slackens. Thus something more appears to be required of government, and we return to the review of the evolution of Federal policy and practice.

With the 1958 recession, the post-war honeymoon with 'full employment' appeared to have ended. National unemployment rose sharply to 6·8 per cent and remained above 5 per cent until 1965. The high average rate obviously reflected quite desperate situations in some areas. In 1958, twenty-three of the nation's 150 major labour-market areas had unemployment rates exceeding 10 per cent, and at least fifty had rates above 8 per cent. The national economy began a hesitating recovery in 1959, but in July of that year the Bureau of Employment Security classified forty-six major labour-market areas and 143 smaller centres as 'areas of substantial labour surplus'. In seventeen of the larger and fifty-three of the smaller areas, unemployment had been 50 per cent or more above the national average for at least four of the previous five years, and these unhappy places were dignified by the title of 'chronic labour surplus areas'. The geographical distribution of these centres is important, for it illustrates the fact that problem localities tend to occur in bunches rather than in isolated situations. Five of the major 'chronic surplus' areas and four of the smaller were in New England, where the textile industry was primarily responsible for employment decline. A further five of the major areas and six of the smaller were in Pennsylvania, where mining was the chief cause of the difficulties, supplemented by problems in steel and railroad equipment centres. West Virginia and Kentucky contained no less than fifteen of the smaller centres, plus Charleston as a major centre, with mining the primary cause of distress. Such examples show that the problem is normally of sub-regional or regional dimensions, and not essentially of individual centres, a fact with implications for aid programmes.

Such conditions brought the problems of the distressed areas to the centre of the political arena in the 1960s. Kennedy had been greatly moved by the conditions he saw in West Virginia on his presidential primary campaign, and determined to achieve more powerful legislation to deal with them, a determination shared with President Johnson, who succeeded him in 1963. Thus between 1961 and 1965 came a series of important acts of Congress designed to overcome widespread problems of chronic economic distress and poverty and to attack these conditions directly in areas where they were most pronounced. The highlights of this legislation were:

1961   Area Redevelopment Act
1962   Manpower Development and Training Act
1962   Accelerated Public Works Act
1964   Economic Opportunity Act
1965   Public Works and Economic Development Act
1965   Appalachian Regional Development Act

The 1962 legislation is self-explanatory. The Manpower Act made

Federal aid available to State and local training systems, and established numerous schemes for training or retraining different classes of workers. The Accelerated Public Works Act authorized funds for a two-year public works programme in an attempt to lower an unemployment rate which had remained obstinately high since 1958, and at the same time provide facilities to serve as a basis for future growth. The 1964 Act provided a great variety of programmes; Jobs Corps, Work Training, Community Action Programmes, Small Business loans, the Domestic Peace Corps, etc. to stimulate local activity. While all this legislation contributed to the considerable erosion of unemployment and poverty in the later 1960s (if not as much as had been hoped), detailed discussion is not possible here. Geographically it is the 1961 and 1965 Acts that are the most significant since, for the first time since the TVA in 1933, Federal money and other aid would be directed to distressed areas as such, in an attempt to provide a basis from which conditions therein could be improved.

The Area Redevelopment Act

In the words of the official description, this Act provided 'a specific kit of tools to help communities rebuild their economic bases'. An Area Redevelopment Administration (ARA) was set up, within the Department of Commerce, to work with private enterprise, community organizations, and State and Federal agencies to aid specified areas of chronic unemployment or poverty. Unlike the comparable legislation in the UK, however, the Act gave the Administration no powers directly to control or influence the location of industry, such powers being still unacceptable to both State and local governments and to business interests generally in the USA. As it was, the supporters of the Act and its administrators had to move warily to find the appropriate frame of reference. The ARA's own description of the Act thus emphasizes the primary reliance on local initiative, local planning and local investment, and on the creation or expansion of profitable private enterprise in developing new employment opportunities. Federal funds were simply to augment local private and public investment and were, in the main, to be loans, repayable with interest.

The ARA had powers to designate Redevelopment Areas (normally whole counties or labour-market areas) on defined grounds of high, long-term, unemployment or very low income – the latter so that rural areas could qualify. Designation entitled an area to benefit from the Act, but the decision as to whether and to what extent to participate rested with the area itself. Additions to and deletions from the list of areas could be made at any time. The ARA could provide low-interest, long-term loans to new or expanding, but relatively high-risk, enterprise in the areas which could not get finance from conventional sources. Loans, and sometimes grants, could also be made to communities for public facilities (water, sewerage, airport improvements, for example) needed to attract, or keep, industry. Various forms of technical assistance were available, and worker retraining schemes could be helped from Federal funds. To qualify for aid, every Redevelopment Area had to establish a committee, representative of important local interests, to produce an analysis of the area and its problems and a reasoned programme for stimulating economic growth, the Overall Economic Development Programme, or OEDP. In its first year, the ARA designated 930 areas and by the end of the programme in 1965, 1,120 areas (embracing over one third of all counties) had been designated. The broad geographical pattern was much the same as it remained in 1968 (Figure 50), although by then some three hundred areas had been removed from the list.

The results achieved under this Act were not spectacular and the system was reorganized under the 1965 Public Works and Economic Development Act. Among the problems of the 1961 Act was that it had to be a compromise measure to gain sufficient support. The total money appropriated was also quite small, especially since a surprisingly large number of areas qualified for aid. The total invested over the whole life of the programme for all types of project amounted to only $322 million – less, for example, than the amount of Federal aid to California alone for highway construction in 1967. Such meagre resources, widely and thinly spread, had little startling impact anywhere. The number of direct jobs created by the

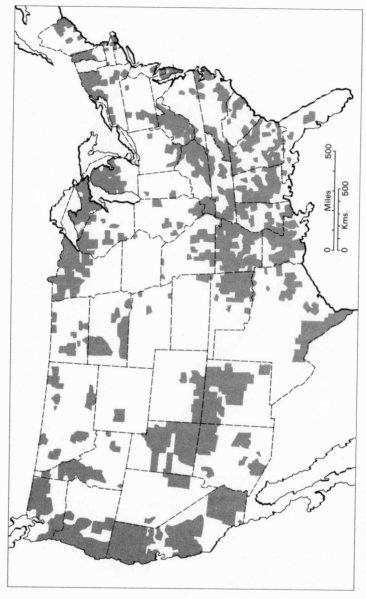

Figure 50. Redevelopment Areas, 1968

programme was estimated in the final report of the ARA at 71,400. On a normal ratio of 0·65 indirect jobs created for every one direct, ARA projects helped provide 118,000 new jobs between 1961 and 1965. Over that period the number of unemployed in the USA fell by 1·3 millions (the rate from 6·7 per cent to 4·5 per cent); measured against this, the ARA contribution certainly appears limited.

The OEDP requirement none the less often proved valuable. The production of the analysis and plan created bodies of a type which many distressed areas lacked. Many of the resulting studies and plans lacked adequate data and proper analysis, however, and the bodies producing them frequently disbanded once the job was done. The OEDP requirement in fact demonstrated the poor quality of local leadership in many distressed areas. People with limited ability and horizons could not formulate plans which would enable their area to benefit fully from the wide variety of Federal programmes. The plans themselves tended to embrace hoped-for developments rather than practical assessment of possibilities. Moreover, the plans were often being produced on an unrealistic area basis. Most development areas are too small, too poor and too poorly led for effective development planning in isolation.

The programme was not completely ineffective, however. Valuable experience was gained, while some of the public works so stimulated, and technical assistance given, would reap a full return only over a longer period and in many indirect ways. Moreover, it proved that in some circumstances a quite modest amount of Federal aid could contribute significantly towards distressed area rehabilitation. In the Scranton and the Wilkes Barre–Hazelton areas of Pennsylvania, for example, total unemployment fell from 29,000 in 1961 to 15,000 in 1965, halving the unemployment rates in both areas. Here, already active local development bodies capitalized on the 'pump-priming' aid that the Federal programmes offered and thus achieved good results. (Unemployment in the two areas was down to 9,000 in 1969 and the rates, while still higher than the national average, are no longer disastrously so.) In sum the Area Redevelopment Act is probably best regarded as a pilot operation, testing out these uncharted seas.

The 1965 Acts

The experiences of the ARA were reflected in the provisions of the Public Works and Economic Development Act and the Appalachian Regional Development Act of 1965. Geographically, the most significant change was in the areas to be embraced by developmental activities. The need for a broader regional approach, involving the cooperative endeavours of numerous communities, and even States, was sensed by Kennedy in his appraisal of the problems of Appalachia. Thus he established the Appalachian Regional Commission in 1963, to prepare 'a comprehensive action programme for the economic development of the Appalachian Region'. The 1964 report of the Commission provided the basis of the 1965 Appalachian Act. A similar concern for a more realistic geographical organization was shown in the Economic Development Act, whose provisions will now be outlined.

This Act gave a new administrative body, the Economic Development Administration (EDA) broadly the same 'kit of tools' as its predecessor, but the funds available (for the initial five-year funding period $3·3 billions) were more generous, and greater emphasis was to be placed on grants rather than loans in appropriate projects. For public works, some $600 million were expended during the first three years of operation (almost six times as much as in the entire life of the ARA), and over 80 per cent was in grants, compared with only a third under the previous dispensation. For private business development, low interest, long-term loans remained available, together with loan guarantees for private loan transactions. Technical assistance is also more generous, and planning grants assist the areas concerned to establish effective planning organizations.

Such assistance is available to areas which qualify by high and persistent unemployment, low family incomes or high population loss through lack of economic opportunity. Further, one county in every State is allowed to qualify – a neat piece of vote-catching! Each qualified area must submit an OEDP before it can be designated as a Redevelopment Area. eligible for EDA assistance.

The OEDP, too, must be updated annually, and the area committee thus becomes a permanent body, normally with professional assistance. In such ways the virtues of the Area Redevelopment Act have been improved upon.

The most significant advance, however, relates to geographical area. The EDA emphasizes the need for planning and coordination across county and State lines. The Redevelopment Areas remain counties or labour-market areas, and the 1968 disposition of these areas is shown in Figure 50. But it is emphasized that, while some problems of such areas may be adequately dealt with locally, advance will generally be possible only if planning is on a multi-county or multi-State regional basis. Redevelopment areas lacking the resources to restore themselves effectively may benefit greatly from help provided to a neighbouring area with better growth potential. Thus the multi-county *development district* has become the chief area planning unit. A 'district' must contain two or more qualified redevelopment areas, and it must include a 'growth centre', i.e. a community with potential for growth to underpin the economic expansion of the district as a whole. To encourage the formation of districts the EDA can make planning grants to assist in their organization, and subsequently pay 75 per cent of the administrative costs of carrying out the programme. The districts must draw up their own OEDPs, have them approved by the State(s) affected (to ensure coordination within States), and revise them annually. By mid 1970, the EDA had authorized the establishment of 137 Economic Development Districts. Of these, 92 (embracing 446 Redevelopment Areas) had had their OEDPs approved and had thus been officially designated.

A yet larger regional base for planning in areas of difficulty was also provided under the Act, recognizing that some parts of the country may face common economic and social problems that pay no respect to State boundary lines and require regional solutions. The same philosophy lies behind the separate Appalachian Act. The objective is comprehensive, long-term planning to bring to bear all relevant Federal aid programmes and assistance in co-operation with State and local efforts. The Secretary of Commerce is thus authorized, with the agreement of the States concerned, to

381

designate *Economic Development Regions* defined by common geographic, cultural and economic relationships and problems. On designation a regional commission, with members from each State, and headed by a Federal nominee, has the responsibility of analysing the region's problems and providing a general strategy for the planned redevelopment of its various parts, using all available aid programmes. Federal grants cover the commission's entire expenses for the first two years, thereafter 50 per cent. Planning, research and technical aid is also provided.

In the first year of the Act, three Economic Development Regions were established: the Ozarks, the Upper Great Lakes and the entire New England region. In the following year the Coastal Plains and Four Corners regions were designated. Figure 51 shows what a considerable area is now covered by these planning regions. If Appalachia is included, about 900 counties are involved. Not all are official Redevelopment Areas, for some are prosperous with few major economic problems. Their inclusion in the development regions is none the less highly important, for they can provide natural 'growth points' to whose good fortunes certain laggard areas can, by careful planning, be linked.

We cannot deal separately with all these planning regions. That designated regions can differ greatly in character and style is shown by the inclusion of New England which, unlike the others, is predominantly urban and industrial, although of great internal diversity. On many counts, New England is a prosperous region, but has for decades faced problems of high, localized unemployment as textile mills and shoe and leather factories closed in their hundreds. In 1961 when the area development programme began, the 'chronic labour-surplus' cities of Fall River, Lawrence, Lowell and New Bedford in Massachusetts had unemployment rates of 9·5, 7·4, 9·1 and 9·2 per cent respectively (US average 6·7 per cent). Even in 1969, after a prolonged period of national economic growth, the respective rates were 5·7, 5·3, 5·3 and 6·0 per cent (US average 3·5 per cent). Other large, and many smaller, New England centres have similar records. In addition there is widespread rural poverty in northern areas, an accumulation of past neglect in many cities which demands a massive urban renewal effort, a

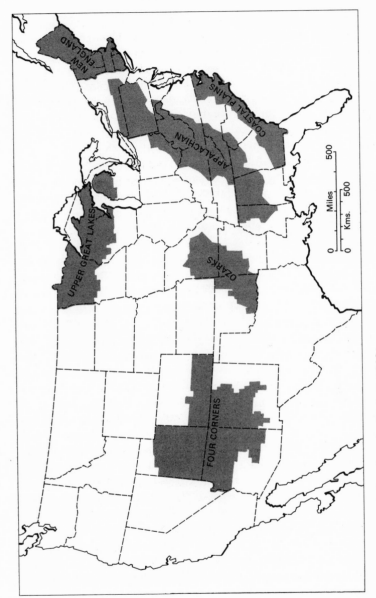

Figure 51. Economic Development Regions. 1968

problem of out-migration in some areas, poor transport facilities in others and widespread water-pollution difficulties. It is right that such issues be analysed on a regional basis, and coherent plans for the benefit of the region as a whole be produced.

The remaining four Economic Development Regions are more consistently poor and rural in character. Farming, mining and forestry have, in various combinations, been important and all have been affected by changing techniques and market requirements. The Four Corners region is interesting as containing large numbers of Mexican Americans and American Indians – minorities even more underprivileged, underemployed and poverty-stricken than the Negro. It also shares with the once-prosperous Upper Great Lakes a serious problem of isolation. Major elements in the difficulties of the latter region were touched upon in Chapter 8. The Ozarks and the Coastal Plains also have their special characteristics and problems but, in essence, each of the four regions is considered to need investment in improved communications, in better public facilities and in education and labour-training schemes. Whether such investment could in every case succeed in improving the prospects remains to be seen. So far the Regional Commissions have been engaged chiefly on the analysis of regional problems and on plan preparation. Some programmes of grant-aided public works have also been started, but no details of the various proposals and plans for each region are yet available.

In Appalachia, however, the general lines of a programme were laid down in the 1964 Report and approved in the 1965 Act. Twelve States cooperated to form the Appalachian Regional Commission, and Mississippi (hardly 'Appalachian' in a physical sense!) has joined more recently. Of these States, West Virginia is the only one included in its entirety. The region covers over 180,000 square miles and contains almost one tenth of the nation's population. While naturally embracing very varied conditions, poor and good, this region has in general been gravely despoiled by farmers, miners and lumberjacks, its once abundant resources plundered, abused and abandoned, leaving behind grave problems of insufficient employment, poverty, malnutrition and despair. In every aspect of its life and economy, as the Presidential Commission clearly showed in its

Report, Appalachia lags far behind the rest of the nation. Two major themes of the Commission's Report greatly influenced the direct allocation of Federal money that went with the passing of the Act. The first was that Appalachia has natural advantages (minerals, water, timber, beauty) on which a thriving economy could still be based; the second that the principal obstacle to the emergence of such an economy was the region's isolation. Both propositions are debatable, but it is true that, despite its position between the generally flourishing and wealthy east coast megalopolis and the Middle West, traffic has always flowed round Appalachia, rather than through it, to its considerable disadvantage. The great weight given to this thesis was reflected in the allocation of the $1,092 millions of Federal money for expenditure in the region over the period 1965–71. Over 75 per cent of the total was allocated to building 2,300 miles of 'developmental highway' and 1,000 miles of local access roads; the balance was to be shared among a variety of schemes for regional health centres, mining-area restoration, erosion control, sewerage plant, water surveys and so on.

Again it is too soon to assess the results of the programme, for economic activities do not adjust themselves overnight to emerging new communications systems, the prospect of tapping new labour markets or material resources etc. In general Appalachia, like the other Development Regions, the Districts and the Areas, has benefited from the great advance of the US economy in the 1960s. There is less unemployment, less poverty and less out-migration, but the contribution of Federal programmes to these advances cannot be separately identified. The broader view now commonly being taken of regions of difficulty, the new bodies created to provide coherent plans for them, the new expertise being created in these matters, the new public facilities being provided and various programmes of aid in education, training and welfare, must surely, however, have had a beneficial effect, and one which will continue when the boom conditions in the national economy have diminished.

It is important to emphasize that planning activities, even for coherent and well-balanced regions, are not a panacea. Various legitimate aims of policy may be incompatible and the successful pursuit of one desirable end may automatically involve the sacrifice

385

of others. Where resources are limited, difficult choices have often to be made. To be effective, also, regional planning must be realistic, though the results may be hard on particular interests. At the end of Chapter 4 it was emphasized that economic growth is not possible everywhere all the time, and that it would be futile and wasteful to attempt to prop up every declining area. Proper planning in fact includes planning for decline – as in assisting migration – but with due concern for human welfare, emotions and dignity. The emphasis on 'growth centres' in the activities of the EDA is thus realistic and vitally important.

Public intervention in distressed areas is not confined to Federal programmes, for State and local bodies are often actively engaged. The first efforts by State governments were in areas, like New England, facing considerable difficulties, and the programmes aimed in various ways at attracting new business. Today every State has some kind of economic development agency, but some of the more recent ones were established as a defensive measure against the loss of enterprise, actual or prospective, to other areas. Fact-gathering, publicity, site preparation, loans or loan-guarantee schemes are the commonest types of operation. At local level, too, numerous quasi-public organizations exist to promote the development of their areas. The existence of such agencies is often taken by business enterprise as indicating a sympathetic and cooperative attitude, and on occasions, no doubt, a finely balanced location decision has been swayed by an offer of special help or a special concession (e.g. in local taxes). Generally, however, the funds available are limited and the ultimate effects of these types of programme at State and local level are not clear. As the system spreads it tends to become self-neutralizing, with the incentives offered in one location offset by those of another. A vexing problem of this kind of activity (and one inherent in the Federal schemes) is whether it is merely transferring activity from one place to another rather than helping to create new business. Federal loans to business are made only when it can be fairly assumed that the enterprise concerned is not simply being poached from another area. No such inhibitions are, or can be, effective at State or local levels. The various activities of State and local government agencies, outside their handling of Federal programmes, are important therefore but, over all, their effect on national geographical distributions is probably fairly small.

At the Federal level, however, while it may also be extraordinarily difficult to assess the precise geographical consequences of activities and programmes, it is clear from the evidence presented in this chapter, and throughout the book, that they are very great indeed. Arguments may continue about the proper role of Federal government or the best arrangement for sharing planning and spending power between the Federal authorities and the State and local areas, but Washington will still command most of the nation's immense tax resources and thus wield a mighty influence on affairs. There seems no doubt that, in a future assessment of the nature and strength of the various forces for change in the economic landscape of our times, the activities of government in the USA, as elsewhere, will prove to be the greatest of all the agents of geographic change.

Some Suggestions for Further Reading

Chapters 1 and 2

Bogue, D. J., *Population of the U.S.A.*, Illinois Free Press, 1959.

Day, L. H. and Day, A. T., *Too Many Americans*, Houghton Mifflin, 1964.

Hart, J. F., 'The Changing Distribution of the American Negro', *Annals of the Association of American Geographers*, Sept. 1960.

Lewis, G. M., 'The Distribution of the Negro in Conterminous U.S.A.', *Geography*, Nov. 1969.

Morril, R., 'The Negro Ghetto: Problems and Alternatives', *Geographical Review*, July 1965.

Taeuber, C. and Taeuber, I., *The Changing Population of the United States*, Wiley, 1958.

US Department of Commerce, *200 Million Americans*, Bureau of the Census, 1967.

US Department of the Interior, *The Population Challenge*, Conservation Yearbook No. 2, 1967.

Zelinsky, W., 'Beyond the Exponentials; the Role of Geography in the Great Transition', *Economic Geography*, July 1970.

Chapter 3

Clawson, M., Held, R. B. and Stoddard, C. H., *Land for the Future*, Johns Hopkins, 1960.

Clawson, M., *Land for Americans* [a shortened version of the major report], Rand McNally, 1963.

Clawson, M., *The Land System of the United States: An Introduction to the History and Practice of Land Use and Land Tenure*, Univ. of Nebraska Press, 1968.

Hart, J. F., 'Loss and Abandonment of Cleared Farmland in Eastern U.S.A.', *Annals of the Association of American Geographers*, Sept. 1968.

Landsberg, H. H., Fischman, L. L. and Fisher, J. L., *Resources in America's Future. Patterns of Requirements and Availability*, Johns Hopkins, 1962.

Some Suggestions for Further Reading

Landsberg, H. H., *Natural Resources for U.S. Growth* [a shortened version of the major report], Johns Hopkins, 1964.

Ottoson, H. W. (Ed.), *Land Use Policy and Problems*, Univ. of Nebraska Press, 1963.

Public Land Law Review Commission, *One Third of the Nation's Land*, Report to the President and to Congress, June 1970.

U.S. Department of Agriculture, *Yearbook for 1958: Land.*

,,　　　　,,　　　　　　,,　　*Yearbook for 1963: A Place to Live.*

,,　　　　,,　　　　　　,,　　Agricultural Economics Report No. 149, *Major Uses of Land and Water in the United States: Summary for 1964*, 1968.

Chapter 4

Hernan, M., Sadofsky, S. and Rosenberg, B. (Eds.), *Work, Youth and Unemployment*, T. W. Crowell, 1968.

Vatter, H. G., *The U.S. Economy in the 1950s*, W. W. Norton, 1963.

Manpower Report of the President (Annual – 1963 to date). Prepared by the US Dept. of Labor.

Zeller, F. A. and Miller, R. W. (Eds.), *Manpower Developments in Appalachia: An Approach to Unemployment*, Praeger, 1968 (the contribution by G. L. Mangum is especially appropriate).

Chapters 5 to 7

Clawson, M., *Policy Directions for U.S. Agriculture*, Johns Hopkins, 1968.

Hart, J. F., 'The Changing American Countryside' and Kollmorgen, 'Farms and Farming in the American Midwest', in Cohen, S. B. (Ed.), *Problems and Trends in American Geography*, Basic Books, 1967.

Haystead, L. and Fite, G., *Agricultural Regions of the United States*, Univ. of Oklahoma Press, 1955.

Higbee, E., *American Agriculture, Geography, Resources, Conservation,* Chapman 1958.

Higbee, E., *Farms and Farmers in an Urban Age*, Twentieth Century Fund, 1963.

Mighell, R. L., *American Agriculture: Its Structure and Place in the Economy*, Chapman, 1955.

A Report by the President's Advisory Commission on Rural Poverty: *The People Left Behind*, Washington, 1967.

Ruttan, V. W. and others (Eds.), *Agricultural Policy in an Affluent Society*, New York, 1969.

Shepherd, G. S., *Farm Policy: New Directions*, Iowa State Univ. Press, 1964.
U.S. Dept. of Agriculture, *After 100 Years*, Yearbook 1962.

Chapters 8 and 9

Bureau of Mines and Geological Survey, *Mineral Resources of the United States*, Washington, 1948.

Caudill, H., *Night Comes to the Cumberlands: A Biography of a Depressed Area*, Little, Brown & Co., 1962.

Christenson, C. L., *Economic Development of Bituminous Coal: The Special Case of Technical Advance in U.S. Coal Mines 1930–1960*, Harvard, 1962.

Davis, E. W., *Pioneering with Taconite*, Minnesota Historical Society, 1964.

Deasy, G. F. and Greiss, P., 'Local and Regional Differences in Long Term Bituminous Coal Production Prospects in Eastern U.S.A.', *Annals of the Association of American Geographers*, Sept. 1967.

Fine, M., 'The Beneficiation of Iron Ores', *Scientific American*, Jan. 1968.

Highsmith, R. M., Jensen, J. G. and Rudd, R. D., *Conservation in the United States*. 2nd edn. Rand McNally. 1969.

Jensen, W. G., *Nuclear Power*, Foulis, 1969.

Landsberg, H. H., *Natural Resources for U.S. Growth*, Johns Hopkins, 1964.

McDivitt, J. F., *Minerals and Man*, Johns Hopkins, 1966.

Munn, R. F., *The Coal Industry in America: A Bibliography and Guide to Studies*, West Virginia University, 1965.

Patton, D. J., *The United States and World Resources*, van Nostrand, 1968.

Perloff, H. S., Dunn, E. S., Lampard, E. E. and Muth, R. F., *Regions, Resources and Economic Growth*, Univ. of Nebraska Press, 1960.

Schuer, S., and Nerscheit, B. C., *Energy in the American Economy, 1850–1975*, Johns Hopkins, 1960.

Shaffer, E. H., *The Oil Import Program of the United States*, Praeger, 1968.

Smith, G. N., *Conservation of Natural Resources*, Part 5, 3rd edn, Wiley, 1965.

U.S. Dept. of the Interior, *Minerals Facts and Problems*, Bureau of Mines, Bulletin 630, 1965.

U.S. Dept. of the Interior, *Surface Mining and Our Environment*, Washington, 1967.

Chapters 10 to 12

Alderfer, E. B. and Michl, H. E., *The Economics of American Industry*, McGraw Hill, 1957.

Alexandersson, G., *The Industrial Structure of American Cities: A Geo-*

graphical Study of the Urban Economy in the United States, Univ. of Nebraska Press, 1956.

Committee for Economic Development, *Distressed Areas in a Growing Economy*, C.E.D., 1961.

Department of Commerce, *Survey of Current Business*, Nov. 1969; 'Input-Output Structure of the U.S. Economy', 1963.

Fuchs, V. R., *Changes in the Location of Manufacturing in the United States Since 1929*, Yale, 1962.

Iden, G., 'Industrial Growth in Areas of Chronic Unemployment', *Monthly Labor Review*, Dept. of Commerce, May 1966.

Owen, G., *Industry in the U.S.A.*, Pelican, 1966.

Perloff, H. S. *et. al.*, op. cit., especially chapters 23–26.

Pred, A., 'The Concentration of High Value-Added Manufacturing', *Economic Geography*, April 1965.

Pred, A. R., *The Spatial Dynamics of U.S. Urban-Industrial Growth 1800–1914*, M.I.T. Press, 1966.

Rodgers, A., 'Some Aspects of Industrial Diversification in the U.S.A.', *Economic Geography*, Jan. 1957.

Zelinsky, W., 'Has American Industry Been Decentralizing?', *Economic Geography*, July 1962.

Chapter 13

The literature on urban problems is massive, and growing rapidly. This list attempts to embrace a variety of approaches and themes.

Abrams, C., *The City is the Frontier*, Harper & Row, 1965.

Campbell, A. K. (Ed.), *The States and the Urban Crisis*, The American Assembly, Columbia Univ., 1970.

Committee for Economic Development, *Reshaping Government in Metropolitan Areas*, C.E.D., 1970.

Gottman, J., *Megalopolis*, Twentieth Century Fund, 1961.

Gottman, J. and Harper, R. A. (Eds.), *Metropolis on the Move: Geographers Look at Urban Sprawl*, Wiley, 1967.

Green, C. M., *The Rise of Urban America*, Harper & Row, 1965; Hutchinson, 1966.

Higbee, E., *The Squeeze: Cities Without Space*, William Morrow, 1960.

Jacobs, J., *The Death and Life of Great American Cities*, Random House, 1961; Pelican, 1964.

Joint Economic Committee Congress of the United States; Subcommittee on Urban Affairs, *Urban America, Goals and Problems*, Washington, 1967.

Lindsay, J., *The City*, Bodley Head, 1970.

A Modern Geography of the United States

Moynihan, D. P. (Ed.), *Towards a National Urban Policy*, New York, 1970.
Murphy, R. E., *The American City: An Urban Geography*, McGraw Hill, 1966.

Chapter 14

Brunn, S. D. and Hoffman, W. L., 'The Geography of Federal Grants in Aid to States', *Economic Geography*, July 1969.
Committee for Economic Development, *Community Economic Development Efforts: Five Case Studies*, Praeger, 1966.
Levin, M. R., *Community and Regional Planning: Issues in Public Policy*, Praeger, 1969.
,, 'New Criteria for Redevelopment Areas', *Land Economics*, Feb. 1968.
,, 'The Economic Development Districts', *Urban Affairs Quarterly*, March 1968.
Levitan, G. A., *Federal Aid to Depressed Areas: An Evaluation of the Area Redevelopment Administration*, Johns Hopkins, 1964.
National Industrial Conference Board, *The Federal Budget: Its Impact on the Economy*, New York, 1970.
Report of the Independent Study Board on the *Regional Effects of Government Procurement and Related Policy*, Dept. of Commerce, 1967.
Robinson, E. A. G. (Ed.), *Backward Areas in Advanced Countries,* International Economic Association Conference, 1967; Macmillan, 1969.
Slesinger, R. E. and Isaacs, A., *Business, Government and Public Policy*, van Nostrand, 1964.
Sufrin, S. C. and Buck, M. A., *What Price Progress? A Study in Chronic Unemployment*, Rand McNally, 1963.
Will, R. A., 'Federal Influences on Industrial Location', *Land Economics*, Feb. 1964.
Wright, D. S., *Federal Grants in Aid: Perspective and Alternatives*, Washington, 1968.

Statistical Sources for the United States

The major source of data in any particular field of activity will usually be the relevant official Census. Those of Population, Agriculture, Manufactures and Mineral Industries have been the most important here. For Population, while the latest available Census details used here were for 1960, the 1970 data will be emerging late in 1970 and throughout 1971. Similarly with Agriculture, while the details are currently available only for 1964, the 1969 Census will be producing its final reports in 1971. The Census of Manufactures was most recently taken in 1967. By mid 1970 only preliminary data were available and detail had, to that time, to be sought in the 1963 Census. The final reports of the 1967 Census will shortly be forthcoming. The Census of Mineral Industries was also taken in 1967, with little detail available by mid 1970, which has made recourse to 1963 Census data necessary on occasion.

In addition to these major sources, for which the time between the gathering of data and publication is prolonged, more up-to-date material is published in various statistical handbooks. The Bureau of the Census produces a series of *Current Population Reports* which give the latest estimates for a wide variety of population data. The Department of Agriculture produces an annual volume of *Agricultural Statistics*; the Bureau of Mines a *Minerals Yearbook*; the Department of Commerce an *Annual Survey of Manufactures* (for non-Census years); the Department of Labor a regular series on *Employment and Earnings*. In addition, special reports of numerous agencies provide specialized statistical sources.

For many normal purposes, the Department of Commerce, Bureau of the Census, annual *Statistical Abstract of the United States* is the most convenient source. It covers an enormous field of statistics (with over 1,000 tables) from all sources. It also contains a comprehensive 'Guide to Sources'.

Index

On completing a teacher's training course at St Mary's College, Twickenham, in the late 1940s, Robert Estall taught for several years in secondary schools in north-east London before entering the L.S.E. to read for the B.Sc.(Econ.) degree in 1952. He graduated with first-class honours in 1955 and joined the staff of the Geography Department at the L.S.E. the same year. He was awarded a Ph.D. of London University in 1964. His first experience of life in the U.S.A. came in 1958, as Visiting Lecturer at Clark University, Worcester, Massachusetts. From that time the weight of his research and teaching interests shifted to North American affairs. He became especially involved in the problems of industrial change in New England and returned there to pursue his research in 1962–3 as a Fellow of the American Council of Learned Societies (which subsequently founded the Readership in the Economic Geography of North America at the L.S.E., which he currently holds). In 1967 he returned again to America, as Visiting Professor at the University of Pittsburgh. He is the author (with R. O. Buchanan) of *Industrial Activity and Economic Geography* (1961) and of *New England: A Study in Industrial Adjustment* (1966). His special interest is in the problems of distressed areas in advanced economies.